* *

THE COFFIN SHIP

**GLUCKSMAN
IRISH DIASPORA**

IN THE GLUCKSMAN IRISH DIASPORA SERIES

Edited by Kevin Kenny

Associate Editor Miriam Nyhan Grey

America and the Making of an Independent Ireland: A History
Francis M. Carroll

The Coffin Ship: Life and Death at Sea during the Great Irish Famine
Cian T. McMahon

* *

The Coffin Ship

Life and Death at Sea during the Great Irish Famine

Cian T. McMahon

* * *

NEW YORK UNIVERSITY PRESS

New York

* *

NEW YORK UNIVERSITY PRESS
New York
www.nyupress.org

References to Internet websites (URLs) were accurate at the time of writing. Neither the author nor New York University Press is responsible for URLs that may have expired or changed since the manuscript was prepared.

Library of Congress Cataloging-in-Publication Data
Names: McMahon, Cian T., author.
Title: The coffin ship : life and death at sea during the Great Irish Famine / Cian T. McMahon.
Other titles: Life and death at sea during the Great Irish Famine
Description: New York : NYU Press, 2021. | Series: The Glucksman Irish diaspora series | Includes bibliographical references and index.
Identifiers: LCCN 2020040679 (print) | LCCN 2020040680 (ebook) | ISBN 9781479808762 (hardback) | ISBN 9781479820535 (paperback) | ISBN 9781479808793 (ebook) | ISBN 9781479808809 (ebook)
Subjects: LCSH: Ireland—History—Famine, 1845–1852. | Ireland—Emigration and immigration—History—19th century. | Immigrants—Correspondence. | Passenger ships—Great Britain—History—19th century. | Immigrants—History—19th century. | Irish—Foreign countries—History—19th century. | Ocean travel—History—19th century. | Seafaring life.
Classification: LCC DA950.7 .M39 2021 (print) | LCC DA950.7 (ebook) | DDC 304.809415/09034—dc23
LC record available at https://lccn.loc.gov/2020040679
LC ebook record available at https://lccn.loc.gov/2020040680

New York University Press books are printed on acid-free paper, and their binding materials are chosen for strength and durability. We strive to use environmentally responsible suppliers and materials to the greatest extent possible in publishing our books.

Manufactured in the United States of America

10 9 8 7 6 5 4 3 2

Also available as an ebook

*This book is affectionately dedicated
to my late mentor and friend,*

Professor David W. Miller

I saw my life and I walked out to it
as a seaman walks out alone at night from
his house down to the port with his bundled
belongings, and sails into the dark.

—Desmond O'Grady, "Purpose" (1996)

CONTENTS

Introduction

In his colorful history of the Kennedys—Irish America's first family—John H. Davis imaginatively reconstructed the "probable shipboard experiences" of JFK's great-grandparents, who sailed on an emigrant ship from New Ross to Boston during the Great Famine. Life below deck, where the emigrants were quartered, was dark and dangerous. "The sick vomited and moaned, women shrieked in childbirth, and men fought over a few inches of bunk or an insult to a county of origin," wrote Davis. Rape was "a common occurrence" as crew members regularly molested female passengers during storms. Worst of all, death ran rampant in these vessels, leaving only one in three passengers to survive the ordeal. "'Coffin ships,' these were called," Davis claimed, "and indeed the only coffins the dead had were the ships they died in."[1]

This one-dimensional portrait of Famine-era emigrant vessels as "coffin ships" has long overshadowed any hope for a true understanding of the voyage. When we use the actual words of the emigrants themselves to scratch its surface, however, we get a much more complicated but clearer picture of what life was actually like. In the autumn of 1847, when shipboard mortality was at historically high levels, Thomas McGinity emigrated with his son from Ireland to New York. Soon after arriving, he penned a letter to his loved ones back home to let them know they had arrived. That note sits, along with hundreds of other emigrant letters, in Belfast's Public Record Office of Northern Ireland. "I take this favorable opportunity of writing to youse to let youse know that I and John arrived safely, thank God, after a passage of thirty days," wrote Thomas. "I never had better health than that which I had at sea." Of course, McGinity ought not to be taken as representative of all emigrants who sailed from Ireland in 1847 (or any other year) for there were many who suffered and died. But his letter is significant because it offers us an intriguing new angle on the strange and complicated story of the Great Famine exodus. And it begs an important question:

what would happen if we used the words and experiences of the Irish emigrants themselves to re-create, and thus more fully understand, that epic moment in modern history?[2]

We need this kind of fresh perspective because historians have long ignored the sea journey, treating it as little more than a brief interlude in the grand drama of human migration. This is particularly true of those who study Ireland's Great Famine. "The miserable epic of the Atlantic crossing in these years has been told so often and well that it hardly seems necessary to recount its dreadful details," explained historian Robert Scally in 1995. "Flanked by the scenes of Skibbereen and Grosse Isle at either end of the voyage, the 'coffin ship' stands as the center panel of the famine triptych." Although most academic historians, including Scally, have long questioned the veracity of the proverbial "coffin ship," their lack of a robust alternative has allowed a range of ahistorical elisions and distortions to survive. It is still often assumed, for example, that the term "coffin ships" originated during the Famine. In fact, the phrase predated the 1840s, was barely mentioned during the Famine, and became popular among Irish nationalists only in the early 1880s as a rhetorical weapon with which to combat landlords and British misgovernment during the Land War. The notion of the "coffin ship" also limits the story of Ireland's Famine migration to a primarily transatlantic one, thus crowding out the smaller but important streams of people (including transported convicts) who traveled to Britain and Australia between 1845 and 1855. Perhaps most importantly, the picture of Irish emigrants as trapped in "coffins" has stripped them of their liveliness, creativity, and agency. I have titled this book *The Coffin Ship*, therefore, precisely as a way to open up and then challenge the accepted truisms that have limited a fuller understanding of not only Irish migration during the Famine but also human migration more broadly. The emigrant voyage began long before one's ship set sail and lasted beyond that first sight of land. My goal in this book is to rescue that process from its historical obscurity and thus resituate the sailing ship, alongside the tenement and the weekly newspaper, as a dynamic element of migration history.[3]

Using letters, diaries, government documents, and newspapers scattered across archives and libraries on three continents, *The Coffin Ship* focuses on the lived experiences of the migrants themselves. My origi-

nal goal was to identify and understand the strategies that Famine-era
Irish emigrants used to survive crossing the Atlantic Ocean. Given that
folks who were headed to Britain and Australia employed many of same
tactics used by their friends and families en route to Canada and the
United States, however, it soon became clear that maintaining strict
distinctions between migratory streams to the northern and southern
hemispheres would only hamper the project's full potential. Nationalist politician John O'Connell's 1854 demand that emigrant vessels be
at least as seaworthy as convict ships points to another important factor: that those Irish who sailed on convict transports (many of whom
did so voluntarily) constituted another trickle in the flood of migrants
during this time period. At a broader level, it also became apparent to
me that the weeks or months one spent on a ship were only part of the
journey. A nineteenth-century sea voyage was actually a long process,
which began with the collection of resources to leave and ended as
one started to settle in one's host community. At every step of the way,
migrants relied on local and international networks of communication
and exchange. This book's core argument, therefore, holds that the migratory process was not merely about enabling individuals to move here
or there. In fact, by encouraging the transnational exchange of money,
tickets, advice, and news, the voyage itself fostered the development of
countless new threads in the worldwide web of the Irish diaspora.[4]

Understanding the context in which the Famine occurred in the first
place is important. On the eve of the disaster, the majority of Irish
people lived precarious lives on the economic fringes of the United
Kingdom. The population was predominantly rural and reliant on agriculture for its income. Farmland, the main means of production outside of industrial nodes in Belfast, Dublin, and Cork, was primarily
owned by a small and mostly Protestant elite whose ancestors had been
awarded it following state-sanctioned confiscations in the sixteenth
and seventeenth centuries. The countryside was not, however, a bustling patchwork of comfortable tenant farms. Sixty percent of the land
was leased by only 25 percent of the country's farmers. Slightly under
half of all farms were small properties (of five acres or less) with short
subleases, often on marginal land. Below these were cottiers and wage
laborers; 60 percent of males working on farms held leases on little or
no land of their own. Visitors to Ireland were routinely shocked by the

seasonal unemployment, food insecurity, and poor housing of many Irish peasants. Despite this material poverty, rural Irish people also enjoyed a rich sense of social cohesion embodied in clachans—tight-knit, local communities of families and neighbors. This solidarity was, in turn, rooted in centuries of land management embodied in the rundale system, whereby land was held in common and redistributed periodically in ways that ensured that each family got shares of the good, bad, and middling land. Although the rundale method and, by extension, the clachans were steadily deteriorating in the mid-nineteenth century under pressure from landowners seeking to rationalize farming practices, most people living in Ireland at the time saw themselves as part of social networks bound by tradition, blood, and reciprocity. When the blight hit the potatoes on which the Irish population was heavily reliant in 1845, it kicked a critical prop out from under Irish life. Many died. Yet many more emigrated, bringing with them these strong notions of kinship and community.[5]

The outpouring of people from Ireland during the Famine years stands as one of the greatest flash floods in the history of human migration. Millions of Germans and Italians left their homelands in the nineteenth century too, but while these groups were bigger in sheer numbers, they were coming from much larger base populations. Considering that the number of people living in Ireland on the eve of the Famine was around eight and a half million, the deaths of one million and the migration of another two million over the following decade were devastating. No wonder the *Galway Mercury* complained in 1851 that "Connemara is become almost a desert from emigration." The sheer scale of this movement also upsets the standard periodization of the Great Famine itself. Most scholars agree with Christine Kinealy that following the blight-free harvest of 1852, "the worst of the Famine appeared to be over in all parts of Ireland." Viewed from the perspective of migration, however, this periodization fails to suffice. Ireland's Famine-era migration only peaked in 1851 when over 250,000 moved away. In fact, migration did not return to pre-Famine levels of less than 80,000 per annum until 1855 (see figure 1.1). As a result, I use 1845 (the outbreak of the potato blight) to 1855 (the end of Famine-inflated migration) as my chronological canvas. My geographical remit is equally broad. Of the over two million Irish who emigrated during the Famine, the larg-

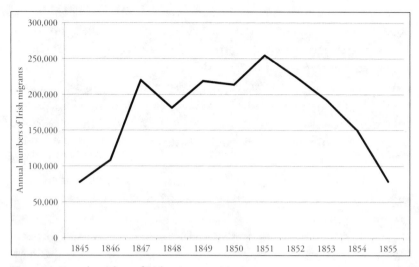

Figure 1.1. Annual numbers of Irish migrants, 1845–1855.

est number (1.5 million) went to the United States. Another 300,000 went to Canada. About the same number ended up in Great Britain, either because they planned to or simply ran out of money en route to more distant destinations. Fewer than 75,000 Irish headed to Australia and New Zealand as emigrants, while over 6,000 were transported as convicts to Van Diemen's Land. Although I have drawn each of these subgroups into my story, the largest ones (headed to the United States and Canada) understandably enjoy the most attention.[6]

The structures of maritime transportation from Britain and Ireland witnessed important changes during the Famine decade. In the early years (up to 1848), there were simply not enough vessels capable of carrying emigrants abroad, especially in 1847, when, as evidenced in figure 1.1, the number of Irish emigrants doubled compared to the year before.[7] Many enterprising businessmen responded by pressing a wide range of ships (not all of which were seaworthy) into service, even in the autumn and winter, when sailing was most hazardous and uncomfortable. They could do so because the government's scattered network of emigration officers was unprepared to regulate the unprecedented deluge of people, ships, and newly active ports. These factors, combined with the government's laissez-faire economic theory and fear of social unrest, allowed many desperate, frightened, and sick emigrants to set sail in dangerously unsuitable conditions, thus setting the stage for the horrors of 1847. A marked dip in the number of emigrants in 1848 corresponded with some changes, which improved conditions and fostered the steady growth of out-migration between 1849 and 1851. When the government instituted a head tax on those landing in British North America in 1848, the tide turned toward the United States. As comfortable farming families elected to leave the country and the panicky streams turned into a committed flood, local businesses responded by working more closely with American packet companies, chartering first-class ships, and competing with each other over shipboard conditions. The UK and US governments also updated their Passenger Acts multiple times between 1847 and 1855, which ensured that the average emigrant ship became less crowded, better ventilated, and more comfortably equipped with supplies during these latter years.[8]

There were also important differences and similarities between the sea routes the Famine Irish followed to their various destinations. Of course, the biggest disparity lay in the lengths of the journeys themselves. The trip across the Irish Sea, which over 75 percent of all Irish emigrants completed en route to their final destinations worldwide, covered approximately 200 miles (from Dublin to Liverpool) of infamously rough waters and could take anywhere from fourteen to thirty hours, depending on where one left from. This could be terribly uncomfortable and even dangerous, but it did not compare to the grand voyage that awaited those heading to North America. A trip from Liverpool to New York, for example, covered about 3,000 miles and took an average of almost six weeks. Sailing direct from Ireland to Canada could save about a week. The journey to Australia was, of course, the longest, taking approximately three and a half months to cover the 13,000 miles from England to Sydney. The divergent lengths of these voyages undoubtedly impacted social relations in different ways. The short trip to Liverpool gave emigrants less time and incentive to develop new relationships. Solidarities were more likely to develop during the weeks people spent at sea en route to the United States or Canada. It is also impossible to quantify but reasonable to imagine that the sheer length of the trip to Australia fostered stronger feelings of both solidarity and hostility than those found on shorter routes. At the same time, all emigrants shared certain formative experiences. They left loved ones behind. They took their chances on the high seas. They made new friends. They managed life and death. They cooked their own meals, slept on wooden platforms, and struggled with seasickness. "I imagined I was the sickest man in creation," lamented James Mitchell as he reflected on his journey from Dublin to Liverpool in 1853, "although there was at least a score around me just as bad." These shared experiences played a role in stitching the Irish diaspora together.[9]

Those who chose, or felt compelled, to emigrate (or enable others to do so) faced the daunting task of collecting enough cash to fund the project. Depending on the year and destination, a Famine-era voyage could cost an adult anywhere from a couple of shillings (from Dublin to Liverpool) to as little as three pounds (direct from Ireland to Canada) to four or five pounds (from Liverpool to the United States) to over eighteen pounds (from England to Australia). At a time when many subsistence-level laborers were paying up to ten pounds a year for one acre of manured land, these fares constituted a major investment. Buying one entitled the traveler to a spot on a shared sleeping platform in the belly of a ship. Passengers were also eligible for a daily allowance of three quarts of fresh water along with one pound of oatmeal, flour, or biscuit, and access to a communal stove to cook on, but while the Australia-bound ships were highly regulated, the enforcement of these rules on the Atlantic was scattershot. Beyond the trip itself, most passengers could expect to spend an additional one pound on an outfit sturdy enough for life at sea and a similar amount on provisions to supplement the ship's allowance. Depending on how far the emigrant lived from the port at which they were to embark, they might also need to spend anywhere from a few pennies to a few pounds getting to the ship, while, preferably, keeping a few shillings in their pocket for incidental expenses along the way. How did over two million people manage to gather these resources in the midst of a collapsing economy? Many, if not most, emigrants received cash or prepaid tickets from friends and family either at home or abroad. Others peddled furniture, tools, and livestock or negotiated reimbursement for improvements they had made by selling their "interest" in their farm. For landlords yearning for profitable estates and lower poor rates, covering the costs of their tenants' emigration served as a way to divest themselves of the impoverished families that one land agent considered "dead weights." During the latter years of the Famine, some local poor law unions, whose workhouses were swamped with starving people, came to see emigration as more cost-effective than feeding and housing the poor. Historians have tended to describe these various funding streams as separate entities, but as we shall see, there was often a large degree of overlap between them.[10]

The circulatory system of nineteenth-century maritime capitalism, which transported timber, pig iron, and fine crockery over long distances, also carried migrants. Much has been made of the fact that many Irish sailed to Canada on empty lumber freighters returning westward for fresh cargo, but the truth is that many ships changed their fittings to suit passengers or goods in the mid-nineteenth century. The very nature of transoceanic trade required that all sailing vessels be flexible, for while they carried bulky raw materials like cotton and wool away from North America and Australia, their return journeys saw them loaded with finer, smaller commodities such as textiles and tools. There was, therefore, extra space available in ships heading to the southern and western hemispheres. When the slave trade was abolished in the early 1800s, underutilized vessels began carrying more European migrants. In short, there were always connections between economic markets and migratory patterns. When Ulster was importing flaxseed from Pennsylvania at the height of its linen boom in the eighteenth century, local emigrants bought berths on the ships as they returned to the Mid-Atlantic states. By the 1840s, ports around Ireland were importing large amounts of wood products from Quebec and New Brunswick, including deals and staves to satisfy the growing needs of the coopers building barrels for Irish eggs, butter, and pork. At the same time, Liverpool served as the gateway for the importation of American cotton en route to textile mills across Lancashire. Laden ships departed from ports like New Orleans and Charleston but often returned with commodities (and paying emigrants) to northern cities like Boston, Philadelphia, and New York. From there, they coasted down south to begin the cycle again. Finally, imperial priorities meant that there was always a cargo deficit between the United Kingdom and the Antipodes. A single vessel "might carry prisoners one year," wrote Charles Bateson in his classic work, *The Convict Ships*, "and the next turn up in Australian waters with cargo and passengers or immigrants, or simply as a freighter." Britain needed wool and Australia needed laborers. A single round trip by one sailing vessel could complete the circuit.[11]

Their multifunctionality meant that the physical layout of these wooden machines was always subject to modification, but they all, including convict transports, shared similar basic features. Most were three- or four-masted, square-rigged barques with at least three top decks (forecastle at the front, main in the middle, and poop at the back, although many also included a raised quarterdeck immediately to the rear of the main mast). The strict class hierarchy, which governed life at sea, dictated that the poop and quarterdecks were reserved for officers and first- and second-class "cabin" passengers while steerage travelers were limited to the main deck. Besides the fife rails, halyards, belaying pins, and other accoutrements of maritime labor, the decks had at least one water closet and a set of open-fire grates where steerage passengers competed for space to cook their own meals at assigned times. There were also one or more small boats for ferrying to and from the shore but no lifeboats in the modern sense of the term. The living quarters were located below these decks. The officers and cabin passengers slept and dined in relatively comfortable apartments located below the poop deck, near the ship's galley and hospital (when there was one). The crew members lived in the forecastle. In the heart of the ship was steerage, also known as the 'tween deck; a long room, accessed from above by hatches on the main deck. This was where average emigrants were quartered during their voyage. They laid their crude bedding on double-decked, roughly carpentered wooden shelves, which ran along the walls of steerage and were arranged into six-foot-by-six-foot berths designed to be shared by four or more people. On the largest ships, tables and benches were arranged in the open space between the berths, and there were water closets at either end. Steerage was sometimes divided into compartments, which positioned the married couples between the single men and women (see figure I.2). Finally, emigrants kept only some of their personal food and clothing in sacks, carpetbags, and trunks or chests stowed near their berths. The rest of their belongings, along with the ship's provisions, water, and any cargo, were stored in the hold, in the bottom of the ship, and accessed infrequently during any given voyage.[12]

The similarity of most deep-sea vessels does not mean that they were all of equal quality. For the most part, American ships were generally

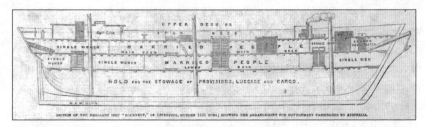

Figure 1.2. A cross-section of the *Bourneuf*, a double-decked emigrant ship bound for Australia in 1852. *Illustrated London News*, June 26, 1852. Image © Illustrated London News/ Mary Evans Picture Library.

considered better than their British counterparts. The latter were usually smaller, slower, and old-fashioned, thanks to decades of trade protectionism and tradition. Following the establishment of Lloyd's Register in 1834, ships were categorized into three classes according to their age, standard at time of construction, and overall maintenance. While emigrants were supposed to travel only in first- or second-class vessels (third-class ships were not even supposed to leave the coasting trade within Europe), the combination of poor oversight, ignorance, ballooning demand, and deception described earlier meant that in the mid-1840s, many Irish emigrants set sail for Canada in unseaworthy vessels. Jurisdictional issues also allowed many poorly equipped British ships to carry passengers to the United States while British captains developed a reputation for challenging the authority of government agents before leaving and for tyrannizing emigrants at sea. The same was not true of British ships headed to Australia. Whether sailing as fare-paying passengers on private ships or as assisted emigrants on vessels chartered by the Colonial Land and Emigration Commission (CLEC), emigrants benefitted from traveling on more highly regulated, quality vessels manned by at least one full-time surgeon-superintendent. Similarly, government policy strictly prohibited the chartering of second- or third-class vessels for convict voyages while insisting on the presence of a medical practitioner and the maintenance of discipline, hygiene, and decent food.[13]

Although American ships were designed to carry raw materials and commodities, they also responded to the growing emigrant trade by redesigning their ships and schedules. Thomas Murdoch, the chairman of the CLEC, testified to a British select committee in the mid-1850s that American emigrant ships were "magnificent vessels" that often carried "bed-places as permanent structures." As these ships and their crews developed a reputation for faster, safer voyages, and the United States became the main destination for Irish emigrants after 1847, American vessels swallowed the majority of the passenger trade. In 1849, twice as many passengers entered New York on American ships as did those on British ones, and the trend continued throughout the 1850s. According to Murdoch's testimony, American ships carried 158,000 of the 175,000 emigrants who sailed from Liverpool to the United States in 1853. This was largely due to the fact that Americans such as the Cope family, whose records I employed while conducting my research, dominated the transatlantic packet sailing business during these years. Regular ships waited until they were full of cargo or passengers before leaving port. While this was convenient for the ships' owners, by ensuring that they carried a maximum payload on every costly journey, it was inconvenient for passengers and merchants, who might have to wait days or even weeks for their ship to leave. By departing on a scheduled day every month, however, American packet ships became very popular. These shipping schedules composed the basis of a complicated system of capitalist exchange, which Irish peasants needed to understand and engage with in order to migrate during the Famine.[14]

Conceiving of the journey in its broadest terms, *The Coffin Ship*'s five chapters trace how the processes of departure, voyage, and arrival developed and repaired complicated strands of communal solidarity among Irish people at home and abroad during the Famine era. From the tearful goodbye at the crossroads to the swindlers and thieves of Liverpool, the first two chapters explore the early stages of the trip. Chapter 1 demonstrates the ways in which complicated networks of relationships, sometimes spanning thousands of miles, enabled prospective emigrants to gather the resources to leave. Earning a spot in steerage was, however, only the first step. One also needed to make one's way to the port of embarkation. Doing so, as shown in chapter 2, often meant relying on the same transnational and local circuits of exchange that had facilitated the journey in the first place. Chapter 3 looks at life at sea in steerage, which one scholar has compared to "a high-density urban environment." It argues that, finding themselves surrounded by strangers in an unfamiliar ecosystem, emigrants broadened their sense of community beyond the traditional confines of friends and family, which had predominated back home. As such, the sea voyage laid the psychological groundwork for the kind of social order, based on collective experience rather than shared kinship, that would serve as the foundation for new communities in the new worlds. Life at sea prepared Irish "emigrants" to become "immigrants." Chapter 4 analyzes death on board the ships. After a detailed consideration of the available statistics on mortality, it turns to consider the impact that death and dying had on both a given ship's micro-community and those living on land. It shows that while shipboard mortality could tear floating communities apart, it could also bring them closer together. Finally, chapter 5 addresses the challenges of arriving in the New World. It illustrates that emigrants began reconstituting relationships back in Ireland as quickly as they formed new ones in North America and Australia. Taken as a whole, the vignettes on which these chapters are based demonstrate that the journey was not an errant thread but rather a critical seam in the fabric of emigrant life.[15]

This understanding of the migrant journey as a connective strand in the global network of nineteenth-century life offers new insight into a critical dimension of modern history. Cormac Ó Gráda and others are certainly correct in arguing that migration has been a mode of relief in historical famines, but this book demonstrates that it has also played a role in how communities have recovered during and afterward. No one who has read the letters and diaries of these Irish emigrants would suggest that a mid-nineteenth-century sea voyage was a safe or easy process, and it is certainly not the goal of this book to understate the suffering, which countless people experienced. Many newspapers at the time definitely did not. "Alas for the victims flung . . . from the shuddering side of the pestilential ship, to feed monsters at whose sight the bravest cheek blanches," lamented the Dublin *Nation* in August 1847, "[or] buried in a strange soil among strange people!" Anxieties over death and dislocation were part of everyday life during the Great Famine. At the same time, these stories of emigrants' intelligence, bravery, and resolve have long remained hidden behind the crude image of the "coffin ship." Pushing beyond the big statistics, official reports, and tired clichés to hear what the emigrants themselves said offers a messier but more honest picture of the experience, and demonstrates how these hundreds of thousands of individual journeys helped to reweave torn bonds of solidarity. Before sending a prepaid ticket back to Ireland in 1846, an unnamed benefactor scribbled words of encouragement on its reverse side. "I hope that your friends will help you to get ready and you will need not be afraid," they wrote, "for the ship that you are to come in is just as safe as if you were sitting at Mr. Magee's fire side." *The Coffin Ship* relies on such lost voices for guidance across the "trackless deep" of a long-hidden history.[16]

1

Preparation

In April 1847, Hannah Lynch of Mountmellick in Queen's County wrote a letter to her brother, John, in Philadelphia. The remittance system on which so many of Hannah's neighbors were relying for the means to emigrate was in full swing. "The Rev. Fr. Healy is after getting I think above fifty letters and money in them all," Hannah explained. "They were sent to his care by people in America to their friends at home to take them out to them. The post office here is full of letters every day, scarcely one without money." This chapter investigates the complicated ways in which people gathered the resources to leave Ireland during the Great Famine. It argues that by successfully exploiting both transnational and local circuits of exchange, emigrants and their friends and families fortified transnational links of community and power. The remittance from family abroad was the beating heart of the emigration process. Whether sent from Toronto, Sydney, or New York, these cash grants were embodied in financial instruments (such as money orders and prepaid tickets) traveling on international networks (such as the packet and postal systems) that were originally built in the service of international capitalism. When combined with the support—bureaucratic, financial, or otherwise—of landlords, poor law guardians, clergy, and government officials, these remittances connected local nodes of community and power to the global networks of commerce, communication, and empire that could carry the people away. Thus did the first stage of each emigrant's journey develop and strengthen transnational links within the Irish world.[1]

"Take Us Out of This Poverty Isle": Family, Friends, and Private Charity

On August 10, 1846, James Purcell of Geelong, Australia, sent a remittance to his sister Bridget Brennan in County Kilkenny. Bridget was helping to prepare James's children to join him in the Antipodes and the enclosed check for ten pounds was to supply them with "clothing and the necessaries for the voyage." In a separate letter, Purcell had sent another twenty-one pounds to cover the cost of Bridget's passage. Such remittances, however, were flexible. If Bridget chose not to come, then "anyone you will recommend can come on the ticket. I suppose it is likely to be Mick." If not Mick, "send Patt Brenan, my sister's son." A year later, Bridget's landlord noticed the remarkable effect that such remittances were having. Many of Charles Wandesforde's tenants had emigrated with help from "members of their families who have sent them money from America to assist them. Many cases have occurred where a brother or a sister will, in the space of one year, assist one or two members of his family and eventually remove the family altogether." This process of family-oriented assistance, often termed "chain migration" by historians, accounted for the vast majority of financial help rendered to Irish emigrants during the Famine. While some people had enough cash on hand, most needed assistance of one sort or another. This explains why, as figures 1.1 and 1.2 illustrate, the annual

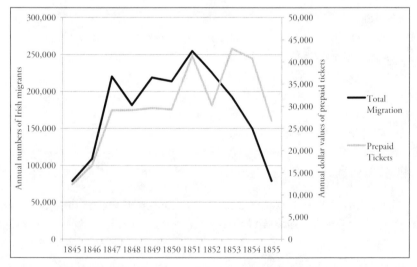

Figure 1.1. Annual numbers of Irish migrants and values of prepaid steerage tickets (in US dollars) purchased from Cope family packet company, 1845–1855.[2]

Sources: The annual dollar values of prepaid tickets bought at the Cope Family office (rounded to the nearest 10) are recorded in the "Inward Steerage Passengers" logbooks (vols. 86–88, HSP).

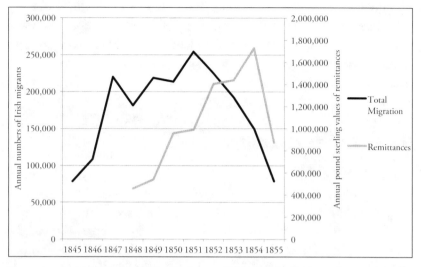

Figure 1.2. Annual numbers of Irish migrants (1845–1855) and values of remittances (in pounds sterling) sent from North America to the United Kingdom (1848–1855).

Source: The annual values of cash remittances from North America to the United Kingdom can be found in *Twenty-Fourth General Report* (1864), 583. Extant data are only from 1848 onward.

numbers of Famine-era Irish migrants, prepaid passage ticket sales in one Philadelphia packet line, and value of cash remittances from North America to the United Kingdom all peaked in the early 1850s, just as the Famine was supposedly ending. As we shall see, this transnational system of remittance served to repair and rebuild disrupted bonds of community within the Irish diaspora.[3]

Although cash remittances did not peak until 1854, they were part of the global conversation on Irish emigration from the early years of the Famine. In 1847, Irish American Quaker Jacob Harvey declared that Irish immigrants had sent over two hundred thousand pounds home in 1846. "The *heart* of the poor Irishman does not change by expatriation," Harvey claimed, "his charity is as deeply seated as his religion, and the very first use he makes of his surplus wages is to assist those loved ones whom he left behind!" In this enterprise, Irish Americans were assisted in New York by the Catholic Archbishop J. J. Hughes, the Irish Emigrant Society, and businesses such as Harnden and Company's Emigration Office, which promised that "persons sending for their friends through the subscribers can rely upon their being treated fairly and brought out as agreed." In an 1846 letter to the Sydney *Morning Chronicle*, which was subsequently reprinted in newspapers back in Ireland, English philanthropist Caroline Chisholm felt that cash gifts sent home by emigrants represented a "generous and praiseworthy feeling." The authorities, she argued, should encourage such efforts at family reunification, "which would be so beneficial to the parties themselves and to the public at large." Those living in Australia, however, found few affordable options available. As late as February 1852, "A Tipperary Man" complained to the Sydney *Freeman's Journal*, Irish Australia's leading weekly, that if their local banks would sell money orders for small amounts of between two and five pounds, "[we] would then, gentlemen, show the world that Irishmen in Australia have as much sympathy for their relatives and friends at home" as those in America. By 1853, the London *Times* was attributing the flood of remittances to the unique characteristics of the Irish people. "All the feelings of family, of race, of language, and religion, that have hitherto kept the Irishman at home, now conspire with equal force to send him abroad," it editorialized that March. "He holds to the multitude either to stay or to go, and as the latter is now the fashion, he will fly as obstinately as before he stood his ground."[4]

In their letters to friends and family abroad, many prospective emigrants sought to secure assistance by describing in stark detail how hard life in Ireland had become and how desperate they were to leave. In a September 1846 letter to their parents in Canada, Michael and Mary Rush painted a bleak picture of life in Ardnaglass, County Sligo. "Dear father and mother, pen cannot dictate the poverty of this country, at present, the potato crop is quite done away all over Ireland," they wrote. "There is nothing expected here, only an immediate famine." The siblings begged their parents to "take us out of this poverty isle." Others tried to exploit family dynamics. When Affy Griffin's husband abandoned her and their four children to go to America, Affy implored his brother "to use that influence I feel you possess with George to induce him to place me above want." The past year and a half had been hard, Affy admitted, and were it not for the charity of some friends, she and the kids would have been consigned to the local workhouse. Although many other men who had left after George had already sent the passage fares for their families, "he has not sent me one penny." Others were nothing short of desperate. In a letter to her son in Rhode Island, a Mrs. Nolan expressed the vehemence with which she and another son, Dicksy, desired to emigrate. "Patt, I can't let you know how we are suffering unless you were in starvation and want without friend or fellow to give you a shilling or a penny," she explained before encouraging him to coordinate with other family members to realize a plan for their escape. "The poor child says," she concluded, "if the letter came in tomorrow for him and his mother, that he would leap into the ship naked as he stands to make haste to see them all."[5]

Prospective emigrants sometimes used guilt to coerce family into sending them money. Affy Griffin thought that her brother-in-law Daniel could use this approach to good effect in convincing her husband George to support her and their children. After confiding that George "drinks a little" and "is fond of cards and other games of chance," she encouraged Daniel not to mention any of this, as she knew her husband wanted to protect his reputation. Instead, Affy suggested that Daniel approach George more obliquely. "Suppose you were to say you heard from Ireland, not to say from whom, that we were badly off and that you wished to have him make a fortune and settle near you," she said. Living near Daniel would "give [George] an object" and render him "an altered man." Others simply demanded that their departed families not leave them behind. Convinced that her brother was on the verge of sending a remittance, Hannah Lynch had sold all of her furniture and now found herself with "nothing but the bare walls of the house." Lynch felt neglected. "I thought nothing would make you all forget me and I the only person left alone," she wrote, reminding her brother that their father had promised to coordinate a family effort to send for her. Lynch also invoked rural traditions of sharing and charity to solidify her case. "Many a time, my father lent money behind the back of the ditch to neighbors and got it again and I am sure he nor you could not turn it to better use than sending for me now," she reminded him. "Everyone is getting money but me. I am quite jealous and ashamed of you all."[6]

Hannah Lynch's reference to lending customs demonstrates that not all emigration remittances were meant as straight cash handouts. Some were more or less temporary loans saddled with the promise, either formal or informal, to repay the amount once the emigrant had settled abroad and begun to earn steady income. In her anger and frustration with her brother, Hannah Lynch offered only a lukewarm promise to repay the cost of her and her family's tickets to Pennsylvania. "I am sure we would do as well as others," she wrote, "and if you would only lend us what you could, with the help of God, we would be able to pay you again, perhaps." By contrast, when Margaret Masterson, a laundry maid in Rahood, County Meath, wrote to her cousin Michael Masterson in Bourbon County, Kentucky, in October 1850, she explicitly promised to pay him back as soon as she could. "I have a great wish for going to America," she explained, "and when I heard the good encouragement you gave in your letter that you would pay the passage of any of your friends that liked to go there, I wished from my heart I could go." If Michael would "be so good as to pay my passage until such time as I could earn it, if God would send me over safe, I'd return it with many thanks as I think I'd do very well there." At other times, emigrants and their supporters borrowed small amounts here and there to supplement remittances saved. Before mailing a prepaid ticket, William Earley apologized for not sending it earlier. "I had not the money," he explained, "I had to borrow part of this now." In 1848, another benefactor sent his prepaid ticket along with a check for four pounds for sea stores. "If it is not enough," he advised, "Bridget or Thomas will lend you what you want and I will send it to them." International cycles of borrowing and repayment kept the remittance system moving.[7]

Given how valuable cash remittances were to both the senders and receivers, it is understandable that they often came with specific instructions on how they should be spent. Lost or stolen prepaid tickets, for example, were a source of constant worry. "Dear sister Ellen," wrote one sender, "if any man got this in his hands, you would lose your passage and I would lose £4 British money, which I paid for you." Those who chose not to take advantage of the boon were instructed to return prepaid tickets back across the ocean. "Please take care of this passage certificate," Mary Quin was told, "and if anything should happen, return it to me by post if you cannot come so that I might have a chance of getting the money back as I cannot get it without it." Benefactors who sent cash for provisions at sea often prioritized certain expenditures. When Mary Duggan, a servant working in Ontario, heard that her sister back in Dungiven, County Derry, was eager to leave

Figure 1.3. Emigrants buy passage tickets at a shipping broker's office in Cork. *Illustrated London News*, May 10, 1851. Image © Illustrated London News/Mary Evans Picture Library.

Ireland, she sent her four pounds sterling, "which is quite adequate to bring you to this country." Accompanying the check were directions designed to enable the sister to spend it most sensibly. Specific costs included two pounds and ten shillings on the passage to Quebec, nine shillings on oatmeal, and five shillings on pork ham, not to mention smaller amounts on sundries such as tea and sugar. Before closing, Mary warned her sister that there would be plenty of people offering her plenty of advice. "Believe them not," Mary insisted. "Stand to what I here tell you and you will be right." The desire to protect precious investments, combined with the donors' firsthand experiences with the migration process itself, discouraged experimentation.[8]

The remittance system was fueled by cash and advice, but it also relied on other kinds of information as well. In situations in which there was literally no money to spare, for example, chain migration required the transmission of accurate accounts of how much was needed. Based in Baltimore, Maryland, in February 1848, John O'Connor sent a letter along with ten pounds to his wife, Judy, in County Galway. "You will be as careful as you can about this money," John wrote, "for perhaps I might get a chance [to send more] before a month." But he still needed accurate information comparing and contrasting current fares. "You will let me know how [much] the passage is in Galway," he insisted. "If you can, you will let me know how much would take ye to Liverpool, for I reckon it's there I must bring ye from." Prospective emigrants planning to start their own links of chain migration needed guidance on how to proceed as well. When John Regan's brother sent him a prepaid ticket on the Cope Line to Philadelphia in 1849, he included some guidance. "If you are coming, I don't advise you to bring your family," he said, "but if you come yourself with Patrick, you might make out and with the blessing of God, you might be able to send for them in a short time." Similarly, Bessie Masterson McManus and her husband sought advice from Bessie's cousin when planning their departure in late 1850. They had saved enough for one adult fare. "My dear cousin, which of us would you advise to go first?" Bessie inquired. Both had their own skills and experiences, but "if it is my husband that you would wish to go, he would care [for] your daughter as well as one of his own if her friends would let her go [with him to America]." Support could be reciprocated in different ways.[9]

While Bessie envisaged a situation in which she or her husband emigrated abroad and then single-handedly raised the fares for the other parent and both children to follow later, the truth is that remittances often relied on the coordinated efforts of several family members. Writing on the back of a prepaid ticket in the early summer of 1848, an unnamed benefactor described how three siblings might work together to get one of them out of Ireland. "As it regards my brother," he explained, "I am sorry he cannot make it suit to come now but I will write again to brother William and see whether we cannot make up enough to bring him in a little while." Between the three of them, they could make it work. "I would be willing to pay one half of his passage money if William would pay the other and leave [the emigrating brother to] find his own provisions." Those who could not contribute to the immediate cost of fares and supplies could promise to help the emigrant upon arrival. In May 1851, Daniel Rowntree was delayed in writing to his sister in Dublin by waiting to hear from another sister, Eliza. "I expected money from her to assist me in bearing your expenses," Daniel explained. "She has changed her mind and will not do so until such time as you arrive. Then, she will provide for your wants." As spending cash on remittances meant less left over for those staying in Ireland, some benefactors took the time to explain the long-term benefits of short-term costs. "We had a notion to send for one of the girls and to send you a few dollars," explained one anonymous letter writer in the United States, "but by sending for the two girls, it will do ten times more good for if they were out in this country, they could have it in their power very soon to relieve and help their parents to bring out the rest of the family."[10]

Beyond contributing cash and tickets, those living abroad also sometimes used the remittance system to assuage the fears of prospective emigrants while rekindling feelings of love and affection with those they left behind. On the back of Mary Kelly's prepaid ticket, for example, her anonymous sponsor assured her not to worry about any of her debts in Ireland. "If you owe Mr. Small or any other body any money," the donor wrote, "tell them I will send home the last penny." Others sought to convince nervous emigrants that they would soon be happy they had made the trip. In a December 1845 letter to his family in Dublin, John Fleming promised to take care of them. "Dear mother and sister, do not be fretting for I will have ye comfortable," he wrote. "Mother, you will have what you always liked, tea, coffee, and everything else." There was often more to a remittance than naked, economic exchange. The process of sending money for passage offered an opportunity to send love as well. When an unnamed benefactor sent prepaid tickets for two adults in early 1847, they included a warm promise to send for others soon. "I send my love to your uncle Thomas Brown," the note read, "hoping that he will pay some attention to Sarah and [the] two boys until November or such time as we shall send for them." In the meantime, the writer nourished hopes of reconstituting the old community in a new land. "Please remember us all to Nancy Dillon, to James Dillon, and his wife and family, also to all our cousins, relations, and inquiring friends," the note continued. "We also send our love and respects [to] Sarah, John, Robert, James, and Thomas, and we hope to see you all in America yet."[11]

For all of the thousands of families that succeeded in generating the cash to facilitate the emigration of one or more of their members, however, there were many others that failed. Letters from abroad sometimes expressed the regret and shame that accompanied not being able to help those still in Ireland. When Patrick Grant, a carpenter's assistant working in Auburn, New York, wrote back to his mother and siblings in November 1851, he painted a sad portrait of his experiences in America. "With the expense of clothes and other things you must know my circumstances are low at present," wrote Grant, who claimed to be making only five dollars a month, probably after room and board. It "grieves me to write this letter without sending something. I had not intended to write until I would but under the present circumstance, duty compels me." Another emigrant promised his mother he was doing the best he could on her behalf. "So, dear Mother, I have no more [money] to spare, if I had you should have it," he wrote. "I deprive myself of many things that I may get you over here." While some of those who left Ireland felt tinges of regret at not being able to support others to do the same, those who could have left but chose not to also felt remorse. "We often say you had good success to leave this unfortunate Ireland," Judith Phelan told her niece in Memphis, Tennessee. "I often wished I had gone with you." In her request for assistance to leave County Tipperary, Elisa Taylor expressed similar regrets. "Dear brother, nothing ever gave me such trouble as I did not go with you [to Canada]," she wrote in June 1847. "I expect that you will not forget the promise that you made me and you going but send me a little help and that will enable me to go to you and if you send anything, no matter what part of the year it is, with the help of God, nothing will stop me from going to you."[12]

Considering the high stakes involved in transferring money across the ocean, and successfully converting it into paid passages, local persons of authority such as parish priests and landowners often served as fulcrums in the remittance system. In September 1851, James Walsh of Melbourne, Australia, sent his former landlord five pounds, which Lord Monteagle had loaned Walsh to fund his departure, along with another fourteen pounds "to defray the passage of my sister" and her six children. Walsh realized that this was not enough to pay their fares, but he hoped that Monteagle would make up the difference "for your Lordship is well aware that a poor, widowed woman could not have greater comfort than to have her family with her to a far distant land." When tickets or money got lost, priests could also help to clear things up. "I went to the parish priest and showed him the letter," Phelim Rooney explained of one such mislaid remittance. "He sent for Bartly Ferguson, Bartly made a declaration to the priest that he got neither ticket nor money or had neither any part or knowledge of it." At other times, landlords and their agents were called upon to help. When James Purcell wanted his sister Bridget to join him in Australia, he sent the cost of the fare to her landlord's business manager who would, Purcell was confident, "agree for your passage and get you the tickets." The Monteagle family papers in the National Library of Ireland contain many promissory notes signed by tenants agreeing to repay money borrowed to facilitate emigration to Australia. At other times, landlord and clergy worked together. In May 1853, Margaret Kelly learned from her parish priest that her sister had sent Lady Monteagle fifteen pounds "for the purpose of emigrating me to Australia." Kelly asked for five pounds immediately to buy her outfit for the voyage and hoped that Monteagle would hold on to the remaining ten "until I am on the eve of going." Trusted landlords could keep precious remittances safe.[13]

When all else failed, a relatively small number of Irish people had their passages abroad paid for, in whole or in part, by private charity. During the Famine era, the British champion of such assistance was the famed philanthropist Caroline Chisholm. The wife of a captain in the East India Company, Chisholm was moved by the plight of British immigrants—especially women and children—when she and her family moved to Australia in 1838. After promoting colonization while helping thousands of newcomers to find secure homes and jobs (and spouses), she returned to England in 1846, where she sought parliamentary support for initiatives to aid indigent emigrants, including the wives and children of convicts, to make their ways to the Antipodes. Over the following years, Chisholm received tens of thousands of petitions for assistance. In January 1847, she told the colonial secretary, Earl Grey, of "the numerous and daily applications, which I receive from country laborers and whole families for a free passage [to Australia . . .]; the majority of these are from Ireland." Unable to secure financial commitment from the government, Chisholm founded the Family Colonization Loan Society in 1849. Funded by charitable subscription, the organization enabled poor folks with meager savings to emigrate by offering them low-interest loans to cover the cost of their passage. In Australia, agents met these emigrants to find them jobs and collect their debt repayments. Over the next five years, the society enabled three thousand people to emigrate. Yet Chisholm's contribution went beyond merely the financial. In a July 1847 letter to the government authorities in Dublin, she described helping a group of women on their way to "homes of plenty" in Australia. "I have six weeks since written to Sydney," Chisholm explained, "in order that their husbands may be prepared to receive them at Hobart Town." Chisholm's transnational connections were as important as her cash.[14]

The remittance system thus rested on a tangle of local, national, and international circuits of communication and exchange. In February 1853, Patrick Danaher touched on this in a letter from Australia to his former landlord back in Ireland. "I am glad to learn that the American as well as the Australian immigrants are taking away as much as they can of their own friends from a land which refuses them a livelihood," he wrote. "Should emigration continue on a large scale for a few years more, I hope poverty will be known only by name in our beloved island." This system of exchange, on which so many Irish emigrants depended, was not a uniform network. Those traveling to Australia needed to wait longer for more money to cover higher fares and associated costs. It was certainly cheaper to brave a winter crossing to Quebec. At the same time, all remittances relied on the successful manipulation of both domestic and global networks of commerce, communication, and empire. Thousands of prepaid tickets and money orders traveled along circuits of capitalist exchange that had been developing for centuries. The reliable postal network that spanned large parts of the world in the mid-nineteenth century facilitated the transmission of up-to-date information on the needs of prospective emigrants while simultaneously allowing those abroad to deliver clear instructions on how best to expend limited resources. There was also more to a remittance than mere cash exchange for the system fostered transnational bonds of community between people on opposite sides of the globe. Sometimes those exchanges looked to the past, as when Hannah Lynch reminded her brother that their father "lent money behind the back of the ditch to neighbors" in the olden days. At other times, they focused on the future and the "hope to see you all in America yet." Finally, the fact that landlords and priests sometimes facilitated the remittance system by coordinating financial exchanges, resolving disputes, and even lending money for fares is a reminder that these broad, transnational networks were often intimately linked to local circuits of power.[15]

"Be So Good as to Send Me to America": Landlord-Assisted Migration

In November 1847, a leading proponent of British emigration, Archibald Cunninghame, addressed one of Ireland's most influential landlords on the twin problem of overpopulation in Ireland and labor shortage in Australia. "Could wise arrangement do nothing here?," he implored Lord Monteagle. Surely, "it would be profitable to pay one half, at least, if not the whole of the passage of poor families, rather than support them three years in a workhouse." From Cunninghame's perspective, the colonies, prospective emigrants, and ratepayers of Ireland would all benefit from such a plan "if it were judiciously managed." During the course of the Famine, several major landlords, caught between dwindling revenues (in unpaid rents) and rising costs (in increasing poor rates), responded by partially or wholly covering the emigration expenses of some of their tenants and workhouse paupers. Although these emigration schemes were encouraged, in part, by amendments to the poor law, the government's laissez-faire approach left it eager not to interfere—and especially not to pay—too much. As a result, despite the fact that it is difficult to gather reliable data on the subject, landlord-assisted emigration probably accounted for the departure of between 50,000 and 100,000 people from Ireland during the Famine (or between 2 and 4.5 percent of the total emigration between 1845 and 1855). The workhouses sent another 22,478 during the same time period, mostly after 1849, and are discussed in greater detail below. The most famous landlord-assisted schemes emanated from estates located in the impoverished west of Ireland such as those of Sir Robert Gore-Booth and Lord Palmerston (both in Sligo), Lord Lansdowne (in Kerry), and Major Mahon (in Roscommon), but similar examples were paid for by Charles Wandesforde (in Kilkenny), Earl Fitzwilliam (in Wicklow), the Marquis of Bath (in Monaghan), and others. While it is true, as popular memory holds, that many of the emigrants in these schemes were pushed out by eviction notices, many others were eager to go and sought to negotiate the best deals they could for themselves and their families.[16]

As Cunninghame suggested, assisted emigration made sense to many landlords and tenants alike. Encouraged by both the Whig government's long-term goal of transforming Ireland from a subsistence to a wage-earning economy, and by their responsibility for paying the rates on farms valued under four pounds, estate managers became eager to clear out poor farmers and paupers despite the short-term costs. In November 1850, for example, William Steuart Trench, who ran Lord Lansdowne's estate, suggested that his lordship offer free passage to any person in the local workhouse or receiving relief. The total cost would run between thirteen and fourteen thousand pounds, which was, Trench argued, "a sum less than it would cost to support them in the workhouse for a single year." Lansdowne agreed and by February 1855 they had spent close to fourteen thousand pounds dispatching a little over thirty-nine hundred emigrants abroad. If the 1847 amendments to the poor laws inspired landlords to pay for emigration, they also induced many tenants and paupers to accept it. Stronger tenants, whose holdings were valued at four pounds and over, were now liable for paying poor rates. Cashing in whatever capital they had and accepting help to leave made sense to many of them. On the other hand, those whose land was worth less than four pounds (and were thus exempt from paying poor rates) but over a quarter acre (and thus not entitled to outdoor relief under the "Gregory Clause") saw emigration as an escape from either the workhouse or starvation. Sometimes, evicted farmers saw assistance to emigrate as compensation for improvements they had made during their tenure. Finally, paupers who were living hand to mouth or consigned to the workhouse had precious few other options. Moreover, in the early years of the Famine, when the numbers of remittances from abroad were fewer and poor law unions less likely to offer assistance to emigrate, landlords' cash was one of the few forms of help available. In sum, that landlord-assisted emigration schemes often went hand in hand with the threat of eviction does not negate the fact that it made sense to tens of thousands of people in Ireland at the time.[17]

In truth, there were two kinds of such emigration programs. The most dramatic, and least common, involved the wholesale eviction and transportation of entire communities. In light of the government's distaste for funding assisted emigration, it is ironic that the landlord in such cases was the British monarchy. Of the five instances of such wholesale emigration from "Crown Estates," which sent a total of eleven hundred people abroad between 1847 and 1852, the most famous is the Ballykilcline removals of 1847 to 1848. Following the lapse of their previous lease in 1834, the hundred or so families on the estate began refusing to pay their rent and physically attacking those bailiffs sent to collect it. This famous "rebellion" finally ended in May 1847, when a stipendiary magistrate backed up by cavalry, infantry, and police showed up to enforce the eviction notices. In the face of subsequent petitions by tenants begging for permission to remain, the Crown responded by offering free passage plus provisions to those who peaceably surrendered their holdings. Between September 1847 and April 1848, over 360 tenants left for New York. In a letter to Thomas C. Knox, the agent tasked with coordinating the departure of the Ballykilcline tenants, the Clerk of the Quit Rent Office explained the stark choice they had. Upon the tenants "voluntarily surrendering their holdings and pulling down their own houses [to render them uninhabitable and thus exempt from poor rate valuation]," John Burke explained, "provision will be made for their emigration expenses to New York." For those who declined to take advantage of the offer, however, "the injunction will at once be issued, the parties dispossessed from their holdings, and their houses demolished." The other Crown Estates that shipped evicted tenants abroad were Boughill and Irvilloughter in County Galway, Castlemaine in County Kerry, Kilconcouse in King's County, and Kingwilliamstown in County Cork, where, one bureaucrat was convinced, "no permanent improvement can be effected until the surplus population of the estate be removed."[18]

The second and much more common form of assisted emigration scheme offered piecemeal assistance to individuals and families whose departure suited the landlord's plans for "squaring" their estates into smaller numbers of large, rational, economically viable holdings. These offers of assistance, often under the implicit or explicit threat of eviction, in some ways mirrored what was known as "tenant right" or "Ulster Custom," whereby a lessee was entitled to financial compensation for both improvements to the holding made during his tenure and the promise to offer the new tenant "goodwill" and undisputed occupancy. Perhaps this notion—that outgoing tenants were entitled to some form of financial compensation—partially influenced the thinking behind assisted emigration. As we shall see, some tenants certainly thought so. Nevertheless, landlords who assisted their tenants' emigration often began by ordering a local census to ascertain in some detail the number and relative wealth of the people living on their estates. The goal of such studies was to identify and target the poor and weak for emigration while encouraging the strong to stay. On the Strokestown estate in April 1847, agent Ross Mahon suggested that the first to go should be "those of the poorest and worst description who would be a charge on us for the poor house or for outdoor relief." This, he figured, would "relieve the industrious tenants." Around the same time, Lord Palmerston's land agent identified "150 families comprising 900 individuals [occupying] 500 Irish acres of land" who were suitable for assisted emigration. The only problem, Joseph Kincaid believed, was in deciding "[which] 400 shall I take out of the 900 candidates, all of whom are desirous to go."[19]

For some landlords and their agents, therefore, the eviction and assisted emigration of weaker tenants and laborers was a synchronized process. The Famine era witnessed a dramatic spike in the number of evictions across the country as landlords took the opportunity to rid their ledgers of insolvent tenants. Between 1846 and 1854, at least 140,000 families (almost 600,000 persons) were formally evicted in Ireland, with some areas hit harder than others. Around 18,000 people living in the Kilrush Union in County Clare were permanently evicted from their homes, for example, between the end of 1847 and December 1852. Most evicted families were left to fend for themselves, but some were offered assistance to emigrate if they did so immediately. One of the biggest and most notorious examples of such evict-and-emigrate schemes occurred on the Strokestown estate of Major Denis Mahon in 1847. Working in concert with a shipping firm in Liverpool, Mahon arranged for the emigration of 1,490 evicted tenants to Canada. They were escorted to the port of embarkation by Mahon's bailiff, John Robinson, whose job was to ensure that every last passenger set sail. Although Mahon's emigrants were supplied with extra food stores, many were nevertheless weak and ill prepared for the voyage. When typhus broke out at sea, they were decimated. Of the 1,490 who left Strokestown in May 1847, almost 50 percent died either at sea or at the quarantine station on Grosse Île. Other evicted emigrants claimed to have been simply deceived. When Hugh Reilly, a stonecutter from County Fermanagh, emigrated to Quebec in 1847, he did so with the assurance that in exchange for surrendering his holding to his landlord, Dr. Robert Collins, he would receive passage, clothing, and food. In fact, he and his family set sail from Derry "destitute of bedding and clothing." In his testimony before a justice of the peace in Quebec, Reilly swore "that he would never have quitted his place of abode but for false promises, and threats of being cut off from all future relief."[20]

Many accepted emigration over homelessness, but others resisted the offer of free passage even in the face of imminent eviction. When William Steuart Trench assumed responsibility for managing Lord Bath's estate in County Monaghan in 1851, he informed the tenants that they could pay their rent, face ejectment, or accept free emigration. Many took him up on the offer of paid passage. "A few, however, stood out," Trench later memorialized, "and would neither emigrate nor pay." Indeed, a man named Traynor told Trench "that he had held the land for six years without paying any rent, that it was worth fighting for, and 'by the powers' he would never pay while he could still hold out against the law!" Similarly, in Cork and Galway, there were reports of relief workers finding it incredible that tenants clung "to their huts with the greatest tenacity, and seem better pleased to perish in the ruins than surrender what they call their last hope of existence." Although Lord Lansdowne in Kerry paid for the passage of over three thousand paupers from his local workhouse in 1851, "some fifty or sixty" remained behind. For its part, the *Limerick Reporter* rued the 1852 eviction and emigration of tenants from the Gascoigne property in Limerick and Kerry. "We have heard that in addition to a free passage to Quebec, they have been provided with the munificent sum of twenty shillings each," the paper complained, "in all, something about £75 among seventy-five human beings to enable them to begin the world independently in the strange and distant land to which they are proceeding." There was often a thin line between eviction and assistance.[21]

It is also true that those who chose to accept landlord-assisted emigration were not necessarily meek and hopeless victims. In fact, the surviving papers of the Prior-Wandesforde estate in Castlecomer, County Kilkenny, demonstrate the ways in which many outgoing tenants used what little social and economic capital they had to negotiate the best deal they could for themselves and their families. When Charles Harward Wandesforde inherited the twenty-thousand-acre estate in 1830, he immediately took personal control of its financial affairs, which included reducing the number of subtenants on small holdings and, from 1840 onward, instituting a program of assisted emigration. Over the course of the next sixteen years, he (working with his son, John) spent a total of £15,432 14s. 5d. to aid 5,769 people to emigrate. Considered in light of the Famine, the statistics reveal some interesting patterns. Between 1840 and 1845, for example, he spent a total of £5,301 6s. 11d. to send 2,692 persons abroad. After the outbreak of the Famine, for the years 1846 to 1855 inclusive, Wandesforde paid another £10,131 7s. 10d. assisting 3,077 persons to emigrate. These statistics suggest that, on average, the number of people who left on a yearly basis decreased after the Famine began. Between 1840 and 1845, for example, Wandesforde aided the emigration of an average of 449 persons per year. During the Famine years, that average dropped to 308. However, after removing from consideration the two years when aided emigration from the estate was at its highest (in 1847 when 1,957 persons left) and lowest (in 1855 when only 29 did so), the average for the remaining Famine years was only 136 per annum, which was remarkably lower than the 449 assisted abroad annually in the five years leading up to the Famine. This drop in the yearly number leaving is obviously attributable in part to the fact that so many left in 1847, but it may also have something to do with costs. The statistics cited above indicate that Wandesforde spent more per passenger during the Famine years (over £3) than he had in the 1840 to 1845 period (slightly under £2).[22]

Nevertheless, as early as the summer of 1847, Wandesforde could boast that whereas before the estate was "crowded with a dense population living in miserable cabins," now the "country is improved [by emigration], and those left behind have benefitted by the change." Although it is clear that many left his estate under the threat of eviction, Wandesforde described the deal he had offered his tenants in generous terms, explaining that he had "paid the passage and allowed each individual a certain sum to assist in procuring food etc. for the voyage" while simultaneously allowing them "to sell the materials of their cabins" and keep the proceeds. Through his business manager, Kildare Dobbs, Wandesforde contracted James and Roderick Miley of the American and Colonial Emigration Office at 22 Eden Quay in Dublin to arrange the emigrants' transportation schedule. The Miley brothers drummed up business by keeping the Wandesforde estate and others like it, aware of what was available by sending along shipping notices, regulations, and news. In August 1845, for example, James Miley sent Dobbs a list of the ships soon heading for Canada. "Please let me know if there will be any for them," he wrote, as "this is the last chance for Quebec until spring." Similarly, in 1850 Roderick Miley apprised the Wandesfordes of the ship *T. Toole*, which was preparing to set sail in less than two weeks. The cost of tickets was "very low," Miley wrote. "I would advise you to make a move . . . as the fare will be twenty shillings dearer next spring." It seems hard to imagine that Wandesforde paid the high fares to Australia, but some of his tenants did emigrate there of their own accord, presumably through the offices of James and Roderick Miley. In a letter to Dobbs, James Miley looked for others. "I hope you will try and get a few more for [the *Nebraska*] as we are getting on rather slowly," Miley pleaded in October 1854. "Any likelihood of an Australian or two from your quarter?" Passage brokers played a role in stimulating assisted emigration.[23]

As news filtered through the estate in early 1847 that Wandesforde was planning to assist a large number of his tenants to emigrate, his office was swamped with hundreds of petitions from tenants asking to be included in the scheme. These appeals, handwritten on scraps of paper and now held in the National Library of Ireland, demonstrate the ways in which these prospective emigrants sought to negotiate the strongest bargain they could for themselves and their families. Many, in desperate straits, did the best they could with what little they had. James Kelly of Moneenroe described himself as "an exceedingly poor man" with eleven people in his family and "without any means of support for myself or them." Under such circumstances, "I hope you will order me to be sent to America as I have a cabin to fall and cannot possibly live at home." By offering to render his home unlivable before leaving, Kelly was reminding his landlord that he would remove another poor rate charge from Lord Wandesforde's ledger. Similarly, Thomas Cloase was "a poor man, having a large, helpless family in great distress." He pleaded "that in the exercise of your benignity, you will send myself and family (in all, ten) to America. I have a house to fall." Wandesforde had evidently made it clear that those facing eviction were eligible for emigration too, for, having recently received a notice to quit his holding, Denis Bowe hoped the landlord would send him and his family to America. For her part, the widow Biddy Dunleary of Ballycomey recognized the landlord's desire to square his estate and offered her departure as a contribution to that plan. She and her five children, who shared a cabin with others, had just learned "that the family occupying the other end of the cabin is emigrating to America." Eager to leave, Dunleary insisted that she and her children "would accompany [the other family] thither sooner than be a source of annoyance or trouble to their neighbors holding land in that spot." On the back of the petition Wandesforde scrawled his reply: "Assist them." Even those with little to work with could use it to their advantage.[24]

After learning that Lord Wandesforde had granted their application for assisted emigration, many tenants subsequently petitioned his wife, Lady Wandesforde, for cash to buy clothing and food for the voyage itself. Through newspapers, public notices, and letters from friends and family abroad, many tenants evidently had a sense of the need for decent apparel on the voyage. "My Lady," wrote John Curry in March 1847, "I am returned, me and my family, for America—I have three daughters and myself badly covered. I hope it will be pleasing to you, my Lady, to order some clothing for them as they are much in need of the same going to a foreign land." In his request for additional support, James Foley of Loon indicated that without it, his plan for emigration could fall apart. "Oh! Do not leave me to languish in this unhappy land," he wrote Lady Wandesforde, "but deign to order me a help of clothing as I cannot go to America if you do not consider me. I have nine in family and no means of clothing them." Bryan McDonald, who was preparing to emigrate in April 1847, begged her ladyship for "some night and day covering as we are at present not fit to appear in society in consequence of our nakedness." A widow named Brenan had obviously heard that the regulations governing foodstuffs at sea were inadequate. In her petition to Lord Wandesforde, she began by thanking him for agreeing to send herself and her children to America but asked for a grant of "two pounds in addition to the usual sum, as she and family are quite destitute of clothing, and they would, after buying necessary articles, have to go to sea without any other than the ship allowance, a thing they dare not venture to do." In such petitions, those preparing to leave were reminding their benefactors that the passage itself was only part of the cost of emigration.[25]

To enable tenants to raise some of their own costs, and in keeping with the custom of "tenant right" whereby outgoing lessees were entitled to compensation for improvements, Lord Wandesforde allowed prospective emigrants to sell their interest to other tenants. When the value of the land involved was not enough to cover their costs, however, tenants petitioned Wandesforde to make up the difference, realizing that their departures would contribute to his plan for rationalizing the estate. Daniel Bryan complained that the person who bounded his holding, Luke Nesbitt, "has not the means to assist me, also no one else wants it." So Bryan offered the holding to Wandesforde himself, asking only "four pounds for the house, which your Honor allowed me to build, and which cost me £6 15s. 0d. and also £1 0s. 0d. for the bere [barley], which is what it cost me for seed and labor." Once paid, Bryan promised, "I will give you no further trouble." Wandesforde was unenthusiastic about such arrangements. A widow named Seymour reminded him that he had granted her application to go to America and that "you are giving six acres, which I held, to Darby Hickey and for which I paid £4 11s. 5d. for I also burned and put on it eighty barrels of lime." Seymour hoped that Wandesforde would therefore "give me compensation as I am very poor having eight children to provide for," but his reply stipulated, "The incoming tenant must allow you for any improvements." Eager emigrants living on expensive properties, for which there was little demand, sought to work out their own deals with the landlord. Daniel Flinne, for example, had "an excellent house [on Kilkenny Street in Castlecomer] well fitted up" but could not find anyone who could afford it. If Wandesforde would "have the kindness to grant me £30 to cover my little encumbrances in Castlecomer and to victual me to Quebec, I will give you up the house until the amount is considered sufficiently paid." To sweeten the deal, Flinne noted there was "a solvent tenant, a native of Castlecomer, proposing for said house that will pay regularly your office £10 a year."[26]

Finally, in a society in which heritage meant so much, some outgoing tenants used their family history as social capital in the scramble for free passage abroad. In particular, the experience of having worked (or having family members who worked) in the estate's colliery evidently had some cachet. James Riley, whose family had already been granted passage to America, hoped that "my long servitude of thirty-five years" would convince his lordship to assist him "with some little means for my sea stores." In her petition to join her husband, brothers, and sisters in the coalpits of Pottsville, Pennsylvania, Mary Wallace reminded Wandesforde, "Tim, my father, was a collier that always worked in his Lordship's colliery until his death." Similarly, Margaret Coogan hoped Wandesforde would "be so good as to send me to America as my forefathers before me were miners under your honorable family and never troubled you before." At the same time, other tenants referred to their ancestry in their pleas for help. The Wandesforde family was originally from Yorkshire in England and settled in Castlecomer, County Kilkenny, in the late 1630s when Christopher Wandesforde, who held various posts in the Crown's administration of Ireland, bought the estate over the objections of the area's original inhabitants, the Brenans. One of the dispossessed owners' descendants, Michael Brenan of Aughamucky, referred to that history in his petition. Brenan begged "to inform you that myself and father and grandfather and ancestors [had all lived] on this estate" but "being no longer able to maintain my family, which numbers seven, I would wish to emigrate with them to America if you, sir, would be so kind as to give me a passage." Centuries of tenure could end with a free passage abroad.[27]

These petitions demonstrate that landlord assistance was a reasonable option for many people seeking to leave Ireland during the Famine. Local networks of communication and community could provide access to the cash required to depart. Tenants were aware of the ways in which emigration suited their landlords as much as themselves, and they manipulated these facts as best they could. True, the tenants brought little to the bargaining table, but they proved adept at making the most of what they had. Coercion certainly lurked in the background (and often the foreground) of these emigration schemes, and historian James Donnelly Jr. is right to decry the notion "that a pauperized tenant without the ability to pay rent or to keep his family nourished had a 'free' choice in the matter [of emigration]." Wandesforde's tenant Billy Cantwell made this clear when he asserted that nothing "but mere necessity and the want of daily or sufficient sustenance . . . could induce me to part

with my bit of land at such an advanced age and think of emigration."
At the same time, others clearly saw in North America the chance for a
new lease on life. There is, therefore, no right answer to the hoary old
chestnut over whether or not evicted tenants were emigrating "voluntarily." Focusing on the dire situation in which many of these people
found themselves, and the cruelty with which some landlords treated
them, should not overshadow the inventiveness and bravery with which
many responded.[28]

There were both advantages and disadvantages to partaking of
landlord-assisted emigration schemes. Developed on a piecemeal
basis by different landlords, they varied wildly. In his annual report
for the year ending 1846, the chief emigration officer at Quebec noted
that while groups of emigrants sent by Colonel Wyndham and Francis Spaight "were generally well-provided" for and granted "landing
money" upon arrival, others sent by different (unnamed) landlords
"landed here in extreme poverty," having received "only a free passage
and provisions." Landlord-assisted emigrants also often departed for
North America without networks of familial support in place to help
when the journey ended and the money ran out. Because the timings
of such voyages were often based on the lowest prices, emigrants sometimes ended up crossing the ocean in late autumn or even winter, the
worst times of the year to be at sea. The destitute and the old, whom
landlords were most eager to send out, also lacked the material and
physical resources to survive the journey. At the same time, there were
some advantages too. For those lacking their own resources, the landlords' cash was hard to turn down. Although they may not have benefitted from family networks at home and abroad, assisted emigrants did
often embark on ships in groups—from a single family to a couple of
hundred people—which served as a transplanted network of protection
and succor. Many petitioners mentioned having family in America to
go to, while local persons of authority sometimes also used their connections abroad to help. Thus did Archibald Cunninghame write to
friends in Australia, asking them to greet and "go on board the [emi-
grant ship] *Lady Peel* and to try to find employment for the families"
assisted to emigrate by Lord Monteagle. All in all, landlord-assisted
migration represented another way in which bonds of community allowed some Irish emigrants to earn their passage abroad. These people

were clearly the expropriated victims of agricultural capitalism, but they were also canny negotiators doing the best they could under difficult circumstances.[29]

"Benevolent Intentions": Government-Assisted Migration

When asked his opinion, in early 1847, of the degree to which the government should interfere with the process of emigration to Canada, the chairman of the CLEC, Thomas Frederick Elliot, counseled a laissez-faire approach. There were so many ports sending so many ships to British North America, Elliot opined, that emigrants could buy their own passages easily, economically, "and in a manner more exactly suited to the circumstances of each individual, than it could be done for them by the government." In other words, as historian Christine Kinealy has suggested, despite the government's "theoretical approval . . . for emigration, in practical terms little support was forthcoming." Things were different when it came to Australia. There, the colonial governments' willingness to financially assist the emigration of able-bodied workers convinced the CLEC to provide the bureaucratic coordination critical to the process. Following a brief cessation of government-assisted emigration to Australia between 1843 and 1847, the CLEC continued facilitating the movement of healthy laborers and their families to Australia. Changes to the Irish poor laws in 1847 and 1849 also allowed workhouse guardians to cover all or part of the emigration costs for their pauperized inmates to Canada and Australia. These systems overlapped in important ways, discussed elsewhere in this chapter, with forms of financial assistance provided by families and landlords as well as the convict transportation system. There were, in other words, both domestic and imperial imperatives at work in the process. As such, government-assisted migration served as another thread in the transnational web of community rebuilding during the Great Famine.[30]

In March 1847, Irish-born colonial reformer John Robert Godley presented the British prime minister, John Russell, with a plan "of systematic colonization, on a very large scale, from Ireland to Canada, and of the assistance of the state to promote it." Cosigned by dozens of dignitaries including several Irish peers and members of Parliament, the memorial proposed to send 1.5 million people to British North America over the course of three years. Calculating the cost of each emigrant's passage at three pounds, his plan called for the government to contribute one pound while leaving it up to the emigrants themselves to procure the remainder, whether through cash savings, remittances, or assistance from one's landlord. On top of the £1.5 million spent by the government on emigrant passages, however, an additional £7.5 million would be required to fund the construction of churches, schools, and stores to help the emigrants get settled in Canada. The total cost to the Exchequer, of £9 million, would be paid for through Irish property and income taxes. Despite institutional suspicion of such large-scale emigration schemes, there was some precedent for it. In 1823 and 1825, the Peter Robinson scheme sent almost 2,600 Irish emigrants to Ontario, Canada, at a cost of £53,000. Such was the success of the Robinson scheme that the government subsequently received over 50,000 applications from people in Ireland seeking assistance to emigrate. Although acknowledged as a triumph at the time, the Robinson program's financial cost dissuaded many in the government from trying to repeat it. When Godley presented his plan in March 1847, he admitted it was expensive but argued that it would both help the Irish poor and "greatly advance the general interests of the empire at large."[31]

Press reactions to the plan for colonization were mixed. The nationalist Dublin *Nation*, citing the seventeenth-century dispossession of Irish Catholic landowners by Oliver Cromwell and his English Parliamentary forces, objected immediately. "In 1647, to Hell or Connaught was the anti-Irish cry," it exhorted. "In 1847, Canada is substituted for Connaught." The Catholic Bishop of Derry, Dr. Edward Maginn, opposed the plan too, in part "because I recognize among the principals in your committee the names of the descendants of those who abetted Cromwell in transporting seventy thousand of the Irish people to the [West] Indies, to die there like dogs, un-anointed." On the opposite end of the political spectrum, the Conservative *Times* of London scoffed at "a scheme for transplanting some thousands of the least educated, the least energetic, and the most helpless of the Celtic population" to the wilds of Canada. "How fearful must be the malady of Ireland when its friends suggest as its best remedy the creation of a pauper and semi-barbarous colony on the confines of a jealous rival and in the heart of an unsettled population!" Irish landlords, by contrast, preferred the idea of state-funded emigration to long-term residencies in workhouses. "The utmost a poor law can do is to make existence tolerable to the pauper, whom it tends to brutify," opined the Cavan *Anglo-Celt*, a Unionist, pro-landlord weekly sympathetic to the poor. "Mr. Godley's scheme proposes to elevate the pauper into the colonist. The poor law provides for the animal—Mr. Godley caters for the man." The proposal enjoyed support from interested in parties in Canada itself and the Antipodes, where the *South Australian Register* was convinced the scheme would, if adopted, "be found so beneficial in every respect, and to all parties, that it will not be long before every colony is enabled to share in its advantages." In the end, despite creating a select committee to investigate its feasibility, Russell and the Whigs ultimately abandoned Godley's colonization scheme.[32]

While the British government was unwilling to fund large-scale emigration, it did prove ready to offer bureaucratic assistance when others were footing the bill. Indeed, emigration to Australia could never have proceeded as effectively as it did without the help of the CLEC. By the late 1820s, it had become clear that the colonies' need for workers was outstripping the convict labor supply. If the colonies were to continue expanding, large-scale immigration would be required, and yet the high cost of the journey combined with Australia's reputation as a "thief-colony" meant that emigrants had to be enticed to go. As a result, between 1830 and 1860, approximately 56 percent of all newcomers received assistance of one sort or another. Funding these fares allowed the colonial governments to filter the incoming labor pool according to their needs, preferring married agricultural laborers (with few or no children) and single, female, domestic servants. The emigrants were responsible for partially covering their costs, however, including a passage deposit, sometimes called "bed-money" or "bedding" (one or two pounds), traveling outfit (approximately two pounds), and the journey to Plymouth, England, the port from which most Australian emigrant ships departed. Emigrants seeking an assisted passage also had to negotiate the CLEC bureaucracy. To begin, applications were sent to London by the prospective emigrants, their benefactors, or one of the selecting agents dispersed around Britain and Ireland. Those whose applications were approved then sent their passage deposit along with certificates of baptism, marriage, and health as well as character references. Upon final approval, the candidate was sent an embarkation order, which often instructed them to proceed to Plymouth within a few days. At times, landlords and family members could help negotiate the system. In January 1855, Melbourne-based Patt Culhane asked his former landlord to use "your influence with the emigration commissioners in procuring a passage for my cousins," the cost of whose bedding deposit Culhane had enclosed in the letter.[33]

James Clements of Crossmolina, County Mayo, negotiated his way through this bureaucracy alone. On October 20, 1846, the secretary of the CLEC, Stephen Walcott, acknowledged Clements's application for assisted emigration to Australia, enclosed the CLEC's rules and regulations, and urged Clements to forward copies of his family's baptismal records "as without these documents, your case cannot be taken into consideration." Two and a half weeks later, a problem arose. The board had noticed discrepancies in the stated ages of Clements and his wife. They would need to send in their original baptismal certificates or withdraw their application. Clements must have done so because on November 14, Walcott informed him that his family had been accepted and could now send in six pounds "to meet the expenses of bedding, etc." When Clements failed to send in the full deposit, however, Walcott wrote again to ask for the outstanding balance of three pounds and to remind Clements of the promises he had made. Were Clements and his wife to arrive in Plymouth without their three children, or if their ages and occupations did not match their application, they would not be allowed to sail. One week later, the long-awaited embarkation order arrived. The Clements family was booked to travel aboard the *Phoebe* on December 16. Clements may have misread or misunderstood the order, or he may simply have gotten stranded en route to Plymouth. Either way, one week later, Walcott wrote to him in the port of Sligo (approximately forty-five miles from Crossmolina), saying that although he regretted Clements's difficulty, "you were distinctly told that you were to proceed to Plymouth . . . and no mention was made of any other port." The family would have to stay put while the government's emigration officer in Sligo inquired "into the circumstances of your case." The surviving records do not reveal what happened to Clements and his family, but the point is that, despite the difficulties inherent in the process, tens of thousands of Irish people managed to emigrate to Australia with the assistance of the CLEC between 1845 and 1855.[34]

Under the Bounty System of the 1830s and early 1840s, burdensome costs and government prejudice against large, young families often compelled Australian assisted emigrants to leave without their small children. When the government reinstated assisted emigration in 1847, however, it also agreed—thanks in part to pressure from Caroline Chisholm—to facilitate the emigration (under the superintendence of married couples) of those children who had been left behind. Nevertheless, as the surviving records indicate, insurmountable difficulties wrought by the dislocations and dangers of Famine-era Ireland had sometimes arisen in the meantime. When the government elected, in the summer of 1847, to charter a ship called the *Sir Edward Parry* for assisted emigrants, it sought to include a number of children left behind by pre-1843 emigrants. In an August 1847 letter to the colonial secretary of New South Wales, Stephen Walcott explained that of the 226 children whose parents had petitioned for their inclusion on the ship, 111 were expected to be able to proceed without much problem. While 40 others could not be located, another 48 were simply too destitute to purchase their outfit and travel to Plymouth. In keeping with the "benevolent intentions" of the colonial authorities, the CLEC agreed to pay the costs of any who could make it to Dublin. The final 27 were "unable or decline themselves of this indulgence" for reasons, which Walcott outlined in his letter "for the satisfaction of their relatives" who would want to know why their children had not embarked. Six were dead, Walcott reported, three were too unwell or too young to travel, and another three had already emigrated to North America. The rest refused to go (or their guardians would not let them) or were already committed to apprenticeships in Ireland. That some Irish parents succeeded in having the CLEC send their children to Australia, however, demonstrates another way in which emigrants used imperial networks to reunite families scattered across two hemispheres.[35]

For those incapable of gathering the ancillary costs required for CLEC-supported travel, the local poor law unions provided another avenue for assisted emigration to North America and Australia. When the Irish poor law system was created by an act of Parliament in 1838, it made little mention of assisted emigration and few unions engaged in the practice. This hesitancy continued during the early years of the Famine, even after an 1847 amendment, which sought to entice small farmers to relinquish their plots and leave the country. Many unions were simply too short on cash to finance emigration, even in cases where it was clear that assisting inmates to leave was more cost-efficient than keeping them in the workhouse. Things changed in 1849, however, when another amendment allowed guardians to borrow the money for emigration from the Exchequer Bill Loan Commissioners. Between August 1849 and March 1855, a total of 17,288 persons were assisted to emigrate under this 1849 amendment act. Although the poor law unions financed much of these expenses, it is also true that remittances from family and relatives played a significant role too. When Rose and Biddy O'Brien's widowed mother paid their passages to Baltimore, Maryland, in the summer of 1851, for example, the guardians of the Gort union agreed to purchase them each "a suit of clothes" while covering the cost of their four-year-old sister Kate's voyage. Later that same year, the Mountbellew union sanctioned the expenditure of six pounds to allow Mary Conlon and her two children to emigrate to America. Conlon's sister, "who emigrated a few years since, has sent a paid passage for Mary Conlon with £1 to take her to the place of embarkation," but when she did not include enough to cover the costs of her children, the union did so. Landlords (who often served as poor law officers) could directly contribute too. In August 1853, Lord Campbell personally offered "to emigrate six or eight of the young women or lads at present in the [Galway workhouse]" if the poor law guardians agreed to pay "one moiety of the expense." In these ways, assistance from family, landlords, and poor law unions often overlapped.[36]

Considering the intrinsic dangers of the emigration process, a closer look at one poor law union's agreement with a shipping broker demonstrates the advantages, which accrued to emigrants traveling on such a contract. In July 1854, Patrick Gibson of Ennis, County Clare, undertook to convey approximately fifty paupers (forty adults and ten children) from the Galway workhouse to Quebec. For fees of a little under four pounds per adult (over fourteen years of age) and slightly under two pounds per child, Gibson agreed to a long list of conditions designed to both protect the poor law union's investment and safeguard the emigrants themselves. Gibson would personally accompany them to

Limerick and make sure that their entire journey from the workhouse to Quebec was completely paid for. He also committed to providing each traveler with "bedding, consisting of a straw pillow, sheet, blanket, [and] quilt" as well as "cooking utensils requisite for the voyage." To ensure that the emigrants' well-being was not sacrificed to cut costs, Gibson promised to ensure that there was "a duly qualified medical man on board" their ship. Delays were part of many emigrants' experiences, but Gibson agreed to pay a penalty of one pound for every day past August 10 that the emigrants' departure was postponed and gave "good security to the amount of £400" for the fulfillment of the contract. On August 25, the master of the workhouse attested "that he saw [the paupers] sail in the ship *Jessie* and that Mr. Gibson treated them most kindly." Two months later, the Galway poor law guardians received a letter from the emigration officer at Quebec, which stated that the *Jessie*'s passengers had "arrived safe and in good health and, with a few exceptions, were doing well." Their welfare was thanks, in part, to the conditions demanded by the workhouse guardians.[37]

While most poor-law-assisted emigrants left in small numbers and at irregular intervals, the Earl Grey (or "female orphan") scheme was unique as it financed the emigration of 4,114 young women on twenty vessels from 118 different unions in Ireland to Australia between 1848 and 1850. Designed to satisfy Australia's growing need for single women, the program was mostly funded by the colonial authorities with bureaucratic assistance from the CLEC and individual workhouses providing each inmate with an outfit for the voyage and passage to Plymouth. Suitable candidates were between fourteen and eighteen years of age, eager to emigrate, and of sober habits and good health. Those with household skills or experience in domestic service were preferred. To ensure the quality of the labor pool, the CLEC sent a naval officer named Lieutenant Henry to visit participating Irish workhouses and select the best candidates. Once word of the program reached the Irish unions, women began volunteering immediately. For its part, the weekly *Limerick Reporter* approved of the scheme, believing it held out "the promise of much benefit to those who are permitted to avail themselves of it." In September 1848, Lieutenant Henry reached the Galway workhouse and selected twenty-five women to go to Australia. A month later, the union paid their bills including £52 10s. 9d. for clothing and

£50 for "expenses in conveying the emigrants to Plymouth." As with the other emigrants traveling with the assistance of their workhouses, these "female orphans" (or "orphan girls") enjoyed a certain level of protection from the system. In October 1849, another batch of women from the Galway union traveled to England to sail on the *Thomas Arbuthnot*. When the government officer at Plymouth noted "deficiencies in the outfit of the emigrants," he supplied the want and charged the Galway union for it.[38]

These examples illustrate that although workhouse paupers occupied the lowest rungs of Irish society during the Famine, those lucky few who secured government-assisted passage were, in many ways, fortunate in the long run. As English-speaking laborers in a collapsing economy, just one ticket away from colonies starved for workers, they found themselves at the nexus of a broader conundrum facing mid-nineteenth-century global capitalism. Their departures were fueled by their own desire to leave combined with the yearning of the colonial authorities, imperial governors, and local poor law guardians to send them away. Previous emigrants played a critical role in the process as well. Mary Conlon's sister must have known that she had not sent enough money to cover the costs of Mary and her children going to America. Yet she also would have known—through personal experience, word of mouth, or the popular press—that her sum would probably be enough to encourage the Mountbellew union to make up the difference. The international administrative reach of the CLEC meant that those who headed for Australia enjoyed more logistical support than those whose local poor law unions sent them to Quebec. But, generally speaking, government-assisted emigrants enjoyed more protection en route to their destinations than did average travelers. When James Clements went to the wrong port, the local emigration officer looked into his case. When Patrick Gibson agreed to ship fifty paupers to Canada, the guardians made sure his passengers were not charged a penny along the way. When the workhouse women from Galway showed up at Plymouth with insufficient clothing, the government bought what they needed. When certain children failed to embark on their ship for Australia, a bureaucrat in the CLEC explained why. For these reasons, tens of thousands of people used government-assisted emigration to reunite their families abroad during the Famine.

"For the Purpose of Being Transported": The Convict Vessel as Emigrant Ship

When the female convict transport *Waverley* left Ireland en route to Van Diemen's Land on July 18, 1847, its surgeon-superintendent was pleased to note that the "prisoners generally, and all other persons, on embarking appeared in tolerable health." Although it may be reasonable to assume that the "all other persons" to whom the doctor made only passing reference were the captain and crew working on the ship, the truth is much more complicated. Beyond the officers, crew, and 134 female convicts on the *Waverley*, there were no fewer than 33 children (of the convicts themselves) as well as 40 "free settlers." This latter group was composed, a bureaucrat in Dublin Castle explained, partly of "the families of certain convicts in the colony," whose passage was being partially funded by the government, and partly of impoverished citizens whose travel was being paid for by Caroline Chisholm's Family Colonization Loan Society. Indeed, the number of free settlers traveling with the Chisholm program would have been even higher, but by the time the *Waverley* was prepared to depart, several of them had "not arrived and [could not] therefore be embarked." Nevertheless, the statistics on the ship's population are intriguing. Of the 207 passengers listed by the surgeon, fully 73 were not convicts either. This means that over one-third (35.3 percent) of the people traveling in the *Waverley* were using it as a form of low-cost travel from Ireland. The pages that follow investigate the ways in which a wide range of Irish people treated convict transports as emigrant ships during the Great Famine. Doing so demonstrates how transnational circuits of discipline could be repurposed into networks of cheap or even free travel for those willing to engage in the risky business of manipulating the British penal system for their own ends.[39]

It is true that the *Waverley's* proportion of non-convict passengers was relatively high by the standards of the day, but such travelers were by no means an anomaly on Famine-era convict ships leaving Ireland. It must be noted here that fears of ill discipline and the government's reticence to allow children to accompany their fathers to Australia meant that male convict ships never experienced the proportions of free passengers that female ships did. Yet the journals of the ships' surgeons render it clear that convicts and crew were not the only people sailing on female convict transports. Of the fourteen female convict ships that sailed from Ireland to Australia between 1845 and 1853, the surgeons recorded exact statistics on passengers for nine of the voyages. Those numbers indicate that the 366 children (not including live births at sea) and 98 free settlers who accompanied the 1,629 female convicts on those ships represented 22.2 percent of the total number of passengers (2,093). Analysis of individual Irish convict ships offers more detail. In September 1846, the *Arabian* conveyed 150 female convicts and 37 of their children to Van Diemen's Land. Of the 187 passengers on that ship, therefore, at least 37 (19.8 percent) were non-convicts. The *John Calvin* left Kingstown in January 1848, carrying 171 female convicts along with 33 children of convicts and 9 free settlers. These 42 souls constituted 19.7 percent of the non-crew on board. When the *Blackfriar* sailed from Ireland to Van Diemen's Land in January 1851, 20.2 percent of its passengers (59 children and 7 free settlers) were not convicts. The final female convict ship to leave Ireland for Van Diemen's Land was the *Midlothian*. When it departed Kingstown in late 1852, its 19 children, 12 free settlers, and 2 "intermediate passengers" constituted 16.3 percent of the passengers aboard. Many families had figured out that networks designed to discipline and punish could also serve as circuits of migration.[40]

Various kinds of government employees also used convict transports to get themselves and their families off the island. Military pensioners retiring to Australia often did so. Respectable, educated women could also hitch rides as "matrons" on female convict ships. These women were hired by the government to maintain discipline and avoid "immorality" among the convicts themselves or between them and the crew. These were not wealthy women in search of volunteer hours. Matrons were entitled to a gratuity of thirty pounds upon landing in Australia, but many needed the cash before leaving. In 1848, Dublin Castle agreed to advance twenty pounds to the matron Mrs. O'Connell to enable her "to purchase her outfit" for the journey, while Mrs. Sproule, matron of the *John Calvin*, was granted ten pounds in advance "to purchase necessaries for the voyage." That these adventurous women thought of the trip as permanent emigration is evidenced by the fact that they often brought family members with them. Mrs. Sproule was allowed to bring her five-year-old child. On the *John William Dare*, "Mrs. Reid's family was permitted to accompany her." When Mrs. Sherlock sailed from Kingstown as a matron on the *Midlothian*, she brought her two daughters. In 1849, Mrs. Lambert brought her sister aboard the *Australasia*. Female convict ships sometimes carried a very different kind of part-time government employee as well. In early 1848, Daniel Kelly, who had "been of some service in bringing to detection seven persons connected with illegal associations in the county of Limerick," was granted free passage on the *John Calvin* along with his wife and five children. The following year, Mr. W. Hart, his wife, and six children were given the same "on account of [Mr. Hart's] services during the late outbreak," presumably the Young Ireland rebellion of 1848. In November 1852, the *Midlothian*'s non-convict passengers including Anne and Mary Giblin, whom the register identified as "Crown Witnesses." In sum, pensioners, matrons, and informers used female convict ships to get themselves and their families off the island.[41]

Male convict ships carried a much smaller proportion of free passengers, but those charged with enforcing discipline could exploit the ship as a tool for migration. Members of the convicts' guard, for example, regularly brought their families with them, presumably with the intention of settling permanently in Australia. When the *Samuel Boddington* left Ireland in the summer of 1845, its passengers included a complement of the "guard's families" comprising twelve wives and twelve children. A year later, five wives and six children accompanied the *Lord Auckland*'s guard. The journals of other surgeons noted that the *Tory*, *Pestonjee Bomanjee*, *Blenheim II*, and *Rodney* all brought guards' wives and children to Van Diemen's Land. Beyond guards' families, male convict ships also carried Catholic priests. During the Famine years, the government appointed clergymen to provide a combination of religious and educational instruction to the prisoners during the long voyage from Ireland to Australia. The hope was that these months of training would better prepare the convicts for work in the Antipodes while simultaneously "impressing on their minds a proper sense of their moral and religious responsibilities." Beyond offering Fr. Robert Downing a free voyage to Australia on the male convict transport *Pestonjee Bomanjee*, the Lord Lieutenant's office directed that he be paid 110 days salary at the rate of £100 per annum (about £30) plus "a sum of £50 for his gratuity." Unlike the convicts he was accompanying, Downing could enjoy a return leg of the voyage as well. "If that gentleman shall <u>remain</u> in the colony for some time," a bureaucrat in Dublin Castle explained, "he may receive the advantage of free passage to Europe <u>whenever</u> he <u>shall wish</u> to avail himself of it." The transportation system was, for a few, an open-ended return ticket.[42]

Many passengers labeled as "free settlers" were actually the wives and children of convicts. Throughout the nineteenth century, the imperial government facilitated the reunion of hundreds of such families (the majority of whom, during the Famine years, were Irish) on the grounds that doing so would both redress the colonial gender imbalance and encourage the good behavior of their male convicts. According to Perry McIntyre, 565 Irish convicts (548 males and 17 females) consigned to New South Wales successfully applied to reunite their families between 1788 and 1852. Whereas the colonial governments paid for the assisted emigration schemes, the imperial government itself funded such convict family reunions. The process relied on the international transmission of multiple documents over the course of several months and even years. The only convicts who could apply where those who "by their good conduct and by the possession of the means of supporting their families, have entitled themselves to the privilege of having their wives and children sent to them free of expense." An application began with the convict's employer who, if satisfied, sent it to the superintendent of convicts, who subsequently forwarded it to the colony's governor. From there, it sailed thirteen thousand miles to London, where the Colonial Office considered it before sending it on to the Home Office, which rendered a final decision. If the application was successful, the convict's family was contacted and arrangements made for their travel to Australia. That so many were successful is a testament to the courage, initiative, and cooperation of various kinds of people from the fringes to the core of imperial power. The initial Australian recommendations often relied upon the words of the local farmers, artisans, and businesspeople for whom individual convicts had been working.[43]

The surviving records of this family reunification system are held in the National Archives of Ireland's Free Settlers' Papers. A specific example from those files demonstrates the ways in which these transnational processes operated. In March 1847, Archibald McIntyre, a comfortable farmer living in Van Diemen's Land, wrote a letter to a person of means named Edmond Carr of Kilbride, County Roscommon. McIntyre was writing on behalf of his convict employee, Pat Mally, who had been working for McIntyre for some time and wished to bring his wife and two sons out to the Antipodes. McIntyre fully supported the plan. Mally hoped, McIntyre explained, that Carr would "be so kind as to let his family know that he is trying to get them out to this country through your influence and also takes the liberty of reminding you of your promise to him when he left Roscommon of sending them to him." McIntyre was also confident that the convict's family would not become public charges in Van Diemen's Land. Mally had always "conducted himself well," McIntyre explained, "and saved a little money and if his wife is industrious, she could maintain herself well by our family washing alone." In a final note, McIntyre added that "Mally sends his love to his wife and children and to all those that wish them well." Even a bureaucratic petition represented a chance to exchange tenderness with kinfolk thousands of miles away. Carr responded favorably and, in a letter to Dublin Castle, forwarded McIntyre's letter from Australia along with a note of his own confirming that Mally's wife was "an exceedingly well conducted and hard working, industrious woman" who would adapt well to life in the colonies. Mrs. Mally was "most anxious" to join Patrick in Australia "but has no means to do so" and would therefore "feel most grateful should the government grant a free passage to Van Diemen's Land to her and her sons in a female convict ship." Although it is unknown if Mally's request was granted, his file demonstrates how the voices of four people, in differential relations of power and thousands of miles apart, could support convict family reunions for their own reasons.[44]

While the majority of such petitions featured women seeking to join their transported husbands, it is also true that men left behind in Ireland could lobby the government for financial support to reconstitute their family in Australia. In April 1850, Bryan Conlon of Limerick petitioned Dublin Castle for assisted passage. His wife Bridget had been convicted of larceny the year before and, while awaiting transportation in Dublin's Grangegorman Depot, had given birth to a baby boy. On foot of her good behavior, the authorities had allowed Bridget to take the baby and their two other children with her to Van Diemen's Land.

Now Bryan, who had managed to save five pounds toward the cost of the journey through his own "indefatigable labor," was desperate to join them. "Petitioner not having a single individual belonging to him in this country and being an able bodied man . . . and ready and willing to work," he wrote, "he may be of use in the country or colony to which his wife has been transported." The authorities agreed, and Conlon was allowed to earn his passage by tending to the livestock on the *Duke of Cornwall* female convict ship when it left Dublin in the summer of 1850. Less fortunate was Con McMahon of Clontibret, County Monaghan, who had, in July 1848, experienced "the inexpressible calamity" of having his son, James, transported to Sydney for perjury. McMahon had recently received a letter from James "saying he likes that colony" and encouraging his father to apply to Dublin Castle for "funds by which any of his brothers and sisters might emigrate to that colony" as his means of assisting them were insufficient. The government denied the request, however, on the grounds that the Australian authorities had not sent the required certificate attesting to James's "good conduct and character." Success relied on the ability to navigate transnational bureaucracies.[45]

Focusing too much on the convicts' families elides another important fact: that the prisoners themselves were sometimes using transportation as a method of free emigration. The Famine certainly forced many to employ jails and workhouses as forms of short- and long-term relief from hunger, but it is also true that for those desperate for a way off the island (and into guaranteed employment) the convict ship offered a way out. The Convict Reference Files in the National Archives of Ireland make this clear. These petitions, often in the words of the prisoners themselves, demonstrate the ways in which people creatively manipulated the system for their own ends. In September 1848, sisters Mary and Johanna Kelleher of County Cork submitted a petition explaining that they had stolen some shirts, "which offence your Memorialists committed for the purpose of being transported with their [mother] who was convicted at the same sessions and sentenced to seven years transportation." The plan failed, however, as the sisters were merely sent to prison in Ireland for twelve months. Their petition, which included a number of supporting letters from men such as their jail's governor and even the judge who convicted them, asked that they be sent to

australian convict attempts
✓s

Australia with their mother. In the end, their petition was successful and they were sent on board the *Maria*, not as convicts but as "free settlers." From the opposite angle, Mary Jane Campbell explained to Dublin Castle that "impelled by hunger, [she had] committed a larceny for the purpose of getting into jail" but found herself transported for ten years. Her petition, which included letters of support from a Presbyterian chaplain and the county inspector in Derry, asked that either her sentence be commuted or her four-year-old child, then lodged in the Newtown-Limavady workhouse, be allowed to accompany her. In the end, she got both. Campbell and her child sailed together as "free settlers" on board the *Blackfriar* in 1851.[46]

Males also used transportation as a form of assisted emigration. "Strong, able men," the *Tipperary Free Press* noted in 1849, were begging judges "for GOD'S sake to *transport them*" and were "in many instances" successful. At a weekly meeting of the Galway poor law union in early June 1851, it was reported that "eight boys were detected in escaping from the workhouse . . . , taking with them the [poor law] union clothes." Upon interrogation, "they stated their object was to get into jail or to be transported" but on account of their "being quite young," the boys were flogged instead. Newspaper reports suggest that while several judges in Ireland were willing to transport convicts in lieu of incarceration, even at the prisoner's own request, others refused to countenance the notion. "It is my duty to punish offenders," Charles Burton told a housebreaker who begged for transportation in 1850, "and not to punish them in the way they think fit to select." In the face of such resistance, those intent on transportation often reverted to open threats. Daniel Callaghan did so when standing before Joseph Devensher Jackson, accused of stealing a cow:

> COURT: If I don't inflict a heavy punishment on you, will you conduct
> yourself for the future?
> PRISONER: I will not, my lord. I'll do something that will get me out of
> the country.
> COURT: Let him be transported for ten years.

Others were simply grateful to go. When James Byrne of Kilkenny was sentenced to seven years' transportation for stealing a silver watch, he thanked the judge. These examples, historian Richard Davis has argued, "suggest that sentencing during the famine period had become almost farcical, with the principles of guilt, punishment, and reform swept away by the great calamity." Many turned punishment into free passage.[47]

These examples demonstrate that prisoners and crew were not the only ones traveling on Famine-era convict transports. A large array of people, from convicts' relatives to matrons, priests, guards, retired pensioners, and even police spies used these ships, particularly those chartered to carry female offenders, to get themselves and their families off the island during the catastrophe. These findings contribute to recent trends in the historiography of the convictism, which seek to broaden how scholars conceptualize the system. There was more to transportation than cops and robbers. As a reliable system of ships and schedules, it provided the opportunity for all kinds of people to head to Australia. Despite transportation's reputation as a "hard sentence . . . beyond the seas," there were several reasons why many poor considered it an option. If nothing else, convict ships were affordable. As we have seen, around 20 percent of the non-convict passengers on any given female transport (not to mention the convicts themselves) were traveling at little or no personal cost. While many prisoners were obviously heartbroken and scared at the prospect of a future in Van Diemen's Land, it is also true that others saw it as an escape from privation and want. As an official government charter with carefully measured provisions and a trained doctor on board, the convict transport was also safer than many of the smaller, private vessels that plied back and forth across the Atlantic. The journey to Australia on a convict transport was longer but was also much safer in many ways.[48]

To earn their free ride to Australia, the Irish poor needed to successfully manipulate several different economic and intellectual strands of British imperial policy. Their petitions for assisted emigration, for example, relied on the good word of Australian farmers, many of whom were eager to hire reliable, hardworking families. The government-assisted emigration of convicts' families provided Australian farmers with the opportunity to source such immigrants before they even left home. At the same time, the system provided rate-paying landlords in Ireland with an outlet for indigent wives and orphans who, if they stayed, would probably remain as public charges for years to come. No wonder that people like Archibald McIntyre and Edmond Carr used their social standing in support of convict petitions to reunite families in Van Diemen's Land. Prospective free settlers also appealed to Victorian mores, which held the nuclear family as the basic building block of healthy society. In her 1852 petition to join her convict husband in Australia, Mary Hayes hoped that the Lord Lieutenant's position as "a married man [with the] the feelings of a husband" would encourage him to grant her free passage. In court, others appealed to their judge's sense of mercy by begging for transportation abroad. Given the desperation so many faced during those years, it is understandable that large numbers of Irish people used convict transports as emigrant ships during the Great Famine. Through a combination of creativity, luck, and bravery, many managed to repurpose these circuits of exile into networks of emigration.[49]

* * *

Famine-era emigrants, regardless of their destination, gathered the resources to leave by employing local and transnational networks of family, commerce, and empire. As such, the process of preparing for departure served to strengthen international connections within the Irish diaspora. These circuits of exchange, often treated in historical literature as separate from each other, were actually often tangled together. The most enduring form of funding came as cash remittances from friends and relations living abroad. These people used their savings to pay for the passage of those left behind. As such, remittances demonstrate one way in which premodern notions of communalism, still entrenched in mid-nineteenth-century rural Ireland, survived the journeys to North America and Australia where market economies were structured around competitive individualism and profit. Many were also moved by deep feelings of love and attachment. "I long to see that long-wished for hour that I will embrace you in my arms," Thomas Garry told his wife when he sent her a remittance to emigrate in March 1848. "There is nothing in this world gives me trouble but you and my dear children, whom I loved as my life." As tenants and laborers, their inexperience in dealing with global networks of commerce and empire (and the insufficient size of some remittances) was mitigated, in some ways and at some times, by local and imperial authorities. Many emigrants successfully engaged a range of powerful figures, from landlords to poor law guardians to bureaucrats to judges, who could connect them and their cash to the international systems of transport and exchange, which were busily moving people around the world. Collecting the resources to leave, in other words, served to develop and expand the transnational tentacles of the Irish community. Once the funds for passage tickets, outfits, and provisions were secured, however, the passengers needed to get to the port of embarkation and settle into the ship. Let us now turn to examine the strategies they employed to complete that next stage of the journey.[50]

2

Embarkation

As James Mitchell of Ahascragh, County Galway, prepared to emigrate to New York in March 1853, he reflected on the anxiety he was feeling. "Mostly all persons who have a journey in contemplation feel a sort of longing for the day to arrive on which they are to depart," he later wrote. "Some persons in order to gratify their curiosity the sooner by a view of the countries, cities, towns, and villages through which they intend to pass or go to! Others from an anxiety to have their (perhaps) long and tedious journey over them!" Mitchell counted himself among the latter. "Having read and heard much of other places and people and never been more than thirty miles from home, I was very anxious to see the 'sights,'" he wrote. "Yet! I dreaded the crossing of the Atlantic and wished it over me as soon as possible." Having gathered the resources to leave, the emigrant's next step was to get to the ship that would take them abroad. This desire to get going was tempered by the need to make sure that they were adequately prepared to undertake a journey, which, depending on their final destination, could last anywhere from five weeks to four months. When and from what port would their ship depart? How should they get there? What kinds of threats should they expect to encounter along the way? Was it necessary to bring extra food or clothing? The needs and expectations of those heading to Australia were somewhat different than those going to Britain or North America, but there was much that all emigrants shared. Published guides, government notices, and shipping advertisements offered many suggestions, but as this chapter demonstrates, Irish emigrants also garnered critical advice from the same people who had funded their fares in the first place. Moreover, when unforeseen challenges arose, these travelers proved adept at employing their own strategies, such as forming new relationships or exploiting the legal system, to get themselves and their families safely onto the ships that would carry them abroad.

Thus did the process of embarkation strengthen and expand threads within the transnational web of the Irish diaspora.[1]

"Use All the Economy You Can": Preparing to Leave Home

After buying a prepaid ticket for two people to sail from Liverpool to Philadelphia aboard the Cope family's *Saranak* packet ship in 1849, an unnamed benefactor wrote some advice on the back of the coupon. Based, perhaps, on personal experience, the scribbled suggestions revolved around ways for the emigrant to prepare for life at sea. Although the extant passenger acts insisted that each emigrant was entitled to a daily food allowance, the person who bought the ticket clearly believed that the prospective travelers should supplement the ship's diet by bringing their own sea stores from home. "You will want some tea and sugar, some oatmeal and flour, some bacon, and a little potatoes if you can get them," the author noted. Otherwise, one should save their money. "Do not bring anything with you," they added, "only what you cannot help to put the expense on you." The note is important for the details it offers on emigrant diets aboard mid-nineteenth-century sailing ships, but it is also useful, more generally, as a reminder that emigrants needed advice and help as they prepared to leave home and begin their journey abroad. As we shall see, travelers getting ready to go employed the same local and transnational networks of community and exchange, which had enabled them to gather the resources to leave. From instructions on how the shipping system worked to suggestions on what to wear, friends and family at home and abroad proved crucial in enabling emigrants to get out the door.[2]

A great proportion of Ireland's Famine-era emigrants were rural farmers and laborers who had little or no experience with the strict systems and schedules that governed international shipping. To successfully complete their journey, therefore, they needed some instruction on the actual mechanics of how these organizations worked. The passage tickets archived in the Historical Society of Pennsylvania's Cope family collection demonstrate that when people living in America bought prepaid tickets for their loved ones, they often wrote advice on how to navigate the packet system on the back of the document. It was important to know, for example, that one could not simply show up at the dock on the day the ship was to leave. "As soon as you receive this letter," an unnamed benefactor explained to Maria Prior in 1846, "you must write to Brown, Shipley, and Co., Chapel Street, Liverpool that you will be there on the 12th of the month." Maria, age twenty, was traveling alone on the *Saranak*. "You will require to give notice before the 8th or on the 8th of the month," the advice continued. "It makes no difference what month within eight months time as the line of sailing packets will sail from Liverpool the 12th of every month." Biddy Brady, age twenty-one, traveled alone on the same ship. Her sponsor, having worked out how long it would take her to get to Liverpool (again, probably based on personal experience), explained that she should "be ready for to leave home on the 1st of April or at last on the 3rd as the vessel will sail on the 12th of April without fail." In a world without electronic records and receipts, the physical ticket itself was precious. "Keep this letter very safe and bring it along with you to Liverpool and show it to the agent," Mary Goodman's sister told her. "Be careful not to lose it, if you do, you lose passage and money."[3]

Shipping brokers, who were licensed by companies to sell tickets on their ships, often used newspaper advertisements to publicize up-to-date information. A sample of ads from the March 7, 1846, issue of the Dublin *Nation* demonstrates the pattern. James Beckett of Liverpool promised that any person who wrote to him, postpaid, would "receive an 'Emigrant's Guide,' which will supply them with every requisite information respecting the manner in which they should act from the time of their leaving home until their arrival in America . . . so as to combine the utmost economy with the greatest probability of success." Similarly, James Miley of Eden Quay in Dublin advertised that those interested in emigrating through his office "can obtain every information respecting rates of passage, days of sailing, etc., on application by letter." Thomas Delany of Talbot Street in Dublin, who sold passages to Australia, Canada, and the United States, made similar commitments. Being cognizant of the costs incurred by many emigrants waiting to sail, these brokers also offered to hold their berths on the ship. Emigrants could "secure their places, without leaving home, by sending their names and a deposit of £1 each . . . to secure berths," promised James Miley, "and then they need not come to Dublin until the day previous to the one named for sailing when they can go direct on board

the ship and thereby save themselves considerable expense and delay."
Those traveling through James Beckett could engage their passage in
advance "in which case they need not be in Liverpool until the day
before the ship is to sail; and they will thereby avoid detention and
other expenses besides *securing a cheaper passage* and having the best
berths allotted to them previous to their arrival." Those traveling to
Australia with the assistance of the CLEC or their poor law unions, as
noted earlier, received their own instructions from Stephen Walcott,
while landlord-assisted emigrants often got their information from estate managers such as William Steuart Trench.[4]

The transmission of information between friends and family, so
critical to the gathering of resources, was especially important once
the decision to leave had been made and preparations put in place.
Overseas sponsors often encouraged their family members to waste no
time. "There is no use in thinking or delaying," Daniel Rowntree told
his sister in May 1851, "the sooner the better." Given the difficulty of
communicating with seaborne emigrants, many family members also
insisted on being notified once the journey had begun. "Write to me
before you start," insisted Hugh Brady's sponsor in 1852, reminding the
teenager to "bring this letter with you to Liverpool to have the certificate to show there." Margaret McCarthy asked her father in Kingwilliamstown, County Cork, to wait until he got his details straight before
contacting her. "When you come to Liverpool, write to me also and let
me know when you are to sail and the name of the ship you sail in," she
wrote in September 1850, "as I will be uneasy until I get an answer." As
Sarah Fleming and her mother made preparations to leave Dublin in
the summer of 1846, her brother John reminded her to let him know
her final destination. "As soon as you come to Liverpool, write to let
me know the day you will sail and whether ye be bound for here [Phila-
delphia] or New York that I may meet ye at the wharf," he wrote. "I
think a month as long as a year until I see ye." Sometimes, newspapers
published information on particular ships. In August 1846, for example,
the *Boston Pilot* notified its readers that the *Jane Black* of Limerick had
recently departed for Quebec with two hundred passengers aboard.[5]

If relationships were crucial to the process of preparing to leave, they
were also important along the route. Indeed, many were encouraged
to begin building personal connections even before leaving home. Jo-

hanna Burgess of County Kilkenny was advised that a neighbor named Ellen Stack "is coming out in the same ship and you [should] go to her and tell her that her sister Mary expects that you will just do as much for her as you possibly can" and thus establish a reciprocal relationship. Similarly, another passenger was told that "Michael Duffey paid his brother's passage the same day . . . I would wish yous were all in the same ship when yous are coming for it would be great company for yous to be together." The economic benefit of traveling with others was rarely far from consideration. A traveler named Mary was informed that "a nice girl" living in her area was coming on the Cope packet line. "I do not know her Christian name but if she did not call to see you, if you had time, I wish you to go and see her and I wish you to come with her because it would save you a few shillings as she will have a bed and cooking things and moreover, I hear that she is a very religious girl and I have knowledge of her two brothers here." Three unnamed passengers traveling together on the same ticket in 1848 were advised to split up before getting to Liverpool. One of them should go to the port alone "and secure your berths" as doing so would mean having to pay lodging in the port for only one instead of all three travelers. "As your means are slender," the writer advised, "you will have to use all the economy you can." In his *Practical Guide for Emigrants to North America*, published in 1850, George Nettle agreed that it made sense for "a family, or a company of friends or neighbors [to] emigrate together . . . not merely on the score of economy but for their mutual assistance to each other during the voyage; as the exercise of neighborly customs and kindnesses will add much to their comfort."[6]

For passengers traveling on a tight budget, the knowledge that there were trustworthy people along the way was comforting as well. Together with their remittances and prepaid tickets, previous emigrants sometimes included notes on whom to trust. To a degree, local authorities could be relied on for the kinds of straightforward instructions that so many emigrants needed. On the back of Thomas Coffey's ticket, his benefactor kept the advice simple: "When you land on the docks in Liverpool," they wrote in 1853, "produce this letter to the first policeman you see in the dockyard and he will direct you." But many more relied on either personal or local connections as the basis for helpful relationships. Oftentimes, these suggestions were based on the previous

emigrant's own experiences. All people traveling from Ireland to Philadelphia on the Cope line first had to take a steamer across the Irish Sea
to Liverpool. The lists of steamships could be confusing, but one passenger was told to "call to Mr. James Kennedy of Dublin as he will see
you in the packet that leaves Dublin for Liverpool as he did your sisters
and when you will see him, give my best respects to him for his kindness." Landing in Liverpool brought its own challenges, but Martha
McGuire was encouraged to "inquire for James Dugan, as he is a friend
to the Rev. Mr. Kane and he will set you right." Another passenger was
given similar help. "Be careful of this ticket," wrote the benefactor, "and
call to Thomas Treacy [in Liverpool] and he will direct you." Considering the violence that such journeys did to communal bonds, a friendly
face was a welcome sight.[7]

As the numbers of people sailing from Ireland rose sharply during
the Famine years, so too did the number of frauds committed by ship
captains eager to cut their costs. The UK and US Passenger Acts, which
were amended six and four times respectively between 1847 and 1855,
were designed to dictate minimum standards in steerage on a range of
issues especially food, fresh water, and living space but remained difficult to enforce, particularly on ships leaving from smaller ports such as
Sligo and Derry. Those preparing to travel needed to understand their
rights. "They will give you a ticket stating what provisions you are to
have from the captain of the ship and also give you all the information
you want," Ann Flanagan was told. Their friends and families disagreed,
however, over how much food each emigrant should bring with them.
Some considered the ship's fare adequate. Catherine Callaghan, who
sailed on the *Saranak* in 1851, may not have been able to read (or understand English) as the instructions on the back of her prepaid ticket
were addressed to someone else. Catherine should travel with "as much
potatoes as she can bring and some salt but she need not want a great
deal of provisions for the captain of the ship supplies them with flour,
rice, and some meat in the week." By contrast, Michael Halloran and
his daughter were told that the weekly provisions were "not sufficient
for you to live on altogether." Some gave detailed lists of what to pack.
"Bring some boiled meat," one advised, plus a six-week supply of "flour,
tea, plenty of sugar, bacon, butter, some dry fish, swedish turnips, some
rice, coffee, oatmeal, some onions, some corn beef" along with "your

pot from home, water can, coffee can, tea pot, spoons, . . . little pan, eggs, oaten bread, salt, soap" and "fresh bread [for] the day you start." Others focused on little luxuries such as "two pints of whiskey." John Delaney's parents were urged to let him "bring what tea and sugar you think he may want for sugar is used a good deal in sweetening gruel and everything." Having something sweet to look forward to at the end of a long, cold day at sea was worth the small expense.[8]

Government regulations and emigrant guides were also sometimes helpful in determining how to manage food and sustenance at sea. For those traveling to Australia with the assistance of the CLEC, many of the basics were provided. "The Commissioners supply, free of charge, provisions, medical attendance, and cooking utensils at their depot and on board the ship," explained a government-issued handbill. "Also, new mattresses, bolsters, blankets, and counterpanes, canvas bags to contain linen, etc., knives and forks, spoons, metal plates, and drinking mugs, which articles will be given after arrival in the colony to the emigrants who have behaved well on the voyage." For those paying their own way, John O'Hanlon's 1851 *Irish Emigrant's Guide for the United States* warned that while the amount of food required by law was "calculated to keep away want and starvation on a long voyage, it will not perhaps suffice for the sufficient support of the passenger." He suggested that emigrants bring with them "potatoes, oatmeal, wheat, flour (fine or shorts), bacon, eggs, butter, etc. in good preservation." The average emigrant should not, however, carry too much luggage with them. Dragging trunks "through crowded streets and bustling throngs" was stressful and left one vulnerable to loss or theft. Inside the ship itself, moreover, the emigrant could only keep "one or two convenient boxes with, perhaps, a few bags containing his sea-store for immediate use, cooking utensils, table equipage, etc." nearby. The rest of one's luggage would be stored in the hold of the ship and accessed infrequently.[9]

Those traveling as convicts or with assistance from their local poor law unions were often caught between their physical need for calories and the authorities' desire to keep costs low. As the *John Calvin* female convict transport prepared to leave Dublin for Van Diemen's Land in January 1848, the local authorities struggled with the price of food. Although Lieutenant Tully, the Admiralty agent in Dublin, had received orders to provide the ship with ten tons of apple potatoes, he found that "from the recent failures in this crop, the supply cannot be obtained but at a very high rate." Instead, Tully replaced the missing potatoes with "a corresponding amount of farinaceous food." When the Mountbellew workhouse paid the passage of thirty young women from Plymouth to Australia in late 1852, it inadvertently sent them out too early. The CLEC subsequently warned the union's guardians that its officer in Plymouth was going to "keep a separate account of the expenses incurred for the subsistence of the young women" as the CLEC "cannot undertake to provide accommodation or provision for emigrants for any period before the day mentioned in the embarkation order." The authorities in Mountbellew were responsible for repaying the CLEC. Sometimes, it was up to the emigrants themselves to cover additional costs. In September 1850, the authorities in Dublin Castle commuted John McKeown's prison sentence "on condition of his emigrating" to the United States. Once the ship was ready to sail, McKeown would be escorted to his port of embarkation by an officer "whose expenses must be defrayed by the prisoner." Coming from a situation of endemic want and malnutrition, food was an important subject that needed to be addressed before departure.[10]

Clothing was another issue that all emigrants had to deal with. Many had little choice in the matter as scarce resources prohibited the purchase of new outfits. These unfortunates headed out to sea in clothing unsuitable for any clime. In this regard, convicts were much better positioned, as they were all clothed in coarse but sturdy new outfits whose quality was inspected by each ship's surgeon-superintendent before departure. Even those independent emigrants who could afford it, however, were discouraged from spending too much money on new vestments. In his *Irish Emigrant's Guide for the United States*, John O'Hanlon insisted that "most of the clothing [the emigrant] takes out is altogether unsuited to the climate and country into which he is about to enter." Previous emigrants often encouraged those following to bring only practical items. Patrick Doran's wife told him not to "put yourself to any trouble about buying anything until you come to Liverpool unless you bring some warm bed clothes, they will be much required." Mary McCollery was encouraged to "bring plenty of bed clothes to keep you warm on the passage," while another was reminded to "be sure to keep yourself warm and comfortable on your passage." When

James Purcell sent money home to Ireland in 1846 to supply the needs of his children and sister who were preparing to join him in Australia, he stipulated that each traveler needed two suits of clothes. "Have one good dress for each landing," he wrote, and a second to "be worn in the ship, have shoes without nails, and in the hot climates, keep light dress." Finally, most people emigrating with the assistance of their local poor law union were, like convicts, provided with new outfits suitable for withstanding the weather. In September 1852, the *Limerick Reporter* noted that a group of pauper women heading for Australia "were warmly and respectably clothed" as they left the workhouse, and several other newspapers in Ireland and Britain made similar notices about pauper emigrants leaving Irish workhouses.[11]

These examples demonstrate that emigrants preparing to leave relied on the continued transmission of information from home and abroad. The same local and transnational networks of exchange that had provided the necessary funds, now served to inform the emigrants on a range of practical issues, from schedules to food and clothing. Although the basic details were printed on the voucher itself, a prepaid ticket on a packet ship was useless unless the bearer understood on what day of the month the ship was set to sail and what their responsibilities as passengers were. The benefactors who sent the tickets sometimes reiterated this information for the benefit of their friends and family. Those traveling with the assistance of the CLEC could refer to the correspondence and printed handbills of regulations sent to all applicants, while emigrants seeking to purchase tickets through shipping brokers such as James Miley could apply for detailed instructions through their offices. Those incapable of reading (or of understanding the English language) could rely on literate friends or family to translate instructions. Finally, emigrant guides by authors such as John O'Hanlon, George Nettle, and others were available to those who could either afford the cost of a shilling or two or borrow them from neighbors or local reading rooms. Finally, once everything was packed and ready to go, the emigrants said their last goodbyes. "The time of parting having arrived," James Mitchell of County Galway diarized, "I brought all the sternness and resolution of my senses to bear on that leave-taking scene but the parting glances of my aged parents completely unmanned me, aye every resolution of mine banished like dew before the morning sun." Eventu-

Figure 2.1. A priest blesses emigrants as they prepare to leave home. *Illustrated London News*, May 10, 1851. Image © Illustrated London News/Mary Evans Picture Library.

ally, the hired jaunting car arrived and "amidst the waving of hats and handkerchiefs, I took a last and lingering look at that little town where I spent some of my happiest days and proceeded rapidly to the railroad station in Ballinasloe."[12]

"One Way or Another": Traveling to the Port

Despite Ireland's levels of poverty during the Famine, its transportation system, which emigrants employed to get from their homes to the seaports, actually enjoyed a period of expansion during those years. In particular, Irish railways developed considerably. The biggest network, the Great Southern and Western Railway, finally connected Cork to Dublin in 1849, and two years later, the Galway to Dublin link was opened. In 1853, Belfast and Dublin were connected when the Boyne viaduct was built. As railways expanded, they steadily replaced canals, which had, since the late eighteenth century, been the best form of long-distance travel on the island. The Grand Canal, completed in

1804, stretched southwest from Dublin to Limerick, while the Royal Canal, which opened in 1817, headed northwest from Dublin to County Longford via Mullingar. For those unable to afford a railway ticket, canals remained an affordable alternative, and the destitute often followed their towpaths when walking across the country. Older forms of long-distance transport such as stage and mail coaches were still used but relatively slow and expensive. Nevertheless, a growing network of "Bianconi cars," designed and operated by Italian immigrant Carlo Bianconi, were very popular. By the early 1850s, these inexpensive, well-organized, horse-drawn conveyances had, according to the *Galway Vindicator*, "brought traveling in Ireland to a comparative trifle compared with what it was among our ancestors." In sum, emigrants reached their points of embarkation via a multitude of vehicles. "One way or another," noted the *Clonmel Chronicle* in the spring of 1849, "crowds are leaving for the United States and a few for Australia and other parts of the world." As they made their ways to the ports, emigrants continued to rely on a variety of relationships.[13]

Horse-drawn jaunting cars, which connected villages and small towns to larger urban centers, often carried emigrants on the first leg of their journey. The most popular were "outside" cars, whose passengers sat back-to-back along the length of the carriage with their luggage stacked down the middle between them. "Facing the scenery and whatever elements accompanied it," writes William Williams, passengers enjoyed some protection from a waterproof apron across their laps. During the second quarter of the nineteenth century, Bianconi expanded his national network of such cars in Ireland. By 1848, his business consisted of, he told an assembly in Cork, "one hundred vehicles including mail coaches and different-sized cars capable of carrying from four to twenty passengers each and traveling eight or nine miles an hour at an average fare of a penny farthing per mile for each passenger and performing daily 3,800 miles, passing through 140 stations for the change of horses, consuming 3,000 to 4,000 tons of hay and from 30,000 to 40,000 barrels of oats annually." The convenience and affordability of these cars rendered them popular with emigrants. "You could scarcely travel a mile on any of our leading roads but you would meet two or three car-loads of people all eager to escape from the land of their birth," reported the *Anglo-Celt* in January 1849. Four years later, the *Limerick Reporter* noted that Bianconi's Dublin-bound cars were "thronged with emigrants." Entrepreneurs subsequently connected those living in outlying areas to larger routes. In Cavan, car operator Peter McCann arranged to meet Bianconi's cars in Crossdoney, thus allowing those living in and around Killeshandra to travel "to and from Dublin by Mr. Bianconi's car and the Mullingar Railway at a very low charge." Those who could not afford a seat on a car sometimes negotiated with draymen, paying for themselves as freight. In one evening alone in January 1852, "seven dray loads of emigrants" passed through Clonmel en route to the port of Waterford.[14]

While horse-drawn cars were popular, those emigrants who could afford it found the speed and convenience of railways worth the cost when traveling a long distance. As noted earlier, railways expanded rapidly during the Famine years. In 1845, only three short routes were operating in Ireland. Together, they accounted for less than seventy miles of track. By 1850, four hundred miles were in operation, with railways stretching outward from major termini in Belfast and Dublin, which were finally joined by a line in 1853. By 1855, the broad outline of an island-wide network was in place. To aid those planning their trips, railway companies advertised their fares and schedules, but newspaper editors sometimes publicized basic information as well. As tens of thousands of people left their homes each season to travel abroad, the railways grew increasingly busy. "The number of emigrants who daily throng to Dublin by the Great Southern and Western Railway is astonishing," remarked a Tipperary editor in April 1849. "All along the line, there is scarcely a station at which there is not a little band waiting for the 'parliamentary' train, with a crowd of their friends and relations to see them off." As the numbers of emigrants increased in the early 1850s, the railways struggled to keep pace. A train heading from Dublin to Limerick in May 1853 found its number of passengers augmented at every station along the way, "so much so that the train due at 11:30 a.m. did not reach Kingsbridge till fully an hour later." As emigrants climbed aboard, their loved ones gathered to see them off. In August 1853, an eyewitness in Galway reported seeing the train platform "densely crowded with the friends and relatives of the emigrants among whom the prevalent sentiment appears to be a passionate desire to regain in America the society of those beloved friends from whom their separation is regarded as merely temporary."[15]

For those unable to afford a ticket on the railway, canals remained an affordable alternative. Throughout the late eighteenth and early nineteenth centuries, indeed, horse-drawn barges along Ireland's two main canals had been the preferred mode of long-distance travel. The first passenger boats traveled along the Grand Canal between Dublin and Sallins in 1780. By the 1820s, boats were carrying passengers seventy miles from Dublin to the River Shannon. The trip took eighteen hours and cost about one pound for a state cabin although the competition from jaunting cars and other conveyances forced the steady reduction of fares. In the 1830s, canal operators sought to reduce travel times through the use of "fly boats." Pulled by two or three galloping horses, fly boats were engineered for speed by reducing drag. For those who could not afford their higher fares, slower, old-fashioned "night boats" remained in use. During the Famine, despite steadily losing some of their clientele to the railways, canals continued to serve large numbers of emigrants headed for points of embarkation. In July 1851, the Ulster Canal Steam Navigation Carrying Company advertised its ability to connect merchants and passengers residing in the north of the island with Liverpool. After being transported along smaller canals to County Down, passengers and freight could transfer to the company's first-class steamers, "which ply regularly between Newry and Liverpool four times each week." Passenger traffic along Irish canals sometimes overwhelmed the systems. In March 1847, several Dublin newspapers reported that the Grand Canal's passenger boats were regularly running behind schedule. "So great is the number seeking for passage by the boats," one reported, "that at the various stopping places along the line of the canal, the constabulary are obliged to be in attendance to prevent the people rushing into the passage boats in too great numbers and multitudes are each day left behind for the next boat."[16]

Walking was a last resort. Those too poor to pay for a seat on a car, barge, or train, however, often lacked the adequate footwear, clothing, and nutritious food required to journey on foot, not to mention the warm bedding and sea stores that would help them survive weeks or months at sea. As a result, those who walked to their ports of embarkation were often the ones least physically prepared to do so. In his evidence before an 1848 select committee, Edward Wakefield reported meeting a large family living under a makeshift shelter made from a "tattered blanket" and some "sticks out of a hedge." Their landlord had given them a small amount of money to give up their holding in Westmeath. "With this pound note," Wakefield told the committee, "they begged their way to Dublin, paid the passage of seven of them to Liverpool, and then begged their way to where I saw them, thirty-six miles from Liverpool." As a national network of flat, level, and well-maintained walkways (albeit for horses), main canals' towpaths provided a ready set of routes for those headed to ships leaving from Dublin. Ireland's roads were, of course, the first alternative for most walking emigrants, but their poor condition in many parts of the country made for hard walking. "Every day—every hour—the inhabitants of this once populous country may be seen thronging the public high roads on their way to England," reported the *Mayo Telegraph* in the spring of 1851, "some to take shipping for America, and thousands more in quest of that labor and support in the sister country denied them in their land of birth." As these destitute persons passed through towns, they were often treated with fear and suspicion. In August 1847, the *Galway Vindicator* lauded its new vagrancy act, which finally protected "the public against being burthened with the support of persons who have no claim whatever upon this district." Later that same year, the Town Commissioners urged the police "to take up and prosecute the beggars now haunting the town under the Vagrant Act to the utmost rigor of the law."[17]

Those forced to walk to their ports of embarkation were often following in the footsteps of spalpeens, the seasonal migrant workers who had, for over a century, been traveling to England and Scotland to work as summer harvesters. Indeed, by the nineteenth century, such Irish workers had become, writes Ruth-Ann Harris, "the elastic supply of labor, which enabled British industry to respond rapidly and efficiently to changes in the demand for goods and services." The first- and secondhand experiences of these Irish sojourners, combined with the knowledge young people gained from their geography lessons in the recently established national schools, helped to prepare some emigrants for the shape and scale of the journey ahead. At the same time, of course, there were important differences between the experiences of migratory laborers and those fleeing the Famine in the 1840s and 1850s. On a physical level, spalpeens were generally young, healthy males traveling unencumbered by dependents. The crowds following the roads to Dublin, Cork, and Belfast during the Famine, by contrast, often included the young, the old, the sick, and the feeble. There were psychological differences too. While migrant laborers saw themselves as vibrant breadwinners looking forward to returning home with cash in their pockets, most of those leaving during the Famine knew that they were going away forever. Their hopes for an uncertain future were surely tempered by the sight, in the words of Robert Scally, "of starving stragglers and wanderers, casual burials, and exposed corpses," which lay along the "long meadow," the seemingly endless, grassy verge running alongside Ireland's roads.[18]

In light of the challenges facing many emigrants in their quest to reach their point of embarkation, the surviving evidence suggests that, whether or not they were traveling voluntarily, most convicts heading to Australia enjoyed a much safer and more comfortable experience than many emigrants. Unlike those families that begged as they walked, for example, convicts were transported in carefully coordinated stages with secure housing and scheduled nourishment along the way. A group of convicts leaving Ennis, County Clare, in early 1848 were to be escorted by a military party "to the jail of the county of Limerick and thence to the jail at Nenagh from whence they will be transmitted in charge of the constabulary to Dublin." At each stage, the prisoners received a dry bed and food. Convicts also rarely, if ever, walked long distances. Instead, they rode on various types of chartered vehicles. In September 1848, the *Limerick Reporter* noted that over three dozen convicts from Clonmel and Limerick were taken by train to the depot in Dublin, where they awaited their transport ship. The following year, the Dublin *Evening Freeman* reported the movement of around seventy female convicts from the Grangegorman depot to the *Maria*. "The convicts were conveyed in covered cars from the prison to Halpin's Pool where the *Isle of Bute* steamer was in readiness to receive them," the paper noted. Once the steamer reached the transport ship, "the convicts already on board (over one hundred) came on deck and loudly cheered the newcomers." Beyond the convenience of traveling in covered cars, trains, and steamers, convicts also had their medical and clothing needs attended to. As a group of male prisoners prepared to leave Galway, Dublin Castle reminded the accompanying constabulary officer to obtain a signed medical certificate for each convict, "so that no prisoner may be removed, except such as may be fit for immediate embarkation." Convicts should also be clothed properly "with the view of avoiding contagion."[19]

Although the poor law unions did not assist paupers to emigrate in large numbers until after 1849, when Famine-related mortality rates had begun to decline, those who traveled with the assistance of their poor law guardians also enjoyed a higher level of comfort and safety than many other emigrants. Workhouse officials often accompanied their emigrants to see them onto the ships and ensure they were not shortchanged on the provisions and articles they were promised. When a group of 140 pauper women sailed from Limerick to Quebec in June 1854, for example, their needs were carefully attended to. The women were, a local newspaper reported, "plainly but comfortably attired in bonnets, shawls, and cotton dresses," which had probably been newly made for the journey. Accompanying them to the vessel were a number of authority figures including the local emigration officer as well as the master, matron, chaplain (who celebrated Mass with the women on the morning before they left), and several poor law guardians of the Limerick Union, all of whom "attended to see that arrangements for the comfort of the passengers were carried out in even the most minute detail." Their ship, the *Theron*, "was much superior to what we have seen in the ordinary class of emigrant ships," reported the *Limerick Reporter*, featuring its own medical gentleman along with above-average ventilation, bedding, and food. Upon landing in Quebec, "the girls will be taken under the protection of the British emigration agent who, it is expected, will have, or already has, situations to which they may at once be appointed." Even those embarking farther afield enjoyed the convenience of an escort. When a group of female paupers departed the Gort workhouse in June 1854, the clerk of the union, James Slator, accompanied them all the way to Liverpool, where he made sure the women were properly embarked on the *Mary Carson* for Quebec. The shipping broker, Patrick Gibson, "performed his contract with every satisfaction, behaved in the most kind manner towards the emigrants, and supplied every article we required," Slator reported.[20]

As emigrants of various sorts said goodbye to their friends and families, some observers read their cries of sorrowful parting as reflective of something deeper in the Irish psyche. These interpretations often reflected the quiet condescension of the urban literati toward the rural poor. "The railway terminus was yesterday the scene of one of those harrowing spectacles whose melancholy recurrence is now so frequent as almost to cease to excite observation," reported the *Galway Vindicator* in June 1853. "Nothing could be more affecting than the passionate demonstration of grief exhibited by those poor people. It is upon occasions like this that the deep and fervid feelings of the peasantry display themselves in all their intensity." Earlier in 1853, a reporter for the same newspaper had witnessed almost twenty Claddagh fishermen climbing aboard a train en route to America. "Their adieus seemed characterized by that fervor that distinguish the parting scenes of the Irish," the reporter noted, "and, in particular, this primitive tribe of people." In October 1852, an English correspondent of the *Hull Advertiser* thought the sounds he heard were reminiscent of the Irish peasant's racial origins. As he waited for his train, he "heard the wail of some score of Irish peasants" saying goodbye to friends. "We never were so fully convinced of the oriental character of the Irish people as while listening to the cry of distress raised at the Limerick Junction," the reporter concluded. "It was, in its character, purely Asiatic." William Steuart Trench, the land agent who organized the assisted emigration of hundreds of poor tenants from Lord Lansdowne's estate, was even less flattering in his assessment. "I do believe that so strange, unmanageable, and wild a crew had never before left the shores of Ireland," Trench later diarized. "But notwithstanding their apparent poverty, they were all in the most uproarious spirits; there was no crying nor lamentation, as is usual on such occasions."[21]

In early 1846, the *Waterford Chronicle* decried the sight of strong youths making their way to the seaports. "It was lamentable to witness crowds of fine, hardy, young men and women rushing along our quays on Thursday night and getting their little substance on board the steamers, which sailed for England next morning, thence to take shipping for America," it mourned. "How long will this state of things continue? When will the severance of family affection, the banishment of the children of our soil, cease to exist?" In fact, the flood of emigration would actually swell over the coming years. In July 1853, the Irish Australian press acknowledged the trend. "Batches of emigrants, often amounting to over one hundred, leave daily by the railway for the seaports," noted the Sydney *Freeman's Journal*, citing unnamed Galway newspapers. "On each Sunday evening, when heretofore the lanes and roads were alive with people amusing themselves according to the customs of the country, including the 'dance at the crossroads,' a stranger might now, but for the occasional meeting with an odd straggler or two, pursue his journey in perfect solitude." Reflecting on a letter from County Kerry, the Dublin *Freeman's Journal* noted that the recent "crowds of human beings" passing through the town of Cahirciveen en route to America had resembled "a second fair." The waves of people traveling to their points of embarkation between 1845 and 1855 put great pressure on Ireland's growing transportation system. The railway network, only recently national in any proper sense, struggled to maintain its schedules as travelers sought passage to the country's coasts. At the same time, Carlo Bianconi's linked routes of horse-drawn cars matured at the very moment when demand exploded. For those unable to afford train or car fares, however, canals, drays, and walking remained viable options. Four years after expressing shock at the number of people leaving its port, the *Waterford Chronicle* likened the crowds of emigrants to the "monster meetings of O'Connell in his halcyon days."[22]

"The Berths Are Crowded": Dealing with Delayed Departures

Delayed departures were a costly and sometimes dangerous part of the emigration process. Whether the delay was caused by weather or sickness or error or fraud, every day meant additional expenditures on food and lodging. For those traveling on a razor-thin budget, the difference between leaving and staying could mean starvation. Those capable of drawing on relationships stood the best chance of success. In July 1852, just two months after their workhouse opened, the guardians of the Mountbellew poor law union in County Galway funded the emigration of thirty of its able-bodied female inmates to Australia. While the CLEC paid for their passages, the guardians agreed to supply the emigrants "with the necessary outfit and with the sum of £1 to each [upon landing] and to have them conveyed to the port of embarkation in England." In total, the union spent £3 5s. 0d. on each passenger. After departing the workhouse in November 1852, however, the women ran into trouble. "The emigrants, after arriving in Dublin," the Mountbellew guardians explained to their superiors in London, "were detained for three days by stress of weather." Beyond covering the women's additional expenses in Dublin as they waited to cross the Irish Sea, the board also ended up having to buy more expensive cross-channel passage tickets and pay for another two days of board and lodging, which the women required while awaiting embarkation in Plymouth. In all, the Mountbellew guardians spent an additional £1 7s. 4d. to cover the costs of each delayed emigrant. The experience demonstrates that relationships, whether formal or informal, proved the best insulation against the dangers and discomforts of delayed departures.[23]

Although weather often played a role, many emigrants found themselves stranded by the simple fact that there were not enough berths available when they were ready to sail. This problem was particularly marked in the early years of the Famine emigration, when new levels of demand overwhelmed shipping brokers. "We are sorry to find numbers of the emigrants who left this port for Liverpool *en route* to America, had to return" to their homes, the *Waterford Chronicle* reported in the spring of 1847, "being unable to procure berths in the emigrant ships advertised for sailing." The following year, the *Galway Vindicator* made a similar observation. "There are five vessels at present in this port bound for America but quite inadequate to supply the demand for emigrants, even at this season," it noted in November 1848. "The berths are crowded and numbers are disappointed." At times, captains actually left passengers behind even after they had embarked. Having departed Liverpool on April 21, 1847, the *Lady Milton* returned over a week later for repairs. When it sailed again on May 5, it left behind 143 passengers. "By this proceeding," one government official complained, "families are stated to be separated, and the passengers left behind, besides the loss of their passage, have been deprived of their clothes, bedding, and provisions." Around the same time, the *Amelia Mary* left Donegal for New York with 111 souls aboard. Once the captain realized that he would be penalized under the US Passenger Acts for carrying too many emigrants, he "suddenly re-landed seventeen passengers on the beach and then sailed." Stranding travelers was illegal, but the government struggled to secure convictions, as getting the suspect and plaintiff together in court on the same day was often impossible. No wonder the

Dublin *Nation* reminded prospective emigrants "to keep their contract tickets in their own possession and not give them up at the time of sailing" as they provided the only grounds for recourse in the event of their mistreatment.[24]

While the shortage of berths and activities of cruel captains could sometimes cause delays, emigrants were also subject to a range of frauds as they passed through Ireland's seaports. The brokers of tickets and provisions, a correspondent of the Dublin *Freeman's Journal* alleged, "do, with perhaps some few exceptions, make it a point to gull and deceive" innocent emigrants. Of particular note were those ticket agents who advertised in provincial newspapers that given ships would sail on given days when, in fact, this was not true. "No man who has not witnessed it," the correspondent lamented, "can conceive the dismay and consternation with which these poor creatures who have, perhaps, only a few shillings in their possession, are struck when they are told that the ship will not sail for another week." In response, the Emigrants' Protection Society was founded in 1851, under the auspices of the Society of St. Vincent de Paul, "with a view of protecting emigrants from the many frauds and impositions to which they are subject." For its part, the Dublin *Freeman's Journal* was delighted to see the formation of such an organization. "Friendless and guideless," the newspaper editorialized, "the wanderer in search of a home in the distant west reaches our metropolis, a fit prey for the harpies who infest every large city." When passengers found themselves defrauded by shipping brokers, they sometimes took the offenders to court. In August 1851, an emigrant named Murray paid Nicholas Herbert Delamere, a ticket agent in Dublin, £12 for passages to America for himself, his wife, and their seven children. Upon landing in Liverpool, Murray realized that Delamere had defrauded him, but as the agent was also in Liverpool at the time, he sued him. The defendant contended that the court had no jurisdiction over business completed in Dublin, but the magistrate disagreed and ruled that Murray be refunded his £12 plus £1 7s. 6d. detention money "and £20 in respect of the damage sustained by the emigrant being delayed."[25]

Nor were fraud-related delays confined to the port of Dublin. Newspaper reports from around the country demonstrate that the threat was alive and well elsewhere too. In Drogheda in April 1847, a number of passengers heading for Maryland climbed aboard a ship only to learn that it was actually cleared for Virginia. When the emigrants complained to the port's comptroller, he ensured that the person who chartered the ship, and misled the passengers, give them eighty pounds to cover their costs from Alexandria to Baltimore. Petty thieves were also a problem. Once the police began, in early 1854, to track the number of emigrants leaving Limerick, travelers were "freed from many little annoyances," a local newspaper claimed, "which they had to endure at the hands of the 'rowdy boys' who prowl about the quays, terrifying the poor emigrants by threats, and oftentimes by assault, to give them money or whiskey." As in Dublin, emigrants sometimes found the courts in port towns capable of protecting themselves and their families. In May 1851, the *Cork Examiner* related the story of a passage broker named John H. Harris who had recently obtained his license and opened an office on Fish Street in the city. "He had no clerk there," the newspaper reported, "but he had what was called a 'man-catcher,' a person [named Cullen] to bring up people for the purpose of taking passages from him." When Cullen subsequently took money from a number of prospective emigrants and absconded, the magistrates found that Harris, "having gone away and left the office in Cullen's care, [was] liable for the contract" made by his clerk. He was therefore ordered to return the amount of the original fares to each emigrant plus compensation as well as "subsistence money for every day since the vessel was announced to sail."[26]

At times, their own troubles with the law could stymie emigrants' plans for departure as well. In March 1847, an affray occurred on board the *Albion* as it prepared to leave Galway for New York. When a bailiff and his police escort attempted to arrest an intending emigrant under suspicion of stealing a hundredweight of meal, the ship's passengers resisted. "The excitement became very great," reported the *Galway Vindicator*, "and at length the emigrants and police got into a collision." Eventually, a military reinforcement was dispatched "to overawe the emigrants," and the suspect was taken into custody after he remonstrated with his fellow passengers not to resist any longer. Reflecting on the event, the newspaper's editor considered the man's arrest "exceedingly harsh if not even cruel" as, given that he had no way to pay for the meal, his arrest meant "the loss of his passage" and would render him, upon his eventual release, "a pauper upon the community." Poor law unions were also eager not to allow their healthy inmates to emigrate while leaving the very young, old, and sick behind for the workhouse to clothe and feed. In May 1854, the relieving officer of the Galway poor law union discovered "an old woman and three children on a cart . . . below at the docks, who wanted to come into the workhouse." When questioned, the woman admitted "the father and mother and an older child were about going to America and were leaving the three children to the old woman." The relieving officer had the father arrested immediately on board the *Waterford*, just as it was preparing to depart.[27]

As we have seen, convicts heading for Australia traveled to their points of embarkation along carefully scheduled networks, but many experienced delayed departures after the imperial government temporarily suspended the transportation of Irish male convicts in 1846. By the time the practice recommenced in 1848, and for some time afterward, the country's prisons were strained under the backlog of delayed transportees. In a letter accompanying a cohort of three hundred male convicts heading to Van Diemen's Land in the autumn of 1848, Dublin Castle notified the colonial authorities of how dire the situation had become. Although overcrowding impacted prisons all over the United Kingdom, it had been "particularly felt in Ireland," where a system designed to manage 350 prisoners had been forced to handle between 800 and 1,000. Such overcrowding "precluded any proper system of discipline being carried out," the official admitted, "the utmost efforts of the officers being sufficient only for [the prisoners'] safe custody." The problem continued even after the establishment of a convict depot on Spike Island in Cork Harbor in 1847. Two years later, in May 1849, the officer commanding the troops guarding the depot's 1,200 prisoners complained that the place was becoming unmanageable. Design flaws in the buildings' layout left open the possibility that "400 convicts could at night, on a pre-concerted plan, congregate together before means to prevent them could be enforced." There were also various nefarious characters hanging about. The "island is at present crowded with workmen, strangers, peddlers, and prostitutes, indeed persons of all kinds, who could without much difficulty hold communication with the convicts when in working parties during the day outside the prison," the guard complained. "It was only last Sunday morning that several drunken men, strangers, were reported to me as being on the island." The state of affairs on Spike Island demonstrates that even those traveling under lock and key were not immune to delayed departure.[28]

Traveling under the auspices of a poor law union, as noted above, could sustain pauper emigrants during delays of days or weeks, but the case of Winifred Kennedy shows that this support could extend over several months. As seen in chapter 1, the Gort poor law union contracted shipping agent Patrick Gibson to organize the emigration of a group of the workhouse's inmates to Quebec in June 1854. The cohort was initially threatened with delay when Gibson struggled to find an adequate vessel leaving Ireland, but he solved the problem by promptly agreeing to send them via Liverpool. To protect the emigrants, the board sent the union's master and its clerk, James Slator, with them "for the purpose of managing the pecuniary transactions connected with this emigration." Two weeks later, Slator reported that all of the emigrants had embarked safely except for one, Winifred Kennedy, "who met with an accident on the way to Athenry and although she was able to proceed to Liverpool, it was ascertained there that her left leg was broken." Unable to proceed to Quebec with the others, Kennedy was admitted into Liverpool's Northern Hospital, where, Slator assured his superiors, "she will be taken care of without any expense to the Gort Union." Badly injured and penniless in a foreign land, Kennedy might have been forgotten were it not for a letter her workhouse received three months later. Written by a John Mahon, presumably on behalf of the hospital in Liverpool where she stayed, the letter demanded payment for five weeks of treatment for Kennedy who "has lately been discharged, cured." In mid-October 1854, the board sanctioned the expenditure of an additional £4 on Kennedy, of which £2 10s. was to pay her hospital fees. The clerk used the remaining £1 10s. "to procure a sailing order in Gort and forward it to Liverpool." Four months after her accident, Winifred Kennedy's journey to Quebec could continue.[29]

Those traveling without the support of government agencies were less fortunate, but some found ways to exploit power relations to their own advantage. One such person was Bridget Reilly of Aughamucky, County Kilkenny, whose emigration was assisted by her landlord, Charles Wandesforde. Reilly left the Prior-Wandesforde estate in the spring of 1847 with her husband and two children en route to Quebec.

They arrived in Athy, County Kildare, intent on taking a passenger boat along the Grand Canal to Dublin, but the vessel was full so they had to wait until the next morning for a train. Having already spent some of their "head money" (traveling cash) just getting to Athy, they realized they did not have enough funds to get to Dublin, so her husband took one child on the train and promised to send Bridget the rest of the money when he got it. "This, your Honor, he never did, and your memorialist has therefore been plunged into deepest misery," she wrote to Wandesforde after returning to Aughamucky. "Deserted by a second husband, who is not the father of her children, who does not care for them, and who ever proved himself idle and worthless—deprived of her child—left without a home—a burden upon public charity," Bridget had nothing left in the world once her plans for emigration collapsed. With "no one under God to look to now but your Honor," Reilly petitioned his lordship for additional assistance. "A word from you will in all human probability, procure her reunion with her child," she pleaded. "A few shillings will take her to Dublin with her remaining child [and] still allow her a passage to America." The Mountbellew pauper girls, without having to write a word or make any plea, received £1 7s. 4d. each to cover their delay. On the back of Bridget Reilly's petition, her landlord instructed his agent to "allow her five shillings." Although many landlord-assisted emigrants were on their own once they left the estate, Reilly's relationship with Wandesforde took the sting out of her delay.[30]

Poor and sickly emigrants, whose departures were delayed but who lacked access to additional support from their poor law unions or landlords, were sometimes saved by local charity. On March 17, 1847, the emigrant ship *Swatara*, which had left Liverpool en route to Philadelphia a few days earlier, put in at Belfast after losing her foremast and bowsprit in bad weather. The ship's passengers, almost three hundred in number, were "principally from Roscommon," and almost half of them were more or less destitute, with "nothing to subsist upon save the mere government allowance of one pound of bread stuff per day." While sitting at anchor, the *Swatara*'s passengers were inspected by medical authorities, who found the ship's steerage compartment badly crowded, poorly ventilated, and so dark "that these gentlemen were obliged to be furnished with a lantern to ascertain the actual state of the passengers." More troubling was the existence of marked cases of typhus fever. Under pressure from public opinion, which feared an outbreak of disease, the local poor law guardians and general hospital agreed to cover the costs of treating the typhus patients. For those healthy emigrants who were lodged on Waring Street while the ship was repaired and fumigated, but lacked the resources to sustain themselves during the long delay, foodstuffs were bought by a grant from Belfast's Relief Fund Committee and a subscription raised by the local emigration officer, Lieutenant Stark. By the time the *Swatara* set out to sea again on April 17, there were, beyond two who had died, around forty-five of its original passengers who were still too ill to sail. Of these, almost half "have, at their own wish, been sent back to their friends with sufficient funds to maintain them for three or four weeks." The remainder, once healthy, would be forwarded to America using funds raised from the sale of their empty berths on the *Swatara*. Although the authorities in Belfast may have been motivated as much by the fear of typhus as by Christian benevolence, the fact remains that public charity could sometimes aid those whose progress was postponed.[31]

These examples demonstrate that relationships, which were crucial to the process of preparing to emigrate, could also insulate travelers against the many problems caused by delayed departure. While it is impossible to calculate, it is undoubtedly true that a number of would-be emigrants whose departures were delayed ended up dying of hunger or disease without ever leaving the country. Consigned to lonely deaths in and around Irish and British ports, their stories rarely appear in the archival records. It is impossible to ever figure out what percentage of the one million people who died during the Famine were prospective emigrants whose departures had been delayed. What the surviving records do suggest, however, is that those emigrants capable of drawing on relationships stood the best chance of dealing with the deprivation and danger, which could accompany delayed departure. Pauper women may have occupied one of the lowest rungs in mid-nineteenth-century Irish society, but their connection with their poor law guardians—patriarchal as it was—protected them against delays, which for other emigrants could prove fatal. This was especially true for a woman like Winifred Kennedy, who, despite finding herself incapacitated and penniless on the streets of Liverpool, had her medical fees paid in full and, upon her discharge from hospital, was provided with a fare to Quebec several months after leaving the Gort workhouse. Similarly, when Bridget Reilly's husband absconded with their money, her landlord took pity on her and gave her just enough to continue her journey. True, considered from the landlord's perspective, giving Reilly a few shillings was cheaper than paying for her upkeep in the local workhouse. Looking at it from Bridget's angle, however, the point remains that she recognized a relationship that might bear fruit at a time of calamity. These people were not mere flotsam and jetsam upon a flowing tide of emigration. Many were intelligent, eloquent operators doing the best they could in a time of need.

"A Strange and Confused Medley": Passing through Liverpool

Although a minority of emigrants sailed abroad directly from Ireland, most passed through Liverpool. Thanks in part to its critical role in the eighteenth-century slave trade, this port city in the northwest of England had grown to become Europe's busiest migration hub. Definitive statistics on the number of Irish who passed through Liverpool during the Famine era do not exist, but Frank Neal's research demonstrates that the vast majority of Ireland's over two million emigrants did so. "During Friday, the appearance of the quays was more like the approaches to one of the monster meetings of 1843," noted the Dublin *Evening Freeman* of emigrants heading to Liverpool in March 1847. "Drays, carts, cars, and jaunting cars . . . piled with boxes, beds, chests, household stuffs, together with pyramids of children—proceeded from early dawn to late at night to the steam packet stations." Seven years later, the numbers were still remarkable. "The multitudes who are daily thronging the pier heads, eager for their departure, are truly wonderful," wrote the Reverend James Buck of the Liverpool Seamen's Friend Society. "Cart loads and wagon loads of boxes arrive in quick succession, accompanied by men, women, and children—Irish, Scotch, English, and German—all mingling together in strange and confused medley." Not all Liverpudlians were as cheerful on the subject, particularly in 1847 when a typhus outbreak gripped the heart of the city. That May, the *Liverpool Mercury* editorialized about the "ruinous burdens and serious personal danger" caused by the Irish influx. For their part, many Irish emigrants did not think much of the city either. "You would hardly believe, were I to tell you, all the tricks, cheats, plots, and chicanery of every kind which I had to overcome," reflected Thomas Reilly, who traveled from Dublin to New York in 1848. "If a man had seven senses, it would take five hundred senses, largely developed, to counteract the sharpers of Liverpool and New York." Irish emigrants employed different strategies when running the gauntlet.[32]

Of all the challenges facing emigrants passing through Liverpool, the first and most dangerous was the physical journey across the Irish Sea. Although steamships did not begin regularly carrying emigrants across the Atlantic Ocean until the 1860s, they were used extensively for cross-channel travel beginning in the early 1820s. The Irish Sea, through which all ships had to proceed, was notoriously choppy, but some routes were more complicated than others. "If you will look at the map of the Channel, you will see that [the route from Cork to Liverpool] requires several changes of winds," noted one passenger in 1853, "so that the voyage generally may be said to be in point of fact a succession of voyages." As the crossing of the Irish Sea was most emigrants' first time on a ship, they were bound to have a sorry time with seasickness either way. Yet the troubles caused by harsh weather and high seas were augmented by the fact that most emigrants' low fares meant they traveled on deck and were therefore exposed to all weather. In 1848, Lord Monteagle complained that there was "not the slightest difference or distinction between the accommodation afforded to pigs and sheep and that afforded to the deck passengers." Moreover, in the face of heavy demand and lax enforcement, he added, the Cork to Liverpool steamers were "dreadfully overcrowded." Those leaving Dublin were often oversold as well. In January 1853, the captain of the *Dundalk* was fined for carrying 120 passengers over the 350 he was allowed. In court, he pleaded that "the night was dark and he was unable to prevent the men from coming on board, it being harvest time in England." Those passengers who took shelter below deck ran a different kind of risk. In December 1848, scores of emigrants traveling from Sligo to Liverpool suffocated to death on the *Londonderry* steamer when its crew battened down the hatches (thus locking the emigrants below) during bad weather.[33]

Having survived the journey across the Irish Sea, the emigrants' next challenge was to avoid being defrauded while waiting to embark in

Liverpool. One class of hustler, known as "runners," "man-catchers," "crimps," or "land sharks," aggressively induced emigrants to follow them to their employer's premises—sometimes by simply grabbing their luggage and running away with it—where the victim was overcharged and the man-catcher awarded a commission. In May 1850, a correspondent of the *Liverpool Mercury* decried the "organized system of imposition and robbery, which is in daily operation" against emigrants. "Large sums of money are extorted from the strangers for pretended services," the author complained, "such as securing passages, finding them suitable lodgings, and introducing them to a certain class of provision dealers from whom they are to purchase supplies to stores." In early 1852, a runner named Cullen sold an innocent emigrant a box of what he called "salt water soap," which, he alleged, one could use to "wash with fresh or salt water." Upon bringing the soap back to his lodging, however, the emigrant "found enclosed in the paper nothing but a piece of salt." When Cullen was brought before the court on charges, the judge declared his determination "to punish to the utmost those guilty of the rascality and frauds now practiced against poor emigrants." While man-catchers operated on the borders between legal and illegal business, there were other hustlers who simply tricked emigrants into handing over their cash. In September 1852, as he loaded his luggage onto the *Jane Henderson*, emigrant James Carrol was approached by Thomas Clansey who described himself as the cook of the ship and offered to pay Carrol "if he would assist [Clansey] on the passage in attending to the [cooking] fires." Carrol agreed and the men repaired to a nearby public house, where Clansey offered to exchange Carrol's shillings for American dollars. The swindler took the money and never returned, but when Carrol complained to the authorities, Clansey was arrested and sentenced to jail.[34]

Shipping brokers, who literally held one's ticket to America, were particularly well placed to defraud intending emigrants. Many used the fact that they themselves were Irish to gain the trust of their fellow compatriots. In an 1848 letter to the Dublin *Nation*, an Irishman living in Liverpool warned of the "system of plunder and bare-faced robbery" to which emigrants were subjected. "I call it a system," he explained, "because it is well organized here and in Ireland, to plunder the poor emigrant of his hard earnings and leave him penniless." After establishing a relationship before the emigrants leave home, the man-catcher meets them in Liverpool and brings them to an office where he "introduces them to one of the clerks as 'old neighbors of his own' from the town of Longford with whom he went to school, etc., etc., and hopes they may be favored with a good ship and at a cheaper rate, on his account" while, in fact, they are overcharged. The correspondent was appalled to see any emigrant being defrauded by "his own country-men and under the appearance of friendship." Other scams were more spontaneous. In the spring of 1846, a number of people in Cork paid the deposits on tickets to New York on board J. W. Shaw's *Mayfield*. In Liverpool, however, a man named Keenan, who represented himself as Shaw, intercepted the travelers and took the balance of their passage fares. When the emigrants tried to embark upon the *Mayfield*, they were refused passage on account of not having paid Shaw the monies owed. Irish newspapers were particularly concerned about the threat to single women traveling alone. One told of a passage broker who induced "a young Tipperary girl" to lodge at his house only to desert her the following day. Unable to remember where the agent lived, the woman lost everything she had and soon "became a prey to the scoun-drels who infest the streets of Liverpool." In some rare cases, emigrants sought to swindle the shipping brokers themselves, as when Ellen Dil-lon fraudulently claimed to have paid Tapscott's office four pounds for a ticket to America on board the *Jenny Lind* in March 1848.[35]

Deportation was another major threat facing Famine-era Irish emi-grants passing through Liverpool. As the closest and cheapest desti-nation outside of Ireland, Liverpool began receiving large numbers of poor Irish soon after the blight hit. By early 1847, a number of au-thority figures in the city were calling for "the removal of the destitute Irish immigrants back to their own country." In June 1847, the British government responded by passing the Poor Removal Act, which ren-dered it easier to deport Irish paupers by streamlining the legal pro-cess and empowering poor law union officers. By 1853, over sixty-two thousand people had been sent back to Ireland. Some of those shipped home were, undoubtedly, preparing or at least hoping to continue on to North America. For its part, the *Liverpool Albion* "rejoiced" to hear the news that "Irish paupers are being re-conveyed to their own country in hundreds, and will be debarked in thousands, in the course of the present week, upon the shores of their native land." When a group of Irish poor refused to leave England, the *Albion* gloated, one stipendiary magistrate told them that "they had long enough been a burden upon the industrious shopkeepers of Liverpool; and that they must go back that night and be supported in the future by the Irish landlords." Soon after, the Dublin *Nation* reported on the arrival of a "wretched" group of deportees. "A cargo of paupers to Cork has come over from England, the first importation under the new act," it announced in July 1847. "The captain of the vessel reports that the majority were out of all the fever hospitals in Liverpool and the authorities were only waiting for the other patients to be sufficiently recovered to ship them off likewise." The *Nation* decried such deportations. "Just fancy us, of Liverpool," it satirized, "who fatten on this people's poverty, who have grown wealthy as they have grown poor—fancy us, indeed, afflicted with the pleasure of their nauseous company or giving a fraction to their maintenance one moment longer than we can avoid."[36]

Despite the many and varied threats facing those passing through Liverpool, emigrants also had a range of strategies available to mitigate the dangers. These tactics, which were usually passed on as advice from one traveler to another or via emigrant guides, often focused on the selection of good ships. In his *Irish Emigrant's Guide for the United States*, the Reverend John O'Hanlon actually encouraged emigrants to choose Liverpool over Irish ports as their point of embarkation for America. Vessels operating in and out of Ireland "are badly provided with those conveniences necessary to preserve the health of passengers and ensure their accommodation," O'Hanlon explained. "They are generally brigs, low between decks, badly ventilated, and small in proportion to the number of passengers taken on board." While the emigrant should acquire advance information on fares, he "must not, however, suppose that the rates of passage given in these documents are set down at the lowest figures; and hence, he must not be in too great a hurry to close with these terms," O'Hanlon claimed. "He should defer this until his arrival at the seaport from which he intends to embark." Personal relationships could facilitate economical savings as well. "I promise you I will do everything that lies in my power for to send your sister-in-law off as cheap and as comfortable as I possibly can," agent C. Graham told John McGinity in September 1848, but he cautioned the woman "not to make any arrangements in Dundalk until she comes to Liverpool where it will be got for the lowest rate." Chartering some or all of a ship was another option. In his *Emigrant's Guide to Australia*, Eneas MacKenzie claimed that "if intending emigrants of a town or district were to meet and sign their names as such, then announce they were ready to negotiate for a ship, they would cause a competition [among shipowners] that would prove beneficial to themselves."[37]

When defrauded, robbed, or otherwise mistreated, Irish emigrants proved capable of seeking justice through the legal system. In his guide, O'Hanlon reminded his readers that the parliaments of Great Britain and America had laws in place to protect them. "These provisions are enforced under heavy penalties," O'Hanlon declared, "and a complaint made by the emigrant to the proper authorities in case of violation will, if supported with sufficient evidence, meet with redress or the infliction of the penalty." That many were willing to follow such advice is demonstrated by the fact that the pages of the *Liverpool Mercury* during the Famine years are replete with examples of Irish emigrants taking swindlers to court. In May 1847, Daniel Harrigan, his wife, and two other women purchased sailing tickets to Canada from a shipping broker named Patrick Gornley. Upon reading the tickets, however, Harrigan realized that Gornley had given him tickets to St. John's, Newfoundland, when in fact they had asked to travel to Saint John, New Brunswick. When Harrigan complained, "Gornley began to laugh at him and said that he could not go to a better place than Newfoundland" and refused to refund his money. The parties went to court, where Lieutenant Hodder, the government's emigration officer in Liverpool, personally represented Harrigan. In his decision, the magistrate decried that Gornley had tried to send Harrigan and his fellow passengers to a place "where they had neither friends nor relatives, and thus pauperism would be entailed upon them and, it might be, death itself." He ordered that Gornley pay a fine and forfeit his license, hoping that the case would serve as "a warning to the emigrants, whenever the appearance of fraud was attempted, to go to Lieutenant Hodder or the magistrates, and they would obtain instant redress."[38]

Personal relationships, which were critical to the process of gathering the resources and preparing to leave home, could ameliorate the threats in Liverpool as well. When Daniel Rowntree of Washington, D.C.,

sent money to allow his sister Ellen and her children to emigrate from
Dublin in 1851, he encouraged her to seek accompaniment on the first
leg of her journey. "It would be well if brother Lawrence could see you
to Liverpool," Daniel wrote. "I fear it will be difficult for you to manage
otherwise from the imposition used [but] if you were once on board,
you would be alright." As C. Graham, a shipping broker on Waterloo
Road in Liverpool, and John McGinity, a linen vendor in Newtown-
hamilton, County Armagh, negotiated over the purchase of a passage
to America on behalf of McGinity's sister-in-law, Graham offered more
than merely a ticket. "Write to me . . . and inform me of the day she
leaves home and when she'll be here," Graham explained, "and it will
enable me to send a person to look for her, by so doing it will keep her
from [being] imposed upon by loafers." John Devine "is a brother-in-
law of mine," Graham assured McGinity. "Him or his boy will be at the
steamer." Emigrants were also encouraged to stick together. In a letter
offering "Counsel to Emigrants," which was originally published in the
New York weekly *People* and reprinted in Ireland in 1849, the author
believed that a large number of neighbors intending to emigrate should
pool their resources, "send a capable and trusty agent to Cork or Liverpool," and charter an entire ship. Traveling as relatives, friends, and
neighbors would be cheaper and more convenient and would protect
them "from the intrusion of vile characters who often abuse the opportunities afforded by an ocean passage for the perpetration of their
iniquities and villainies."[39]

As the numbers of Irish emigrants began to crest in the early 1850s,
the Catholic clergy recognized the need for a lodging house capable
of protecting emigrants from "the heartless frauds and demoralizing
influences to which they are exposed" in Liverpool. In May 1851, an
Emigrant's Home was opened on Vulcan Street, close to the docks.
Owned and operated by Fred Marshall, the lodging house enjoyed
the blessing of the Society of St. Vincent de Paul's Emigrant Protection Society in Ireland. Although the organization offered to place all
Irish Catholic emigrants "under the immediate and constant care of
their natural guardians, the clergy of their own church," the house also
promised Protestant travelers that "particular care is taken not to interfere in the slightest degree with their religious convictions." Priced at
sixpence a night and capable of accommodating eight hundred lodgers

in dormitories designed to keep married people, single women, and single men "entirely separate," the house included washing and drying rooms, luggage storage, and a dining hall "furnished with writing tables and . . . supplied with American maps and guide books." To distinguish themselves from runners, the home's porters met the steamers dressed in "blue jackets and red collars" to bring the emigrants safely to the house where they could get provisions, bedding, and assistance buying passage tickets. Within a few weeks of opening, however, the new place attracted the attention of a "formidable array" of man-catchers. One night, a group of these swindlers surrounded the carts carrying emigrants to the Vulcan Street home and sought to take them away to their own rooming houses. A riot broke out, and several were arrested. For its part, the *Liverpool Mercury* strongly supported the idea of protective homes for emigrants. The Dock Estate made forty thousand pounds a year from the dues on passenger vessels, the newspaper editorialized, and might continue to do so unless, "from the unenviable notoriety, which the port has obtained, emigrants, dreading to encounter the difficulties here, select other ports as the place of embarkation."[40]

The Vulcan Street home reiterates the role that relationships played in helping Famine-era Irish emigrants negotiate their way through the dangers of Liverpool. The columns of the popular press demonstrate that many emigrants successfully employed the legal system to seek redress when mistreated. Others relied on interpersonal networks formed through family, neighborhood, or even business connections to insulate themselves or their loved ones against the "land sharks, crimps, and other dishonest characters" who plagued Liverpool's docks. Their Catholicism represented another kind of connection to which emigrants could turn for support. Regardless of whether or not any given emigrant was a pious Catholic, their clergy provided a connection to an instrument capable of providing succor at a time of need. "We trust that every parish priest throughout the country will make the [St. Vincent de Paul's Emigrants' Protection Society] known to his flock," editorialized the *Limerick Reporter* in 1851, "and recommend those who leave his district for the purpose of emigrating, to put themselves under its care." From the perspective of the clergy, institutions like the Vulcan Street home provided an outlet for exercising its moral and religious power over a fluctuating community on the move. To the average emigrant, however, religious affiliation could simply serve as a support network during the journey. Indeed, the importance of relationships was manifest in the fact that so many man-catchers used their Irish background to portray themselves as a "false friend." A few days after the Vulcan Street home opened, the *Galway Vindicator* suggested that prospective emigrants embark at Irish ports to avoid being "fleeced by the swarm of sharpers that infest every seaport in England." Once the Great Southern and Western Railway connected Dublin to Galway, emigrants would find in the latter an excellent port of departure for America. "At all events, let them shun England as they would a lazar-house," the paper opined, "for it is death to the men and dishonor to the women to sail in any of her liners."[41]

"Put Matters to Rights": Settling into the Ship

The last step every emigrant took before heading out to sea was settling into the ship itself. "Having secured his passage and laid in his sea-stores, the emigrant should go on board the ship a day or two before sailing, if possible," explained *Wiley & Putnam's Emigrant's Guide*. "He should then prepare his bedding matters, arrange his chests, and see that the conveniences, which he will need when seasick, are at hand. In short, let him put matters to rights as much as possible." The nineteenth-century sailing ship—whether emigrant or convict—was, in many ways, a miniature model of contemporary class relations. The captain, his officers, and the cabin passengers slept in their own apartments (often called state rooms) at the back of the ship, were served by a cabin boy or steward, and dined at a private table. The crew had their own accommodations in the forecastle. The majority of passengers traveled in steerage. Because the 'tween deck was used to carry cargo when heading from North America to Europe, the fittings and furnishings of steerage were often roughly carpentered affairs. "The sleeping place (called *berth*) furnished by the ship consists of nothing more than a sort of shelf made of unpainted deals [cheap pine planks]," warned Wiley and Putnam, "with a strip of deal at the outside to the keep the occupant from rolling out." To maintain Victorian strictures of gender and sexuality, steerage was often compartmentalized by temporary bulkheads designed to separate married couples, single men, and single women from each other "for the preservation of morality" (see figure 1.2 in the introduction). Their relationships with others impacted how passengers settled into this new environment.[42]

For many emigrants, getting onto the ship itself did not protect them from theft or violence. The sailors themselves, after all, were often the perpetrators of such abuse. In May 1852, an American packet ship named the *Rappahannock*, carrying over five hundred passengers "principally of the humbler class of Irish," was preparing to leave for New York. On the day it was to depart, while the captain was busy mustering the emigrants on the main deck, the crew broke into the passengers' chests and stole whatever they fancied. "They also got a quantity of whiskey, the property of the passengers," one newspaper reported, "of which they imbibed so large a quantity that they became not only drunk but infuriated." When the captain went ashore to file a report with the police, the crew attacked the passengers with knives, threatening to murder them. At one point, when a sailor named Burns knifed an emigrant, he "was severely maltreated, the passengers jumping on him and bruising him dreadfully." Evidently, some land-based thieves specialized in preying on emigrants' luggage. In July 1851, a "rough-looking character named George Kerr" was charged with plundering an emigrant's boxes on board the ship *Leviathan* as it sat at the dock. Caught in the act by a passing policeman, Kerr was described in court as "a noted thief and a plunderer of emigrant ships." The following year, two "rough-looking Irish youths" named Harrison and Coutbrett were charged with a more violent theft. After coming across an emigrant sitting on his chest, they dragged him off the box, opened it, and took two articles of clothing. When a police officer searched the vessel, he "discovered the prisoners concealed in the ship with the coat on one of them and the trousers upon the other."[43]

In light of these threats, and the length of most voyages, emigrants were often advised to carefully secure their luggage in the ship. "As soon as possible, get your berth assigned to you, this done, be sure you tie all your boxes and things fast, so that they may not tumble about in the rocking of the ship, otherwise they might be broken and lost," wrote an unnamed benefactor on the back of a prepaid ticket in 1848. "Mind to keep everything under lock and key, both in Liverpool and on your passage." Seven years later, another advisor, perhaps mindful

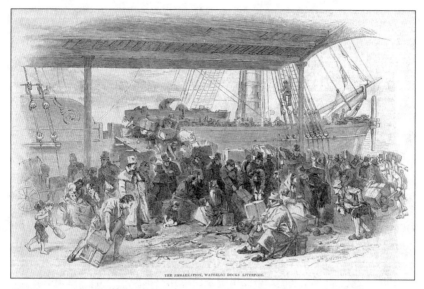

Figure 2.2. Emigrants embark at the Waterloo Docks in Liverpool. *Illustrated London News*, July 6, 1850. Image © Illustrated London News/Mary Evans Picture Library.

of the thefts reported in the press, was even more specific. "Mind and lock everything up," they warned, "and don't leave the ship while your things are on board." Each emigrant carried two kinds of luggage. The first, composed of bulky items not needed on a daily basis, were locked in the hold below the 'tween deck. The second, stored in smaller boxes or bags, were for daily use and kept close at hand, usually near one's berth. As Bridget Brennan prepared to emigrate to Australia in 1846, her brother James told her to bring "two good-sized chests [as well as] two small ones to hold anything most necessary as you cannot get at the large boxes but seldom." Emigrant guides agreed. Nonessential items should be packed into "clean, dry trunks or boxes," suggested Wiley and Putnam. "Fasten the trunks securely and mark upon them, in two or three places, the owner's name. These should be stowed away on board the ship in as dry and convenient a place as possible." Meanwhile, "clothing and other little matters in daily use at sea should be kept in a common wooden chest properly furnished with tills, locks, and the like." Such boxes suited steerage passengers as they "are cheap, capacious, easily fastened to the floor" and "answer very well for a table and a settee." As Mary Sullivan prepared to sail in 1851, her benefactor suggested that "any old, strong box will do," but J. C. Byrne's *Emigrant's Guide* insisted that all chests be "sound, strong, and water-tight."[44]

Besides securing one's luggage, picking one's berth was the most important task an emigrant needed to attend to on the eve of departure. Berths were, as noted earlier, essentially rough wooden shelves running lengthwise along the sides of the 'tween deck and arranged in a two-tier fashion, one above the other. The Passengers Acts dictated that each emigrant was entitled to a berth, but this did not mean that all travelers enjoyed their own bed. In fact, most berths were designed to handle at least four or more bodies at once. Passengers were also expected to provide their own bedding. "A good *straw* bed is . . . as good a kind as one would wish to have for steerage use," explained Wiley and Putnam. "It is easier to lie on than a hair mattress (no small consideration in a heavily rolling ship) and it can be thrown away on arriving at quarantine without loss." Comfort and health at sea were always at a premium. "Nowhere is a fresh-made bed more prized than in a confined steerage," they advised, "and we would recommend that the sheets be changed as often as the nature of the case will allow." The berth's physical location on the ship itself was no small consideration either. In his guide for emigrants heading to North America, George Nettle stipulated that it was "of some importance to select a berth where there is light and ventilation, and as near the middle of the ship as possible, where the motion is always the least perceptible." MacKenzie's *Emigrant's Guide to Australia* agreed that passengers should seek berths "as near to the center as possible." Easy access to the rest of the ship was important too. "Be sure and take an under berth," wrote an anonymous benefactor on the back of a prepaid ticket, "and take it as near the hatchway as you can." In case of emergency, personal relationships could play a role in the process as well. In 1851, Ann McMullen was advised to tell Luke McHenley to ask Harden and Company "to keep a berth for you if you do not get [to Liverpool] before the 8th of May."[45]

With the luggage and berths sorted out, emigrants and convicts alike were organized into messes, which served as the basic unit of administration for the cooking and consumption of food at sea. On emigrant ships headed for Australia during the Famine years, messes were compulsory for all passengers. After arriving in Melbourne in December

1853, an "Affectionate Nephew" sent a letter to his aunt describing life at sea on the *Beulah* with approximately 150 other emigrants. "We were divided into messes of eight persons and out of each mess there was one appointed as captain of the mess to receive the provisions when they were issued, attend to the cooking, make puddings, grind the coffee, et cetera," he explained. Convicts going to Australia were organized along similar lines, with well-behaved prisoners appointed as captains. Messes were not compulsory on ships heading for North America, but O'Hanlon believed that emigrants sailing in that direction should adopt them anyway. "Single persons emigrating would do well to combine in parties of two or three, being joint partners in outfit, cooking, and expenses," he argued. "Better if they were neighbors or acquaintances at home as in such cases greater confidence would be established and mutual good offices rendered in case of sickness on board." Wiley and Putnam believed that organizing into messes would ensure "greater regularity," "better cooking," and "a greater variety of eatables than each alone would have" while also being "more social than for each individual to live by himself." For those adverse to cooking and capable of affording the small luxury, it was sometimes possible to pay someone to do it. "On board the larger ships there is usually a *second* cook who undertakes such work, if desired," Wiley and Putnam pointed out. "A small fee, say a dollar or two (four to eight shillings sterling) will secure his services for the whole voyage."[46]

As ships at sea were self-contained, isolated communities, the medical examination of each and every member was critical to the long-term safety of the whole. The Passenger Acts demanded that a medical practitioner inspect all passengers to ensure they were free of infectious disease. Those deemed healthy enough had their passage ticket stamped or signed accordingly. Anyone identified as ill was disembarked immediately (along with their luggage and any dependents) and their fare refunded in full. The US Passenger Acts also dissuaded captains from embarking the sick and elderly by threatening them with bonds and commutation fees. When a group of over one hundred emigrants from the Crown Estate of Ballykilcline embarked in Liverpool en route to New York in March 1848, they had to leave behind "Francis Stewart, who, on account of his aged appearance, would not be permitted by the captain of the *Channing* to embark in that vessel." In spite of these laws, several factors set the stage for excess mortality on many voyages in the second half of the 1840s, as discussed in chapter 4. In particular, the long-term malnutrition and illness of many emigrants, their strong desire to leave the island, and the inability of emigration officers (and unwillingness of many captains) to rigorously enforce regulations laid the groundwork for many deaths. Although the actual number of emigrants leaving Ireland increased in the 1850s, their health and safety simultaneously improved thanks to several amendments to the American and British Passenger Acts between 1847 and 1855. Nevertheless, loopholes remained and enforcement was uneven. For example, from 1848 onward, all ships carrying a hundred or more steerage passengers were required to either have a physician on board or grant each passenger the equivalent of fourteen (instead of twelve) square feet of surface space allowance. Passengers were often powerless, however, to stop unscrupulous captains sailing without a doctor, or taking one aboard to pass customs before relanding them, or employing dodgy formulae when figuring out their ship's surface space.[47]

Emigrant guides sometimes offered advice on how to prepare one's body for the rigors of a sea journey. In his book for those heading to Australia, Eneas MacKenzie explained that there were things the emigrants could do themselves. Each person, for example, "should take one or two calomel pills and some gentle aperient medicine" to forestall seasickness. One's diet in the lead-up to departure was equally important. "The food should also be very plain, that the stomach may be in good order and we assure our readers that the 'cup o' kindness' taken for the sake 'of auld lang-syne' is apt to have anything but a pleasing recollection afterwards," the guide insisted. "A week's abstinence from rich food and irritating drinks is amply rewarded; the self-denial prevents many an hour or day's suffering of agonizing pain." Similarly, Wiley and Putnam urged their readers to keep their own little stash of medicine handy. In the till of their wooden chest, each emigrant should keep towels, soap, a comb, a small mirror, shaving equipment, and "a box or two of simple purging pills, as the change of diet may render the use of them necessary." When children fell ill close to departure, other passengers sometimes helped out. As the *George Seymour* prepared to leave Gravesend for Auckland in August 1847, its surgeon-superintendent, Harry Goldney, struggled to treat the Donovan family's sick infant.

"The mother from the period of embarkation has suffered greatly from debility," Goldney diarized, "and the infant has been pallid and emaciated [but was taken] soon after embarkation under the care of various emigrants, who would offer to take charge."[48]

As symbols of Victorian order and discipline on a voyage of over one hundred days, convict ships and their passengers were subject to especially rigorous medical examinations before departure. As we saw earlier, convicts heading to their point of embarkation were subjected to inspection before they even left their local jail and once again before they embarked on their transport. The children of female convicts were also regularly vaccinated against smallpox. Despite these regulations, sick convicts often slipped through for various reasons. According to Harvey Morris, surgeon-superintendent of the male convict ship *Bangalore*, which sailed from Kingstown to Hobart in 1848, there were two reasons why he did not strictly apply the letter of the law. First, as the pre-embarkation medical examination was an "ordeal, [which] was conducted almost in the open air on exceptionally cold days, it was not possible to remove the men's clothing and consequently persons were passed" who should not have been. Second, Morris explained, "the crowded state of the jails [in Ireland] and the necessity that exerted of clearing them of some of the worst criminals rendered it absolutely necessary to dispense with many of those forms, which under other circumstances ought to have been observed." Other convicts simply disguised their illness. By the time Charles Byrne embarked at Kingstown in April 1852, he had been suffering from diarrhea for several months but made "the least of his symptoms to others from a desire to proceed in the same ship with his brother, also on board." John Moody, the medical official assigned to the female ship *Blackfriar* in 1851, complained that a teenaged girl he had rejected due to an eye disease was embarked anyway because her mother and sister were prisoners aboard the ship.[49]

Finally, as emigrant and convict ships prepared to set sail, they were often visited by a member of the clergy who performed a religious ceremony to wish the passengers a safe journey. While certainly seen by the authorities as an opportunity to reify the need for discipline and obedience at sea, these ceremonies could also, from the perspective of the convicts themselves, be considered an opportunity to socialize, take a break from the routine of work, or simply engage in prayer. As the female convict *Earl Grey* prepared to depart Kingstown for Hobart in December 1849, the Grangegorman depot's Catholic chaplain, the Reverend Bernard Kirby, visited it to conduct such a ceremony. A devout eyewitness saw prisoners united by faith. "Pariahs of their sex, condemned by the law, and outcasts of the world," he wrote, "there was yet consolation and hope for those who wept in that kneeling crowd and deeply and trustfully did they seem to feel it." For those heading to Australia on the emigrant ship *Miles Barton* in April 1853, the predeparture religious ceremony provided one last opportunity to communicate with their loved ones back home. After celebrating such a service, the Reverend James Buck offered to send an account of the ceremony to the families of any emigrant who requested it. He soon received forty-five addresses. "The homes to which they pointed embraced as many points as the compass itself," Buck exulted, as he reflected on the wide range of sympathies "radiating from the deck of that one emigrant ship." At the same time, from the opposite perspective, Buck also considered these emigrants' friends and families, whose "eyes and bosoms were looking and throbbing toward that promiscuous community who were, *pro tempore*, the dwellers within the wooden walls of that city afloat."[50]

Settling into one's ship and preparing to depart was, in other words, an important part of the journey. The night before James Mitchell departed Liverpool in March 1853, he secured his berth, loaded his luggage, and went to sleep on the ship that would carry him to New York. "I slept as sound on board that night as ever I did at home," Mitchell later reflected. The next morning, he awoke "to witness the greatest bustle and confusion I ever saw." Various little rowboats and steam tugs kept transferring passengers and luggage from the shore to his ship and it was soon so crowded "that I could not for the life of me see how they were all going to be accommodated." Despite Mitchell's bafflement, relationships were the key to settling into the ship. To begin, emigrants often relied on the same interpersonal networks that had helped them to leave home in the first place, especially friends and family who offered critical advice on the particularities of life in a floating wooden box that few, if any, would have had any previous experience with. Once on the ship itself, getting settled required the creation of new relations. The physical layout of the 'tween deck imposed some division between the passengers, based on Victorian notions of gender and sexuality, but more imposing were the class distinctions between those in steerage and the captain, officers, and cabin travelers in the state rooms. This encouraged those on the 'tween deck to stick together. Whether protecting each other from violent sailors, tending to sick neighbors, or organizing themselves into messes, steerage passengers realized the value of solidarity on the 'tween deck. "Nothing tends to make a voyage pass rapidly and pleasantly so much as unity and sympathy amongst the passengers," J. C. Byrne insisted in his emigrant guide, "and it should be the business of all, particularly heads of families, to promote such a state of things by every means in their power." As each emigrant ship prepared to depart, the broad outlines of this new, "city afloat" were already in place.[51]

* * *

Irish Famine–era migrants faced a number of challenges en route to their ports of embarkation. For peasants and laborers unfamiliar with modern systems of transportation, simply calculating where they had to go and how long it would take was difficult. Timeworn bonds of trust and recognition meant nothing to meticulously scheduled networks of railways, steamers, and packet ships. When accidents happened or the money ran out, people were left behind. They also faced a plethora of thieves, frauds, and bullies eager to prey on them in ports such as Liverpool. At the same time, however, migrants also had some weapons at their disposal. First and foremost was their determination. Reading these stories, one appreciates the fortitude with which so many embraced the massive drama of traveling so far on so little. When defrauded of their precious cash, emigrants successfully exploited the legal system to find the redress on which their journeys and, often, their lives relied. Ultimately, the most important resource available to emigrants was their relationships. From a family member offering advice on the eve of departure to a landlord providing an abandoned wife with a few shillings to the succor of a newfound mess-mate on the 'tween deck, emigrants relied on personal connections, old and new, to mitigate the difficulties and dangers they encountered. In this way, the process of embarkation played a role in the development of communal solidarities within the broader Irish diaspora. Once the ship weighed anchor and pulled away from the pier, many emigrants reflected on who and what they were leaving behind. When Samuel Harvey was leaving Belfast for New York in 1849, he borrowed a telescope for one last look at his homeland. "Oh thou spot of earth, endeared by a thousand tended ties and fond recollections," he wrote, "your receding form but little knows with what sad feelings your unhappy exile bids you his last farewell!!" As emigrants like Harvey left behind communities in Ireland, however, they founded new ones at sea.[52]

3

Life

As Alexander McCarthy prepared to emigrate from County Cork in the autumn of 1850, his daughter, Margaret, sent him a letter from New York. In it, she included some advice, probably based on personal experience, on how her father should manage his relationships with the crew and fellow passengers aboard the ship that would carry him to America. "Bring some good flour and engage with the captain's cook and he will [bake] it better for you for very little [cost]," Margaret explained. Alexander should "also bring some whiskey" to share with the cook and any sailors "that you think would do you any good. . . . Give them a glass once in a time and it may be no harm." Life at sea was going to be difficult, especially at first, but with the right mind-set, her father could make it. "Take courage and be determined and bold in your undertaking as the first two or three days will be the worst," Margaret warned him. Most importantly, Alexander should be considerate of the feelings and prejudices of the other emigrants on the ship. "Keep your temper, do not speak angry to any," Margaret told him. "The mildest man has the best chance on board." McCarthy's letter took for granted what many historians have tended to forget: that relationships were a key dimension of the ocean voyage experience. Instead of suffering alone in the bellies of their ships, people nurtured maritime relationships to mitigate the dangers and uncertainties of life at sea. As such, emigrant vessels were unique environments where everyday structures of solidarity and control were both duplicated and defied. They thus served as floating links in the transnational chains of Irish diasporic life.[1]

"A World of Wonders": The Beauties and Dangers of Life at Sea

Every emigrant ship—regardless of its size or destination—shared one common dynamic: the open ocean. The strangeness of this natural environment heightened many emigrants' sense of isolation and left them open to developing new relationships. While the majority of Ireland's Famine-era migrants had no experience with oceanic travel and probably feared it, they were often taken aback by the beauty of life at sea. "How strangely I feel this moment, as I sit lonely on the forecastle, and gaze around on the dark heaving billows of the Atlantic, which I have pictured in many a dream of the imagination," diarized Samuel Harvey, the day after Ireland sank from view. "So novel is my situation that I can scarcely believe its reality. What a world of wonders are ye, thou mighty expanse of waters!" Many were struck by natural phenomena such as the glow of bioluminescent algae in the seawater. "The phosphorescence of the sea at night is very beautiful," Harvey wrote, "the vessel's bows dashing into the waves, which meet her, scatters them on each side in hissing, snowy foam, which at night look to the eye of a spectator like sheets of sparkling, liquid fire." In the absence of familiar formations such as mountains, trees, and rivers, the ocean and sky became the emigrants' new landscape. On his voyage to Australia in 1852, John Clark used familiar shapes to characterize the sunrise he saw one day. "In the east, some small, dark clouds were laid out as a plantation, with mountains and rivers etc. to complete the picture; this was beautiful enough," he wrote, "but when the sun arose, and tipped the trees with the grandest colors imaginable, changed the rivers to lakes of fire, made the mountains all volcanoes, it formed a sight, which can only be seen in the tropics." Alone in his gloomy apartment aboard a convict ship to Van Diemen's Land, even Irish exiled '48er John Mitchel derived some pleasure from the natural environment. "The sun is drawing near his evening bath," he wrote in June 1848, "a grand, imperial ceremony, at which I always *assist*."[2]

The sea's unique wildlife also provided emigrants with both entertainment and nutrition. As belief in the supernatural comprised, writes S. J. Connolly, "a very real part of the mental world of large numbers of Irish Catholics in the decades before the famine," it makes sense that many attributed magical powers to the fish and birds they encountered on the high seas. When a large number of porpoises passed the *Middlesex*, a packet ship traveling from Liverpool to New York in the spring of 1853, it caused great excitement among the emigrants on board. "One man swore they were sharks and that some one was going to die on board certain! as it is a sure sign of death to see sharks follow a vessel," complained an Irish emigrant. Another passenger "asserted that they were young whales and that should the 'old one' happen to be about, our vessel would be in great danger." The sailors themselves often contributed to these nautical superstitions. On board the *Rienze*, headed from Belfast to New York in 1849, the crew members taught the passengers about the various birds that followed the ship in search of scraps of food. These included storm petrels, nicknamed Mother Carey's Chickens, which, some claimed, embodied the souls of dead sailors. "It is all nonsense about Mother Careys predicting storms," remarked one emigrant. "The sailors, however, are all afraid that any of the passengers should injure them." Wildlife also provided a ready source of nutrition capable of bringing variety to each ship's humdrum diet. On his voyage as surgeon-superintendent on the *Thomas Arbuthnot*, which carried a complement of 194 Irish "orphan girls" to Australia in 1849, Charles Strutt enjoyed some of this fare. "Caught a shark about six feet long and had some of him for dinner," Strutt wrote in his journal. "Very good white fish, though a little strong and rich, which perhaps is owing to the butter and mode of cooking." Several weeks later, they caught a number of birds as well. "Some sea fowls alighted, almost exhausted, on the rigging," he noted, "they were immediately caught and stuffed."[3]

Although many Irish emigrants suffered from ill health during their voyage, some actually found the experience beneficial to their constitutions. Those traveling in the comfort of first or second class obviously had a better chance of having such an experience. In an October 1853 letter to his brother in Ballymoney, County Antrim, William McElderry explained that despite a "very long and rough passage" on a steamship to Quebec, "I was not sea sick nor did I know what want of health was since I left home." Even those traveling on limited budgets sometimes had similar experiences. Soon after arriving in Canada, having had her passage paid for by her landlord, Johanna Kelly offered a mixed report on how she and her fellow travelers had fared. "We had six weeks passage, during which time myself and John had good health," she told her father back in County Tipperary, "but Johanna and Margaret were sick during the voyage." The journey to Australia was around three times longer than the transatlantic trip, but the fact that these ships were more carefully regulated and staffed by a medical professional meant that those traveling on these vessels often enjoyed good health too. When the *Hercules* sailed from Cork to Adelaide in 1853, its surgeon-superintendent, Edward Nolloth, was happy to report that "the general health of all on board continued to improve and by the time we arrived at the Cape [of Good Hope], nothing could be more satisfactory in this aspect." Nolloth pointed to the strict routine of cleanliness he maintained on his ship as the reason for this success and boasted that, with a few exceptions, the emigrants disembarked in Australia "in a robust state of health." Others found life at sea downright agreeable. "I never wanted one minute's health since I left my native home," Jonathon Smith told his parents back in Antrim in the autumn of 1845. "I never was happier in all my life than I have been ever since I left you."[4]

As the majority of Irish convicts came from backgrounds pock-marked by deprivation and want, many responded well to the regulated systems of cleanliness and nourishment that abounded on transports. Troubled by his Irish female convicts' propensity for developing scurvy, surgeon-superintendent R. Whitmore Clarke opined in 1852 that "this scorbutic tendency" was attributable "to the fact that the female prisoners had been imprisoned for very long periods and that (according to their description), potatoes and vegetables seldom formed part of their diet." The journals of the ships' surgeons indicate specific examples of female convicts benefitting from life at sea. During Mary O'Connor's 1850 voyage to Van Diemen's Land aboard the *Duke of Cornwall,* she was treated for menorrhagia. Upon disembarkation, however, the ship's surgeon said O'Connor now felt "stronger than when she first came on board and is much improved [in] general health." The following year, Honora Corcoran, age twenty-two, sailed aboard the *Blackfriar* under the watchful eye of John Moody. When she left Ireland, Corcoran was a "tall, delicate-looking girl subject to epileptic fits and seldom free from headache," but during her time at sea, Moody reported, "she had neither headache nor fits and got both stout, fat, and healthy." Male convicts often enjoyed relatively good health as well. This was especially, but not only, true of those prisoners who earned extra privileges through good behavior. Soon after arriving in Sydney in November 1849, prisoner Jonathon Quin wrote a letter to his parents back in Newry in which he described his "very pleasant voyage" aboard the *Havering* transport. "I have not had one day's sickness since I left," he reported. This was, in part, thanks to his having been appointed as a constable. He and nine other prisoners were chosen "to keep order and regularity in the ship so that I had a very pleasant time of it," Quin told his parents. "We were at as much liberty as the soldiers and no want of food, wine twice a week, and I may say, if I paid for my passage out, I could not have been more comfortable."[5]

Some emigrants clearly discovered much beauty, wonder, and even good health aboard their ships, but many also struggled with the challenges that came with life at sea. The most common complaint was, of course, seasickness, which could last anywhere from a couple of hours to several weeks. Seasickness, along with all motion sickness, derives not from the movement of the body itself but rather from how the senses perceive it. When the inner ear notices that the body is in motion but the eyes (of someone, for example, in windowless steerage) fail to perceive movement, the brain becomes disoriented and nausea results. Although the causes of seasickness were imperfectly understood at the time, previous emigrants did advise newcomers that staying on deck (which would have synchronized how the inner ear and the eyes perceived the ship's motion) could delay its onset. "Keep yourself clean on board a ship and if you get sea sick don't stay in your bed as a great many will do," advised Ellen Thornton's unnamed benefactor. "When the days are fine, stay as much on deck as you can." While seasickness was uncomfortable for many, it could contribute to the demise of those who were in poor health before they started their voyage. As the convict ship *Kinnear* sailed from Ireland to Van Diemen's Land in 1848, the surgeon-superintendent reported that Catherine McNamara, who was weak and delicate to begin with, "was excessively sea sick and suffered greatly from its depressing effects . . . fancying every moment that the vessel was going down with her." Ultimately, he noted, "she became greatly reduced and continued for a considerable time in a helpless state of imbecility, her feces and urine passing involuntarily, when death put a period to her miserable existence." For most passengers, however, seasickness was not fatal. Some even considered it a necessary part of the journey. "Numbers of passengers sick and throwing off," wrote one Irish emigrant headed for New York in 1849. "Yet they are content to bear it all as they know it is bearing them the more swiftly forward to their desired haven."[6]

Beyond the nausea induced by motion sickness, the sheer physicality of life below deck brought its own daily inconveniences. Many emigrants found sleeping on rough wooden shelves designed to hold several people at a time to be an awkward experience, especially in bad weather. When Thomas Patterson and his friend, James Garrett, sailed from Belfast to New York in the spring of 1848, they struggled to sleep during a storm. "The ship was tossed at such a rate that it nearly pitched us out of our bed," Patterson complained, "and was very uncomfortable with the one rolling on the top of the other." In a letter entitled "A Fat Woman in Trouble at Sea," which was published in the Cavan *Anglo-Celt* in July 1852, a woman who traveled as a cabin passenger to California described the difficulties she encountered in her bed. "Our cabin has two boxes in it called berths, though coffins would be nearer the thing," she remarked, "for you think more of your latter end at sea a great deal." Her berth being situated directly over her roommate's, "I have to climb up to it, putting one foot on the lower one, and the other away out on the wash-hand stand, which is a great stretch and makes it very straining; then I lift one knee on the berth and roll into it sideways. This is very inconvenient for a woman of my size, and very dangerous." Climbing back down off the berth was just as bad, but getting dressed was even more difficult. "Lacing stays behind your back, and you on your face, nearly smothered with the bed clothes, and feeling for the eyelet hold with one hand, and trying to put the tag in with the other, while you are rolling about from side to side, is no laughing matter," she wrote. But "putting on stockings is the worst, for there ain't room to stoop forward, so you have to bring your foot to you, and, stretching out on your back, lift up your leg till you can reach it, and then drag it on." All in all, the writer believed, life in a berth had to be experienced to believed. "You will pity me if you could conceive," she concluded, "but you can't—no, nobody but a woman can tell what a woman suffers being confined in a berth at sea."[7]

The physical layout of sailing ships also rendered them rife with possibilities for accidents. When James Purcell paid for his sister Bridget to join him in Australia, he warned her to stay below deck during storms "and at all times have care. There is good care wanting in a ship, the danger can be easily seen. Look sharp at all places." The existence of open hatches in the deck, which led to passenger accommodations up to twenty feet below, endangered those walking above, especially the young, old, and weak. On his journey to New York in 1849, Samuel Harvey reported that a child fell down one such hatch, cutting its head severely. "Children are exceedingly troublesome in a ship," Harvey complained. "They are continually in danger of getting hurt." Even the sturdiest passengers could experience terrible injuries. As the *Tory* convict transport sailed from Ireland in December 1846, a twenty-five-year-old prisoner "of a strong, robust constitution" named James Ross lost his footing on the slippery deck and landed heavily on his right shoulder, breaking his clavicle. Ross ultimately recovered, but others were left with long-term disabilities. On the *Australasia* in 1849, twenty-two-year-old convict Ellen Doyle was thrown to the deck when the ship rolled hard. The keg of water she was carrying struck her thigh and "dislocated the femur downwards and forwards," reported the ship's surgeon, who tried to help by tying her legs together. By the time they reached Van Diemen's Land, however, Doyle was "unable to use the limb." Finally, despite their familiarity with the perils of life at sea, sailors were, as an 1848 article in the New York *Sailor's Magazine and Naval Journal* acknowledged, susceptible to great danger. Seamen "live upon the very confines of death [with] but a board partition between them and eternity," wrote H. J. V. "If at any time a plank should spring, a bolt give way, or a cable part, their bodies may sink, shrouded into a watery grave, and their souls, with scarce a moment's preparation, appear before the Eternal Judge!"[8]

Although storms killed a relatively small percentage of emigrants, their power and unpredictability meant that they featured prominently in many survivors' letters and journals. Thomas Reilly's account of a storm that lashed his ship on its route from Liverpool to New York in 1848 gives a colorful account of the disorder caused by a squall. "We were tumbled out of our berths, the hold was two feet full of water, a leak was gaining an inch a minute on us, [and] our topsails were carried away," Reilly wrote to a friend back in Ireland after making it safely to America. Down in steerage, with the hatches above them nailed shut, the passengers were "quaking with fear . . . some praying, some crying, some cursing and singing, the wife jawing the husband for bringing her into such danger, everything topsy-turvy—barrels, boxes, cans, berths, children, etc. rolling about with the swaying of the vessel—now and again might be heard the groan of a dying creature and continually the deep moaning of the tempest." Above deck, things were even worse. The ship was practically capsized, lolling to one side, as sheets of rain and great billows of wind pounded away at her. "She would screech with every stroke of the waves, every bolt in her quaked, every timber writhed," Reilly remembered; "the smallest nail had a cry of its own." Nevertheless, not all passengers saw storms as negative experiences. When Henry Johnson traveled from Antrim to Canada in 1848, he considered the benefit of such an event. "We had some very hard gales before but this surpassed anything I ever thought of," he told his wife back in Dungonnell of one particular storm. "Although there was some danger, yet the wind being with us and going at the rate of thirteen miles an hour through mountains of sea, I enjoyed it well." The six days of stormy winds carried them farther, he claimed, than the previous six weeks of nice weather.[9]

As the journey to Australia was much longer than its transatlantic equivalent—and thus passed through several different climate zones—emigrants on that route regularly experienced several storms during the course of any one voyage. The upset it caused to those living below deck could be similar to that which Reilly witnessed on the broad Atlantic. Describing the steerage floor of the *Nepaul*, headed for Victoria in 1852, one emigrant reported seeing "in graceful negligence, the plates, mugs, cups and saucers, galley pots, water kegs holding three gallons of water, stone jars of like dimensions, tubs, slop-pails, etc. etc., all without owners, running about, as if glad for a holiday, and as soon as you recover your legs, you find all the latter articles have relieved themselves of their contents, the former to the great detriment of dry feet and the last to the disgust of the morals also." On his voyage to Australia in 1855, Charles Moore's ship encountered a storm so violent that each wave that hit the ship's hull sounded "like a cannon." As it struck the ship in the dead of night, "most of us were up, mothers and children crying, and things rolling in all directions. Tea pots, mugs, plates, water kegs, meats, flour, rice, plums . . . in fact, everything between decks, and you never seen such a mess in all your life and still laughable to see things rolling about. If we set down, the next minute, [you were] thrown off your seat." For his part, Irish political exile Thomas Francis Meagher noticed a change in the weather once his ship, the *Swift*, rounded the

Cape of Good Hope en route to Van Diemen's Land. While the first leg of the journey from Kingstown had been relatively calm and dry, the leg across the Indian Ocean was rather unpleasant. "Heavy falls of rain, accompanied by the wildest gales, frequently occurred," Meagher later recounted, "the latter driving us considerably to the south and introducing us—at a distance, to be sure, but unmistakably enough—to the white bears and icebergs of the bleak Antarctic."[10]

Although icebergs were a potentially lethal factor of life on the high seas and caused the wreck of a few emigrant ships during the Famine era, many passengers found them strangely compelling. Unfamiliar with the sight, they sometimes disagreed over what they were. "A large iceberg in sight caused great excitement, expected it was land, had the appearance of an island at a distance," wrote one passenger en route to Australia in 1853. "Was a beautiful sight, the sun shining right upon it, something similar to a solid mass of white marble. . . . Some of the passengers said it was a wreck. Had a very strange appearance in the wide ocean." When John Burke sailed to New York via Liverpool in 1847, he acknowledged how unique his experience of seeing an iceberg was. "On a fine May morning, I arose early to witness what the captain said the previous night would be the grandest sight of my life," Burke later memorialized, "and true it was for as the sun rose above the horizon, it fell on a sight to inspire awe! delight! wonder! and magnificence! For there, as if [at] anchor, yet quietly and majestically moving was an immense iceberg—bright as a mirror, reflecting the golden rays of the rising sun. Such a sight is not often seen by man to such good advantage as we were treated to this morning." When M. A. Beggs thanked the guardians of the Dungannon poor law union in January 1846 for having paid her passage out to Ontario, she described the wonders she saw in terms that her rural neighbors would understand. "On the 2nd of May, we saw the first iceberg, as large as a little village," she explained, "and when we came to the Gulf of St. Lawrence, the icebergs were as thick around us as stacks in a meadow . . . had God not wrought a miracle, we never could have got into America."[11]

Ultimately, however, one of greatest challenges of life at sea might also have been the one that emigrants mentioned least frequently in their diaries and letters: boredom. As demonstrated later in this chapter, emigrants practiced various forms of improvisational entertainment among themselves, but they also experienced long bouts of ennui about which few had much to say. In his letter back to friends and supporters in Ireland, exiled '48er Thomas Francis Meagher described the tedium in an article that was subsequently published in Irish newspapers at home and abroad. He and his three traveling companions (fellow political prisoners Terence Bellew McManus, Patrick O'Donohoe, and William Smith O'Brien) had brought with them some books and games in their luggage. "Occupations like these served in great measure to relieve the monotony of our sea life and render it something more than endurable," Meagher admitted. "Were it not for them, indeed, the voyage would have been most tiresome and insipid." Although willing to countenance working in the coasting trade or perhaps taking the odd cruise through the Mediterranean, Meagher asserted he "would not be a sailor for all the world. The sameness of the life would be my death before long." For the benefit of his land-bound readers, Meagher described the repetitious nature of life at sea. "One day's sailing is just the same as a three months' voyage and from a sketch of one, an excellent outline of the other may be conceived," he explained. "Breakfast: tea without milk, dry biscuit, and brown sugar; dinner: salt-beef, preserved potatoes, bottled porter, a joint of mutton, perhaps, and a bowl of pea soup; shifting of sails; yarn-spinning; rope-splicing; hands-to-quarters; hammock-scrubbing; singing, drumming, dancing, fifing at the forecastle; the first watch, lights extinguished; there's a complete history of a voyage around the world!"[12]

Life at sea was, in other words, a strange, wonderful, and sometimes frightening experience with which most Famine-era Irish emigrants had no previous experience. From warm, glowing waves of bioluminescent algae to towering mountains of ice and snow, the Atlantic, Pacific, and Indian oceans contained wide varieties of sensual experiences that challenged migrants in new and complicated ways. At times, the sheer strangeness of it all could remind some of what they had left behind. "Sky beautifully dappled with little white clouds, high in the atmosphere," diarized Samuel Harvey en route to New York in September 1849. "Several of the passengers remarked that since we took our departure, it is the only sky, which they have yet seen, like that which they have seen at this season o'er canopying home." As his fellow Irish passengers stood there, "thoughtfully looking upwards," the scene seemed "to awaken, in their minds, a train of pleasing though tender recollections." At other times, the bizarre new world in which emigrants found themselves elicited feelings of isolation, loneliness, and fear. In his 1850 *Practical Guide for Emigrants to North America*, George Nettle cautioned that this would happen. "As the emigrant leaves 'the lessening land' and passes over the 'trackless deep,' a medley of feelings and sensations will naturally occupy his mind," warned Nettle. "He will feel that he is parting from his associates and friends and from those endearing ties and circumstances of his childhood, the comforts and enjoyments of which he was not aware of, for the true value of friendship is never properly estimated until it becomes lost forever." Having left behind their friends and relations, and finding themselves in an unfamiliar floating community, many Irish emigrants soon began developing new social networks rooted in these shared experiences.[13]

"The Order of a Well-Regulated Family": Power and Resistance at Sea

In early 1846, former workhouse pauper M. A. Beggs wrote a letter in which she thanked one of the guardians of the Dungannon poor law union for paying her passage to Canada. "We had a very rough passage for the first few weeks but the all-wise God took care of us," Beggs assured her benefactor. One of the officers who commanded the ship particularly impressed her. "I never saw a man act with more attention, activity, sympathy, and wisdom than the mate of the vessel," Beggs noted. "He was just like yourself and acted on board as you do in the workhouse." By drawing operational comparisons between a sailing ship and a workhouse, Beggs's letter demonstrates that the hierarchical structures of both were based on a similar premise. Believing that firmly established social hierarchies were the only antidote to the anarchy and disorder, which lay dormant in modern society, eighteenth- and nineteenth-century legislators made sure that social organization was even more patriarchal and rigid at sea than it was on land. As such, the authorities saw the emigrant ship as a miniature version of Victorian society at large. Standing on established military traditions of discipline and obedience, Western maritime law had long recognized the captain as sole commander of his ship. Supported by a small coterie of officers, he enjoyed near autocratic power, especially on the kinds of long voyages that carried emigrants to North America and Australia. This, combined with a daily schedule—marked by the ringing of bells—of when to clean, eat, and entertain oneself, kept emigrants and convicts in line. Indeed, building on the work of famed sociologist Erving Goffman, historian Marcus Rediker has conceived of sailing ships as "total institutions" where the rules, hierarchies, and everyday schedules of the voyage regulated all aspects of life. The following pages show that although these strict hierarchies dictated the outlines of maritime social organization, the crews and emigrants themselves found ways to redefine and resist power at sea.[14]

The similarities between British and American laws governing discipline and disorder at sea derived in part from the fact that both were rooted in a medieval code known as the Rules of Oléron, which bound a seaman to his ship for the duration of its voyage and legalized harsh punishments for desertion. Throughout the eighteenth and nineteenth centuries, successive admiralty laws in Britain and the United States upheld the power of captains over their crews and passengers. The master's "first duty is to preserve order and discipline on board of his ship under the guidance of justice and moderation," explained the New York *Shipmaster's Assistant* in 1851. "To enable him to do this, he is clothed with extensive authority over the officers and crew; and in case of necessity, over the passengers, who may be compelled to conform to the rules of good order and propriety." As flogging was not formally outlawed in the American navy until 1862 (and suspended in the Royal Navy in 1879), individual captains and their officers often used violence (threatened or actual) to enforce discipline throughout the Famine period. British emigrant ships headed to Australia operated under similarly strict hierarchies. Although the captain enjoyed ultimate control over the operation of the ship and the activities of its crew, the surgeon-superintendent was responsible for maintaining order among the emigrants. He was, the CLEC made clear in their official instructions, "not only charged with the medical care of the emigrants, but . . . on him devolves also the maintenance of discipline among them, and consequently, the enforcement of regulations for securing cleanliness, regularity, and good conduct." Each surgeon should therefore establish "fixed days and certain hours for as many purposes as he can," thus

Figure 3.1. Roll call on the quarterdeck of an emigrant ship. *Illustrated London News*, July 6, 1850. Image © Illustrated London News/Mary Evans Picture Library.

bringing "the whole of his system into a settled routine capable of insensibly uniting itself with the daily life of the emigrants as a matter of course." The religious instructors, teachers, and matrons on board such ships were always subject to the authority of the surgeon, who worked in cooperation with the captain.[15]

The structures of hierarchy and discipline, which organized society on emigrant ships, were more or less mirrored—albeit with greater degrees of severity—on the convict transports, which the Home Office and Admiralty chartered to carry male and female prisoners to Australia during the same time period. The role of the surgeon-superintendent who sailed on every convict ship was originally conceived of merely in terms of medical service, but their remit expanded during the early nineteenth century. As the status of the medical profession elevated in society at large, ship surgeons came to be seen as critical to the overall management of the ship's company, and by the mid-1820s the surgeon-superintendent became the primary organizer of discipline on the ships. In their official instructions, surgeons were reminded that they were being entrusted with the "entire management, as well as the medical treatment" of the prisoners. Captains still had the final say on everything that happened aboard their ship, but they were expected to comply with the surgeon-superintendent's decisions regarding the management and treatment of the convicts. In maintaining good behavior, surgeons had a range of options available to them. "In order to promote the utmost attention to cleanliness and good order among the female convicts who may be embarked," for example, each surgeon was empowered to dole out gratuities of tea and sugar "to the most orderly and cleanest mess." If violent punishment was required, the surgeons were ordered "to cause it to be done in the most public manner possible, in order that the example may have the effect of deterring others from the commission of offences." In May 1846, for example, Irish convicts Quigley, Storey, Lowry, and Mulligan each received numerous lashes on board the *Lord Auckland* "for fighting and repeated misconduct and disobedience of orders, tending generally to produce a mutiny among the convicts."[16]

Religion's perceived role in maintaining social stability on land—by defining a hierarchical moral code for all to follow—meant it was employed at sea for the same reasons. Indeed, thanks to most sailors' reputation for godlessness, many authority figures believed that a healthy dose of religion was needed on ships more than anywhere. Of the over fifteen hundred seamen and cabin boys whom one evangelical Protestant preacher encountered on the quays of Dublin on the eve of the Famine, he was disgusted to find "three hundred and sixty-seven without Bibles or Testaments, or even a religious tract, and entirely without better clothes for the Sabbath. In three vessels, the whole crew was drunk and the captains had been out all night." In this context, the Sunday religious service was considered a key element of every maritime weekly calendar. Even before leaving port, the service could prove an effective tool for imparting respect for the social hierarchy. After performing one such ceremony on the deck of the *Asia* before it departed Liverpool for Australia in April 1853, the Reverend James Buck was presented with a unanimous vote of thanks by the passengers. "I again ascended my barrel pulpit," Buck later wrote, to tell the passengers that the most effective way to show their appreciation was "to maintain a spirit of perfect subordination to the rules of the ship, and a habit of respectful and accommodating courtesy among themselves throughout their long voyage." At sea, divine service operated as a weekly reminder of each person's place in the ship's pyramid of power. "By all means, fail not in attending divine service," urged *Wiley & Putnam's Emigrant's Guide.* "It is not only proper in itself, but it is a mark of respect, which is due to the preacher and the captain."[17]

Religion was seen as the great bulwark against anarchy and disorder on convict ships as well. British naval surgeon Colin Arrott Browning, who served as surgeon-superintendent on several convict voyages to Australia through the 1830s and 1840s, was convinced that Christianity lay at the heart of any reform system. "If we would see an efficient system of moral discipline in operation in our prisons, penitentiaries, and convict hulks, we must provide for the effectual instruction of their inmates in the great facts and doctrines of Christianity," he wrote in 1847. Any "attempt to reform our criminals by any means short of those which God himself hath provided and ordained to that end, as set forth in the Scriptures, involves not only ignorant presumption, but practical infidelity." As on emigrant ships, a priest or religious minister often visited convict transports prior to their departure. On Palm Sunday 1849, Catholic priest Bernard Kirby visited the female convict transport *Maria* as it lay anchored in Kingstown Harbor. After praying with the women and handing out sprigs of palm, Kirby "enjoined them to be peaceable and orderly on their voyage—mild and submissive to the authorities on board." While surgeons were responsible for running all schooling for convicts on most transports, the authorities did sometimes hire religious instructors to assist in the project. In September 1848, Dublin Castle appointed a Catholic priest named Robert Downing to accompany a cohort of three hundred male convicts to Van Diemen's Land aboard the *Pestonjee Bomanjee.* Whereas "no systems of moral and reformatory discipline can be effectually carried out without efficient instruction in the doctrines of Christianity," Dublin Castle explained to the Home Office in words that echoed Colin Arrott Browning, Downing had been hired to induce "a more prompt and ready attention on the part of the convicts to the instruction imparted to them during the voyage, and to the duties expected from them on their arrival in the colony."[18]

Considering the skewed ratio of emigrants to officers on board any of these ships, the maintenance of order often relied on a number of passengers adopting leadership roles as well. Within a week of departing for New York in the spring of 1847, Irish emigrant John Burke's ship, the *Symmetry*, encountered a mighty storm, which blew it back "near the coast of Cork" over the course of two long days. Once the storm had calmed, Burke later memorialized, the ship's captain called "all he had faith in, whose intelligence he might rely on among the passengers, to provide order, cleanliness, and economy in the use of food and prepare for a long voyage." Burke agreed to do so. "I acted as captain between decks and a most trying and uncomfortable position it turned out to be," he wrote. "Some, I felt, must enforce order and cleanliness or we were at the mercy of typhus and some [other] disease, which was at any moment likely to break out from lack of food and all its concomitants." For others, including adults heading to Australia under the auspices of Caroline Chisholm's Family Colonization Loan Society, their active, patriarchal participation was part and parcel of the charitable assistance they were receiving. [We] "pledge ourselves, as Christian fathers and heads of families, to exercise a parental control and guardianship over all orphans and friendless females," exhorted one such resolution, and "to preserve the order of a well-regulated family during our passage to Australia." Naturally, there were others who enjoyed adopting roles of authority. Indeed, some seem to have enjoyed it too much. When the emigrant ship *Beejapore* sailed from Liverpool to Sydney in 1852, its passengers included John Reid Miles, a schoolmaster "whose voice can be heard all over the ship, and who takes a very active part in looking after the passengers and carrying out the general arrangements of the ship." Miles was, another emigrant admitted, "a very useful man on board" but one who took "cognizance of too many trifles, as he is constantly appearing before the surgeon-superintendent with some unfortunate culprit."[19]

Some emigrants' participation in the maintenance of discipline and order at sea was loosely defined, but others had formalized roles on the ship. Indeed, during his infamous voyage as a steerage passenger to Quebec in the spring of 1847, Limerick landlord Stephen de Vere identified the lack of passenger involvement as part of the broader problem of underregulation at sea. "I would earnestly suggest the arrangement of every passenger ship into separate divisions for the married, for single men, and for single women," he told the CLEC, "and the appointment, from amongst themselves, of 'monitors' for each ward." By investing individual emigrants with a particular responsibility, the authorities would create miniature hierarchies within steerage that mirrored the ship's structure at large. On both convict and emigrant ships headed for Australia, such formal positions were taken for granted. Well-behaved convict prisoners were assigned to favorable tasks such mess captain, hospital attendant, cook, or barber and thus permitted to elide harder jobs like scrubbing the floors, bunks, and tables of their prison with holystones and sand to keep them clean and dry. After making sure that his emigrants were inspected, messed, and berthed before leaving for Sydney in July 1852, surgeon-superintendent Thomas Willmott appointed several passengers to positions of authority including one matron, one teacher, six constables, one cook's assistant, and a "hospital man." On board the *Pestonjee Bomanjee*, which sailed to Adelaide in 1854, an emigrant recorded the gratuities paid to such helpers. Those with fewer responsibilities such as the constables and sub-matrons were paid two pounds each, while the water closet constable, who was accountable for clearing blockages and regularly flushing the toilets with chloride of lime, was paid five pounds. The schoolmaster, matron, and baker were all granted free passage plus ten, five, and three pounds, respectively.[20]

Although the captain, his officers, and the surgeon were responsible for arresting and punishing those who committed crimes during the course of the voyage, it is also true that, at the discretion of the master, passengers could sometimes perform such duties. In his guide for Irish emigrants, John O'Hanlon encouraged passengers to anticipate the role they might play in a confined environment containing a multitude of people. "In all efforts to produce harmony and order, which are frequently disturbed amongst so many persons," O'Hanlon explained, "each passenger should consider himself a guardian of peace and good fellowship." While forms of deck justice were often meted out on the spot through negotiation, strong words, or even fisticuffs, they could also get quite complicated and mimic the justice system on land. During his journey from Belfast to Melbourne via Liverpool in 1852, emigrant Samuel Pillow described one such case. When a passenger named

Cooper was accused of beating his wife, "a Mr. Newton (one of our saloon passengers) who was a barrister, or solicitor, was appointed judge, a jury was empanelled, and witnesses examined." Cooper was found guilty "and sentenced to be taken to the lee side of the ship and there to receive twelve bucketfuls of water on his head, which sentence was duly carried out." When Cooper met one of his principal accusers, a man named Baker, on deck that same evening, they got into a fight, which quickly escalated. Baker ran to his room and grabbed a gun. "The captain now appeared and ordered Baker to be put in irons on the poop [deck]," Pillow wrote. "He was released the following day." Ultimately, the master of the ship always had the last word and reserved the right to punish problematic passengers.[21]

In light of Victorian society's existential fear of female sexuality, the separation of the sexes was seen as key to the order and security of every ship. Indeed, both American and British passenger laws stipulated that unmarried males were to be divided from the other passengers by, in the words of the British legislation, "a substantial and well-secured bulkhead." The evidence presented before an 1854 select committee on emigrant ships suggests, however, that these rules were loosely applied on the Atlantic voyage. Dr. George Douglas, who had been serving as medical superintendent at Grosse Île since the mid-1830s, said that the separation of the sexes "is not enforced in vessels coming from the ports of Ireland." Delaney Finch, who had recently traveled from Liverpool to Quebec, felt that the lack of "propriety" in emigrant ships meant young women traveling alone frequently "become mothers before they are wives." An American select committee admitted that single females were vulnerable to "the advances of the dissolute and unprincipled." No wonder that the advice on the reverse of Ellen Thornton's ticket to Philadelphia warned her not to "have anything to say to the sailors, stay in your berth at night. It is a great custom with young girls coming to this country to be chatting to the sailors." On emigrant voyages to Australia, where such rules were more strictly enforced, matrons were expected to help preserve discipline, hygiene, "and that propriety of demeanor so becoming in young females." Surgeons traveling on convict ships were instructed to use their "utmost endeavors to prevent [the female convicts'] prostitution." Indeed, such were the fears surrounding female sexuality that women could forfeit their passage to Australia unless escorted by a male companion. In November 1846, the CLEC denied prospective Irish emigrant Catherine Hough's application for free passage to South Australia when it realized that her brother had moved to America, thus depriving her of "the requisite protection on the passage out."[22]

The separation of the sexes also provided a battleground for those passengers and crew members who sought to challenge the patriarchal system that governed life at sea. Captain Scobell of the UK select committee on emigrant ships was horrified to learn that the louvered bulkheads on some ships allowed "unmarried men [to] view the married women dressing or undressing, and see what is going on." Even in the more carefully regulated ships heading to Australia, where the crew were instructed to have no intercourse whatsoever with the women, people found ways to defy the system. Soon after the *Thomas Arbuthnot* departed for Sydney in October 1849 with almost two hundred female domestic servants, the ship's surgeon, Charles Strutt, ordered that some boards on the fore lattice work be removed to facilitate ventilation. After a couple of months at sea, however, he had the woodwork replaced "to prevent some of my girls from talking too much with the sailors on deck." The renewed restriction gave rise to "much commotion and some crying," Strutt noted, "nevertheless, it was done, and a general admonition given to [the women] to stay in bed quietly at night lest worse should follow." The officers themselves were sometimes slow to reprove sailors for fear of undermining their morale. In March 1849, the carpenter on board the *Digby*, another ship carrying young, single Irish women to Australia, was caught pulling "Biddy Murray's clothes completely over her head to the exposure of her per- son" but escaped punishment as the surgeon feared it would only cause more trouble than it was worth. At other times, sailors found creative ways to fight back. When the *William Money* sailed for Adelaide in late 1848, the surgeon annoyed the sailors when he insisted they stay away from the single women. One evening, a week after departing Plymouth, "one of the sailors dressed up as a woman with another sailor [taking] hold of his arm, and walked aft round," diarized an eyewitness. When the surgeon confronted the couple on the deck, the sailors "turned round and laughed at him, then all of them clapped their hands and hooted him."[23]

The underregulation of ships crossing the Atlantic was partly rooted in the ports of embarkation themselves. As business operatives, captains were tasked with minimizing the overhead costs of their ship's owners or charterers by saving money on the provisions, water, and renovations required for passenger safety and comfort. At the same time, they were under pressure to keep revenues up by taking (and sometimes exceeding) the maximum number of passengers allowed, which varied between 1845 and 1855 but was generally between two (US) or three (UK) passengers per five tons of ship's burden. While the CLEC recognized the need for the regulation of passenger traffic, it operated within the broader laissez-faire mentality, which governed imperial economics at the time. Strict regulation bred contempt. When the government hired Charles G. E. Patey, a former naval commander, to raise the standards of emigrant regulation in Liverpool in 1851, it "caused some excitement," wrote Daniel Molony, a captain on the Cope packet line. The man was "a positive Tartar," complained Molony. "He has been all around Liverpool, condemning boats, galleys, cabooses, passengers' water casks, and tanks." British legal jurisdiction over American ships (and vice versa) proved another obstacle to effective regulation. In January 1851, Thomas Murdoch admitted that the CLEC felt "powerless" to prosecute acts of emigrant mistreatment committed "on the high seas by foreigners under a foreign flag." Later that same year, the collector of customs in New York told the British consulate that, beyond cases of passenger overcrowding, he "could not undertake to carry out British laws." In light of these difficulties, Irish landlord Stephen de Vere believed that any ship carrying more than fifty passengers should include a government-paid surgeon "invested during the voyage with the authority of a government emigration agent, with power to investigate all complaints at sea on the spot."[24]

An eyewitness account from Limerick demonstrates the difficulties facing those tasked with inspecting ships leaving that port. On February 6, 1849, Richard Lynch, the government's sole emigration officer in Limerick, acknowledged a letter from the CLEC in which it was alleged that sixteen ships, which had sailed from Limerick in 1848, were found to have large numbers of stowaways on board upon arrival in Quebec. In his own defense, Lynch asserted, "it is utterly impossible for me to prevent such occurrences, so many facilities are afforded to persons anxious to obtain a passage by stealth for getting on board vessels in this river after their departure from the quays of Limerick." The problem was partly rooted in the local geography. The port of Limerick actually lay "a distance of sixty miles from the sea, with a facility of communication from both sides of the [River] Shannon, nearly the whole distance," rendering it even more difficult to arrest surreptitious embarkations. Ships leaving Limerick were also often windbound for a week or more in the Shannon Estuary, Lynch explained, "where there is constant communication with the shore" and thus opportunity for people to sneak aboard. Many prospective stowaways were also deeply motivated. "Instances have been known of persons having been turned out of vessels when mustering in the port of Limerick," Lynch noted, "who afterwards followed her by land and got on board at Tarbert or Scattery, a distance of nearly fifty miles, at night, and secreted themselves in her." It was up to captains and their officers to stop fare dodgers and complete a final, strict roll call of everyone aboard before taking to the open seas. Referring to a previous letter, in which the CLEC directed him to remain at the Limerick port at all times, Lynch argued that without the appointment of additional staff "to accompany the vessel down the river, and muster the passengers prior to their final departure," he could not be held "accountable for what he cannot in any degree control."[25]

The near autocratic power of the captain and his officers aboard nineteenth-century sailing ships meant that those who chose to abuse their passengers could often do so with impunity. Irish landlord Vere Foster learned this when he sailed from Liverpool to New York aboard the *Washington* in December 1850. While serving drinking water on the first day, the mates "cursed and abused, and cuffed and kicked the passengers and their tin cans." When Foster gently remonstrated that such behavior was "highly improper and unmanly," the mate vowed to "knock me down if I said another word." On their third day at sea, when Foster protested the lack of sufficient provisions, the first mate honored his promise and felled Foster with a punch to the face. "I said not a word, knowing the severity (necessarily so) of the laws of discipline on board of ships," Foster later recounted, but he did complain to the captain who said "I was a damned pirate, a damned rascal, and that he would put me in irons and on bread and water throughout the rest of the voyage." After the journey had ended, Foster notified the government, but Stephen Walcott of the CLEC admitted that legal recourse was unlikely "both from the difficulty of obtaining evidence in the case, and from the doubt as to the jurisdiction of a British court over acts done at sea under a foreign flag." Even officers sailing on the more highly regulated routes to Australia could similarly dodge the laws. In one famous case, the surgeon-superintendent of the *Ramillies* flogged four young women for using bad language and stealing another emigrant's biscuits and butter. "The mind can hardly dwell on the revolting idea of men holding a half naked girl and flogging her till the blood starts from her skin," editorialized the Adelaide *South Australian Register* soon after. "We read of such horrors in Russian dungeons but scarcely give them credit." Nevertheless, given the length of time since the offense, the fact that the surgeon had probably left the colony, and the difficulty of gathering evidence, the CLEC had to admit that further inquiries "could not lead to any practical result."[26]

If the captain and his officers sometimes undermined the order and discipline they had sworn to uphold, the working-class seamen under their command could be equally troublesome. Correspondence between the Cope family and its captains demonstrates, for example, that seamen sometimes overrepresented their abilities. In June 1848, as he prepared to depart for Liverpool, Captain Theodore Julius fired his cook who "turned out good for nothing as he cannot even cook for the sailors." A year later, the same captain discharged another sailor before departing the Capes of Delaware. The seaman was "by his own confession entirely unfit to go in the ship," Julius wrote. "He is just out of the hospital, still sick, and a cripple by nature and says he was drunk and did not know he had shipped in the ship at all." The association between seamen and depravity was common at the time, especially among evangelical Christians. "A ship is a dreadful nursery for immorality and ungodliness," cautioned the London *Sailors' Magazine* in November 1847. "It is a circle in which vice acts with celerity, vigor, and success." The multiethnicity of many crews also drew a symbolic line between the working class and their white officers. "The sailors are English, French, Dutch, Greeks, Yankey," noted Charles Moore on his journey to Australia on board the *Constitution*. Other Australia-bound emigrants noticed seamen of color including

Lascars from India. Deeply troubling, from the point of view of the authorities, were subversive activities that brought the crew and passengers together. When the captain of the *Niagara*, which sailed from Liverpool to New York in the summer of 1846, found out that the steward had been stealing food from the officers' table and giving it to some of the emigrants, he immediately had the man put in irons. The steward had "repeatedly used insolence to the officers of the ship besides robbing the ships' stores," complained the carpenter whose own fare had suffered as a result. "His conduct has been mean in every way, he neglected his business [in order] to fool with the steerage passengers."[27]

When the emigrants themselves challenged the ship's authorities, they often did so by banding together. Sometimes, especially when mutiny threatened, officers employed the threat of overwhelming violence in the face of such challenges. "Our paddy passengers are getting quite quarrelsome [and] some of them began to talk of taking the ship, which they thought they could do in spite of officers and crew," wrote one sailor en route to New York in 1846. In response, the captain, his officers, and one of the cabin passengers produced pistols, which they loaded in sight of the emigrants. They also "had what things [the passengers] could get for shillelaghs brought aft so that I should not wonder if we put a stop to fighting." More often than not, officers responded with less coercive actions. When a few of the single men refused to take their turns cleaning the water closets on board the *Irene* in 1852, the surgeon "sent them on to the poop, separate from each other and allowed no communication to or from them." The following day all three relented and returned to their duty "in good humor." During such moments of antiauthoritarian solidarity, class hierarchies among the passengers often remained intact. It was, after all, Vere Foster, a wealthy landlord from a privileged background, who complained on behalf of his fellow passengers when they failed to receive their foodstuff allowances. "We, the undersigned passengers on board the ship 'Washington,' paid for and secured our passages in her in the confident expectation that the allowance of provisions promised in our contract tickets would be faithfully delivered to us," the letter asserted. They demanded to know when they could expect to have them. When the captain received the letter, Foster later noted, he "abused me foully and blasphemously, and pushed me down" but the following day, the passengers all received their provisions.[28]

Although women were treated as "the weaker sex," they could sometimes exploit this sexism to their own advantage at sea. Upper-class Victorian society's preoccupation with female sexuality revealed, as Michel Foucault has illustrated, a new "technology of power" embodied in a "science of sexuality," which codified and legitimated structures of class and gender domination. Viewed as a manifestation of the anarchy and disorder that threatened civilized society, "hysterical" women were seen as particularly dangerous. To be sure, many surgeons responded to such women with physical coercion and violence. When John Henry Read, surgeon-superintendent of the Australian emigrant ship *Steadfast*, encountered an eighteen-year-old with "very eccentric habits and conduct quite wild" in January 1849, he considered it necessary to "place her under restraint, shave her head, and blister the nape of her neck and [give her an] emetic." Six weeks later, "she again commenced wild wanderings and tearing and throwing her clothes overboard," Read noted in his journal. "She was consequently again bandaged down in her bed." While some of the women identified as "hysterical" may well have been suffering from undiagnosed mental illnesses, it is also probable that others used the doctor's fears of female mania to garner special treatment. Due to concerns over sexual misconduct (both between the women and sailors and among the women themselves), female convicts were rarely allowed out of their steerage prison at night despite the fact that it was greatly uncomfortable down there in warm and humid weather. On the *Duke of Cornwall*, which sailed from Dublin to Hobart in 1850, however, a "great number" of women were granted the privilege. "They were allowed to do so in consequence of being attacked with fits when the hot weather set in," prisoner Jane Woods later told an inquiry. Yet in the last few weeks before arriving in Australia, the women returned to sleeping in steerage. "The weather had become cold," Woods explained, "and most of the women had got better."[29]

The letter from M. A. Beggs, in which she compared the discipline on board a sailing ship to that which she experienced in an Irish workhouse, demonstrates that some Irish emigrants (especially the very wealthy and the very poor) had previous experience with the hierarchical structures of organization and control that governed much of life, especially in cities and at sea, during the early Victorian period. Nevertheless, it is also important to bear in mind that for many Irish peasants, a sailing ship's strict schedule represented their first introduction to the "time, work-discipline, and industrial capitalism," which E. P. Thompson analyzed in his seminal 1967 article. From the bells that demarcated the changing of work shifts to the musters, meals, and Masses that scheduled their weeks, the structure of each ship's organization served as a primer for those moving from fields to factories. The bedrock of this system was a patriarchal hierarchy in which a tiny number of well-placed, literate white men enjoyed almost total control over the bodies of hundreds of passengers and crew members at a time. The ever-present fear of anarchy and disorder, which threatened the social order they ruled, encouraged these men to use a combination of religion and violence to maintain their position. At the same time, the peasants and workers occupying the lower rungs of this social ladder did not always do so peaceably. True, some played important roles in the maintenance of discipline at sea. Many others, however, had competing senses of fairness and equity, rooted in collective action, which did not conform to those held by the authorities. Finding solidarity in new relationships that had not existed at home, and employing combinations of explicit and subtle resistance, these migrants helped shape the way power and community actually worked at sea. These new kinds of interpersonal networks and communal bonds could also help to foment the resilience Irish emigrants needed to withstand the dangers and difficulties of life at sea.[30]

"Finding Friendly People to Assist": Resilience through Relationships

Just a few days into his voyage from Belfast to New York in March 1847, a polite Presbyterian named James Duncan was troubled by the confusion and disorder he encountered in steerage. "Down below . . . there is somebody swearing or some indecency passing around you every moment," he complained in his diary, "but it could scarcely be otherwise where all the management of fifty families is to be done in one apartment." A week later, with their ship still "beating about in the channel," Duncan's assessment of his neighbors grew less kind. "Things are getting on better on the whole but we are far from being comfortable," he wrote. "We have a very obscene set of characters in the opposite berths, they live like swine and talk like brutes, lying together without any respect to sex." When a storm hit during the second week of April, however, the sense of shared danger brought sniping passengers together. "All the saints and dearest friends were called on for a light," by the passengers cowering below deck. "Children appealed to their parents, wives to husbands for help." A quick change in the wind, which caught an inexperienced helmsman off guard during the third day of rough weather, inspired communal activity among the emigrants. "The mighty sails flapped like thunder, making the vessel stagger like a little boy when a man has hit him hard on the side of the head," Duncan explained. "By the assistance of the passengers and great exertion, the sails were taken in without much damage and the vessel sailed away on the other tack." Surviving life at sea often required great hardiness, bravery, and strength. Their letters and diaries demonstrate that Irish emigrants also developed new relationships to buttress this resilience.[31]

Surviving the range of illnesses and injuries, which lurked at sea, often relied on assistance from others. By helping each other through tough times, emigrants rebuilt bonds of reciprocity, which had been left behind on land. A month into the *Pestonjee Bomanjee*'s journey from Plymouth to Adelaide in 1854, one of its young female passengers began suffering from chest pains and violent spasms. The surgeon cupped and blistered the patient in her berth but could not remain by her side through the night. "The matron and a few others, including myself, remained up to render her every assistance," wrote one of her fellow emigrants. The following day, the woman was awake but in great pain so they transferred her to the hospital where two other women agreed "to take turns with her tonight." Although male convict ships were governed by strict discipline, some were willing to break the rules to aid others in need. Among the convicts on board the *Bangalore*, which sailed from Dublin to Hobart in 1848, was a twenty-two-year-old prisoner named Martyn Baynes who had disguised his dropsy so that he could accompany his father and brother as convicts on the same ship. When his breathing became so labored that he required constant supervision, Baynes's own family members nursed him tenderly. The surgeon soon learned that these men even "stole tea, sugar, and other things" to comfort their patient, but as he was improving under their care, Morris admitted to his superiors, "I could not dispense with their services and consequently was obliged to pretend ignorance of their crimes." Fellow emigrants also often tried to save each other from impending danger, sometimes with mixed results. As the *Nepaul* sailed to Victoria in 1852, a charcoal burner weighing over ten pounds slipped from its hook and crashed to the floor, narrowly missing the head of a man sleeping below. When his fellow passengers apprised him of his close call, the man responded with annoyance. "What utility was there in waking [me]," he cried, "when the danger was over?"[32]

In times of great peril, many found solace in communal religious practices carried from home. After arriving safely in Saint John, New Brunswick, in the summer of 1847, Catholic priest John Mullawny wrote a letter to his family in which he described how he had responded to a violent storm that rose up soon after he left Ireland. During one night in particular, "I did put on my habit and surplice and went round all my friends and neighbors to leave them the last farewell," Mullawny remembered. "I went to my bed and gave myself up to the Lord but thanks be to God, we arrived safe on land." In visiting with his neighbors at sea, Mullawny trod the same kinds of social footsteps he would have followed had he been in a similar situation at home. Trauma could draw friends and families closer together. Though mindful of the ways in which they were different from the Catholics passengers, the Protestant faithful also used religion during treacherous storms. Despite it being a Sunday during one particular squall, Jonathon Smyth told his parents back in Ballymoney, County Antrim, in 1845, "Some were singing, some dancing, some praying." As for Smyth and his friend, "[We] read our Bible and sung the 107th Psalm . . . , I never troubled nor pain, I put my trust in the Lord and saved me from all distress, he kept me in good health." When the weather was merely rough but not stormy, however, it could play havoc on scheduled religious services. While reflecting on the nightly worship service shared by the second cabin's Protestant passengers on board the *Rienze* from Belfast to New York in 1849, one minister lamented the effect bad weather had on their little communion. "It is greatly annoying to those leading in prayer when the ship is heaving much," he wrote. "It is very difficult to maintain composure of mind and feelings."[33]

When passengers contributed free physical labor to save a ship in danger, they were protecting themselves but also demonstrating the ways in which maritime life could threaten the pyramid of power. "Had a very rough night," remarked one emigrant traveling from Ireland to America in 1847. The "crew could not tack the ship without the help of the passengers." With their lives on the line, everyone aboard a sailing ship had to help each other. In 1848, Thomas Reilly reported that "most of the male passengers were all night relieving each other at the pump" to save their ship from sinking during a storm. At other, less dangerous times, passengers could treat the work as a form of leisure. In March 1854, W. Philipps, a shipowner based in London, told a select committee about "emigrants sometimes assisting in navigating the ship." One afternoon, while traveling down the English coastline on a ship his company owned, Philipps recognized Lord Yardborough on his yacht and challenged him to a race. As the ships surged forward, it quickly became apparent that Yarborough's lighter vessel was gaining on the larger, 570-ton vehicle that Philipps was traveling in. "We saw that would not do," recounted the gentleman, "so I enlisted some of the emigrants." Twenty were assigned to the main tack, with another ten forward and thirty or forty left "to pull and haul." The emigrants "were much delighted," Philipps remembered, and soon, "we were able to go about as fast as his Lordship." Such moments of teamwork flattened—if only temporarily—hierarchies on the ship as well. When asked if he thought the emigrants felt an interest in the vessel after helping to run it, Philipps concurred that the ship became "an amusement and exercise" to them. He was quick to add, however, that having so many workers all of the time would only sow confusion. "It is only thew and sinew that you want for the working of a ship in ordinary circumstances," concluded Philipps. "Supposing we had four men to the 100 tons, you would not send them all aloft to reef topsails, for they would be in each other's way."[34]

Many of Ireland's Famine-era emigrants used their abilities to develop new relationships based on work and employment in other ways. For those living only a shilling or two from abject poverty, even a menial paid position on board a sailing ship could help to cover their costs until they reached the other shore. In answer to a query from a businessman who wanted to send some livestock overseas, the owners of the Cope packet line responded favorably. "We have spoken to Captain Turley about bringing over thy sheep and he thinks there is little doubt that he can secure the services of a competent man among the passengers to take charge of them," they explained in August 1852. At other times, emigrants could earn free provisions doing the kinds of work that were required on every ship that sailed. "I had good success in that the captain found I was a carpenter and set me to work," Christopher Kelly told his brother John of his late voyage from Liverpool to Boston in 1846. "From that time, I wanted to cook nothing but had no pay." Others, wary of being bound by a cash contract, insisted on being paid in kind. During his journey from Portadown to New Orleans via Liverpool in 1853, Andrew Collin and his fellow passengers were reduced for several days to living on bread and water when their communal cooking stove was broken during a storm. Finding themselves tasked with cooking for every soul on the ship, the cook and steward offered to hire Collin to help. "I did not wish to be bound to it," Collin later told his parents, "and so I offered my services on condition that they would cook our victuals free and that was agreed to." His labor benefitted himself and the others in his traveling party. "We had a very comfortable time for the balance of our voyage," Collin reminisced. "We had a surfeit of good victuals and we all enjoyed ourselves." Finally, as seen in chapter 1, the spouses of transported convicts sometimes earned their passage to Australia by working during the journey. In his evidence before an 1851 board of inquiry, Bryan Conlon explained that he had done so on board a female convict ship, which had sailed from Dublin to Hobart the year before. "I had charge of the fowls and [live]stock," he said, and "messed and slept with the sailors."[35]

Personal charity had a way of bringing people together too. "Among the steerage passengers, there will often be those who are extremely poor," warned one emigrant guide. "As you hope for success in the New World, and for kind hearts to meet you there, and for the smiles of Providence, fail not to minister to the wants of any poor fellow-passenger." When possible, those needing assistance were encouraged to travel with someone they could rely on. In August 1850, the Cope family dissuaded John Peters from expecting his disabled friend to make the voyage to Philadelphia alone. A person in his situation "could not be comfortable on board ship unless he had some one with him to take care of him," they explained, "as there is no one attached to the ship whose duties would permit them to give him the attention he would require." The following year, the same company's managers did help an illiterate traveler named Eliza Donohough after she landed in Philadelphia en route to Wilkes-Barre. "If she gets along safely it will be owing to her finding friendly people to assist her," mused Henry Cope, "as she appears to have no ideas about traveling." On board the ship itself, spontaneous acts of kindness united previously unattached emigrants. When the captain allowed four days to pass without doling out the food allowance on board the *Washington* in 1850, the poorest passengers suffered most, wrote Vere Foster, "as they had no means of living, excepting on the charity of those who had brought extra provisions." Such acts of kindness, often related to food, could serve as a social adhesive. In July 1849, the religious instructor on board the convict transport *Mountstewart Elphinstone*, which was also carrying two exiled Irish '48ers, was glad that his wife had insisted he bring sherry and marmalade on the journey. "I did not care much for these things when she was collecting them but I have indeed felt the benefit of them," Joseph Walpole admitted. "I have given some pots [of marmalade] away, for instance, to the soldiers' wives and children, and to a sick man in the hospital."[36]

When threatened by the officers and crews, emigrants often relied on relationships to protect themselves. That some of the men working on these ships considered female prisoners and passengers as easy targets for sexual harassment is undeniable. In an 1847 letter to a friend, an experienced ship officer named William H. McCleery described his own behavior on a recent trip from Belfast to Quebec, in which he was traveling as a passenger. "We had a splendid lot of girls and perhaps I did not have some fun among them," McCleery boasted. "I used to rouse them up in the mess, pull the clothes off them, and run away with their clothes." In the context of Victorian concerns surrounding femininity, young single women were seen as vulnerable outsiders at sea. The perceived antidote to this condition was the development of fictive kinship between single women and their married fellow passengers, which placed girls and young women under the protection of a father or mother figure. In October 1846, the CLEC allowed Mary Allen and Alice Bailey to buy their way on board the *Princess Royal* to

Australia. The ship was chartered to carry only assisted emigrants, but Mary and Alice were allowed to proceed on it as they had other family members aboard and the CLEC had "no wish to separate parents from their children." To return the favor, however, their older family members were expected "to protect and advise the [other] single women who will be berthed in the same compartment with them on the passage out." The presence of a matron could also enable single women to travel alone. In November 1846, the CLEC asked one of their passage brokers in Ireland, Samuel Ellis, to assess the suitability of two teenagers for free passage to South Australia. As Ellis was aware, the CLEC preferred not to allow young, unaccompanied females to set sail without the protection of married relatives, Walcott told Ellis, "but as the board intend to appoint a matron for their December ship, they propose to afford passages to a larger number than usual of single females."[37]

As Vere Foster's experiences en route to New York in 1850 demonstrate, passengers often found strength in numbers. Those committed to resisting maltreatment alone and in rude or disorderly ways faced longer odds and were unlikely to receive support from their social betters. "One of the female passengers played the dirty trick this evening of committing a nuisance on the deck at the top of the steps," diarized Foster one night. "Being caught in the act, she was (very properly) made to take it up with both her hands and throw it overboard." Acting collectively invested emigrants with greater potential energy, but they sometimes disagreed over how to channel that power. On board the *Washington*, for example, one of the cabin passengers, a Mr. Williams, suggested that the passengers raise a cash subscription for their ship's poorly behaved surgeon "as an inducement to him to conduct himself well during the rest of the voyage." The bulk of Williams's fellow passengers responded with scorn. Indeed, some suggested "that they would not mind each contributing a shilling to buy a rope if they thought [the surgeon] would be hanged with it." Finally, at a time when the transnational popular press was expanding at an unprecedented rate, Foster and his fellow passengers also employed the printed word to voice their collective displeasure. Their resolution was framed in terms of advice and support for those following behind. "We testify, as a warning to, and for the sake of future emigrants, that the passengers generally, on board of this noble ship, the 'Washington,' Commander A. Page, have been treated in a brutal manner by its officers," it read, "and that we have not received one-half the quantity of provisions allowed by Act of Parliament and stipulated for us in our contract tickets."[38]

While men of wealth and prestige, such as Vere Foster, could be expected to employ the popular press as a weapon against maltreatment, it is also true that regular emigrants of modest means often used the press in the same way. A sense of unity was key to success. Otherwise, as Stephen de Vere wrote in 1847, few Irish emigrants would formally protest, finding themselves "ignorant, friendless, penniless, disheartened, and anxious to proceed to the place of their ultimate destination." Soon after arriving in Philadelphia in the summer of 1851, Ellen Rountree told her brother back in Dublin about the way she and her fellow emigrants had been treated. Their passage broker, James Miley, had taken responsibility for victualing the ship before departure but had supplied them only with the cheapest fare. "The oatmeal was the worst India buck, the flour was red wheat," Ellen complained. "The only thing we could use was the tea, such as it was." From her perspective, on the other side of the ocean, the popular press remained the emigrant's last response. "Let me know if Miley was inserted in any of the Dublin newspapers," Ellen asked her brother, "as the passengers were determined to do so to prevent others from meeting with the same." Rountree's point that the emigrants' letter was designed to protect those coming after them demonstrates that emigrants sometimes thought of themselves as members of a resilient, transnational community. When a shipload of hungry passengers arrived in Quebec in the summer of 1846 aboard the *Elizabeth and Sara*, having voyaged directly to Canada from Killala, County Mayo, a handful of them penned a public letter, which was printed in their local press back home. They, too, described their protest in terms designed to protect other passengers. "The suffering, which we have undergone in our late voyage across the Atlantic, and our desire to save others from experiencing similar treatment, induces us to address this letter to you, and to request you will publish it," they wrote. Indeed, they deemed it "a duty that we owe to our fellow countrymen."[39]

These examples render evident that passengers' resilience in the face of the dangers, mistreatment, and loneliness to which they were exposed on their voyage depended in part upon their ability to develop and maintain relationships with others going through the same thing.

Whether helping to haul ropes, tend to the sick, or challenge malefaction, Irish emigrants found themselves building new—and rebuilding old—social relations to deal with the difficulties they encountered at sea. It reminded them that they were not alone. "It is among the keenest of trials to bid farewell, perhaps forever, to the friends and home of one's childhood, and to see no more the old, familiar scenes," Wiley and Putnam acknowledged of the lonely emigrant. "Tens of thousands, however, have done so before him. . . . Tens of thousands will do so after him." Those without support on the ship found it immensely more difficult to handle challenges such as homesickness. After embarking on the steamer, which would carry him to his Bermuda-bound convict transport, exiled Irish '48er John Mitchel was met by a naval officer who "conducted me to the cabin, ordered my fetters to be removed, called for sherry and water to be placed before us, and began to talk." Prohibited from communicating with the outside world and facing fourteen years of exile, Mitchel felt deep pangs of loneliness while the naval officer prattled on about his experiences in South America and Asia. "No doubt, he thought me an amazingly cool character; but God knoweth the heart," wrote Mitchel. "There was a huge lump in my throat all the time of this bald chat, and my thoughts were far enough away from both Peru and Loo Choo." While Mitchel's status as a political prisoner was atypical, his sorrow over disrupted communal bonds was not.[40]

"A Community of Feeling": Emigrant Solidarity at Sea

From the very first moments of embarkation and departure, emigrants participated in a series of rituals, which drew them together as a seaborne community. Three days before the *Marco Polo* was set to depart Liverpool for Sydney in 1853, a number of its passengers began climbing aboard to get settled. That night, while some returned to their lodgings on shore, several others bedded down on board the ship. "I fancied I was at the bazaar," wrote one emigrant the following morning; there was "dancing, singing, and all kinds of music playing most of the night." Such festivities, restricted only to those with tickets, drew a clear line between the passengers and those staying behind. As the *Marco Polo* prepared to pull away from the dock a few days later, a more formal, hierarchical ritual was enacted when the passengers were mustered on deck by a government inspector who examined their berths and checked their names against the ship's manifest. When a stowaway was discovered in the third cabin, he was arrested and taken back to shore. These kinds of actions reinforced the distinctions between those going and those staying. The "band commenced playing 'Off She Goes,'" remembered the emigrant eyewitness, "the cannons firing, the people on shore cheering, shouting hurrah, and waving their handkerchiefs" as the passengers waved back in tears. Although the ship's departure signaled a new phase in these Old World relationships, it also marked the start of new, maritime ones. Most historians of migration have tended to consider the sea voyage as merely a short-term, in-between phase in the emigrant experience—a thing to be endured and then forgotten—but the truth is that it represented an important moment in the development of diasporic communities. By creating the space for new, collective solidarities based not only on history and blood but also on shared experience, life at sea constituted another filament in the nineteenth-century Irish world.[41]

Even before leaving home, emigrants began fostering relationships that would help them at sea. Guidebooks recognized the importance of such contacts. "Families about to embark should provide a common store," encouraged *The Irish Emigrant's Guide for the United States*, "and a community of feeling should induce them to band together on board with a view to economize in the regulation of their affairs." When benefactors in North America and Australia sent remittances back to Ireland, they sometimes encouraged prospective emigrants to connect with others going out. As sixteen-year-old Ann McMullen prepared to sail to Philadelphia in 1851, her unnamed benefactor used a note on the back of her prepaid ticket to advise her to keep an eye out for potential traveling partners. "You will have to be very careful of yourself and be particular what company you keep on board of ship," they wrote. "If there was anyone from the neighborhood coming, it would be company for you." Benefactors who had information on other emigrants planning to travel often communicated these details along with their remittances. "Patrick King's brother and sister will call on you," explained a message on the back of one prepaid ticket, "and will be with you in the same ship." Finally, the remittance system could sometimes help to protect the young and the weak by coordinating information between benefactors and emigrants. When James Purcell sent money in 1846 to allow his sister to join him in Australia, he passed on some information he had recently received. "Patt Purcell wrote to me that he was sending for his two children," James explained. "[Take] care [of] them too, as well as you can, if no one be with them."[42]

On board the ship itself, messes provided the basis for the fictive kinship at the heart of seaborne communities. Those traveling to Australia with Caroline Chisholm's Family Colonization Loan Society were reminded of the social value of such units. "Each body of emigrants is divided into groups containing twelve adults who can take their meals together during the passage," explained Eneas MacKenzie's emigrant guide. "The object of this arrangement is that friends and relatives may unite and aid each other in their common emigration and induce a social intimacy among strangers previous to embarkation." Those "friendless" young men and women traveling alone were introduced to family groups prior to departure "to ensure mutual responsibility for good conduct during the passage." For those heading to North America, John O'Hanlon agreed that a level of democratic organization among the passengers, separate from the ship's own hierarchy, was a good thing. "Two or three influential persons on board should call the passengers together before clearing the port and represent the advantages derivable from regularity and cleanliness, draw up a set of rules on the following plan, and then submit them for general approval," he suggested. "An energetic, active, influential person or number of persons should [also] be named with irresponsible powers to put these regulations, or such others as might be deemed advisable, in force." In a letter to a New York newspaper, which was subsequently reprinted in the Irish press in 1849, an anonymous author agreed that emigrants should travel "under the guidance of capable and upright men chosen from among themselves, apportioning the space afforded them in such manner as would best comport with convenience, delicacy, and good order, and settling all differences by an appeal to an arbiter chosen from their own ranks."[43]

In the face of the homesickness, which inevitably accompanied most voyages, emigrants often reflected on the relationships they had left behind. Some sadly conflated their lost relatives with the landscape of Ireland itself. During his first full day at sea after departing for New York in 1850, George Ritchie gazed mournfully at the coast of Ireland.

"It seemed to me that I was then gazing for the last time upon those hills, which pointed out the land of my forefathers," Ritchie later wrote. "I felt a degree of loneliness that I never before experienced." As Ritchie drew connections between his family and his homeland, the emotional pain of the one was transposed onto the other. "Many a deep sigh have I wafted across the deep water to that dear spot where a kind father and a fond mother first gladdened the happy period of my boyhood," Ritchie told his parents. During his journey from Belfast to New York in 1849, Samuel Harvey committed similar observations to his diary as he peered at the receding Irish coastline through a telescope. "Yonder is the 'Gravel-Hill'—the old Fairy-Thorn too, where, mid the gloom of darkness of night, I have often stole by with tremulous apprehension, in years long gone by," he reminisced. "Yes, aged and venerable tree, you are the remembrance too, of many an innocent and happy scene." When the weather turned for the worse and danger was about, the feeling of disconnection between emigrants and their families in Ireland was exacerbated. One month into his journey, Samuel Harvey and a fellow traveler, Mr. Henning, found themselves watching over an old, dying woman during a dark and stormy night. "In that lonely hour, I could not but think how much more comfortable were the inmates of Rockmount Cottage than their wandering friend who was once as happy as they," reflected Harvey. "'If' (said Mr. Henning to me), 'our friends at home could but know how we are situated at this moment, I don't think they would envy us much.'"[44]

Many emigrants used religious ceremonies to ease bouts of homesickness. Not all such rituals were of the hierarchical, formal variety favored by the authorities. When a complement of almost two hundred Irish single women, part of the "female orphan" scheme, sailed to Australia on board the *Thomas Arbuthnot* in 1849, a number of them expressed their sadness over missing home in ways reminiscent of rural Irish funereal folk practices. Christmas Eve "was devoted to keening that is, to deploring their fate, old Ireland, and their friends and relations," complained the ship's surgeon, Charles Strutt. "Seven or eight would get together in a little circle and keep up a dismal howling, without any distinct words that I could catch." Sensing disorder in such expressions of communal grief, Strutt stepped in. "I dispersed one or two of these clubs, and Mrs. Murphy routed the rest by giving public notice that the keeners should have no pudding today," he noted in his journal on Christmas Day, "which proved an effectual remedy of their grief, so they fell to dancing and singing instead." Considering the fact that both mirth and mourning were integral parts of traditional Irish wakes, the women's reversion to "dancing and singing" suggests that Strutt's victory may have had its hidden limits. On other ships, as the Protestant captains and surgeons did not officiate over Roman Catholic religious services, those passengers who did so found an opportunity to consolidate leadership over their impromptu constituencies at sea. Nationalist newspaper editor Charles Gavan Duffy, who would later become a politician in Australia, sold his popular weekly Dublin *Nation* and emigrated in 1855. "On the first Sunday at sea, I may be said to have begun my Australian career," he later wrote. After receiving permission from the captain, Duffy read prayers for "some hundred Irish Catholics in the second class and steerage . . . and continued the practice till the end of the voyage."[45]

In order to foster communal harmony on board the ship, steerage emigrants were encouraged to travel on terms of perfect equality with each other. An anonymous letter to the New York press argued that passengers crossing the Atlantic should band together in a democratic society of equals. "As their first experience of republican rule," the writer exhorted, "the attempt would be of decided interest and value." When Caroline Chisholm chartered ships to bring needy families to Australia, she fomented equality by ensuring that there were no cabin passengers aboard. "Much personal comfort arises from the feeling that all the passengers are on a footing of equality," explained Eneas MacKenzie in 1853, "there being no classification in the Family Colonization Society's vessels, and all possess the privilege of walking on the poop [deck]." Beyond enjoying freedom of the ship, MacKenzie added, Chisholm's emigrants could prepare their meals without being disturbed by cabin passengers who would usually have preference in terms of time and resources. John Mitchel, the Irish political prisoner and heartfelt foe of church and state, was glad to hear two convicts complaining of the special treatment he received, as a gentleman, on board the *Dromedary* prison hulk. Such anger was only natural among men "who have to take off their hats when they speak to the pettiest guard of the ship" and dare not step onto the quarter-deck, yet "see me marching up and down the same quarter-deck, with my hat on, and those very guards and officers, now and then, when they meet me in a quiet place, touching their caps to *me*." This infuriated the prisoners, sneered Mitchel, but "[I] venerate their black looks, trusting that their wrath will fructify into an intelligent and wholesome hatred of [Britain's] damnable 'institutions.'"[46]

Sober entertainment was considered one of the key requirements for a happy community at sea, and on ships heading to Australia under the watchful eye of the British authorities, entertainment was programmed into every voyage. Surgeons traveling on board ships chartered by the CLEC were formally instructed "to promote music and dancing, and every harmless means of combining exercise and amusement." Ever fearful of the sexual disorder that they believed was lurking under the surface of working-class life, the authorities emphasized that all entertainment must be strictly moral. Parents were encouraged, "for the sake of the young, to be present on such occasions, so that there may be mirth without danger and amusement without remorse." When L. S. Cunningham sailed as a surgeon on a convict ship to Van Diemen's Land in 1849, he noted that while the prisoners were generally glad to be leaving Ireland, they were also prone to periods of ennui. "Everything I could think of was done during the voyage to keep their spirits up," Cunningham told his superiors at the conclusion of the voyage. "I had one or two musical instruments in the vessel and I had them up to dance and sing [after their work was finished], whenever the weather permitted." Rambunctious entertainment could, of course, sometimes cause trouble. As many passengers danced on the *Irene* en route to Australia, one insisted they stop doing so as a child was dying in steerage. The surgeon overruled the complainant, however, on the grounds that "the emigrants do not take exercise enough." When permitted to do so, the passengers themselves often organized their own entertainment. "A public meeting [was] heard at three o'clock to consider the best means of advancing the moral and intellectual wellbeing of the community," wrote one emigrant headed to Australia in 1852. Several passengers offered to perform, including one man who proposed to deliver a lecture but refused to disclose its subject, merely promising "he will be prepared at the evening time."[47]

On the less-regulated ships heading to Canada and the United States, communal entertainment almost completely relied on the initiative of the passengers themselves. Alcohol often played a role, especially in the early days of the voyage, before supplies were exhausted. As he sat waiting to depart in July 1847, one emigrant told his brother back in Fermanagh about the ways in which the other passengers carried on. "I have seen a Sabbath Day past such as I never saw," complained Joseph Carrothers. "All confusion and drinking as the captain was not on board, there was no regularity." The things he saw during his voyage from Belfast to New York similarly troubled devout Presbyterian James Duncan. "This was Patrick's Day," he wrote on March 17, 1847, "so his friends were up by the break of day to pay the customary devotions in the shape of drowning the shamrock." A couple of weeks later, Duncan fell in with a group of sober passengers, one of whom suggested "having a bit of amusement in the shape of a public meeting." Duncan soon found himself chairing the evening's entertainment, which "was carried on with as much foolery as possible until the whole of the passengers were engaged in it or attending to it." Various songs were sung and a "sailor told some of his adventures, which was worth all the rest." Physical exercise was an important part of many entertainments, and Samuel Harvey's voyage to New York witnessed much dancing and even "gymnastic feats at which the First Mate is matchless." Indeed, Harvey described the mate, Mr. Pratt, as "a fine, little, agreeable fellow and capital dancer." En route to New York in 1853, Galway emigrant James Mitchell remarked on the ways in which passengers entertained themselves at sea. Many "dressed gaily in the evenings, promenaded the deck, while some tripped the light fantastic or gathered in groups listening to the strains of some gifted songster. All, according to their different tastes, trying to while away the weary hours of their confinement on ship's board."[48]

The working-class culture of sailors included its own rituals, which symbolically drew the crew (and, at times, the passengers) together in ways that transcended the usual shipboard hierarchy. In the mid-nineteenth century, one of the most popular ceremonies was known as "Crossing the Line" and occurred when a ship passed through the Equator. This was, as Marcus Rediker has shown, "essentially an initiation ceremony that marked the passage into the social and cultural world of the deep-sea sailor." Those who were crossing the Equator for the first time could choose to either pay a fine or suffer a range of

Figure 3.2. Emigrants enjoy music and dancing on the 'tween deck. *Illustrated London News*, July 6, 1850. Image © Illustrated London News/Mary Evans Picture Library.

physical humiliations at the hands of the experienced sailors. Although emigrants were formally protected from such ceremonies, ships' officers often remained aloof during the proceedings. As the emigrant ship *William Money* approached the Equator en route to Adelaide in late 1848, one eyewitness noticed the sailors "busy getting razors and lather and pills and wigs and dresses ready." The next day, the events began. "Was a bit of fun to see [the sailors] blindfold [the novices], ask where they were from and if they opened their mouth in went a pill of the tar brush and if he would not speak they would give him a draught, which was a bucket [of seawater over the head]." The sailors were instructed not to accost the passengers, but everyone understood that those who chose to "go on deck had to stand the consequences." The following year, a group of Irish single women had a similar experience when they crossed the Equator on board the *Thomas Arbuthnot*. "We had a visit from Neptune with his fair spouse, Amphitrite, accompanied by his constables and barber," noted the ship's surgeon. "They did not meddle with the emigrants but they caught the junior passengers and, finding their answers very unsatisfactory, ducked them soundly in a great tub. The whole affair went off very well."[49]

The monotony of life at sea was also periodically broken when ships passed each other. Captains often exploited such opportunities to exchange resources or compare notes and news, but the passengers themselves got much out of the experience too. "Speaking a ship is an event of exciting interest to passengers," Samuel Harvey remarked during his voyage from Belfast to New York in 1849. "Every available place is crowded in order to have a good view. . . . Such an event considerably ameliorates the loneliness of position." En route to Victoria in 1852, John Clark recorded similar feelings. "There is something peculiarly romantic about speaking with a vessel at sea," Clark thought. "The hurry and bustle of hauling in the sails, the shouting of captain and boatswain—the passengers running here and there to catch the best glimpse of the coming vessel—a dozen or so running as to break their necks with letters to the post office—the shouting of the captains of 'where are you from?' and 'where bound to?' through their trumpets— all combine to render it a scene highly exciting." Passing ships sometimes provided opportunities otherwise unavailable. As the *Emperor* sailed to Australia in 1851, it encountered a French ship carrying three Roman Catholic priests. One of the clergymen, according to a first-class passenger, "came on board our ship to attend to our Irish emigrants. All of us English were ordered on deck" during the service along with the few Irish Protestants traveling in steerage. Finally, communicating with ships headed to Europe provided a chance to send letters back to those at home. "As we expect daily to meet with a homeward bound vessel," the same emigrant traveling on the *Emperor* wrote to his parents, "I have taken the present opportunity of addressing these lines to you, which I earnestly hope will find you in possession of good health." The global network of sailing ships provided precious prospects for communicating with home.[50]

As noted earlier, emigrant ships generally duplicated the strict hierarchies of class that dominated Victorian life on land. It is also true, however, that during moments of great danger and distress, such structures could sometimes temporarily dissolve into a state of equality reminiscent of what cultural anthropologist Victor Turner called "communitas." In February 1852, the *Saint Kieran* steamer departed Dublin for Liverpool with almost two hundred impoverished Irish emigrants confined to its open deck, "some of whom were going to join their friends in America, others to England." Soon after leaving Ireland, the ship encountered a terrible storm, which left the passengers exposed to wind, rain, and waves throughout the night. The following morning, one eyewitness reported, the deck was "covered with men, women, and children, all of whom appeared lifeless from hardship and exhaustion, and their clothes were quite saturated with the water." As large numbers of deck passengers lay on the floorboards, insensible from the cold and exhaustion, "Captain Collis ordered an enormous fire to be heaped on in the cabin and calling all his hands together, and begging the cabin passengers to assist them, all commenced to carry the wretched creatures into the state cabin." Soon, the "berths, sofas, and floor were filled with women, children, and old men, all of whom appeared as lifeless as if in their coffins." As the deck passengers slowly recuperated, they expressed their gratitude "in tears and sobs and prayers to the Almighty for their good friends on board." Captain Collis received particular praise as a commander "not only of first-rate ability but possessed of the finest feelings of our nature."[51]

While many passengers on emigrant ships found ways to foment solidarity with others at sea, it is also true that disharmony was part of life as well. J. C. Byrne's *Emigrant's Guide to New South Wales* reminded passengers that "quarrels should be avoided with care, all exercising mutual forbearance; otherwise, discord will increase until comfort will be at an end, [and] the vessel will become a hell afloat." With so many people from various backgrounds thrown together on a single vessel for weeks or months on end, disagreements could erupt over the smallest trifles. "A fight originated through cards," remarked one emigrant en route to Australia in April 1853. One of the combatants "received a beautiful black eye." In other cases, difficult personalities simply struggled to get along with others. As the *Tasmania* sailed from Dublin to Van Diemen's Land in late 1845, a thirty-year-old female convict named Mary Griffon, who was on the sick list for a variety of maladies, steadily grew "more vindictive . . . threatening everybody," and hiding an iron bar in her bed. Two months later, the surgeon reported that Griffon "has occasionally been in a very excited state, quarrelling and fighting—it has been found necessary to separate her from the others by confining her in the solitary box on three occasions." For those Irish planning to cross the Atlantic, John O'Hanlon suggested that a trustworthy passenger be paid "to attend to the lighting of fires, supply[ing] of coal, [and] regulation of turns for cooking purposes [as most] differences among passengers arise from the undue monopoly of fires." As hot meals were central to the comfort of life at sea, the communal grates on which emigrants cooked often caused hassle. On board the *Rienze*, bound for New York from Belfast in 1849, a scene almost erupted when "a few drops of gravy [flew] from the frying pan of a Protestant into the saucepan of a Roman Catholic female. The unfortunate offender, in order to save his head, had to beat an immediate and hasty retreat."[52]

Although religion was perceived as important to the maintenance of social control, one of the most enduring forms of division among Irish emigrants at sea was sectarianism. While it is important not to overstate the prevalence of such animosity during most people's day-to-day lives in Ireland, it is also true that during times of stress and difficulty, sectarianism was heightened. Hence, when Catholics and Protestants were stuck together in a ship for weeks and even months on end, trouble sometimes arose. Immediately after finishing a prayer service at sea one Sunday, Samuel Harvey found himself struggling to prevent a fellow Protestant named Magill from attacking two young Catholics "who [had] trampled and made much noise on deck above our heads during worship." On board the *Massachusetts*, which sailed from Belfast to New York in 1847, a standoff occurred when a number of passengers celebrated Saint Patrick's Day by singing a song, "a Catholic one, and [gracing] it with many an oath. . . . We had a show of numbers and the Protestants had the day." Protestants also sometimes denigrated Catholics as superstitious during times of danger. Henry Johnson of County Antrim was disgusted by how the Catholics behaved when their ship sprung a leak during a storm in 1848. "Some praying and crossing themselves, others with faces as white as a corpse," Johnson wrote to his wife after arriving safely in Canada. "On deck, they were gathered like sheep in a pen crying on the captain to save them. I asked some of them what was wrong but they were so frightened they couldn't speak." In the throes of danger, "they would do nothing but sprinkle holy water, cry, pray, cross themselves and all sorts of tomfoolery instead of giving a hand to pump the ship." Johnson's outrage pushed him to the brink of suicide. "I got such a disgust at the party of papists at this scene," he insisted, "that I felt almost as if I could have submitted to go down if I had got them all with me."[53]

On individual ships in which they predominated, Irish Catholics were largely insulated from the scorn of the Protestants they encountered along the way. In situations in which they were a minority population, however, Irish Catholics found themselves more likely to suffer the barbs of either religious or ethnic denigration. As the *Pestonjee Bomanjee* sailed from Plymouth to Adelaide in 1854, one of its English passengers, a woman named Eliza Whicker, kept a diary in which she recorded her efforts to help maintain discipline and order at sea. As they passed the Fernando de Noronha islands off the coast of Brazil, Whicker's attention focused on one family in particular. "A family of Irish people were obliged to be cropped and washed in the bath from head to foot," Whicker complained, "their beds and bedding thrown overboard, and themselves moved to another part of the ship, having infested their neighbors with vermin." Whicker's decision to highlight the national origin of the family in question—they were the only Irish family on the ship—suggests that she saw a connection between their nationality and their filthiness. When Protestant missionaries encountered immigrant children, they often considered their Irish background as important to their intellectual and moral shortcomings. One missionary in New York, for example, found that children working on the Delaware and Hudson Canal were often well versed in the Bible's teachings. "This arises from the fact (as we learn from themselves) that they are sought out by the city tract distributors, and taken to Sabbath schools," explained the minister, "and although their parents in most cases were ignorant and degraded (being mostly Irish) . . . , they are still influenced by their early instruction." At other times, of course, the Irish were simply the ethnic butt of maritime jokes. "The very last Irish case we have heard," sniped the New York *Sailor's Magazine and Naval Journal* in 1847, "is that of a cook who, happening to let some candles fall into the water, put them in the oven to *dry*."[54]

The class distinctions inherent in the various grades of passenger status—from the wealthy and comfortable in the first- and second-class cabins to everyone else in steerage—sometimes played itself out in tension and division as well. When it came to drafting public resolutions in praise of captains, for example, it was often taken for granted that the gentlemen traveling in the state rooms would write the words, sign the document, and make the presentation while those in steerage stood quietly smiling in the background. When the *Rienze* sailed from Belfast to New York in 1849, however, those traveling between the decks had their own ideas. In truth, class tensions had bubbled under the surface from relatively early in the journey. A woman and her young daughter were the only passengers traveling in the first-class cabin, "the last of whom the First Mate hates tremendously on account of her pride and affectation," diarized one eyewitness in the second-class cabin. Toward the end of the voyage tension also arose between the passengers themselves when a group in steerage, "who have during the voyage imagined that the second cabin passengers kept too much aloof from the society of those in the steerage, got up an address of thanks to the captain" without informing their social betters. After administering "a pretty sharp reproof to the leaders of the other part for their foolish and impolite conduct in this affair," the second-class passengers drafted, signed, and submitted their own address, which the captain gratefully accepted. "The leaders of the steerage passengers hung around, listening to every word," noted the eyewitness, "and seemed much dissatisfied at our polite reception."[55]

Irish steerage passengers sometimes divided among themselves as well. They often did so for reasons and in ways that were reflective of the rural society from which they came. Although the most famous case of ostracism in Irish history occurred during the Land War in the early 1880s when a landlord named Charles Boycott was shunned in protest over evictions he had ordered, social isolation had long been a weapon of the weak in rural Ireland. Exclusion was used to sanction those who transgressed the mores of peasant society. On board emigrant ships, these values, and the punishments for transgressing them, remained alive and well. As a ship headed from Ireland to Quebec in 1846, one of the officers reported coming across a woman whom the other passengers were threatening to throw overboard. When the mate challenged Pat Battle, the leader of the steerage passengers, he was told that the woman in question "is a bad wench; we will never have good luck while she's on board; we will never get to land with her in the ship; sure enough, the priest told us bad luck to us, with her on board." Upon further inquiry, the officer learned that the young woman "had disgraced her character in her own land, and was sent by her master, who had led her into sin, as an emigrant to a distant country." This was what led her fellow Irish to consider throwing her overboard. In the end, thanks to the officer's threat to anyone who injured the woman, "the poor creature was no more interrupted, though none would speak to her." Such ostracism could have marked effects. One evening, as the *Digby* sailed to Australia with over two hundred fifty Irish domestic servants in 1849, "a girl named Rose Riley, Cavan Union, [unsuccessfully] attempted self-destruction by throwing herself over the ship's side." Rose had allegedly carried on "an improper intimacy" with one of the sailors, explained the ship's schoolmaster, and "been upbraided by the girls of the union on the day previous to the rash act." Shame and fear were particularly powerful at sea, especially for those whose social identity was strongly rooted in the group they were traveling with.[56]

With the ship captains formally enjoying almost dictatorial power at sea, the crews and officers sometimes divided among themselves over issues of power and control. The captain's workforce was rarely a united group, and cracks regularly appeared in the ship's hierarchy. At times, the struggle erupted at the top of the pyramid where the closely related responsibilities and duties of captain and leading officers created friction between them. On board the *Digby*, for example, the surgeon, William Neville, described the captain, Mr. Tabor, as "a low, illiterate man constantly boasting . . . of his own skill in deception and cunning, stating he knew himself to be a blasted rogue and rejoiced in it and believed all others to be equally so." The ship's schoolmaster, George Binsted, agreed that Tabor was a corrupt liar. In his journal, Binsted stated that Captain Tabor had encouraged the First Mate "to put lead on the scales with a view to defraud the emigrants of their allowance." At other times, the sailors themselves protested poor treatment by refusing to work. When the first mate of the *Saranak* packet ship struck the boatswain in the face "with a policeman's mace" as they were ready to begin their journey in 1851, three of the ship's sailors "refused to do duty or to go in the ship." The captain subsequently had the men lodged in jail. Even when seamen were brought before the courts, they often preferred to stick together rather than turn on one another. When two sailors were arrested in New Orleans in 1846 for fighting on the levee, the judge let one go but fined the other five dollars on the grounds that he was much bigger than his opponent. Upon hearing the decision, the smaller man protested that they had "just come ashore after a long voyage and had been merely sky-larking," but the judge upheld his verdict. "Never mind, Jack," smiled the smaller one as he slapped his comrade on the back, "I'll pay half the fine myself."[57]

* * *

The Irish Famine–era emigrant ship was, in other words, more than merely a wooden vessel for transporting people across oceans. It was also a seaborne community, a "city afloat," with many of the same dynamics present in landlocked societies. The authorities strove, with great success, to shape these communities into miniature duplicates of Victorian patriarchal society, with religion and violence as the lowest common denominators of social control. Captains and officers employed their crews, and even many passengers, as agents in this process. But the emigrants themselves, most of whom were traveling in difficult conditions below the deck, also found ways to defy authority and cooperate collectively. In a strange and sometimes dangerous environment, emigrants developed new kinds of social relations—based on shared experience rather than kinship—that would serve them well in their new homes. This was an important, and often overlooked, stage in the dynamic process by which diasporic communities grew in the nineteenth century. Soon after arriving in Canada in the autumn of 1848, Henry Johnson wrote a letter to his wife back in County Antrim, in which he described his struggles with food during his voyage across the Atlantic. Upon opening his box of provisions, which had been stored in the hold for a few weeks, "I found the ham alive with maggots and was obliged to throw it overboard." He soon found himself relying on the ship's basic food allowance. "The pigs wouldn't eat the biscuit so that for the remainder of the passage I got a right good starving," Johnson admitted. "There was not a soul on board I knew or I might have got a little assistance 'but it was every man for himself.'" Although Johnson made it safely to Canada, his lack of shipmates made life at sea more difficult for him. When it came to managing death and dying, such social isolation was even more dangerous.[58]

4

Death

In 1847, Patt Brenan of County Kilkenny petitioned his landlord for inclusion in his lordship's assisted emigration scheme. "Fever and plague [are] so . . . spread amongst the people in Quebec that it is frightful for a man with a heavy family to think of landing there," Brenan wrote. "Desolate of all friends and without one shilling for [my] pocket," he hoped Charles Wandesforde would "give me my passage to New York where I will be near to my friends in hopes they may relieve my distress." While the threats facing those headed for Quebec in 1847 were known far and wide, they have also often been popularly accepted as representative of the Famine as a whole. Although held at arm's reach by most professional historians, many popular accounts continue to casually peg the death toll among Famine emigrants at around 20 percent, with 1847 being treated as the only year worth talking about. When ultra-runner Michael Collins completed a solo run of 550 miles from Grosse Île to Toronto in 2016, he sought to memorialize "the fated journey of some 100,000 Irish" who set sail for Canada in 1847, of whom "one-fifth—some 20,000—died." This chapter both clarifies and broadens our understanding of emigrant mortality during the Great Famine. The first section employs hard data from a range of primary and secondary sources to demonstrate that the high mortality rates on some ships headed to Quebec in 1847 were extraordinary exceptions to the rule. In fact, over 97 percent of Ireland's Famine-era emigrants probably made it to their destination alive. Moreover, as Stephanie Smallwood has pointed out, bare statistics fail to capture the ways in which historical actors "experienced and understood shipboard mortality." In keeping with my commitment to foreground the words and experiences of the emigrants themselves, the second and third sections of this chapter investigate the implications that death and dying had on community life at sea and on land. Mortality was an everyday part of the emigration process and tore many families apart. Yet it could also bring Irish emigrants, their friends, and their relations closer together.[1]

"Ship Fever": Calculating Irish Emigrant Mortality

A generation of quantitative analysis by scholars such as Raymond Cohn, Ralph Shlomowitz, Robin Haines, and others—combined with surviving statistics in primary sources from the period—paint a fuller and more complicated portrait of mortality at sea in the mid-nineteenth century than is commonly understood. As these scholars admit, the extant documentary evidence from official sources is problematic in several ways. There are periodic gaps in the data, especially earlier in the period. Discrepancies and errors of calculation and interpretation sometimes appear in the primary sources themselves. Nor should one assume that the clerks recording the original data had full access to all information. Some captains were accused of underreporting mortality figures to bolster their own reputations. Emigrants often scattered before they could be properly counted. Government officials did not always record the deaths of passengers who died soon after disembarkation, from diseases caught at sea. Jurisdictional issues could also make it hard to accurately track deaths on shipwrecks or on vessels that returned to their original port of embarkation. Sometimes, the information was simply never recorded. When a US Senate select committee sought to collect data on immigrant illness and mortality from custom-house collectors along the eastern seaboard in 1853, it had to admit that because such officers were primarily focused on ascertaining the value of merchandise, "the returns relating to the health of passengers have engaged but a secondary importance." A British select committee formed the following year to gather data on the same subject struggled with both "the absence of anything like complete returns from the ports of the United States of the condition in which emigrant ships and their passengers arrive in those ports" and "the almost impossibility of procuring evidence from the emigrants themselves as they hasten to disembark and disperse at once upon landing."[2]

The process of calculating the mortality rates of Irish Famine–era emigrants in particular comes with its own challenges. The main issue is that it is often impossible to definitively say what proportion of a given ship's complement of emigrants was actually Irish because the vessels' manifests rarely noted individuals' nationalities. Ships that left Irish ports were obviously peopled primary by Irish natives, but the vast majority of Ireland's Famine-era emigrants to North America (and almost all of those heading to Australia) traveled through English ports such as Liverpool and Plymouth, where they were often mixed up with other emigrants coming from Britain and continental Europe. Officials sometimes attempted (with varying levels of success) to collate the numbers of English, Irish, Scottish, and other emigrants traveling the seas in the 1840s and 1850s. This was possible on the smaller, more highly regulated routes to Australia, but their methodologies for doing so on ships crossing the Atlantic were necessarily crude. In its thirteenth annual report, for example, the CLEC explained that it calculated a given year's number of Irish emigrants to Canada by adding all of those who left Irish ports, 90 percent of those who departed Liverpool, and 33 percent of those who sailed from Glasgow. The inaccuracy of doing so was evident in 1854 when a party of 191 German paupers (half of whose passage was paid by the inhabitants of their village in the Duchy of Baden) sailed from Dublin to Quebec aboard the *Enterprise*. All in all, as Marvin McInnis has admitted, "one has largely to despair of sorting out the numbers [of emigrants' ethnic composition] in this period." Cross-referencing official sources with anecdotal evidence in letters, diaries, and newspaper accounts can serve to mitigate these challenges, but the point remains that the statistics on emigrant mortality in the mid-nineteenth century are, by their very nature, inherently flawed.[3]

While historians disagree over how to calculate nineteenth-century emigrant mortality, they unanimously concur on its leading cause: infectious disease. As Raymond Cohn has argued, "if an epidemic did not break out on a ship, few deaths typically occurred." A deadly mixture of medical misunderstanding, poor hygiene, weak regulation, and fatalism provided the perfect breeding ground for contagious illness. This was especially true in the cramped environment of steerage, whose Famine-era Irish passengers were often already malnourished and seasick. Whether at sea or on land (where the majority of Famine deaths were caused by infectious diseases, not outright starvation), typhus was the leading cause of death and often colloquially referred to as "road fever" or "ship fever," although it was often undoubtedly confused at times with the less common relapsing fever and typhoid. Typhus was the main killer in 1847. A bacterial infection carried from rodents to humans (and then from humans to humans) via body lice—whose infected feces entered the skin through abrasions and cuts—typhus inflicted terrible headaches, fever, and bouts of nausea on its victims. The survival rate was up to 75 percent, but the disease's long incubation period of over one week meant that seemingly healthy people could pass medical inspection and carry the disease onto a crowded ship. Those struggling with typhus were also susceptible to other maladies such as dysentery, which carried off many people as well. The second major killer was cholera, whose scariest attribute was the speed with which it moved. One could fall sick in the morning and die that night. A global phenomenon of the mid-nineteenth century, cholera appeared at a time when, as one historian explains, "public health and medical science were catching up with urbanization and the transportation revolution." Cholera was, like typhus, a bacterial infection carried by contaminated water and food and characterized by vomiting, diarrhea, and cramps followed by dehydration, organ failure, and death. It enjoyed two major, transnational outbreaks during the Famine era, in 1849 and 1853.[4]

Although infectious disease was the leading cause of death at sea among emigrants, the malnutrition and exhaustion that accompanied life in Ireland during the Famine left many Irish vulnerable to these maladies. Glazier and colleagues found a slightly complicated correlation between emigrant and "inland" mortality rates, but Mokyr believed that "the already-emaciated condition of many emigrants, . . . compounded by the contagious diseases, which raged in Ireland [during the Famine], led to many deaths of emigrants." This accords with the findings of scholars working in other fields. In his analysis of mortality rates among east Indian and Pacific Island migrant laborers in Queensland and Fiji in the late nineteenth and early twentieth centuries, Ralph Shlomowitz partly blamed seaborne excess mortality on "infectious diseases being brought aboard vessels through the inadequate screening of recruits." Eyewitnesses often came to similar conclusions. According to an 1847 select committee, the excess mortality among Irish emigrants that year was attributable to "the past sufferings and privations of the emigrant, latent disease, and the effect of a sudden transition from a stinted and unwholesome diet to food of better quality and supplied in greater abundance" at sea. As conditions in Ireland improved in the early 1850s, the seaborne health of emigrants rose as well. In December 1852, Dr. George Douglas, the medical superintendent at Grosse Île, noted "the almost total absence of ship fever," which had plagued Irish emigrant vessels in previous years. "The source and cause of fever no longer exists in Ireland as formerly," concluded Douglas, and, as a result, "the sickly and starving are no longer to be met in multitudes." As hundreds of thousands of tired, malnourished, and frightened Irish people streamed onto emigrant ships during the early years of the Famine, the conditions they were escaping, combined with the underenforcement of regulations discussed in previous chapters, exacerbated their vulnerabilities.[5]

The emigrants' weaknesses were also aggravated by the fact that most Famine-era sailing ships lacked a qualified physician. Here, again, those traveling to Australia were in a better position. From 1815 onward, every convict ship was required to carry a surgeon, and from the mid-1830s, government-chartered Australian emigrant vessels had to as well. By the time emigration from Ireland spiked in the mid-1840s, therefore, those ships headed for Australia had clear, regulated medical systems in place even if the quality of these surgeons was uneven. Many were physicians who had retired after years in the British navy. These men understood how ships were run but were not necessarily trained to handle emigrants. Following the founding of the CLEC in 1840, civilian surgeons were preferred for emigrant vessels, but many of them lacked either experience or qualifications. On the Atlantic route to North America, which most Famine-era emigrants sailed on, ships' surgeons were few and far between. The UK government baulked at insisting that North America–bound ships carry doctors because they realized that the position's low esteem and poor pay would make it more or less impossible to meet the demand, especially when the numbers of emigrants swelled during the Famine. When the Canadian authorities complained about the issue in the summer of 1847, the CLEC's Thomas Frederick Elliot replied that he doubted "whether a sufficient supply of lawfully qualified surgeons could be obtained on such terms as would alone be compatible with the low charges at which the humbler class of persons can afford to emigrate." In 1852, the new UK Passenger Act required all ships carrying more than five hundred emigrants be staffed by a surgeon as well, but because the complements of so many ships failed to reach that threshold, most remained without one. Of the 362 emigrant vessels that sailed from Liverpool to North America in 1853, only 116 carried a surgeon. It was not until 1855 that all emigrant ships crossing the Atlantic were required to carry a medical professional.[6]

Years of careful work by trained scholars have provided us with a relatively clear picture of the mortality rates of seaborne travelers in the mid-nineteenth century. Slavery's transatlantic Middle Passage, that hideous benchmark for maritime mortality, witnessed a gradual decrease from 15.6 percent in the first half of the 1700s to a fairly consistent 10 percent in the nineteenth century. Some other migratory people around this time had elevated mortality rates too. Chinese contract laborers sailing to Cuba in the third quarter of the nineteenth century died at a rate of 9.9 percent, although the long nature of that voyage may partly account for this high figure. Among indentured servants heading from Calcutta to the West Indies between 1850 and 1856, the mortality rate was 4.3 percent. By contrast, Europeans sailing in these years generally enjoyed much safer journeys. According to Raymond Cohn, the mortality rate among Europeans en route to the United States between 1820 and 1860 was about 1.56 percent. Only 1.36 percent of those Europeans who headed to New York City between 1836 and 1853 died. In 1854, the mortality rate among passengers from Britain and Ireland to New York was 1.19 percent. Most of the time, Canada was even safer again. The annual reports of the chief emigration officer in Canada suggest that between 1845 and 1855, 444,377 souls sailed to Quebec, of whom 11,998 (2.7 percent) died. When the statistics from 1847 are discounted (for reasons explained below), however, the mortality rate across those years drops to only 0.96 percent. Ships sailing from Britain to Australia during the 1840s and 1850s were about the same. Those carrying emigrants (both assisted and unassisted) lost somewhere between 1 and 2 percent of their passengers. Male and female convict ships sailing between 1846 and 1855 lost a total of 227 out of 22,113 embarked, or slightly over 1 percent. Taken together, these statistics suggest that 1 to 2.5 percent serves as a useful benchmark or "normal" range of average mortality rates for Europeans at sea in the late 1840s and early 1850s.[7]

Although this death rate is very high by today's standards, the surviving data suggest that the vast majority of Famine-era Irish emigrants experienced mortality rates within or below this "normal" range. Raymond Cohn's analysis of 1,077 European immigrant voyages to New York, for example, demonstrates that, between 1845 and 1853, the annual mortality rate exceeded 1.6 percent only once—in 1849—when it hit 3.1 percent. Moreover, this spike impacted ships sailing from the European continent (3 percent) as well as those coming from Britain and Ireland (3.1 percent) and is attributable to both the potato blight and an outbreak of cholera, which erupted in Europe in 1848 and had spread to the United States by 1849. Cohn concludes there is a "lack of correlation between mortality and nationality" on immigrant ships headed to New York during the Famine years. In a related study of over 28,000 European immigrants to New York between 1836 and 1853, Cohn found that, overall, "the immigrant's country of origin had no effect on mortality." Cormac Ó Gráda has also demonstrated (based on data from an admittedly small sample supplied by Raymond Cohn for 1845–1853) that in only two of those years, the cholera years of 1849 and 1853, did New York–bound ships leaving from Liverpool or any Irish port record mortality rates higher than 3 percent. In 1847, the average mortality rate on ships headed from Ireland to New York was 1.33 percent. For those Irish who sailed to Quebec during the Famine, 1847 stands apart and is discussed in detail below. Judging from the annual reports of the government's chief emigration officer in Canada (cited above), however, Irish emigrants to Quebec otherwise enjoyed relatively safe passages. In only one year (again 1849, when 3.25 percent perished, largely due to cholera) did Irish emigrants have an average mortality rate higher than "normal." Indeed, for the years 1846 and 1850 to 1855 inclusive, the annual Irish average mortality rate never went above 0.75 percent. In 1855, of the 4,114 passengers who either embarked in Irish ports or were born at sea en route to Quebec, only 8 (0.19 percent) died.[8]

Those Irish headed to Australia during the Famine era could also expect to experience a relatively safe journey. The statistics for 1845 to 1846 are less reliable, but the extant numbers suggest that most traveled within the "normal" range of emigrant mortality. Assisted emigrants, who were more likely to come from deprived backgrounds, had slightly higher death rates. The scholarship of John McDonald and Ralph Shlomowitz, combined with statistics published in an 1854 British parliamentary select committee on emigrant ships, demonstrate that of the 136,846 assisted emigrants who embarked for Australia between 1847 and 1855, 3,381 (2.47 percent) died. According to the chairman of the CLEC, the worst year was 1852, when 4.48 percent of all assisted emigrants died, although he attributed this, in part, to the elevated numbers of young children who had been allowed to travel that year. Focusing on the annual reports of emigration officers at specific ports of arrival allows us to compare how Irish assisted emigrants fared in relation to those of other nationalities. Of the 1,836 Irish who embarked (or were born) en route to Sydney and Port Phillip, New South Wales, in 1848, 32 (1.74 percent) died. This rate was only slightly higher than those experienced by the 4,648 English (1.46 percent) and 1,534 Scottish (1.43 percent) assisted emigrants that season. Two years later, even though the number of Irish embarked for New South Wales had increased to 3,148, only 21 died, representing a mortality rate of 0.67 percent. That same year, the mortality rates for English and Scottish assisted emigrants to New South Wales were 1.9 percent and 1.09 percent, respectively, although their sample sizes (633 and 92) were relatively small. When emigrants to Australia fell prey to a cholera outbreak in 1852, the Scottish fared the worst. The death rates for the Irish, English, and Scottish assisted emigrants to New South Wales in that year were 3.97 percent, 2.86 percent, and 6.21 percent, respectively. Using only these three years (1848, 1850, and 1852) as a sample, the overall mortality rate of Irish assisted emigrants to New South Wales was 2.04 percent.[9]

Contrary to popular belief, Irish convicts generally enjoyed much safer rides than assisted emigrants en route to Australia. As demonstrated above, the average mortality rate for all convicts between 1846 and 1855 was 1.03 percent, but Irish transports during that period did better, at 0.92 percent. The deadliest Famine-era Irish convict ships both arrived in Van Diemen's Land in 1847. Of the two hundred male convicts who sailed on board the *Tory*, five (2.5 percent) died. The female transport *Waverley* lost 3.73 percent of its complement of 134 female convicts. These official statistics counted only the number of dead convicts. Tabulating the number of deaths among the non-convicts is more difficult as they are usually only found, when listed at all, in the surgeon's journal. Recalculating the death rates on the Irish ships just mentioned to include these passengers, however, does not drastically change the ships' mortality rates. Beyond the 200 male prisoners on board the *Tory* were 7 wives and 13 children of the ship's guard. Among these 220 souls were a total of 7 deaths (3.18 percent). The *Waverley's* passengers included 134 female convicts, 33 of their children, and 40 settlers. The voyage witnessed a total of 7 deaths, which represented 3.38 percent of those who embarked in July 1847. English convict ships actually recorded the highest mortality rates during the Famine years. The male ship *Hashemy* (1849) and female transport *Cadet* (1848) lost 7.02 percent and 4.67 percent of their convicts, respectively. Although the voyage to Australia was longer, and therefore more likely to witness deaths, the stricter government regulation of passenger comfort and safety ensured that Irish travelers, whether journeying as emigrants or convicts, generally experienced very average mortality rates. In sum, given the fact that 95 percent of Ireland's Famine-era emigrants did not sail to Canada in 1847, it is clear that the vast majority of Ireland's passengers, regardless of destination, experienced mortality rates within the boundaries of what was considered "normal" at the time.[10]

Does the legend of 20 percent mortality hold up for those Irish who headed to Canada in 1847? A definitive answer will never be possible due to the evidentiary problems explained earlier in this chapter. The question is also complicated by the fact that A. C. Buchanan, the Irish-born chief emigration officer in Quebec, endured a bout of typhus himself in 1847, which further hampered his efforts to collect and tabulate information. While indisputable data are hard to find, however, the annual reports of Buchanan (in Quebec) and M. H. Perley (the government's agent in Saint John, New Brunswick) do offer excellent eyewitness accounts and lots of statistics to work with. According to their figures, a total of 115,895 emigrants of all nations either embarked as passengers (steerage or cabin) or were born en route to Canada during the year ending December 31, 1847. Of these, 11,071 (9.55 percent) died either on the voyage or in the quarantines established on Grosse Île and Partridge Island. How many of them were Irish? Answering that question requires parsing out the numbers of people who embarked at both Irish ports and Liverpool given that, as Buchanan stated in the text of his 1847 annual report, "emigration embarking at the port of Liverpool is almost exclusively Irish." In his report for the same year, Perley agreed that the New Brunswick–bound passengers from Liverpool "were very nearly, without exception, all from Ireland." Using these numbers, it appears that of the 98,749 Irish emigrants who embarked or were born en route to Canada in 1847, 10,820 died either at sea or in quarantine soon after arrival. This represented a mortality rate of 10.96 percent.[11]

This rate of over 10 percent is certainly high (indeed, it mirrors the slave trade in the 1800s), but it does not hit the threshold of 20 percent. To approach that number, one must narrow the focus even further onto a smaller cohort of emigrants. In his list of every ship that sailed to Quebec in 1847, Buchanan included details on its port of departure, total passengers embarked, and total deaths. These records demonstrate a high level of variability in the rates of mortality on ships that left Irish ports. Generally speaking, the more busy a given port of embarkation, the more likely its passengers would fall ill and die at sea. Only 66 people left Ballyshannon. Not one of them died. Of the 73 who traveled on two ships from Westport, one (1.37 percent) died. Less than 1 percent of the 318 emigrants who sailed from Youghal perished. Such correlations were not, however, always straightforward. Although Newry and Killala shipped almost the same number of emigrants (1,498 and 1,349, respectively), their mortality rates (2.27 and 7.78 percent) were very different. Limerick, Ireland's second-busiest emigration port in 1847, lost only 301 (3.28 percent) of its 9,174 emigrants, while Sligo, which shipped about half as many emigrants as Limerick, lost 11.18 percent. Belfast and Dublin, the third and fourth busiest ports, lost 4.36 and 7.72 percent, respectively. The microbial regimes in given port towns were more important than mere population density in determining risk of infection. The two deadliest ports in 1847 were Liverpool and Cork. Of the 27,051 who went from Liverpool to Quebec that year (Liverpool being considered an Irish port for reasons explained earlier), fully 4,156 (15.36 percent) died. Cork was even worse. There were 1,904 deaths among the 10,205 people who sailed from Cork to Quebec. This staggering loss rate of 18.66 percent represented the high tide of mortality on any given Irish route to Quebec in 1847 and explains the 20 percent so often cited. At the same time, these 10,000 emigrants represent only 10 percent of the total Irish emigration to Canada that year and less than 0.5 percent of the total Irish emigration during the Famine.[12]

Closer analysis complicates our understanding even further by demonstrating that these high rates of mortality did not occur in equal proportion across all ships. Thirty-three vessels sailed from Cork in 1847.

Of them, five (representing 13.05 percent of Cork's total number of emigrants for that year) experienced mortality rates within the "normal" range of 2.5 percent or less. Another five ships (carrying 1,250 emigrants) suffered mortality rates of between 2.5 percent and 5 percent, while an additional six ships (with 1,332 emigrants) experienced between 5 and 10 percent mortality. In other words, 38.31 percent of all Cork emigrants (3,910 of 10,205) sailed on ships that experienced mortality rates, which were at or below the 10 percent average for all Irish ports (including Liverpool) in 1847. Five other ships (carrying 1,716 emigrants) bore death rates of between 10 and 19 percent, which means that over half (55.13 percent) of all Cork emigrants sailed on ships with loss rates that were at or below the average for the Cork-to-Quebec route in 1847. This also means, however, that 4,579 (around 45 percent of Cork's total) sailed on ships marred by loss rates of 20 percent or more, figures reminiscent of some eighteenth-century slavers. Indeed, writing in December 1847, one magistrate in New Brunswick described the swindling shipping brokers of Liverpool and Ireland as "traffickers in human beings . . . with not half so much feeling as those engaged in the slave trade, the latter having a motive to land their cargo in good order, the former having nothing further to expect than the passage-money received." For his part, A. C. Buchanan struggled to find similarities among the deadliest ships. "No general law can be inferred as having governed the ratio of sickness and mortality, with any reference to the period of the ship's sailing, or the length of her passage," he wrote in his annual report for 1847; "disease has occurred in no regular proportion to the numbers embarked together" nor the relative population densities in steerage. This adds weight to the conclusion that the microbial regime of Cork and its hinterland was uniquely deadly.[13]

The names of those ships that experienced the highest mortality rates en route to Quebec in 1847 have—for good reason—entered the pantheon of Irish folk memory. Perhaps the most famous are the *Virginius*, *Naomi*, *Erin's Queen*, and *John Munn*, whose passengers included the 1,490 tenants induced to emigrate from Denis Mahon's Strokestown estate in County Roscommon that May. When Mahon contracted a Liverpool shipping broker to carry his tenants to Quebec at a cost of slightly over three pounds sterling per adult, he ensured that they would receive more than the minimum amount of shipboard provisions.

Nevertheless, neither he, nor the bailiff who accompanied to them to Liverpool, nor the brokers who issued their tickets, nor the captain who accepted them, nor the emigration officer who signed off on their embarkation adequately ensured that the travelers were all physically prepared for the voyage. As a result, when typhus broke out at sea, many were unable to stave off its ill effects. Of the 1,490 Strokestown emigrants who embarked in Liverpool, over 700 died at sea or at quarantine in Grosse Île. The mortality rates on their ships were all far above the terrible average for Irish emigrant vessels that season. The *Erin's Queen* lost 136 of 493 (27.59 percent), the *John Munn* lost 187 of 452 (41.37 percent), the *Naomi* lost 196 of 421 (46.56 percent), but the *Virginius* was the worst of all ships that year, losing 267 (56.09 percent) of the 476 passengers who embarked. A few other Irish ships had similarly high mortality rates en route to Quebec in 1847. The *Avon* of Cork lost over half (55.28 percent) of its passengers, while the *Bee*, also of Cork (46.88 percent), *Larch* of Sligo (44.55 percent), and *Triton* of Liverpool (40.26 percent) all suffered exceptionally high death rates as well. The year 1847 was unique because so many ships had such high death rates, but there are scattered examples of individual ships experiencing comparable rates in other years too. In 1849, 1851, and 1853, the *Sarah* (from Sligo), *Blanche* (from Liverpool), and *Fingal* (from Liverpool) all suffered mortality rates of over 10 percent.[14]

Finally, controlling for the age of the migrants adds more texture to our understanding of mortality at sea. This was true for all passengers in the nineteenth century. In his annual report for 1847, A. C. Buchanan found that although the overall mortality rate for all immigrants was 8.77 percent (see above), the death rate for adults was only 7.21 percent, while children under fourteen years of age died at a disproportionate rate of 11.86 percent. Looking at the Irish in particular for that year, the death rates for adult males (6.37 percent), adult females (6.05), male children between one and fourteen (8.62), female children between one and fourteen (8.69), and infants under one year (14.42) show the skewed ratios in which emigrants died. In his analysis of more than 28,000 European immigrants to New York between 1836 and 1853, Raymond Cohn came to similar conclusions. "Mortality was not significantly affected by [the] sex" of a given person, Cohn wrote, but the "immigrant's age was the most important factor affecting mortality." Infants less than one year old and the elderly were more likely to die than others. Scholars of Australian immigration agree. According to Ralph Shlomowitz and John McDonald, "the most noteworthy demographic characteristic" of government-assisted voyages to Australia throughout the 1800s "was undoubtedly the extraordinarily high death rates suffered by children." On a typical voyage between 1838 and 1853, "nearly one-quarter of the infants embarked or born on the voyage would have died." Colonial Office records suggest that when typhus broke out on the emigrant ship *Ticonderoga* en route to Australia in 1852, killing 20.64 percent of the passengers, the disproportionate impact on children was particularly marked. While adult males (17.98 percent), adult females (15.41), and male boys between one and fourteen (16.67) all died at below-average rates, female girls (28.57) suffered more. Infants under the age of one year (71.43) were practically wiped out. During the Famine years, the UK government responded by periodically restricting the number of children allowed as passengers aboard assisted emigration vessels.[15]

Although shipwrecks were the most dramatic, and highly publicized, causes of migrant deaths in the mid-nineteenth century, they accounted for a relatively tiny proportion of the overall mortality. This is partly because so many happened either on or near the coast, which allowed passengers to scramble, swim, or be shuttled to safety. Even when lost on the high seas, stricken ships were often on the equivalent of maritime highways and therefore capable of receiving succor from passing vessels. In his analysis of the Atlantic route during the Famine years, Raymond Cohn agrees with other historians that shipwrecks killed relatively few people. They—like airplane crashes today—"received a lot of press and occasionally resulted in large numbers of deaths, but were not very likely to occur." The CLEC's official statistics on shipwreck-related mortality, which were published in its annual reports, support this conclusion. Between January 1847 and December 1855 (the only years for which complete shipwreck records were compiled during the Famine), a total of 2,809,067 souls sailed from Britain and Ireland. Of this number, only 3,185 (0.11 percent) were killed in shipwrecks. In his work on emigrant mortality en route to Australia during these years, Robin Haines concludes that loss of life by shipwreck "was rare." Beyond sensational cases such as the *Cataraqui* (which went down in

Figure 4.1. The wreck of the *Edmond* at Kilkee, County Clare, in 1850. *Illustrated London News*, December 7, 1850. Image © Illustrated London News/Mary Evans Picture Library.

1845), *Tayleur* (1854), and *Guiding Star* (1855), very few ships sank at sea. Indeed, according to Haines, of the 281,378 government-assisted emigrants who traveled to Australasia and South Africa on CLEC-chartered ships chartered, only 0.2 percent were lost by shipwreck. Finally, the number of convicts killed by shipwreck was, according to Charles Bateson, "trifling." Of the 160,023 convicts sent to Australia between 1788 and 1868, fewer than 550 (0.34 percent) died as a result of shipwreck. The seaworthiness of the ship itself, the skill of the captain and his crew, and the season of travel could all play a role in causing or preventing shipwrecks, but the truth is that these terrible events were few, far between, and rarely catastrophic.[16]

Taken as a whole, these statistics lay bare the intellectual danger of allowing the terrible suffering experienced by many of those who traveled to Quebec in 1847 to crowd out our general understanding of Irish emigrant mortality during the Famine. The truth is that horror ships such as the *Virginius* and the *Avon* were the exceptions that proved the rule: the vast majority of Irish emigrants who sailed to Britain, North America, and Australia between 1845 and 1855 experienced mortality rates that were within or below the normal range for European seafarers in the mid-nineteenth century. This is not to demean or debase the suffering of those who fell ill and died in 1847 (or any other year). Compared to twenty-first-century air travel, their voyages were dangerous and on par with those faced by African migrants on the Mediterranean today. Their deaths were and remain important threads in the fabric of the Famine era. But it also remains incumbent upon us not to allow such sorrowful fragments to overshadow our understanding of the whole. Terrible and sad as many of their stories were, the 37,256 people who traveled from Liverpool and Cork to Quebec in 1847 represent slightly over one-third of the 98,749 Irish who sailed to Canada that year and less than 2 percent of the over two million who emigrated during the Famine at large. Finally, it is critical to remember that these bare statistics tell only part of the story. For a fuller understanding of death at sea during the Great Famine, one must examine how mortality was interpreted and experienced at the time by the emigrants themselves. A poem "written on the death of an Irish emigrant girl at sea" and published in the Australian press in November 1850 laid bare the social dislocation engendered by a maritime burial.

> No eye upon that grave shall weep,
> No sigh shall linger there;
> Nor faithful friends their vigils keep,
> Nor faithful love repair.

Let us turn now to consider how mortality shaped the social dynamics of seaborne emigrant communities.[17]

"The Ocean Is Their Cemetery": Death and Dying at Sea

The funerary rites surrounding death, which were imbued with great symbolic importance on land in the nineteenth century, were layered with profound meaning at sea as well. Incapable of preserving dead bodies long enough to return them to land for a "decent Christian burial," long-distance seafarers developed rituals designed to replicate the social cohesion imbued by traditional, terrestrial funerals. The lack of a burial spot was particularly troubling for many at the time. "It is rather strange that the average of human life on the sea is ever half as long as on the land since seamen are constantly so much nearer death's door," reflected the *Sailor's Magazine and Naval Journal* in December 1851. "The ocean is their cemetery, the vessel is both their hearse and coffin." In such a strange natural environment, many felt threatened by the thought of themselves or their loved ones dying at sea. In his classic memoir, *Two Years before the Mast*, American writer Richard Henry Dana reflected on the ways in which death and dying impacted shipboard communities. "Death is at all times solemn but never so much as at sea," he wrote. "A dozen men are shut up together in a little bark, upon the wide, wide sea, and for months and months see no forms and hear no voices but their own, and one is taken suddenly from among them, and they miss him at every turn. It is like losing a limb. There are no new faces or new scenes to fill up the gap. There is always an empty berth in the forecastle." Many of those Irish emigrating during the Famine era were leaving their homes at a time when the social practices surrounding death were becoming undone by the combination of mass mortality and grinding poverty. Unburied bodies and lonely deaths were part of the Famine experience. In this context of social and psychological insecurity, the experience of death and dying at sea was often particularly charged with symbolic meaning. For this reason, while mortality could tear at the fabric of these floating communities, it could also stitch them together in new ways.[18]

The appearance of dangers such as disease and stormy weather often immediately struck fear into shipboard societies. When, after one week at sea, smallpox infected two children on board the *Hottinguer*, en route from Liverpool to New York in 1845, the impact on the 395 other passengers was immediate. "It is impossible to describe the dismay, which prevailed through the ship," reported Dr. Richard Fraser who was traveling as a cabin passenger. The captain responded by taking swift action. "The bodies were thrown overboard the instant that life had ceased," Fraser wrote, "their beds, bed clothes, and linen were also thrown into the sea, and their berths purified with burnt tar." When sudden, violent deaths had unsettling effects on the passengers, surgeons and other officers often interpreted their respective reactions in terms that contrasted masculine strength with feminine weakness. As the emigrant ship *Irene* sailed from Liverpool to Sydney in 1852, its passengers "were much affected by one of the crew falling overboard and being lost." The ship's surgeon spent "a long time in the evening among the single women, trying to divert their attention from the melancholy accident." The abrupt onset of a storm could have a similar effect. When the Irish female convict ship *Kinnear* was caught in a heavy squall in 1848, its surgeon, John Williams, reported that the prisoners engaged in such "bitter wailings and lamentations . . . that it was fully an hour afterwards before they could be quieted." Others expressed calm resignation at moments of great danger. As the steamship *Arctic* steadily sank off the coast of Newfoundland in 1854, one of its stewardesses sat "almost paralyzed with fear," saying "she might as well die there as anywhere else." For his own part, a Mr. Foy of County Antrim refused to leave his berth when his ship's galley caught on fire, telling a fellow passenger "that his father and grandfather had died in their beds and that he would die there too."[19]

For those traveling alone, slowly dying at sea was an isolating experience. In his account of the *Rienze*'s voyage from Belfast to New York in 1849, Samuel Harvey described the depressing final hours of an anonymous woman stricken by dysentery. Her daughter had died a few days earlier, leaving the woman all alone. "Most of the passengers [are] frightened to go near her," Harvey diarized. "She has no friends on board now, has left her clothes, some webs of linen, and seven sovereigns of gold to a son in New York." As the patient was removed to the ship's hospital, Harvey recoiled at the state of the room. "This is a little place partitioned off the steerage at the very bows of the vessel, and is the most miserable place in the whole ship for a sick person," he opined, "owing to the continual noise of the waves and the dreadful tossing to which this part of the vessel is peculiarly exposed." In the absence of a ship's surgeon, it fell to her fellow passengers to take turns spending the night attending to the dying woman. When others refused, Harvey reluctantly agreed to do so. After accepting a glass of brandy "to prevent us from feeling the smell so much," Harvey and a friend "entered on our duties, which [were] extremely disagreeable from the nature of the disease and the pitching of the vessel, it blowing hard at the time." Consigned to the darkness for four long hours, Harvey and his companion "sat listening to the moans of the sick and dying, the whistling of the winds among the creaking rigging, and the melee of rats . . . while to crown the picture, wave after wave broke like thunder at our ear, shaking the vessel from stem to stern." Watching the woman die alone in the darkness was a troubling experience. "I hope I shall never again witness such another sight as that dying woman," Harvey wrote. "Reason had resigned its throne . . . and while she grasped at everything within her reach, she would sometimes fix her eyes on us with a fierce, unearthly glare, and mutter something between her teeth, as if cursing us." She died two days later.[20]

Even on convict ships, which carried trained and equipped surgeons, loneliness, neglect, and depression could contribute to the rapid death of those who fell ill. When two-year-old James Woodley, the child of a military pensioner, died of tuberculosis on board a transport headed from Cork to Van Diemen's Land in 1851, the ship's surgeon attributed his demise, in part, to the parents' disinterest in the child's health. Considering the "the unnatural treatment evidenced towards this child by his parents since coming on board," Harvey Morris wrote in his journal, it was reasonable to infer "that the first seeds of the disease had been planted by their neglect and nurtured by their cruelty." Among the prisoners themselves, depression could have negative impacts too. When Irish prisoner Ellen Sullivan died of dysentery aboard the *Tasmania* in 1845, the surgeon noted that she "had been in a low desponding state since her embarkation." Sullivan had often refused food, "seldom spoke to anyone, and expressed a wish to die." Once a prisoner grew convinced that his or her life was ending, it could be difficult to persuade them otherwise. After James Fitzsimons was diagnosed with tuberculosis on board the *Bangalore* in 1848, he positively refused "to admit the possibility of his recovery," the surgeon lamented, "no matter how I attacked him or what means I used to erase his melancholy forebodings." One day, while the physician was waxing eloquent about the healthful climate of Van Diemen's Land, Fitzsimons sincerely thanked him for his kind words before solemnly assuring him that he would never see land again. This "proved literally true for although we sighted Tasmania before he died, the poor man never saw it." In the face of imminent death, surgeons often used food and drink to cheer up their patients. As he lay dying on board the *Hyderabad* in 1849, Irish prisoner Charles Oakes "takes his medicine as directed and eats a little," his surgeon observed, "but takes all the wine that is offered to him."[21]

In pre-Famine Ireland, funerary customs were one of the many ways in which communal bonds were rebuilt and reified. By respecting and caring for the dead and dying, rural people demonstrated their respect and care for the living as well. As mass mortality and destitution overwhelmed these communities during the Famine, therefore, the inability of friends and families to properly bury their dead reflected a deeper and highly troubling disruption of community bonds as well. Referencing a story told by famous *seanchaí* Peig Sayers, in which a woman was forced to single-handedly carry her own daughter to the cemetery for burial during the Famine, Patricia Lysaght has noted "the erosion of social customs and norms, especially in relation to the burial of the dead, to which both the literature and folklore of the Famine testify." The surviving archival record demonstrates that people living in Ireland at the time recognized the social implications of disrupted burial practices. Fr. Theobald Mathew rued the steady stream of paupers interred in the "free ground" of his local cemetery in 1847. "Each day, there was a large pit dug and all that died that day were put down," explained Mathew. "Some days, there were sixty or seventy a day buried, and some days more." In an 1851 editorial, the *Galway Vindicator* expressed its disgust at the poor law commissioners' refusal to buy coffins for those penniless poor who died outside the walls of the workhouses. "It is as essential to bury the dead as to feed the living," proclaimed the editor, "and we do not, therefore, see on what principle of economy or humanity the poor law commissioners can object to supply coffins to deceased paupers." Private charity often proved the last resort. An eyewitness in County Mayo in 1849 referred to the hundreds of "living skeletons, men, women, and children" tramping the roads in search of food. When five of these unfortunates died, they "lay exposed on the road side for three or four days and nights, for the dogs and ravens to feed upon, until some charitable person had them buried in a turf hole at the road side."[22]

In the context of social relations at sea, where communal bonds were of heightened importance, emigrants often struggled to adapt to maritime funerary practices, especially when they contravened standards of decency and respect. In June 1854, a number of passengers who had recently arrived from Liverpool on board the *Chapin* complained of the captain's behavior at sea. "When the dead bodies of the passengers were thrown overboard, there was no religious or other ceremony," they asserted in a public letter to the *Boston Herald*. "Every movement was heartless and eminently calculated to annoy the survivors." At first, heavy pieces of metal were tied to the feet of the deceased to ensure their bodies sank but the captain soon gave up the practice, exclaiming "I'll be d—d if I waste any more of my pig iron on such miserable devils." His blasphemous words and conduct "appalled the stoutest hearts." Even when considerate burial practices were adopted, the speed with which they proceeded at sea unnerved many. When a young girl died on board the *Nepaul*, a ship chartered by Caroline Chisholm to take emigrants to Geelong in 1852, the social implications were noticeable. "It seemed very strange—to one accustomed to see or rather hear of corpses laying a week or more in charge of honest friends—to see them carried in two or three hours to their resting place," bemoaned one eyewitness. "She died about 8 a.m. and was buried at half past three p.m." The angled platform "upon which was laid the corpse, sewn into a canvas bag with about one hundredweight of ballast, differed so much from the ordinary mode of burial that a chill seemed to creep upon you when beholding it." Deaths impacted the whole community. "When it became known . . . that death had visited our ship, solemn quiet came over us all," wrote another emigrant after a sailor fell from the rigging. "All spoke for some time almost in whisper."[23]

Sailors generally took their responsibilities to dead fellow tars very seriously, but when faced with the option of following their captain's orders or fleeing disease, they often chose the latter. Working at sea was always a dangerous vocation, but many considered voluntarily exposing oneself to typhus, cholera, and other infectious diseases as beyond their job description. Even in the face of physical punishment, fines, and imprisonment, sailors protected themselves when necessary. "Fever is raging in Quebec at present," William H. McCleery told a friend soon after arriving from Belfast in 1847. "There is scarcely a ship but that their crews and captain et cetera are in the hospital. . . . Five of our men ran away the night after we came here and there is just one man, cook, carpenter, and [the] boys left." When disease broke out at sea, not all captains agreed that they and their crews were responsible for burying the dead. Soon after departing Liverpool for Quebec with over three hundred Irish emigrants in the autumn of 1853, the *Fingal* experienced an outbreak of cholera for which it was not prepared. There was no surgeon aboard, wrote passenger Delaney Finch, and the captain "did not consider himself bound to look after [the emigrants'] health and he refused, to my knowledge, to attend to the passengers when they were in bad health." After a week and a half, the water closets broke down, which forced the passengers "to come up with their nuisances over the side of the ship." The captain's treatment of the people who died on the voyage was equally objectionable. Finch recounted one situation in which a corpse was not sewn into a shroud of canvas but rather "thrown over in the clothes it had on" and another in which a dead body lay on the deck for six hours as "they could not get anybody to throw it overboard." Finch said the sailors "were afraid of the disease in the first place, and did not think it was a duty they were bound to perform." In the end, "they left it to any person of feeling to do what they thought proper."[24]

When mortality put pressure on the fabric of floating emigrant communities, it often did so along preexisting lines of division. In light of the religious context in which nineteenth-century emigrants made sense of death and dying, it is understandable that the experience often gave rise to sectarianism carried from home. While sailing from Belfast to New York in 1849, Protestant Samuel Harvey was disgusted by the response of a Catholic fellow emigrant whom the ship's officers invited to take a turn watching over the woman dying of dysentery. "He being a proud, young puppy and the task so extremely disagreeable, he gave the captain an unmannerly refusal," Harvey wrote, "whereupon the captain, in as polite a way as he could, gave [the Catholic's] piety as severe a castigation as I have ever heard, much to the amusement and satisfaction of those who heard it." Luckily, a newlywed Protestant "who is pious and kind-hearted instantly sprung out of bed from his young wife and volunteered his services for the first watch," gloated Harvey, "leaving unthinkingly his little wife in the berth with the hard-hearted Roman Catholic, which was a topic of much jesting and merriment to the passengers of the second cabin." When Irish landlord and philanthropist Vere Foster sailed aboard the emigrant ship *Washington* in 1850 to gain "insight into the condition and prospects of Irish emigrants," he found himself troubled by the lack of religious observance at Catholic burials. "No funeral service has yet been performed, the doctor informs me, over anyone who has died on board," Foster later told Parliament, "the Catholics objecting, as he says, to the performance of any such service by a layman." Instead, after a dead passenger was "sewn up, along with a great stone, in a cloth," the ship's steward waited until the sailors began singing at work before throwing the child's body overboard, thus using their sea shanty "as a funeral dirge."[25]

We saw earlier that crews and emigrants often duplicated social conventions they had learned on land. Epidemic illness and mass mortality at sea could, however, overthrow such frameworks, leading to the total collapse of shipboard society. When the fever-wracked *Blanche* finally completed its voyage from Liverpool to New Orleans in March 1851, horrified eyewitnesses testified to the ways in which the ship's entire population was virtually incapacitated. Dr. Frederick Hart, the port's health officer, immediately noticed a total lack of leadership on board the vessel. "I found the captain sick in the cabin and unable to report himself," Hart told the local British consul. The first and second mates were also sick and, "with the exception of an old cook, the steward, and two sailors, the rest of the crew [was] down with the ship fever." In the absence of social order, chaos had prevailed. The deck of the ship was "completely strewn with filth and feculent matter" and populated by "two hogs and about fifty of the most squalid-looking wretches I ever beheld," Hart wrote. The scene in steerage was just as bad. "On descending between decks, the stench and the groans of the sick and dying beggar description. There were about seventy cases of ship fever, two of which died the first twelve hours after her arrival." There was also at least one corpse on board the ship and two passengers had committed suicide en route from Liverpool. No one knew how many had died "as the log book was not written up," but the passengers themselves estimated that "some fifty must have died," although the captain disputed such a high figure. The city's mayor, disgusted by the *Blanche*, framed his anger over immigrant destitution in terms of social cohesion. "If hitherto a generous community has overlooked this grievous evil in the desire to extend a cordial welcome to the natives of other countries," Abdiel Crossman told the British consul, "there are certain limits to this indiscriminate hospitality, which a due regard to our own protection will compel us to adopt."[26]

At times, emigrants could become totally demoralized by the death and disease that had become part of their everyday lives. When Limerick landlord Stephen de Vere traveled as a steerage passenger to Quebec in early 1847, he described the collapse of many people's spirits in one of the most oft-cited eyewitness accounts of the Famine era. "Before the emigrant has been a week at sea he is an altered man," de Vere told the CLEC. "How can it be otherwise? Hundreds of poor people, men, women, and children of all ages, from the driveling idiot of ninety to the babe just born, huddled together, without light, without air, wallowing in filth, and breathing a fetid atmosphere, sick in body, dispirited in heart." In his evidence before a US Senate select committee on sickness and death aboard emigrant ships, Dr. John H. Griscom struggled to describe the squalid state of a ship from Liverpool, which he had inspected in New York in 1847. "The indescribable filth, the emaciated, half-nude figures, many with the petechial rupture disfiguring their faces, crouching in the bunks, or strewed over the decks," Griscom related, "presented a picture of which neither pen nor pencil can convey a full idea." In the same report, Ambrose Dudley Mann suggested that "the Black Hole of Calcutta was mercy" compared to the holds of ships like the *Virginius* and *Larch*, which had sailed from Ireland to Quebec in 1847. In the face of such difficult circumstances, some emigrants found themselves urging their friends and relations not to follow them across the ocean. "I am very glad that you did not come out here," Ference McGowan told his parents after landing in New Brunswick in 1847. "They are coming here and dying in dozens. There is not a vessel comes here but the fever is on board." Later in the same letter, amid news and updates on friends and neighbors, McGowan reiterated the point. "Let none of you attempt to come here this season," he wrote, "as there are so many here and the fever is in every house almost."[27]

Even those strictly disciplined and carefully organized French Canadian religious, who worked tirelessly throughout 1847 to succor the sick and dying Irish in the fever sheds, found themselves and their system of pastoral care overwhelmed at times by the sheer scale of suffering, which engulfed Quebec that summer. The surviving records of the Grey Nuns of Montreal, which include lengthy accounts by the sisters themselves, testify to the ways in which they struggled to maintain a semblance of control along the banks of the Lachine Canal in Pointe Saint Charles. "Hundreds of people were laying there, most of them on bare planks, pell-mell, men, women and children," wrote one eyewitness. "The moribund and cadavers are crowded in the same shelter, while there are those that lie on the quays or on pieces of wood thrown here and there along the river." The sheer number of dead bodies, and the difficulties faced in transporting them to a burial ground, presented a logistical problem with ethical implications. "Before we could build a hangar to store the dead bodies as the sick expired, we would take them outside of the sheds and the bodies would be left in the open air on planks prepared to that effect in a courtyard," explained one nun. As the cemetery was some distance from the sheds, the bodies remained there, exposed to the elements, until a large enough number had accumulated to warrant loading a cart of them for interment. "What a spectacle when entering the courtyard, to see on one side all these inanimate corpses," the nun reminisced, "and on the other all the caskets ready to receive them." Even in such a morbid environment, however, dark humor could serve to alleviate human spirits and restore a sense of fellowship among those committed to helping the sick and dying. As they stood contemplating a number of empty coffins stacked in the courtyard one day, a French priest asked one of the nuns if she thought their own coffins had already been built. "They are yet to be made," the nun replied confidently, "but it is certain that their planks have already been sawed."[28]

The social dislocation that all migrants faced, in one form or another, was worse for those stricken with an infectious disease while traveling alone as their illness only encouraged further isolation from the host community. In an 1849 letter to the editor of the *Armagh Guardian*, a Benjamin Workman described in some detail the sad case of a forlorn Irish immigrant he had recently encountered in Montreal. He had seen her the previous Saturday, "walking in the streets of this city, evidently laboring under severe disposition; her gait was feeble and tottering, her visage pale, eyes sunken, and the whole aspect bespoke great bodily exhaustion." After noticing the woman entering and exiting several shops along the road, he made some inquiries and learned she had asked each proprietor "only for some cold water." When the woman sat down to rest, Workman approached her and discovered that her name was Eliza Johnson, from Armagh. She was stricken with cholera. Johnson had recently sailed from Belfast to Quebec and had been in Montreal for only two days, but when the owner of her lodging house realized she was ill, he turned her out in the rain, urging her to visit the immigrant hospital. "Being a total stranger in this city, she knew not where to go to find this hospital," Workman explained, "and wandered through the streets till her clothes were as wet through as if she had been dipped into water." Moved by the poor woman's plight, Workman procured a vehicle and, with the assistance of two policemen, transported her to the emigrant sheds where she died two days later. "After her removal to hospital, everything was done for her that could be resorted to," Workman assured the editor, "to save her life and make her comfortable." By offering to help Eliza Johnson, and sharing her sad story with others, Workman demonstrated that while death and dying could push people apart, it could also bring them together.[29]

When family and friends had the energy to spend with their dying relations, the experience could sometimes unite them. In the spring of 1847, Irish emigrant James Duncan and his friends, the McKees, sailed aboard the *Massachusetts* en route to New York. By the end of their fourth week at sea, however, one of McKee sisters had fallen ill and was sinking quickly. Unnerved by the thought of being buried at sea, she asked Duncan if he would join her brother in convincing the captain to have her remains preserved and buried ashore. Duncan figured this was probably impossible, but when he promised to do so, Miss McKee "seemed much relieved and lay easier for a while." When she died early the next morning, traditional gender roles dictated that her female fellow passengers should help to prepare the body for interment. "The women that were standing by were slow to go near her," diarized Duncan, "but some of the men spoke to them and they had to for shame so they changed her clothes and fixed the place up." That evening, Duncan screened off a little room below deck and lighted a lamp. "I then invited a few to the wake," he explained. "Mr. McMullen made a prayer and read for some time. The conversation was kept up on scripture subjects until 12 o'clock when the greater part went to bed." The ship still being some distance from its destination, the captain gently insisted on burying Miss McKee at sea, but the funeral was delayed as a raging sea tossed "boots, shoes, pails, boxes, clothes, and everything, almost lifting the corpse out of the berth." Finally, two days after her death, Miss McKee was sewn into a canvas shroud and lowered into the sea. Afterward, Duncan stood quietly on deck with John McKee, her brother. "I intended words of consolation but we stood for hours, spellbound, no word was uttered for the scene was strange, nothing to remind us of the busy world that we seemed to have left," Duncan wrote. "We turned in but the ladies below were all in gloom, sitting in the dark, so we got a light and prepared some hot drinks and then got to our berths."[30]

Faced with the various dangers presented by a transoceanic voyage, many found unity in their Christianity, which promised eternal bliss to all who believed in God. From the perspective of the religious clergy, who were locked in a constant struggle to convince sailors to embrace the faith and turn away from blasphemy and alcohol, religion was presented as a way to quell both their everyday and metaphysical fears. In a report to the *Sailors' Magazine and Nautical Intelligencer* in London, the Reverend T. Muscutt, a Protestant evangelical missionary with the British and Foreign Sailors' Society, explained that piety was the only way for sailors to fully prepare for the dangers that attended them at sea. "They, like other men, have immortal souls to be saved or lost," Muscutt explained. "With the grace of God in their hearts, they are ready for a blessed eternity, and have not, when the storm pours forth its fury around them—*then*, for the first time, to seek God." Irish emigrants themselves often relied on their religious faith to quell their worries about the voyage. After settling in Buffalo in 1849, Sarah Carroll wrote a letter to her cousin in Tennessee in which she explained that her uncle's letter encouraging her to emigrate from Queen's County had been delayed in the post "and did not reach me until the middle of winter [but] I being so [eager] to come, I started at that time." Carroll spent ten treacherous weeks at sea and was "often expecting a watery grave only I put my confidence in that good God that is as good on sea as on land." In an original poem titled "Mary Astore; or, Irish Emigrants at Sea," which was published in the *Boston Pilot* in May 1852, a Mrs. Crawford depicted the healing potential of prayer at sea:

> Altar nor Priest have we, Mary Astore!
> Yet on this stormy sea, Mary Astore!
> We can our vespers say,
> We can for *Ireland* pray;
> God wipe her tears away, Mary Astore!

In the context of ever-present danger, religious faith offered relief as much in the then and there as it did in the everlasting.[31]

While the authorities recognized that professional medical knowledge and skill could save lives at sea, those coming from rural societies were often afraid of what was in the doctor's bag. In his report on the excess mortality of children on certain ships headed to Australia in 1852, Thomas Murdoch of the CLEC apportioned a large part of the blame to the parents themselves. "The extent of the mortality is in part ascribed to the insurmountable objection of the Irish and Scotch parents to the medical treatment of their children," Murdoch explained. When three-year-old John Cadogan died aboard the Australia-bound emigrant ship *George Seymour* in 1847, its surgeon described the child's mother as "the lowest caste of Irish and endeavors to conceal any ailment the child may have." Just two days before John died, "the mother stated the child was much better." When deaths occurred, surgeons often preferred to conduct autopsies to confirm their suspicions regarding cause of death. The friends and families of those who died, however, being already upset by the person's passing and the thought of their committal to the "trackless deep," often objected to such a procedure. When Patrick Begg, an ordinary seaman, died after a nasty fall aboard the Irish convict ship *Hyderabad* in 1849, the surgeon sought to dissect the body but demurred as it was blowing a heavy gale of wind at the time "and the man's shipmates objected to there being a postmortem examination." Similarly, "the indomitable prejudice of the prisoners against necrotomy" persuaded Jonathon Ferrier not to proceed with one on board the Irish female convict ship *Earl Grey* in 1850. Finally, some surgeons respected the sorrow caused by sudden deaths. When Irish convict Lucy Gorman died on board the *Midlothian* in late 1852, David Thomas admitted that from "the general despondency produced by this unforeseen termination, I did not think it advisable to examine the body but have no doubt that it was a case of metastasis to the heart and lungs."[32]

Coming from a society in which wakes and other preburial practices played important social roles, nineteenth-century Irish emigrants often attempted to follow these customs at sea. During his tenure as US consul to Bremen in 1847, Ambrose Dudley Mann explained the connection between emigrant beliefs and the transmission of disease. "In all Catholic countries there is an extraordinary degree of devotion—proceeding from the best impulses of the human heart—to the memory of the departed; and nowhere, perhaps, does this sentiment prevail to a greater extent than in Ireland," wrote Mann. "The humblest peasant, so destitute as to be unable to enjoy any other visible remembrance of the lost ones dearest to him, fondly clings to the garments, however ragged and worthless, worn by them when living." It was from such clothing, he believed, that a fatal effluvium arose on board the ships. Others interpreted Irish beliefs less favorably. One observer, writing from Saint John, New Brunswick, in October 1847, blamed the *Avon's* extraordinarily high mortality rate on the Irish emigrants themselves, whom the author contrasted unfavorably with the gallant Protestants aboard. Despite the bad weather they encountered in crossing the Atlantic, "all would have been comparatively well but for the quality and perverseness of the passengers themselves, who were the most unruly, turbulent, and wild set that ever Ireland sent forth." These "infatuated beings, moved by some inconceivable and demoniacal spirit, would not separate themselves from the dead, until the infection rose to such a pitch on board" that the crew and Presbyterian passengers intervened, only to discover "above sixty dead bodies stowed away in chests or sewed up in beds!" Although this was probably not actually true, the letter does demonstrate the low esteem in which Catholic beliefs were often held. Nor were emigrants necessarily ashamed of their customs. When the surgeon ordered an Irish convict to wash her child aboard the *Blackfriar* in 1851, she replied, he wrote, "Glory be to God, she had reared nine of them and had never put a drop of water on one of them."[33]

Putting aside religious beliefs and practices, the physical act of dealing with dead bodies sometimes brought seaborne communities together in strange ways too. As Henry Johnson of County Antrim sailed from Liverpool to New York in 1848, the father of a family berthed near him died during a storm, and his body laid on the steerage floor. "After a while, the boxes, barrels, etc. began to roll from one side to the other, the men at the helm were thrown from the wheel, and the ship became almost unmanageable," Johnson reminisced. "At this time I was pitched right into the corpse, the poor mother and two daughters were thrown on the top of us, and there corpse, boxes, barrel, women, and children all in one mess were knocked from side to side for about fifteen minutes." Once the crew regained control of the ship, "we sewed the body up, took it on deck, and amid the raging of the storm, [the captain] read the funeral service for the dead, and pitched him overboard." On strictly hierarchical ships, it was hard for passengers to challenge authority figures over the treatment of other dead officers. As the *Elizabeth and Sara* sailed from Killala to Quebec in the summer of 1846, the captain and a number of emigrants died. "Their bodies were, of course, immediately committed to the deep but the mate, as if to add to our misery, notwithstanding our most urgent requests to the contrary, persisted in keeping the body of the captain," a group of surviving passengers later complained. For almost two weeks, "the body lay upon the quarter deck in a most horrid, disgusting state of decomposition," thus causing the prolonged transmission of fatal disease. As landfall loomed closer, most agreed on the benefit of burying bodies as soon as possible. When the woman, over whom Samuel Harvey had kept watch at night, finally died just hours from New York City, the captain asked the passengers if they would be willing to delay their imminent arrival by bringing the ship to a halt for the burial service. They unanimously declined and, after reading "a small and appropriate extract from a funeral sermon, . . . launched her body into the sea."[34]

While the authorities often looked down on the Irish dead and dying, they sometimes treated them with a kindness rooted in a sense of social duty. After gaining permission to accompany her imprisoned mother aboard the convict transport *Maria* in 1849 (see chapter 1), fifteen-year-old Johanna Kelleher fell ill with tuberculosis. Kelleher's appetite was "very good," the ship's surgeon noted, but she "cannot be persuaded to eat arrowroot or any of the medical comforts." Eager to nourish her as best he could, Nolloth gave Kelleher "an egg every morning for breakfast and a piece of fowl for dinner with a quantity of porter or wine," and even an occasional "opiate draught at bed time." Nevertheless, Kelleher succumbed to the disease. Although it is impossible to confirm its veracity, a story originally published in Boston and reprinted in the *Sailor's Magazine and Naval Journal* demonstrates the ways in which captains could take pity on bereaved emigrants. Allegedly written by a humble female Irish emigrant, the letter described her sadness at seeing dead passengers buried at sea, each wrapped in a "narrow shroud" and "committed to the deep, with no requiem but the bursting sigh of a fond mother, and no obsequies but the tears of fathers and brothers, and pitying strangers." When her own baby died, the woman refused to allow it be "given to gorge the monsters of the deep" so she hid it from view, "gave evasive answers, . . . and sang to it, as if my babe was only sleeping for an hour." When the captain found out, he took pity on the woman and had the child put in "a rude coffin," which he placed in a small boat and had towed behind the ship. "It was then I thought of my dear cottage home, and my native land," the woman wrote, "and of the kind friends I had left behind me, and longed to mingle my tears with theirs." When the crew spied land three days later, the captain fulfilled his promise by bringing the child ashore, burying it, and writing the name of the place on a piece of paper, that the mother might remember it. "I thanked him for his care," she reminisced, but "told him the record was already written on my heart."[35]

Burials were a sad part of life at sea and liable to undermine the morale on which peace and order rested. As a result, captains and other authority figures sometimes concluded interment services with announcements and news designed to lift everyone's spirits. As the emigrant ship *Digby* sailed for Australia in 1849 with a complement of young women traveling under the "female orphan" scheme, one of their number, Ann Ferguson, succumbed to fever. In his journal, the ship's schoolmaster, George Binsted, noted that three other Irish female emigrants were subsequently given the dead woman's clothes "as a reward for good conduct during the time they have been hospital assistants and for great kindness to the sick." Music could also be used to deflect negativity. When a troubled young woman attempted suicide on board the *Beejapore* in late 1852, the captain had her taken to the hospital and handcuffed until the sail maker could stitch together a straitjacket for her. "The doctor got the fiddler to work as soon as possible," wrote one eyewitness, "to get the passengers . . . dancing, and detract their attention as much as he could from this sad affair." Nevertheless, nothing lifted an emigrant's spirits like the sight of land. As the *Constitution* sailed for Australia in 1855, one of its passengers died of smallpox. "She was placed between two beds, which are not very wide, and sewn into quilts, and a large stone at each end, which was done close to our berth," a fellow emigrant observed. It being a rough night, the prayers and hymns were sung in steerage. "All being done and ready, she was taken on deck and buried by ten o'clock, which was very mournful," remembered the passenger. "At the time, the captain told us that we should be in Sydney tomorrow, three weeks." At other times, the co-incidence of burial and arrival was simply fortuitous. By the time Irish convict James Deegan died of scrofula aboard the *Hyderabad* in 1849, his body was "one entire mass of disease." The corpse was quickly sewn into a canvas shroud "and very soon cast into the sea," the surgeon remarked in his journal, "immediately after which, land was descried from the masthead."[36]

While many sailors looked upon their emigrants as either an annoy-ance or a subservient population subject to their control, it is also indu-bitable that many acted with great bravery and kindness when disaster struck. Mid-nineteenth-century newspapers are replete with firsthand accounts of officers and crewmen saving the lives of endangered pas-sengers. Soon after embarking on her maiden voyage en route to Mel-bourne in January 1854, the iron clipper *Tayleur* and its 650 emigrants and crew ran aground along the coast of Ireland. "The scene then was of the most frightful character," described an eyewitness, "all the pas-sengers . . . screaming and crowding together in the most heartrending manner." According to one contemporary report, the ship's problems were compounded by the fact that some of the crew were "Chinese and Lascars who could neither speak nor understand English and, as he thought, were inadequate to work the ship." Nevertheless, when the vessel struck the rocks, "a black sailor at once jumped on shore and five or six of the men immediately after followed his example." Coordinating with their crewmates still on the clipper, these men tied the ship to the shore "and by these means, and these means alone, the single rope and the plank, were many lives subsequently saved." All in all, about 370 people died in the accident including those who insisted on clinging to the wreck, although one man climbed so high into the rigging that he remained above the waves and was saved the next day. Nor did sailors necessarily save only their own passengers. When the Boston packet ship *Ocean Monarch* caught fire just five hours after leav-ing Liverpool in August 1848, several nearby ships bore down on it immediately. The heat and smoke rendered approaching the burning wreck very difficult, reported one local journalist, but a "noble fellow, a foreigner . . . went to the wreck when there was little hope of saving any more [passengers], and stuck to the hull of the vessel till every soul had left her. It is said this praiseworthy individual, by his own hand, lowered one hundred persons to the boats below."[37]

Indeed, shipping companies, their crews, and their passengers were regularly brought together through acts of reciprocal assistance in times of death and destruction. When the brig *Hannah* of Newry hit an iceberg off the coast of Canada in April 1849, a number of emigrants went down with the ship, but over one hundred scrambled onto the ice, where they remained throughout the night. The following morning, the survivors "were rescued from their perilous situation through the courage and humanity of Captain Marshall of the *Nicaragua*" and several other passing ship captains who carried the poor people to Quebec. Getting refunded for such seaborne acts of charity was not always easy. "The delay and difficulty, which masters of vessels experience in obtaining a reimbursement of the expenditure incurred by them in their humane act of saving the lives of their fellow-creatures has subjected them to much inconvenience, and even to personal loss," A. C. Buchanan complained in his 1854 annual report. "It is needless to observe that the true policy in such cases is to encourage instead of throwing impediments in the way of efforts specially made in the spirit of humanity." When lightning struck one of the Cope family's Philadelphia packets in 1846, its owners thanked the company whose ship had come to their rescue. "May we ask of you to continue to extend to Captain Miercken your kind offices and, as he may stand in need of funds, to pay him such sum as he may want, and draw on us for that amount and the expenses to which Captain Caldwell and yourselves have been put," the Copes wrote. "If at any time it is in our power to render you any services in this place, we shall be happy to reciprocate the kindness." When passengers died suddenly, the Copes also attempted to tie up loose ends with their families. In an 1853 letter to a Mary Bateman, the Copes fulfilled the "painful duty" of informing her that her husband Thomas "had become deranged" on board the *Tonawanda* and committed suicide. In order to recover her husband's possessions, she should, they advised her, hire an attorney "acquainted with all the law requires."[38]

When they needed to, emigrants could also save themselves. As the *Ann* traveled from Limerick to Quebec with over one hundred emigrants in late 1848, it collided with the *Hampton* going in the opposite direction. Rather than save the passengers, Captain M'Fie and his crew allegedly locked them in steerage and departed aboard the *Hampton.* "Thus was the mass of men, women, and children—not one of them capable of managing the vessel—totally abandoned to their fate," decried the Quebec *Morning Chronicle* "by one who, as captain, should have stood by his ship." When the passengers managed to escape to the main deck, however, "they hoisted a light on the mast-stump as a signal of distress." The following morning, a ship picked them up and brought them to Quebec. As shipwrecks usually happened on reefs and rocks close to land, survivors could often scramble ashore. When the *Cataraqui* crashed upon "the iron-bound coast" of King's Island, Tasmania, in 1845, 9 of its 423 souls managed to swim to safety. Finding only "one small tin of preserved fowl" to eat, reported the *Sailor's Magazine*, "they lay down in the bush, having got a wet blanket out of the water for their only covering, and being almost destitute of clothes." The following morning, they met with a Mr. Howie "and his party of sealers, who reside upon King's Island" and who provided the survivors with food, drink, and help burying the dead bodies that washed ashore, "the mangled condition of many of which it is too painfully horrible to describe." Indeed, shipwrecked passengers often took it upon themselves to bury the remains of their fellow shipmates. When the *Annie Jane* was wrecked off the Hebrides in 1853, "Christian sepulture was deemed impracticable, for the churchyard was ten miles distant, and there were neither carpenters to make coffins nor proper timber to fashion them from." Instead, the survivors buried the dead, "a great many being naked and mutilated," in "capacious pits." At the time of writing, over 260 bodies had been buried "but a great many still remain unburied, and indeed every tide [throws more corpses] up."[39]

In moments of great danger, the lines between bravery, desperation, and human instinct often grew messy. When the Liverpool barque *William and Mary* foundered en route to New Orleans in the spring of 1853, one of the sailors later claimed "that some of the passengers may have formed a raft and saved themselves upon it, or by floating on some fragments of the vessel." Had they done so, he surmised, they would not have been waiting in the water too long "as the place where the *Wil-*

liam and Mary foundered is a general highway to vessels bound south."
At other times, individual acts of heroism saved lives. The captain of the
emigrant ship *Charles Bartlett*, which collided with the *Europa* steamer
two weeks after departing London en route to New York in the summer
of 1849, was impressed by the actions of one passenger in particular.
"I saw him let himself overboard and clench a man in his arms and,
finding him dead, let him go," the officer reported. "I next saw him
on the bow of a boat, hauling a man from under water with a boat
hook, who was afterwards restored to life on board." Adults often did
whatever it took to save children, especially their own. Only one child
was saved from the wreckage of the *Annie Jane* when it ran aground in
1853. "It belonged to a humble Irish woman, who, with her two children, was about to join her husband in America," the press reported.
"She struggled hard to preserve them both by binding one on her back
and grasping the other in her arms; but when the ship [broke apart],
the latter was dashed into the sea, and the other remained." Similarly,
when the *Tayleur* was wrecked off Lambay Island in early 1854, the
ship's surgeon "attempted to swim to shore with his child on his back,
and supporting [his wife] with one arm while he swam with the other;
the three, however, unfortunately perished." Others on the same ship
were more fortunate. When a five-month-old baby's parents drowned,
another emigrant saved the child "by bearing it in his teeth from the
wreck to the shore."[40]

Finally, even in Grosse Île and Montreal—in the darkest days of
1847—death had a way of fomenting a sense of community among the
people consigned to the fever sheds. At one level, the sheer scale of the
challenge embraced by the Grey Nuns of Montreal, and the discipline
with which they faced it, brought them together as a group. According
to the religious order's annals, the nuns' Mother Superior called on "the
courage and the generosity of her girls . . . to combat in a new field
of sacrifice": the immigrant hospital. "All, like intrepid soldiers who
wince at the sound of a bugle, [answered] this call." At the same time,
a June 1847 pastoral letter by Joseph Signay, Archbishop of Quebec,
sought to bring Canada's Catholics together in support of their destitute Irish co-religionists. Responding to an encyclical letter by Pope
Pius IX, Signay urged his flock to join in three days of public prayer
for those facing famine back in Europe. "Together, Dear Brothers, you

shall entreat the Lord to put an end to the suffering of the Irish nation," Signay exhorted, "so long tested by adversity, but still so attached to the Catholic faith." Ultimately, while many considered themselves lucky to at least have learned the fate of their dead relatives, others who visited the fever sheds were pleasantly surprised by what they found there. One man, who had been separated from his children when he fell ill with the fever, was fortunate to have found his son soon after recovering. Together, they visited the immigrant hospital in Montreal and encountered a girl whom the son "recognized as his little sister, and both of them embraced each other in tears, to the great content of the father." In another case, a woman, having survived the sheds and reconnected with two of her children, had almost given up hope of ever finding her last daughter only to stumble upon her in St. Patrick's Church one day. "Let us judge the emotion and the happiness of this tender mother," exulted the Grey Nun's annals, whose whole family had reunited "in this land of exile."[41]

These examples demonstrate the complicated ways in which death and dying impacted seaborne Irish emigrant communities during the Famine era. Mortality was always and everywhere difficult as it reminded the survivors of their own vulnerabilities. Yet at a deeper level, Irish emigrants came from a society in which funerary practices were an important part of community life. The dead lay in their own homes, under the care of friends and family, for at least a couple of days as neighbors and relations came to pay their respects. Although church attendance in pre-Famine Catholic Ireland was not particularly high, certain elements of the church's rituals remained important to the laity on both sides of the sectarian divide. Formal burials in cemeteries provided closure for the survivors while adding another stitch to the local community's sense of place and belonging. When "a man dies on shore," intoned Richard Henry Dana, "you follow his body to the grave, and a stone marks the spot." By contrast, those buried at sea were forever dislocated from the land and its community. As such, death and dying on the ocean could bring out the worst in people. As the *Digby* carried over 250 Irish "orphan girls" to Australia in 1848, the ship's surgeon, William Neville, decried the captain's behavior on a previous voyage. "The dead were taken by the hair of their heads," Neville claimed, "and cast overboard like dogs." At other times, however, death and danger brought out the best in people. When a ship suddenly sank in the Irish Sea in late 1853, a local fishing smack raced to the scene. "A more heroic action never was recorded," recounted one eyewitness. "Two dauntless and brave men, with immense difficulty and infinite risk, were seen hanging over the side of their small boat, hauling the drowning men out of the water, every wave threatening them with instant death." Mortality, which shaped communal bonds at sea, also played a role in connecting emigrants with home.[42]

"Their Parting Has All the Bitterness of Death": Interpreting Maritime Mortality on Land

As deep, personal connections existed between migrants and their friends and relations on land, the impact of seaborne mortality was felt beyond the bulwarks of the ships themselves. Indeed, for many living through the Famine, emigration was a direct response to death. "I had to put my family into the poor house where they have all died within a month back," explained Thomas Corby of Crutt, County Kilkenny, in his petition to his landlord for assistance to emigrate in March 1847. His mother and family had all been sent to America three years earlier, and Corby now figured that the deaths of his wife and children signaled it was time for him to leave too. Contemporaries similarly drew comparisons—both metaphorical and literal—between departure and death. While watching a crowd of emigrants loading onto a train in Galway, an eyewitness concluded, "their parting has all the bitterness of death." Forced to quit their desolated homes, "they set their lives upon the 'desperate cast' of emigration, and the many shipwrecks and other fearful disasters that so frequently occur, too fatally attest that self-expatriation is but a despairing alternative." For some, emigration and death literally went hand in hand. At the same railway terminus, a delicate man struggled through the crowd "in order to bid his brother farewell," but, "exhausted and overcome by his struggles and intense emotion, he fell into a swoon, and shortly afterwards expired." The following paragraphs demonstrate that the mortality and disease that often plagued Irish emigrants abroad indubitably kindled bigotry in their host communities. At the same time, however, the news and updates on death and dying, which migrants and their relatives sent back and forth across the oceans through letters and newspaper clippings, served as important threads of reciprocal exchange in the fabric of Irish life.[43]

As the tide of Irish passengers, many of whom were sickly, ran high in 1847, the authorities and publics of their host cities often grew fearful and protested their arrival. This was especially true on mainland Britain, whose ports were the entrée point for most emigrants heading to North America and Australia. In a March 1847 petition to the Home Office, a citizens' committee in Liverpool complained of "the alarming spread of epidemic disease in the thickly populated districts of the town and more especially in the neighborhoods occupied principally by the lower orders of the Irish people." The letter entreated the government "to arrest the influx of the multitudes from Ireland whose emigration tends in no way to their own relief from distress while it threatens the health and life of the residents of Liverpool with the most alarming consequences." Yet when British towns enacted laws and policies to deport paupers back to their homes, the receiving Irish seaports often protested too. "These persons have no claim on us, more than what humanity and Christian charity dictate," James Mathews, the lord mayor of Drogheda, told the Home Office in July 1847, "and I trust that the government will interfere to prevent our town from being turned into one vast lazar-house; or if such persons must be removed, let them be sent to the places on which they are legally chargeable." Cities on the far side of the Atlantic expressed similar concerns. An April 1847 letter to the editor of Quebec's *Le Canadien* feared the impact an influx of Irish emigrants might have. "If emigration this year is triple or quadruple what is has been in years past, as is forecast; if these emigrants bring with them, as is very, likely the germs of contagious diseases," A Citizen wondered. "I ask you, what will be the fate of Quebec and Montreal if we do not work assiduously to protect ourselves against these dangers?" In response, however, the paper's editor decried the "strict and isolationist" immigration policies adopted by the United States, hoping "that Canadians will be more generous, more hospitable, and more Christian than their neighbors to the south."[44]

In its assessment of the underlying causes of emigrant mortality, the government was hampered by its own laissez-faire philosophy. Those who worked with the ships themselves often generally agreed what the most dangerous dynamics were. When the *Elizabeth and Sara* and its fever-wracked emigrants arrived from Killala in August 1846, Quebec's chief emigration officer, A. C. Buchanan, claimed the vessel "fully [realized] the worst state of a slaver." The medical officer at Grosse Île, Dr. George Douglas, agreed, having found the passengers "in the most wretched state of filth and disease." According to Dr. Douglas, the three leading causes of death among transatlantic emigrants were, in order of importance, a lack of cleanliness and adequate ventilation, insufficient and unwholesome food and water, and overcrowding in the berths. The British government was unwilling, however, to strictly regulate the passenger trade. When the legislative assembly of Canada demanded that health guidelines be more strictly enforced on emigrant ships, the CLEC claimed that the ravages of 1847 "are owing to the peculiar condition of Ireland this season, and . . . cannot be viewed as examples of an evil that can occur in ordinary times." Enforcing the Canadians' suggestions "would involve too much interference with the liberty of the subject" and contrast with what had "been found requisite in any ordinary or average period." There were also, as the chairman of the CLEC explained to an 1854 select committee on mortality aboard emigrant ships, complicated jurisdictional issues at play. Foreign vessels were only subject to British laws while they were in British ports. Once they were three or more leagues from the shore, they were bound only by the rules of the country whose flag they bore. At the same time, although British vessels remained subject to the UK Passenger Acts throughout their whole voyage and while in Canadian and other imperial ports, there was "no means of punishing any infraction" in American or other foreign harbors.[45]

At other times, British and American authorities blamed disease and death on the Irish themselves. "The emigrants embarked from Liverpool are in a great measure from Ireland and the north of Scotland," the CLEC's Thomas Murdoch explained in his analysis of excess mortality on ships to Australia in 1852. They were, he concluded, less clean, less healthy, and less nourished "than the average English emigrants, and consequently far more liable to contract and propagate disease." The typical shipboard diet also contrasted unfavorably with the potatoes and milk to which the Irish were accustomed. While shipping brokers were required to provide each passenger with a pound of oatmeal, flour, or biscuit a day, noted Buchanan, the truth was that "one-half of this allowance is replaced by Indian corn meal, an article of food wholly new" to the Irish emigrants "who do not know how, indeed, to prepare it." As evidence of the advantage served by a varied, wholesome shipboard diet, Dr. Douglas cited the robust health of recent German emigrants who had left Europe "supplied abundantly with animal food, bread, flour, lime-juice, and beer." Some officials also blamed the deaths on the moral bankruptcy of the Irish. "It is doubtful whether the frightful extent of mortality among the Irish emigrants at sea has not been in great part chargeable to their own want of moral energy," concluded Buchanan in his 1847 annual report. The "lower classes of the Irish emigrants have failed on their arrival to make the exertions, or to take advantage of the opportunities, which promised them the earliest certain benefit." In his evidence before the US Senate's 1854 select committee on emigrant mortality, New York public health official Dr. John H. Griscom went further. Cholera moved through steerage much faster than typhus, he proclaimed, as if "Providence deemed it necessary to send a swifter, winged messenger of death, in these latter days, to punish his creatures for their continued violation of the laws given for the preservation of their health and lives."[46]

When Irish nationalists referenced emigrant mortality during the Famine era, they often did so using evocative language designed to both blame it on British misgovernment and elicit sympathy for its victims. Contrary to popular belief, the phrase "coffin ships" was almost never used in these years and was popularized only decades later. Nevertheless, cognizant of the public sensitivity over funerary practices, nationalist leaders sometimes used terminology that linked emigrant ships with instruments of interment. At an assembly of the Irish Confederation in March 1848, Thomas D'Arcy McGee protested the state of Ireland under British misrule. "The towns have become one universal poorhouse and fever shed, the country one great graveyard," he told his audience. "The survivors of the famine and pestilence have fled to the sea-coast and embarked for America, with disease festering in their blood. They have lost sight of Ireland, and the ships that bore them have become sailing coffins, and carried them to a new world, indeed; not to America, but to eternity!" The Catholic clergyman and popular lecturer Dr. Daniel W. Cahill liked to use similar language. At an 1854 meeting of Irish nationalists in Liverpool, Cahill recalled the sight of embarking emigrants. "I always bid these poor exiles a last farewell with my eyes full of tears and my heart bursting with unmingled feelings of Irish sympathy and legitimate political anger," Cahill said, "and when I take my place on the shore, and see the ships weighing their anchors, swell their canvas, and move slowly on through the foaming deep, I hear my heart foretelling as she clears the river, that she is a large ocean hearse, and that before the sun sets twice, she will bury her living cargo in the foundations of the sea." A year earlier, at a similar meeting in Glasgow, Cahill told his listeners that the track of the emigrant ship "is marked by the whitened bones of the murdered Irish that lie along the bottom of the abysses of the moaning ocean."[47]

When emigrants, their friends, and their families discussed the dangers attending the transoceanic voyage, they did so in language that was less flamboyant than McGee's or Cahill's but equally evocative. Upon leaving home, many acknowledged that things would never be the same. After emigrating to New York in 1848, Thomas Reilly expressed to his friend "the deep regret I feel at being separated from you." Letter writing was, perhaps, "the only way in which I shall ever again converse with you." At a more basic level, however, part of the remittance process on which so many journeys relied involved shoring up the prospective emigrant's courage as they prepared to embark on a potentially fatal journey. "John tells the boys to have good courage, not to fret for anything," one unnamed benefactor wrote on the back of a prepaid ticket, "and not to get frighten[ed] if a storm comes." At other times, benefactors on the other side of the ocean assuaged the travelers' fears by combining references to home with fragments of insider knowledge on the process itself, gleaned from personal experience. "Don't fear the passage, you will just be as comfortable as if you were in Johnstown [County Kilkenny]," assured one letter writer. "Keep all the time on deck if you possibly can as it will be of great good to your health." The purchaser of a prepaid ticket on the Cope packet line assured their relations that the ship on which they were to sail "is one of the best ships that ever crossed the sea. . . . Take courage and come here, you will be as safe as if you were at home." Another benefactor used their knowledge of the Atlantic's weather cycles to reassure a prospective traveler. "You will be as safe on shipboard as you will be at home, unless the dangers of the sea," they remarked on the reverse of a ticket before posting it home. "You need not be affeared as it is a good season of the year."[48]

The popular press was one of the ways in which Irish readers stayed abreast of the dangers facing emigrants at home and abroad during the Famine era. By the mid-nineteenth century, a transnational Irish reading public had developed around a lively network of newspaper exchange. It was in the columns of these weekly papers that Irish readers learned of the epidemics that periodically raged in port cities around the Atlantic. In July 1847, the *Galway Vindicator* announced having "received files of Canadian papers to the latest dates, [which] give appalling accounts of the suffering of the Irish emigrants from fever and dysentery." The paper cited a recent report of the situation in Quebec. "There were then 21,000 passengers at Grosse Isle," the statement read. "960 died on the passage out; 700 died at the station; there were 1,500 sick on board the vessels; 1,100 sick on shore; and 90 died on Saturday [alone]." Later that month, the *Vindicator* quoted a recent editorial in the *Montreal Pilot*. Thousands of Irish emigrants "have found graves on the banks of the St. Lawrence," the editor admitted, "far, far from the friends of their childhood, and from those early associates, which, even in the dying hour, bring consolation to the sufferer." Similarly, when diseased emigrants arrived on the New Orleans levee in the early 1850s, Irish newspapers clipped and reprinted articles from its local press. "Creatures of tender years, the beardless youth, and the half-grown maiden, are thrown, like carrion, upon our shores," grumbled the New Orleans *True Delta* in an article reprinted in the Dublin *Nation*, "shirtless, shoeless, hopeless, reduced, by famine and disease, to a state of almost idiotic inanition." Such newspaper accounts impacted the lives of those with friends and family back home. In an 1849 letter to a cousin living in Philadelphia, John Montgomery of Portadown said he had received two letters from his brother William, who had recently moved to Louisiana. "I see by the papers there has been great mortality in New Orleans," Montgomery wrote. "I pray he may be preserved through all."[49]

Considering the fact that so many thousands of emigrants died anonymously overseas, and that imperfect communication networks, illiteracy, and psychological trauma further hampered the transmission of personal updates, those whose friends and relations had emigrated were often left assuming that no news was bad news. After reaching Peekskill, New York, in 1848, Thomas Garry sent a letter to his wife back in County Sligo. News of the mass mortality that had impacted Irish emigrants in New Brunswick the year before left him concerned about family in the area. "I feel very sorry for my brother Francis that lived at Saint John," Garry lamented. "I fear he is dead." Unanswered personal correspondence was often taken as evidence that the intended recipient had passed away. "I, with great enjoyment, sit down to answer your letter, which is indeed a great consolation . . . as we gave up all hopes of hearing from you," Judith Phelan told her niece, Teresa Lawlor, in 1851. Phelan had received no answer to her three previous letters and had even urged other people she knew "to seek after you or to write to your parish priest to know if you were dead or alive." When they heard nothing back, it seemed to confirm "that something happened to you." Anne Kelly of Knockcommon, County Meath, grew annoyed with her brothers in Canada when they failed to answer her letters. "I often think they are not living," she complained in July 1850. "Christopher would often write until he heard of Ellen Moss getting married. He was then struck dumb and wrote no more." When letters did arrive from abroad, they served to confirm or deny rumors of death. "Dear Michael, your friends all thought you were dead, it is so long since they heard from you," Margaret Masterson told her cousin in Kentucky, "but thanks be to God, you are doing so well." When all else failed, many turned to the transnational popular press for answers. In March 1849, a Mrs. Brice of Little Mary Street in Dublin took out an ad in the New York *Nation* seeking intelligence of her brother, James Beatty, "as a rumor of his having died in Boston has reached her."[50]

Beyond ads and reprinted articles, newspapers on all sides of the oceans often took it upon themselves to publish information on emigrant mortality as a form of public service. At a local level, they often confirmed the safe arrival of ships that had recently left their particular seaport. "It affords us the utmost satisfaction to be enabled to state . . . for the information of those whose friends have emigrated from this port in the present season," announced the *Galway Vindicator* in June 1846, "that the *Sarah Milledge* and *Lively* arrived safe at Quebec, the *Kate* and *Clarence* at New York, the *Victoria* at St. John's, and the *Midas* at St. Andrews early in May with the emigrants and all hands quite well." This gratifying information would, the paper hoped, "allay the fears of several in consequence of the painful but unfounded rumors put into circulation relative to the passengers in the *Sarah Milledge*." Nor did local newspapers publish only good news. A year later, the same paper admitted "the total loss of the barque *Maria* of this port, which was launched in July last, and sailed for Quebec on the 22nd of August." Luckily, "the passengers, with the exception of one man, were safely landed with their stores, etc. and transmitted to their destination at the expense of the ship." When catastrophic shipwrecks killed dozens or even hundreds of people, newspapers sometimes published long lists of the names of both the dead and the living in the knowledge that the news would get back to their relatives one way or another. The wreck of the Australia-bound *Tayleur* in early 1854 prompted the *Limerick Reporter* to publish the names of those who were saved as "there were many passengers from Tipperary, Limerick, Clare, and Waterford on board" the ill-fated vessel. Among those who died were two young Galwegians. "The melancholy news," rued the *Galway Vindicator* that week, "has flung a gloom over the whole town."[51]

Businesses and government officials also sometimes attempted to disseminate information on those who had died for the benefit of their loved ones. On occasion, the Cope family did so by personally reaching out to survivors. When William Nichols, a steerage passenger aboard the *Tuscarora*, drowned while attempting to land in Philadelphia in late 1853, the Copes told George Nichols about it. "We have written to thee as we find thy name on a card in his trunk," the Quakers explained, "and presume he may have been a relative of thine." In his reply, George Nichols thanked them for their kind attention and asked them to send the death certificate and kindly confirm "whether the body has been found or not." At other times, the Copes coordinated with their business partners in Liverpool to transmit important information. In April 1854, one of their packet ships lost forty emigrants to disease. "We regret much to perceive the number of deaths on board the *Tonawanda*," admitted Tapscott and Company, which coordinated the registration and embarkation of Cope passengers in Liverpool. "If you can furnish us with the names of the deceased to enable us to answer inquiries, we shall be much obliged." At the height of the fever crisis in Quebec in 1847, the CLEC also made some attempt to gather and share information on those who died. "I hope you are still bearing up under the frightful calamity, which surrounds you," secretary Stephen Walcott told A. C. Buchanan in September 1847. Walcott had noticed that the Quebec *Morning Chronicle* of August 28 had published a list of those who had died in quarantine between May 8 and July 3. "Now, as the relatives of emigrants in this country are very anxious to know the fate of their friends," Walcott continued, "I should be much obliged if you could get and send me eighteen or twenty copies of this number of the *Chronicle* for distribution amongst our naval agents, and likewise the same number of copies of any subsequent lists that may have been printed." These lists, Walcott noted, covered only quarantine mortality. "Is there any means of getting the names of those who died on the passage?"[52]

Ultimately, direct correspondence was the surest way in which emigrants and their families shared the fates of their kin. Indeed, such updates on life and death constituted an important filament in the web of transnational community. "Dear father and mother, I take the present opportunity of letting you know that I am in good health, hoping this will find you and all friends in the same," Catherine Hennagan told her parents, a few months after arriving in New Brunswick in 1847. "I wrote you shortly after I came here but received no answer, which makes me very uneasy until I hear from you and how you are and all friends." Catherine and her neighbors, who had traveled with the assistance of their landlord, Sir Robert Gore-Booth, had enjoyed a favorable passage, but after three weeks in quarantine, "my dear little Biddy died." Worrying about one's relatives could exact a heavy emotional toll. "You will send me all particulars about the children, for I am very uneasy until I hear from ye; if any of them are dead, do not [deny me the news]," John O'Connor told his wife back in Galway in 1848. "Dear Judy, I am as well as any man but the uneasiness for you and the children is wearing me." Others acknowledged having delayed contacting their families at home but found life in America moved quickly. "My dear brother, you must have imagined that I was dead or considered me the most ungrateful of brothers," admitted Edward McNally in a letter from Pennsylvania in 1851, "but it is wonderful all the poor stranger has to encounter when they first land in this country." Besides letters and remittances, copies of local newspapers were perhaps the most commonly posted item among Irish emigrants and their relations in the mid-nineteenth century. For those without the energy or inclination to write a letter, sending a newspaper could serve as a token of remembrance. "On last Friday, when we heard the American mail had arrived and we had no letter from you, we were extremely disappointed," Jane Ellen told John Orr in Chicago. "We had a paper, however, which prevented us from thinking you were dead altogether."[53]

To complete these circuits of personal exchange, newly arrived emigrants often sent home updates on mortality with explicit instructions that the news be widely disseminated among the families living in their old neighborhoods. "I take the liberty of writing these few lines to you, hoping to find you in good health as this leaves me in at present, thanks be to God," Ference McGowan wrote his father and mother after arriving in Saint John as part of the Gore-Booth assisted emigration program in 1847. "Write when you receive this and let me know how the family is and also all my old neighbors." Many friends and relations had fallen ill and died since leaving Ireland. "The people are lying out here on the shores, under sheds," McGowan told his parents, "and going to the grave, numbers of them every day." In this context of high mortality, Ference felt compelled to send detailed updates home. "Catherine McGowan of Gurthnahowle died of fever, also Paddy McGowan of Drynahon, Paddy Clancey's daughter Biddy, [and] Frank McSharrey's wife. Paddy McGowan of Gurthnahowle is lying ill of the fever" as was Molly McGowan. It was, however, not all bad news. "Let Paddy Connoley know that his son and daughter are in good health," McGowan added. "Biddy McSharrey is in good health. Frank McSharrey and family are getting well of fever. Larry Runian and wife are on [the Partridge Island quarantine]. Mrs. Dolan Connor and family are well, the husband is in the [United] States." Emigrants often made sure their news reached specific people. "Give my most affectionate love to Mary," Daniel Murphy told his brother back in Dublin in 1849, "and tell her to write to Edmond informing him of our safety and that I will write to him from our new settlement." Many felt gratified to know their sad news at least brought some closure to those left behind. "I wrote [our mother] an account of my dear brother's death [and she] seems quite reconciled," Eliza Fitzgerald told her brother Michael Cahill a week before Christmas in 1848. "It would be a blessing if our heavenly Father saw fit to call her to himself."[54]

To assuage fears and sensitivities surrounding funerary rites, family members often took it upon themselves to assure those living abroad that their kindred had been granted respectable burials. In an October 1850 letter to her son in Rhode Island, a Mrs. Nolan of Clara, County Kilkenny, described the depth of her destitution. "Patt, I can't let you know how we are suffering unless you were in starvation and want without friend or fellow to give you a shilling or a penny," she complained. Nevertheless, "thanks be to God, whatever me or his children that's here is suffering, your father died and was buried the way that he lived, that's respectable and decent," and she hoped "you and the rest of his children will do the same under the merciful hand of God." Just as settled emigrants often sent remittances home to facilitate the migration of their friends and families, they also sometimes posted money for funerary costs. "I enclose an order for twenty dollars," Daniel Rowntree told his brother Laurence in March 1852. "I request of you to see that the graves of our dear father and mother and brother are preserved, which I have no doubt you have already done. By paying some little, you can have them registered until such time as I can get a headstone ordered." For most emigrants and their relations, these exchanges over mortality and its pain were always rooted in deeper conversations about family and life. After purchasing a prepaid ticket for their children on a Cope vessel, a parent in Pennsylvania described the final moments of a dying child. "I had the consolation of wetting his lips when he was departing in his beloved brother's arms," they remarked on the back of the ticket. "I purchased a lot for his interment, paid 20 dollars for it, where we hold the title forever, it will be a family lot that nobody ever can encroach on." By sending the enclosed remittances, they hoped to reunite a family scattered by emigration and death. "Dear Jon, I trust I have discharged my duty towards you all," they wrote, "and I trust I may be spared to see you all gathered together."[55]

Death and dying was, in other words, an ongoing topic of conversation among the world-scattered Irish during the Famine era. In the public sphere, politicians and government officials described mortality in ways that fit their own agendas. Buchanan attributed excess mortality to the emigrants' own "want of moral energy," while nationalists such as McGee and Cahill blamed the proliferation of "sailing coffins" on British misrule. On a personal level, however, news about death played a role in community building on all sides of the oceans. Carefully transmitted through newspapers, letters, or word of mouth, the names and circumstances of those who died provided a way for emigrants, their friends, and their relations to mend interpersonal networks disrupted by the Great Famine. Whether worried about their loved ones, saddened by their news, or reconciled to their fates, Irish people found in death and dying a way to stay in touch. When Ference McGowan instructed his parents to share specific details on those who had died with his neighbors back in Ireland, he did so because he wanted to maintain reciprocal relationships capable of transcending the vast distance that separated them. Press reports of sensational shipwrecks played a similar role in bringing communities together too. When the *Arctic* sank near Newfoundland in September 1854, 350 lives were lost. "The sympathies of the whole community are deeply aroused towards these afflicted families," intoned the Quebec *Morning Chronicle*, "as well as toward all who have lost relatives and friends by this terrible disaster." In a letter to a friend back in Strabane, emigrant William Hutton reflected on the public impact of the *Arctic*'s sad fate. "The loss of life in every way by these horrendous battles, shipwreck, cholera, yellow fever, plague, etc. etc. must inflict a vast amount of deep and widespread woe amongst God's creatures," Hutton wrote. In the midst of such calamity, "who can measure the depth of gratitude that ought to warm the hearts of those who still continue in a happy land unscathed in self, family, or friends?"[56]

* * *

As this chapter has demonstrated, the Famine-era emigrant voyage was a relatively dangerous and frightening experience in ways that mere statistics fail to capture. At the same time, there was more to these vessels than one-dimensional "coffin ships." The popularity of that phrase undoubtedly rests, to some degree, on the fact that those two simple words ("coffin" and "ship") neatly encapsulate excess mortality and mass migration, those twin pillars of popular memory surrounding the Famine. This has played an important role in Irish identity building, at home and abroad, since the nineteenth century in ways that have often crowded out nuanced understandings of the actual experience. In particular, the truism of "20 percent" emigrant mortality has loomed large in the popular mind. As the primary and secondary sources presented in this chapter make clear, the average mortality rate on the ships that carried one hundred thousand Irish emigrants to Canada in 1847 was definitely very high, at around 10 percent. It is only when we zoom in on one port in particular (Cork) for one year in particular (1847), however, that we see an average mortality rate close to 20 percent. For the more than two million emigrants who did not travel to Canada in 1847 (in other words, for around 95 percent of all Irish migrants during the Famine years), the average mortality rate generally fell within the "normal" range for Europeans on the high seas in the mid-nineteenth century. Paying attention to the words of the emigrants themselves also offers a new and deeper understanding of what mortality meant to these people at the time. After journeying from Galway to New York in 1853, James Mitchell reflected on the lives that had come and gone at sea. "There was one death, that of an infant, and a birth," Mitchell diarized, "which left matters just as they were when we left port, at least as far as numbers were concerned." Irish emigrant letters and diaries show that while death could undermine relationships at sea, it could also bring people together in new ways. This process of repairing and rebuilding interpersonal solidarities was also one of the first thing emigrants did when they arrived in their new worlds.[57]

—————————— 5 ——————————

Arrival

In later years, Irish emigrants would sometimes struggle to articulate how they had felt when they first laid eyes on their destination. "No words can describe it," reminisced John Burke who had sailed to New York in 1847. "To the nearly-emaciated, forlorn emigrant, [it] is about the happiest moment of his life." This joy was often tarnished, however, by the realization of how far one was from home. "A painful sense of loneliness is often felt by emigrants during the first two or three days after landing," warned Wiley and Putnam's emigrant guide. "Having looked forward during a long passage to the time of arrival, with their curiosity and hope much excited, they experience a sinking of the spirits when they actually find themselves in a land of strangers and of strange customs." Leaving shipmates behind was especially hard. "A community of feeling has existed in the crowded steerage," Wiley and Putnam admitted, "and when the time to part from each other has come—some to go North, some South, some East, some West—no more to meet, it gives rise to painful emotions." This chapter investigates the ways in which immigrants responded to the challenges of arriving in their new destinations. While many previous historians have shown how migrants established connections within their new worlds, the following examples demonstrate that they also used various strategies to restitch their transnational communal bonds at home and abroad. Some did so by fostering relationships they had developed with fellow passengers. Others accepted the help of the authorities and "social betters" who looked upon immigrants as disadvantaged dependents in need of firm guidance. The popular press also provided a network for migrants to communicate with each other and those still living at home. The most important strategy involved staying in direct contact with their own friends and family on all sides of the oceans. As such, the steady stream of new arrivals provided another way in which the emigrant journey kept the world-scattered Irish in touch during the Famine era.[1]

"We Should Land Together": Preparing to Disembark with Other Passengers

After spending so many weeks in close proximity to each other, it was natural that many emigrants were sad to leave each other at the end of their voyage. When the *Thomas Arbuthnot*, a government-chartered emigrant ship carrying almost two hundred Irish domestic servants, landed in Sydney in early 1850, its surgeon-superintendent noticed how sad the young women were upon disembarkation. "Landed all the girls in a large steamer and walked at their head to the [Female Immigration] Depot," reported Charles Strutt. "There was such weeping and wailing at leaving the ship; when on board the steamer, an effort was made to give three cheers, but with very indifferent success." Although many were disoriented by the dissolution of their shipboard community, others found ways to repurpose those relationships. After all, fellow passengers provided an immediate source of solidarity, friendship, and economy. When he arrived in San Francisco from Belfast in 1849, E. H. Lamont noted the small boats offering to ferry passengers from their sailing ship to the dock. "I had made arrangements with a party of ten that we should land together, and for two dollars we procured a boat," explained Lamont. "I was among the first over the ship's side; soon we were all right, and I gave the word, 'Pull away, my hearties.'" Lamont's fellow travelers, "joining in the laugh that emanated from our overflowing spirits, took up the word, 'Pully way, marties,' increasing our merriment; and, brimful of mirth and happiness, we reached the shore in less than no time." While the process of disembarkation could leave many feeling lost and alone, therefore, it could also open new opportunities for freshly arrived immigrants. The following paragraphs examine the ways in which fellow passengers worked together to ease their arrival in the New World.[2]

Emigrant literature often encouraged solidarity among newly arrived passengers to insulate them from the threats, which lurked in every port city. "Families in all cases should cling together and provide, if possible, against separation," remarked J. C. Byrne in 1848, "and parents especially should endeavor to guard against their daughters being removed beyond the reach of their influence." Given that most emigrants were traveling on limited budgets, the economic advantages of such unity were usually emphasized. "It is best for a small party to agree to aid each other with their luggage, arranging it on deck as it is hauled up from the hold, then to join together, and agree with the steamboat people to convey the whole to [the port]," suggested Eneas MacKenzie in his *Emigrant's Guide to Australia*. "By so doing, there will be a considerable saving." In his guide for Irish emigrants, John O'Hanlon agreed that passengers ought to stick together. "In traveling, no division of members of the same family or party, nor of their luggage, should be admitted," he wrote. "Separation of persons and effects, destined for the same place, will cause at least trouble, expense, and delay." Moreover, O'Hanlon reminded his readers, passengers were usually entitled to stay on the ship for at least a night or two after casting anchor at their destination. Doing so was wise for it gave the immigrant "an opportunity of looking out for a respectable and suitable lodging, by leaving some member of his family or company on board, to take care of his effects." At the same time, individual migrants should not forget the dangers of placing too much trust in their fellow passengers. "Dishonest men frequently take occasion of the intimacy, which naturally springs up during a long passage, to engage an emigrant who has money, in some foolish scheme or other," warned Wiley and Putnam. "Let it be your rule to make no engagements for business, of any sort, until you arrive in America."[3]

Emigrants also sought to make a good first impression on their hosts by working together to clean their ship and themselves before landing. When a variety of Australian government officials greeted Charles Strutt and his group of prospective domestic servants on board the *Thomas Arbuthnot* in 1850, they inspected the vessel and its occupants. "They were greatly pleased with the order and regularity of the ship, the fatness of my girls, and the cleanliness of their berths, tables, decks, etc.," Strutt wrote in his diary, "and to do the poor wretches justice, they deserved the praise, for they had exerted themselves and worked like horses. Not a dirty spot was to be seen, and we carried off the recommendation and praise of being the cleanest ship that had arrived with emigrants, whether male or female." Convict ships were held to very high standards, as a vessel's cleanliness was considered representative of its orderliness as a whole. Indeed, scrubbing the deck and berths was often prioritized over educational practices, especially on the eve of arrival. "In consequence of the prison being washed out and many of the prisoners being engaged in it during the whole day, no school was held," diarized the Reverend Charles Woods aboard the *Blenheim II* as it approached Van Diemen's Land in 1851. The process of cleaning occurred on the less regulated routes to North America too. The captain of the *Yeoman*, which carried a complement of Sir Robert Gore-Booth's assisted emigrants to New Brunswick in 1847, was delighted to see "all hands employed scraping, washing, and cleaning the ship, [and] passengers washing and cleaning their clothes" to prepare for disembarkation. Respectable outfits were an important part of the landing process.[4]

Having permission to spend one or more days and nights aboard their sailing ship allowed emigrants to come and go from the port city and thus learn something about the place without getting fleeced by lodging house runners and draymen. This was critical as every time luggage moved from one vehicle to another, it ran the risk of being lost or stolen. When the *Nepaul*, which Caroline Chisholm had chartered to bring working families to Australia in 1852, arrived in Geelong, its passengers were annoyed to hear that they would have to hire a steamer to bring them to their final destination in Melbourne. It was not, however, "the 2/6 per head that people demur about," noted one passenger, "it is the moving from boat to boat, the chance—the almost certainty—of losing your packages." Whenever possible, passengers learned about their destinations while safely on their ship. After spending a few hours in Melbourne in 1852, a passenger returned to his vessel to share what he learned. "This is the news he brought: the inhabitants are dreadfully independent, if you happen to go and buy anything, they never think of giving you change," recounted a fellow passenger, "and as for walking through the streets in the night time, you can't do that without being well armed." Some emigrants hired their labor to fellow passengers in order to earn privileges and gather information. After arriving in New York in 1847, John Burke temporarily left the other members of his traveling party. "One of my shipmates had the address of a relative on the Bowery and I volunteered to pilot him to his friend and done so admirably," Burke later wrote, "and had a good supper cooked on a stove—the first of its kind . . . as we had no such convenience in Ireland."[5]

As they prepared to formally disembark and find lodging on shore, passengers continued to share information and watch each other's backs. When Thomas Langford sailed as a cabin passenger from Ireland to New York via Liverpool in late 1853, he coordinated with a few other trustworthy emigrants to complete the entire process of disengaging from the ship and settling into a lodging house. "I joined with two other respectable passengers and while two carried out the luggage, one watched it on the wharf," wrote Langford. "We then got a cart, something like your dray cart, and put our luggage on it and came to this place, 'Edinburgh Castle,'" on Cedar Street. Social class clearly played a role in Langford's choice of fellow travelers, but regionalism and gender could also contribute to emigrant solidarity. After arriving in Adelaide in 1854, a group of Channel Islanders formulated a plan before leaving the ship. "The Guernsey men went all together ashore and went to town to seek for lodgings and work, some got some and others were not successful," noted another passenger. "When they returned, the women were getting up the water, which they had been left without all day, the men going ashore in the morning before the water was served out." Others made the transition from the ship to the shore by connecting with fellow emigrants on the basis of labor and employment. Soon after landing in Australia in 1853, Edwin Francis and two of his shipmates—fellow boot makers by trade—had "a look around and a talk with some previous arrivals and got a little information." They learned that while they could find lots of work at good wages, the "trouble was that we must have a place to work in." They first leased a small cottage "in a back slum" but eventually bought their own "canvas house" for twenty pounds.[6]

When the gold rush hit Australia in 1851, many prospective gold diggers found economy and safety in cooperation. Though still three weeks from Melbourne, the emigrants aboard the *Fanny* were excited by the prospect of finding some of the great wealth hidden in the hills of Victoria. "The gold fields are now the chief topic of conversation among the passengers," remarked Joseph Claughton in July 1852. "We are busy forming ourselves into parties [for] when we arrive at Melbourne, to go to the Gold Fields, if there be any encouragement from them." Upon arrival and disembarkation, Claughton's luck enabled him to quickly find comfortable lodging at a reasonable rate. "I had made an agreement with a messmate called Charles Lindbergh, a native of Sweden, while on board the *Fanny*, to go to the Bendigo goldfields with him, in consequence of which, we were in company together," Claughton explained. When Lindbergh got a tip on great accommodation, the two of them went straight there, thus saving themselves time and money. Later that day, as Claughton strolled around Melbourne, he was struck by the sheer energy of the place. "The town is crowded with men from every part of the world," he wrote in his journal. "Gold and the diggings is the all-absorbing topic of the day." Almost every shop window had the same message painted in large letters: "Gold! Gold is bought here. The highest prices for Gold! Gold!" When the *Fanny's* luggage finally arrived a few days later, Claughton noted the high prices being charged for cartage. Luckily, "there was some nine or ten of us, all of the same neighborhood. One dray took the whole lot." Finally, a week and a half after casting anchor, Claughton and his associates were ready to head into the hills. There were six of them, all "bearing firearms of some description; some pistols and guns with a large sheath knife fastened to our belts, looking more like robbers than anything else."[7]

Emigrants who traveled together as a party often enjoyed special relationships that transcended the ties they had formed previous to departure. Soon after arriving in New Orleans in late 1853, Andrew Collin recounted to his parents some of what he and his friends had experienced since leaving Portadown, County Armagh, six weeks earlier. Collin admitted that leaving was hard. "I am not the least discontented about the ramble I took only for one thing, that is that it seemed to go so hard against your will and the will of my friends for me to leave home," he confided, "but I believe I could not have settled at home without seeing it out." He was, however, happy to report that "all our party has arrived safe, in the best of health, thank God." They had crossed the Atlantic in only five weeks, "which, I believe, is one of the quickest [journeys that] has been made from Liverpool to New Orleans." Having arrived in the United States and disembarked from their ship, the time had come for the traveling party to disperse. "Pat McAliece and wife, and Mary McAliece and Bridget are all going up to St. Louis tomorrow and I intend going to Mobile," Collin explained. "For Francis Devlin, William Mackle, and Samuel Wilson, I cannot say exactly what they will do yet." These men were considering following Collin to Mobile, but he was hesitant to encourage them in case things did not work out for them. Nevertheless, as things stood, Collin had only good news to report. "I wish to inform you that we all landed in as good friendship as we met in at the Portadown Station," Collin wrote, "and it was so all the way, which made everything go along sweetly and I think so far as I see that all our party are well satisfied with each other."[8]

The disadvantages of traveling alone became even more pronounced after disembarking. Many found foreign bureaucracies, for example, difficult to navigate. When Henry Johnson landed in New York in 1848, he was soon struck down by dysentery. "I went to a doctor and he gave me a small bottle, told me to use with it a glass of burnt brandy, three times a day," Johnson told his wife back in Antrim. When the remedy had no effect, Johnson resolved to admit himself to a medical institution. "I made application to get into the hospital but on account of a wrong name being on the ship's books, they would not let me and were going to fine me into the bargain," Johnson recounted, "only I started off as fast my legs would carry me." Many lonely emigrants simply wandered out into their new country in search of work. "When I landed in [Philadelphia], I remained there for the space of ten days, constantly looking for work but no chance," Edward McNally explained to his brother back in County Down in 1851. He decided to head for Pittsburgh "but I had not money enough to carry over all the way so I began to work on the Central Railroad where I remained for some time until I got a little money and then I started for Pittsburgh but on my arrival there, the cholera was bad . . . so I took the steamboat for Cincinnati . . . but there I searched in vain for trade and could not get a single day's work and I found myself without a single cent in a short time." After arriving in New York from Belfast in May 1847, James Duncan was surprised to see how quickly his shipboard community fell apart. "Mr. and Mrs. Morrison and Mr. Whitesides stopped in the neighborhood of where we landed and I did not see them again," Duncan noted. "Mrs. Battersby and family went on the steamer for Albany. Mrs. D. went to 272 Bowery where I saw her safe and now all is scattered." On his second day in America, Duncan "walked about all day today, seeing one and another but no friends."[9]

Passengers often united at the end of their voyage to make landing easier for themselves, but they also sometimes came together to commend or condemn their treatment by the ship's captain. By publishing such resolutions in the popular press, emigrants sought to draw public attention to the behavior of particular officers and their crews. Soon after arriving in New York from Liverpool in April 1849, Richard Flynn and over seventy of the three hundred passengers aboard the *Elizabeth Bentley* protested that they had "not been provided sufficient medical assistance—there being no surgeon or duly qualified medical officer on board; and we are of the opinion that the lives of several who died on the passage would have been saved had there been a proper supply of medicine dispensed." Yet more often than not, such public statements were issued in recognition of good service. When the *Jeanie Johnston* made it safely to Quebec in June 1851, a number of its emigrants joined together to offer their "sincere and heartfelt thanks" to Captain James Attridge and to the ship's medical officer, Dr. Richard Blennerhassett, "who has well preserved the character he has long since earned for himself as emigrant doctor." Such glowing commendations of ship's officers sometimes situated the relationships formed at sea in broader terms of family and community. The passengers aboard the *Dunbrody* thanked Captain Williams for bringing them safely from New Ross to Quebec in the late summer of 1853. "You were like a father to us," their resolution stated, "and the many amusements you afforded us kept us from fretting about our dear children and friends we left after us [in Ireland]." Indeed, personal relationships had brought them together in the first place. It was, after all, "hearing from our dear children and friends who had sailed with you before, [which] caused us all to come in the *Dunbrody*."[10]

Finally, the sailors themselves, on whose skill and labor the entire shipping system relied, were capable of uniting against their officers upon the conclusion of their voyage. Under constant threat of physical punishment, imprisonment, and heavy fines, seaman employed solidarity to improve (or escape) their working conditions. Their rough culture sometimes rubbed passengers the wrong way. As James Mitchell's ship approached New York in 1853, he noticed the sailors preparing to cast anchor. While completing their tasks, the sailors "made the ship ring with their songs and merriments," Mitchell diarized. "Their songs, however, were grossly obscene and entirely unfit for the ears of a Christian, showing most forcibly what a depraved and reckless class they generally are who follow a seafaring life." Sailors who united to challenge the authorities through desertion or mutiny risked not only being arrested by the police but also being physically assaulted by their officers. When the seamen aboard the *Queen of the West* emigrant ship attempted to mutiny, the captain attacked them with a sword. One sailor "had his arm nearly severed just below the elbow." Faced with the dangers and indifferent wages of life at sea, many sailors deserted their ships after arriving in Australia during the gold rush. When the emigrant ship *Georgiana* arrived in Geelong in October 1852, about eighteen crew members announced "that it was their intention to go ashore and proceed to the gold diggings." The captain offered to grant them two months' leave of absence if they completed the ship's voyage to Sydney. When the crew refused, he asked the emigrants for their support, but they declined. Ultimately, a fight broke out, and although the captain shot the cook dead, the main body of sailors "put ashore in the life boat, and made their escape towards the Bellerine Hills, and have not been heard of [since]."[11]

These examples demonstrate that otherwise unrelated emigrants often worked together upon arrival to ease their way through the difficult and dangerous transition from the ship to the shore. Practical considerations were always at the forefront of such cooperation. The economic advantages of sharing the cost of a boat or dray to carry luggage were obvious. Emigrants also often shared information about where to go and whom to trust in order to save time, money, and effort. Other forms of collaboration might not have been as apparent to those emigrating for the first time. Although passengers traveled as individuals and small parties, the truth is that the medical and customs officials who first greeted them often judged their shipboard community as a whole. By scrubbing the ship and their bodies on the eve of arrival, emigrants projected an image of themselves as clean and orderly and thus suitable for admission to their new society. Once ashore, passengers regularly reorganized themselves into small parties to save on lodging, find work, and protect each other from robbery and assault. Many stuck together to maintain friendships formed either before departure or at sea. Nevertheless, there was only so much that fellow passengers could do to help each other negotiate the process of arrival. Ultimately, most realized that their shipboard relationships would not last long after disembarkation. "I cannot now describe my feelings but they were strong as we sat together for the last time, who had been such intimate friends for eight weeks, hoping and fearing alike," lamented James Duncan after arriving in New York from Belfast in May 1847. He and his fellow passengers looked, Duncan imagined, like "a nice dish for the land sharks who were waiting their arrival." Luckily, there were also helping hands, in various positions of authority, awaiting their arrival too.[12]

"Respectability and Useful Designs": Social Authorities and Emigrant Relief

In light of the hierarchical nature of Famine-era Irish society, where many poor people relied on clergymen, landlords, philanthropists, and government officials for succor during hard times, it makes sense that vulnerable emigrants often turned to such individuals soon after disembarking. Their "social betters" had the experience, connections, and pecuniary means to help emigrants get their bearings and develop a plan for where to live and work. Some Irish landlords, for example, sent information and funds to assist those tenants whose emigration they had funded. On the other sides of the oceans, government officials based at the ports of disembarkation were the first people in positions of authority whom many newcomers encountered, and their responsibilities often included helping needy migrants. Similarly, emigrant societies were very important too. Yet there was more to such acts than mere kindness. For many in positions of power, helping emigrants served as a way to reify their own positions of authority and consolidate their vision of an orderly, hierarchical society. In an 1851 open letter to the American Emigrants' Friend Society in Philadelphia, Irish landlord and philanthropist Vere Foster assured its directors that their organization would enjoy the support of "of the public authorities of the city of Philadelphia, of the clergy of the different denominations, of the British consul, and of other individuals in high station, when they shall have satisfied themselves of the respectability and of the useful designs of your Society." Emigrant relief found favor with a wide range of stakeholders in the mid-nineteenth century.[13]

In Canada, for example, the government's emigration officers were mandated to expedite passengers searching for work and lodging. The government's chief emigration officer at Quebec, A. C. Buchanan, connected such financial assistance to the maintenance of social order. Disharmony would result, Buchanan warned in 1846, from "any relaxation of the system with which the superintendence of the emigration has been conducted, or any inability in the department to maintain its course of assistance, to the full extent of the claims that may arise." In particular, he feared an accumulation of destitute workers and their families in and around port cities, an increase in crime and disease, and the concomitant rise of "a hostile feeling . . . between the inhabitant and the stranger." His report from May 1850 gives a sense of the kind of assistance his office provided. "On board many of the vessels from the ports of Limerick, Dublin, Waterford, and Sligo, there were a number of very poor families, consisting either of widows and orphans or helpless women and children coming out in search of their husbands or other relatives," Buchanan explained to his superiors in London. "These parties chiefly emigrated voluntarily, landed here destitute, and in some instances without any correct knowledge as to their destination; they consequently became chargeable on this office, and I found it necessary to grant free [inland] passages to 1,375 persons." Some feared that poor families were exploiting the fund. In 1846, A. B. Hawke, the emigration officer in Upper Canada, claimed that many remittances sent from British North America were accompanied by the private assurance that any emigrants who could make it as far as Quebec would be "assisted [by the emigration officers] to get to their friends."[14]

When it came to dealing with indigent emigrants, Buchanan had several interrelated responsibilities. He was in charge of ensuring, for example, that entitled emigrants received their "landing money," cash allowances sometimes earmarked by their landlords or workhouses for emigrants upon arrival in Canada. In July 1847, for example, the secretary of the CLEC sent Buchanan a list of the eleven families who had, with the assistance of their landlord, sailed from Dublin to Quebec aboard the *Naparima*. The CLEC had been informed "that each family is to receive on arrival at Quebec the sum of £1/10/0 and that the money for this purpose has been supplied to Mr. James Miley, the passage broker at Dublin," Stephen Walcott explained. "I am therefore to request that you will have the goodness to ascertain if the parties receive the amounts intended for them and to acquaint me with the result in order that it may be communicated to [the emigrants' former landlord,] Sir Edward Walsh." Buchanan was also responsible for enabling poor emigrants to travel inland, even when the United States was their intended destination. When a number of poor Irish women and children arrived in Quebec en route to their families in Missouri, Kentucky, Tennessee, and Louisiana in 1853, Buchanan considered it expedient to pay their fares some of the way. The families had sailed only to Quebec "as their means did not permit their taking shipping to New York or New Orleans," Buchanan noted in his annual report, "and, having landed here destitute, it was found necessary to forward them, which was generally effected within the range of steamboat travel, either to Cleveland on Lake Erie, or Chicago on Lake Michigan." Finally, Buchanan worked with local authorities to find work for prospective laborers. In 1853, the mayor of Port Hope told Buchanan that the arrival of fifty female paupers from the Limerick poor law union benefited everyone in town. The local inhabitants finally had domestic servants, while the women themselves were now "placed in a position, which will give them all a fair start for a living in the New World."[15]

When landlords assisted their tenants to emigrate, they sometimes used their transnational connections to ensure that the immediate needs of their passengers were met or, at least, that the emigrants were not completely destitute upon arrival. In the summer of 1847, Lord de Vesci, an MP for Queen's County, attempted to employ the bureaucratic machinery of the CLEC to good effect after sending a number of emigrants to Canada aboard the *Wandsworth*, *Odessa*, and *Brothers*. In a letter to Buchanan, Stephen Walcott forwarded the landlord's request. If Buchanan would watch out for the emigrants in question "and transmit to me the account of any reasonable expenditure you may incur in this service," Walcott explained, "the [CLEC] will remit to you the amount, which his Lordship may hand to them for the purpose." Personal relationships could play a role too. Before sending wives and children to reunite with their husbands in Australia, Caroline Chisholm often sent letters ahead, giving the authorities and family members notice so that they could prepare to host the new arrivals. As seen in chapter 1, at least some of Lord Monteagle's powerful friends in Ireland and Britain used their connections to notify Australian employers that respectable laborers were coming from his lordship's lands. After learning that a number of Monteagle's tenants were sailing aboard the *Lady Peel* in late 1847, Archibald Cunninghame "addressed two letters to friends in the colony, enclosing copies of your Lordship's list and description of the emigrants" to see if they could help them find good work soon. Those in positions of power were duty bound, Cunninghame figured, to restore "prosperity to the British Empire by a just and equitable distribution of its labor."[16]

At other times, Irish landlords personally employed ship captains and other agents to oversee the voyage itself, help the emigrants get settled into jobs, and report back on their progress. Sir Robert Gore-Booth did so when he sent hundreds of former tenants to New Brunswick aboard the *Aeolus*, *Yeoman*, and *Lady Sale* in 1847. According to the letters he received from the authorities aboard the ships, his emigrants had all been given ample opportunities upon arrival in Canada. In his testimony before a select committee on emigration, Gore-Booth read aloud from a letter by Mrs. Purdon, whose husband had served as captain aboard one of the ships. "Captain Purdon got 150 [of the ship's 396 emigrants] sent off to Fredericton yesterday, where there is plenty of work," Mrs. Purdon assured Gore-Booth. "The Misses Gilmour are with a dressmaker who has undertaken to get situations for them; their brother is engaged for £20 a year to go to a farm in the country. . . . I have two girls on board, Mary Brine, who took charge of the cow, and the gamekeeper's sister, for whom I will get situations when the ship goes up to town." In his own letter to Gore-Booth, Captain Purdon claimed to have done what he could to help. "Poor things, I am sorry to see some of them landing without friends or money on a foreign shore," Purdon wrote. He planned to give away all of the remaining provisions (instead of selling them for profit) while, "to those who seem most needful, I will give a little money, say from 2s. to 2s. 6d. each, and I know under the circumstances you will not find fault with me." Gore-Booth also heard from John Robertson, his shipping broker in Saint John who was in charge of handling the disembarkation of the immigrants and the subsequent loading of the ships with timber to sail back to Ireland. According to Robertson, it was not Gore-Booth's fault if his tenants failed to make a living in Canada. The *Aeolus*'s Captain Driscoll had been remarkably successful at helping the immigrants find work. Only the "deluded dupes" among them remained unemployed.[17]

Despite such claims of generosity, it is also clear that many landlord-assisted Irish emigrants were often woefully underprepared for arrival in Canada. In his annual report for 1849, Buchanan complained that those helped by landed proprietors generally "landed in extreme poverty. In some instances, a small sum of money had been given each family to aid their outfit; but generally, nothing beyond a passage had been provided." Such was Buchanan's annoyance at the practice that he actually wrote letters to those Irish and Scottish landlords who were known to have sent underresourced emigrants to Canada, warning them of the poor conditions in which those emigrants ended up. Two years later, Vere Foster made a similar observation while visiting Brantford in Canada. In a letter to this mother, Foster described having witnessed, over the course of a few weeks, the arrival of several hundred Irish emigrants who were assisted by their local poor law guardians and generously granted one pound each upon disembarkation. In contrast, however, "those sent out by Irish landlords arrive in the worst condition," Foster noted, because they usually showed up "without a farthing or any arrangement for receiving assistance" and "generally consist of large, helpless families, none of whom, of course, are in a condition to earn anything." In July 1847, the government's emigration officer in New Brunswick, M. H. Perley, singled out Gore-Booth's Irish tenants as particularly poorly treated. Those sent aboard the *Aeolus* had been, he charged, "exported" by a landlord intent on disencumbering his estate, and would likely become permanent charges on Canadian public funds. Perley decried this "'shoveling out' of helpless paupers, without any provision for them here."[18]

Those unassisted emigrants who headed to the United States were particularly susceptible to fraud and robbery as the country lacked a formal immigration processing station until the founding of Castle Garden in New York in 1855. Another part of the problem facing newly arrived immigrants was that they were often hunted down by dishonest brokers and agents, who specifically used connections of ethnicity and language to earn and then betray their trust. At a time when familiar faces and voices were few and far between, immigrants were vulnerable to being tricked by fellow Irish men and women. When a select committee was appointed by the New York legislature in 1847 to examine "this nefarious business," it was "shocked to find that a large portion of the frauds committed upon these innocent, and in many cases ignorant, foreigners are committed by their own countrymen who have come here before them; for we find the German preying upon the German—the Irish upon the Irish—the English upon the English, etc." A year later, the *Limerick Reporter* reprinted a circular from the Emigrant Society of New York. "In landing in New York, the ship is always boarded with a class of persons called 'runners,' many of whom are Irish and speak the Irish language," the circular warned prospective emigrants. "These persons pretend to find good lodgings and cheap, for the emigrants, and invariably fleece them." In his 1851 emigrant guide for those Irish headed to the United States, John O'Hanlon told them to expect similar treatment to that which had greeted them in Liverpool. "No sooner has the emigrant landed, than he finds himself exposed to a repetition of the frauds practiced before his embarkation," O'Hanlon wrote. "The runner employed is generally a countryman, and ready to profess a sympathy and desire for the wellbeing of the unsuspecting passenger."[19]

Although New York lacked an immigration depot in the 1840s and early 1850s, its legislature did fund the establishment of the Commissioners of Emigration in 1847. The goal of these volunteer state appointees was, as with the Canadian officials, to maintain the regulations at their nation's primary port of entry, where disease and lawlessness were threatening the social order. Their responsibilities included licensing boardinghouse keepers and their runners, supervising ticket agents, and seeing to it that the masters of all vessels submitted their ship lists and paid their bonds. They also ensured that sick immigrants received any assistance they required. Protecting new arrivals from getting swindled was also part of the commissioners' remit as there was, they admitted, a "regular and systematic course of deception and fraud . . . continually in operation." The commissioners watched Manhattan's piers closely and in July 1847 appointed an agent in Albany to greet and protect "unsuspecting foreigners" heading upstate. The following April, a law was passed to strengthen their hand against fraudulent ticket agents and runners. The Commissioners of Emigration also did more than merely combat deception and robbery. In its annual report for 1854, the board listed a number of ways in which it helped newly arrived passengers. In common with the Canadian emigration officers, these commissioners offered very practical forms of assistance. When friends and family sent money for inland travel, for example, the commissioners helped new immigrants to get the most value out of that cash, and when such sums were insufficient to cover the total costs, the commissioners often covered the balance themselves. According to their 1854 annual report, they helped immigrants "by procuring labor or places of employment in city or country, by writing and receiving letters for the uneducated or those ignorant of our language, . . . and in numerous other ways assisting and protecting the newly arrived stranger."[20]

With immigration control still in its infancy, private benevolent organizations were especially influential. Manned and funded primarily by first- and second-generation, middle-class immigrants, these emigrant societies aimed to combat deceit and robbery at every stage of the voyage. The New York Irish Emigrant Society, which was founded in 1841, for example, opened an account with the Bank of Ireland, upon which it could draw drafts. Anyone who sent a sum to the society's office on Spruce Street in Manhattan, along with "plainly written directions" regarding to whom and where it should be paid, could have the amount safely remitted abroad. Similarly, the Philadelphia Emigrant's Friend Society, founded in 1848, was designed "for the purpose of securing emigrants from imposition upon their arrival here" and helping them to find good jobs and homes. In the spirit of transatlantic cooperation, which played such an important role in other mid-nineteenth-century benevolent movements such as abolitionism, the middle-class friends of poor emigrants sought to develop transnational connections whenever possible. Although Liverpool did not witness the creation of emigrant societies on the scale of New York or Philadelphia, some of its citizens, agents, and newspaper editors did work with North American groups to disseminate emigrant guides and information. Such protective services were often laden with the moral imperatives of the people running them. When the Emigrants' Protection Society was founded in Dublin in 1851, for example, the *Nation* newspaper highlighted more than its ability to combat fraud. "To place an unprotected young female of rustic simplicity within the careful circle of an emigrant family" before, during, and immediately after the voyage, remarked the *Nation*, "is a priceless guardianship." Meanwhile, back in Boston, exiled '48er Thomas D'Arcy McGee urged immigrant societies to go beyond pecuniary assistance by helping newcomers to become American voters. "To prevent beggary is excellent," McGee opined, "but to make citizens, more so."[21]

While the captains and crews of sailing ships often considered their passengers as little more than human cargo, it is also true that the companies that operated shipping lines sometimes did their best to help their passengers when difficulties arose after disembarkation. The records of the Cope family packet line in Philadelphia demonstrate that the owners considered themselves accountable in various ways. In a letter to one of their captains, for example, the Copes sought to retrieve a passenger's lost luggage. James Richie, who had sailed from Liverpool to Philadelphia in 1852, had forgotten "a red chest with black handles and a barrel of stores (both without mark)" aboard the *Saranak*. If the captain found them, he was asked to deliver them to a John Gallagher in Liverpool. The Copes also answered letters from the public requesting status updates on family members who were supposedly traveling on the company's ships. Unfortunately, because the ship's manifest traveled on the vessel itself, the Copes could not confirm or deny any individual's arrival in advance. "As we receive no list of passengers until the ship arrives here, we cannot tell whether the persons thee inquires for are in the *Saranak*," they told Patrick McAleer in 1845, although they did predict that the ship itself "will probably be here in a week or ten days." Once the ship arrived, they could be more helpful. "Sarah Keenan's name is on the list of passengers per the ship *Wyoming*," the Copes told Mary B. Thomas in July 1850, "which arrived here on the 20th instant." The company even agreed to pass on information to newly arrived immigrants on behalf of their friends and relations. When Thomas Donaldson learned that some people he knew had planned to sail to Philadelphia aboard the *Wyoming*, the Copes promised "to give the directions thee desires to the Keegan family should they arrive in that ship."[22]

Those Irish who landed in Australia generally encountered a more highly regulated environment, which left them less susceptible to fraud and abuse. From 1848 onward, the Female Immigration Depot, located in an old barracks on Macquarie Street in Sydney, served as both a temporary shelter and a labor exchange for unaccompanied single women. A similar depot was built in Birkenhead in 1852. While wait-

Figure 5.1. The immigrant depot at Birkenhead, Australia, which opened in 1852. *Illustrated London News*, June 26, 1852. Image © Illustrated London News/Mary Evans Picture Library.

ing to get collected by family members (or seeking employment in the depot's "Hiring Room"), the women were fed and housed in dormitories. When the *Thomas Arbuthnot's* complement of almost two hundred Irish "orphan girls" arrived in Sydney in February 1850, this was where they stayed. After a week in Sydney, the ship's surgeon-superintendent, Charles Strutt, accompanied over one hundred of them on the two-week journey by horse-drawn cart to Yass in search of jobs as domestic servants. Many Australian settlers feared that the influx of Irish female paupers would degrade colonial society, but the Sydney *People's Advocate* believed these women would become "nursing mothers to an empire, which we believe is destined to be one of the most potent that the world e'er saw." Their close confinement meant that convicts were both restricted and protected upon arrival. When three hundred Irish male prisoners sailed to Van Diemen's Land aboard the *Pestonjee Bomanjee* in 1848, Dublin Castle sent a letter to the colonial authorities, advising them to enroll the men in industrial and moral training and thus prevent them from "being too suddenly exposed to the temptations of the colony without some degree of control or superintendence." Those convicts granted tickets of leave could hire themselves out as laborers. Before Jonathon Quin had even disembarked from his transport in 1849, a number of employers came aboard. "I hired myself . . . as a shepherd, and to make myself generally useful, for a period of twelve months at twelve pounds a year," Quin told his parents in Armagh. After that he was "at liberty to go to any part of the country I think fit."[23]

In sum, whether landing in Canada, the United States, or Australia, many thousands of Ireland's Famine-era migrants received help from various types of authorities and "social betters." It made sense that Irish immigrants, finding themselves in a foreign land on a tight budget, would seek support from people of means. From the perspective of the benefactors themselves, moreover, there were various reasons why aiding the poor made sense. For those in positions of power within the British imperial government, helping indigent immigrants find work and lodging served as an antidote to the allegedly ever-present threat of disease and crime in Canada and Australia's growing port cities. Doing so also reified the extant social hierarchy through the exercise of "benevolent" patriarchy. When a number of landlord-assisted emigrants sailed from Londonderry in July 1847, the CLEC's Stephen Walcott asked A. C. Buchanan to help them in any way consistent "with the fair claims of all emigrants of the humble classes equally to the care and advice of the department established for their protection." Matthew Gallman and others have suggested that middle-class benevolent organizations such as emigrant societies also contributed to the development of North American capitalism, by directing newly arrived workers toward labor-short regions, and of bourgeois democracy, by encouraging immigrants to assimilate, naturalize, and follow their leaders. As such, the migration of millions of poor people provided a grand opportunity for those wishing to strengthen the social structure of the mid-nineteenth-century Anglophone world.[24]

"Everything That Is Enlightened and Beneficial": The Popular Press as Emigrant Resource

The weekly newspaper provided another resource for the newly arrived immigrant. Although Ireland's literacy rate in the mid-nineteenth century was approximately 50 percent (and subject to considerable regional variability), the popular press played an important role in Irish society. Those who could not afford the full price often shared subscriptions with their neighbors or visited the reading rooms and libraries, which proliferated across the island during this period. The public reading of newspapers, in which one person read the columns aloud for the benefit of his or her listeners, was also a popular pastime and a common way for the illiterate to hear news and opinion. The transnational circulation of newspapers also served as a way for the Irish at home and abroad to stay in touch. Friends and families often sent copies of their local papers as tokens of their feelings for one another. A few months after John Orr left Belfast for New York in early 1847, his sister urged him to stay in touch. "Mamma desires me to say," Jane wrote, "that any time you do not write, if you would send us a paper, directed with your own hand, it would be almost as satisfactory [as a personal letter]." In the Antipodes, even political prisoners found ways to access newspapers from home. "The Irish extracts [reprinted in Australian papers] are generally very meager and unsatisfactory," complained exiled '48er John Martin in June 1850, but his confederate Thomas Francis Meagher "has received a good many [Dublin papers] and an old school fellow of [John] Mitchel's and mine, whom we have lately met here" shared some too. Over in North America, emigrants often enjoyed sharing any Irish papers they received. In an 1849 letter to his friend back in Antrim, John Mulholland remarked on a small community of people from the north of Ireland, whom he had encountered in Windsor, Nova Scotia. "They take great pleasure in reading an Irish paper," Mulholland noted, "and as Miss Cunningham kindly sends on a Coleraine paper, I circulate it among them." In these and other ways, the popular press proved a vital asset to those seeking to transition into their new societies.[25]

The editors of Irish weekly newspapers, whether located at home or abroad, often lauded their papers as circulatory systems of information and ideas. Irish-born publisher Patrick Donahoe, for example, used his office in Boston as an international node of Irish exchange. After publishing O'Hanlon's *Irish Emigrant's Guide for the United States* in 1851, Donahoe printed the book's first few chapters in the columns of the *Boston Pilot*, which he owned and edited. When the issue sold out unusually quickly that week, Donahoe printed extra copies, which he encouraged his readers to share with their friends and families back home.

"Persons sending [remittances] for their friends [in] Ireland," Donahoe wrote, "would do well to send them the *Pilot* containing [O'Hanlon's] guide." Newspapers traveled in the other direction too. Soon after publishing their first issue in late 1842, the editors of the wildly popular Dublin *Nation* mailed free copies to various editors in the United States and Canada. That December, Donahoe told his readers that he had received "the three first numbers issued" of the *Nation* and was happy to add it to the list of newspapers with which the *Pilot* held reciprocal exchange agreements. Closer to home, editors such as Donahoe supported libraries and reading rooms as places of relaxation and learning. When a new one opened in Boston in the autumn of 1849, Donahoe encouraged young men to visit and support it. "What more agreeable and interesting resort could be found than a clean, cheerful reading room full of intelligent people and stored with books and newspapers?" asked Donahoe in the columns of the *Boston Pilot*. Reading rooms were intellectual nurseries, he concluded, "of everything that is enlightened and beneficial."[26]

For the middle-class leadership of emigrant communities, the popular press served as a key dynamic for the propagation of bourgeois ideals and values. A few months after founding the New York *Nation* in 1848, Thomas D'Arcy McGee urged his readers to use his newspaper as a training tool for naturalizing into respectable, American citizens. "The deepest research, the purest eloquence, the loftiest morality are none of them unfit for a newspaper," McGee declared in February 1849. "Most of all are they needed among us now, when society is assuming permanent forms in America, and all the lights the human mind can furnish are needed to guide it right." A year and a half later, after moving to Boston in the wake of a public spat with the Roman Catholic bishop of New York, McGee used his new paper to vaunt the broad value of a good weekly journal. "The newspaper is one of the great engines of modern civilization," McGee exhorted in the *American Celt*. "From the reading of it, a great amount of useful information and pleasant pastime may be obtained." O'Hanlon, who enjoyed a close working relationship with Donahoe, extolled the role of the popular press in his guide for Irish emigrants. In his mind, a good newspaper served the entire family. Heads of households should subscribe to one or two respectable weeklies, O'Hanlon advised, and if unable to afford the full cost, encourage a neighbor to share the price of one subscription. Families that regularly read newspapers were "much more intelligent, respected for general information," declared O'Hanlon, "and better calculated to turn marketable, moneyed, business, and political transactions to good account."[27]

Coming from a conservative rural country, public voices often portrayed America's teeming cities as critical threats to the Irish body and soul. In a public letter reprinted in the Dublin *Nation* in May 1852, a P. Mulligan recounted having seen "as much misery and want" during his recent travels through American cities as he had ever seen in Ireland. Many emigrants found themselves stuck in America, unable to find work yet lacking the funds to return home. "About seaport towns in particular, there are swarms of idle persons . . . who resort to any and every scheme for obtaining a livelihood," Mulligan warned. "[There is] murder and robbery, even in the open streets and in broad daylight." Even those who managed to find work often lived hard lives subject to low pay and constant abuse. There were also spiritual dangers of life in urban America, which the Catholic clergy remained vigilant against. In an open letter to a Dublin newspaper, the Reverend Mr. Mullen decried the fate of thousands of Irish emigrants. "Multitudes settled in the suburbs of the large cities, where thousands of the most depraved and abandoned of every sect were congregated, where infamy was sweltering and crime of every species abounding," Mullen lamented. Watching their children descend into spiritual destruction, older Irish immigrants "wept and thought of Ireland, its village churches, its priests, its religion, constituting happiness, even amidst privations and poverty." Some friendly, native-born editors likewise encouraged newly arrived Irish emigrants to avoid the cities. In an open letter to Vere Foster, Horace Greeley advised newcomers to bring their labor and skills out to the country. "No one should board or stop in [New York City] a day unless he has friends here," Greeley wrote in 1852. "If he lands without a penny, let him walk immediately northward until he leaves the city out of sight and then begin inquiring for work on any terms."[28]

While cities were portrayed as sinkholes of danger and depravity, the open plains of western states such as Illinois and Wisconsin were seen as wholesome beds for the planting of new Irish communities. Owning a farm had been practically impossible in Ireland, where a relatively small sliver of the population controlled the majority of the land, but in America, independent proprietorship was at least possible. In an open letter to the editor of the Dublin *Nation*, an immigrant in Philadelphia was heartened to see recent arrivals heading straight out west. "They face towards the great western lands in little swarms, and this is what they should continue to do, for in the cities they are slaves, while in the west they become lords of the soil," An Exile explained. Armed with the right social values, these emigrants could find happiness. "With the charity of religion, the steadiness of temperance, and the industry of Irishmen," he wrote, "they cannot fail to establish themselves happily in the vacant lands westward." Letters from Irish farmers who had successfully started their own farms in the western states were often reprinted in the popular press. In May 1850, the conservative *Times* of London published a letter by a Limerick farmer in Wisconsin. Although most Irish emigrants lacked the funds to buy a farm outright, as this man had done, his description of rural life was compelling. "You need not mind feeding pigs, but let them into the woods, and they will feed themselves until you want to make bacon of them," the farmer boasted. Wisconsin truly was a land of plenty. "Here, the meanest laborer has beef and mutton, with bread, bacon, tea, coffee, sugar, and even pies, the whole year round," he declared. "Every day here is as good as Christmas Day in Ireland."[29]

The emigrant press certainly reflected the values of its bourgeois editors, but it also served as a font for the technical instructions one needed to make it across the ocean. As such, the shipping brokers' advertisements, which took up columns of space in all of the major newspapers during the Famine, contained large amounts of critical information. In 1846, for example, James Beckett of Liverpool ran a successful business selling steerage berths aboard "first-class, fast-sailing, American packet ships" headed for the United States and Canada. As many prospective emigrants probably did not understand the basic premise of the packet system, Beckett used his advertisement to describe it to them. "All these ships sail punctually on their appointed days," he explained, "or the passengers are allowed one shilling per day each until the ship sails." This strict schedule allowed emigrants to save time and money. Having received their application, Beckett would reply with a letter listing what day and time the vessel was scheduled to depart so that passengers "may, on their arrival in Liverpool, go on board the ship and thereby avoid all expense of lodging, etc." Once emigrants had settled into their new homes and saved enough to enable others to follow, they could also use the advertisements of shipping brokers for instructions on how to safely send remittances home. Tapscott's was one of the biggest such agents in the mid-nineteenth century. In an August 1851 ad in the New York *Freeman's Journal*, the company notified its readers that any persons living in the United States or Canada could "send for their friends" through its offices in New York, Liverpool, and Dublin. With so many remittances bought on tight budgets, it was important for people to know that their investment was protected. "Should those sent for decline coming out," assured another brokerage, the Roche Brothers of Fulton Street, "the money will be refunded to the parties without any deductions, on producing the passage certificate and receipt."[30]

At a more basic level, weekly newspapers also notified their readers of the safe arrival of particular ships. By publishing status updates on these vessels, newspapers repaired frayed threads in the fabric of the transnational Irish community. In the interests of economy, many such notices merely listed the basic details of such ships. In May 1848, for example, the Quebec *Morning Chronicle* noted the arrival of the *Envoy* from Londonderry with one cabin passenger, 214 in steerage, and a single death on the voyage. Likewise, on October 26, 1850, the *American Celt* of Boston remarked upon the arrival of the *David* from Galway "after a passage of forty three days, bringing with her eighty passengers, all well." When the emigrant ship *Faneuil Hall* arrived in March 1849, the *Boston Pilot* did not mention its port of embarkation but did list the names of all 173 passengers aboard including the Donnell family ("James, Mary, Margaret, and Mary") and "John Murphy (dead)." Back in Ireland, newspaper editors used the safe arrival of local ships as evidence of their port's suitability for emigration. The *Galway Express* was pleased to announce, for example, the safe arrival in New York of several emigrant ships from Galway in August 1854. "If any proof were wanting of the superiority of Galway over Liverpool as an American emigration port," declared the *Express*, "it is now supplied by the short passages of the *Clarence*, the *Waterford*, the *Triton*, and the *Eva*." Such news reports were also designed to bring relief to worried relatives left behind in Ireland. In July 1853, the *Limerick Reporter* announced that the *Africa* had safely completed its route from Liverpool to Melbourne with all passengers on board in good health. Considering that "so many respectable passengers from Limerick and Clare and other parts of Ireland" had sailed aboard the *Africa*, the *Limerick Reporter* was delighted to impart "this gratifying intelligence to many anxious families."[31]

The popular press was also a critically useful tool from the perspective of the recently arrived immigrants themselves. In particular, many bought space in the Information Wanted columns of local newspapers as a way to reunite with loved ones. The most famous of these columns ran in the *Boston Pilot* between 1831 and 1921, but many weekly newspapers published similar ads as a way to both generate revenue and connect people throughout the Famine era. In 1847, the editor of the *Boston Pilot* boasted of his paper's success rate. "Every day, we hear of persons being found" through the column, he claimed. "Our paper is the best medium in the country for this purpose, as it circulates largely in every town [throughout North America] where there is an Irishman." Littered with specific details designed to catch the attention of casual readers, these ads were aimed not only at the person being searched for but also at their friends, families, relatives, workmates, and acquaintances—anyone who could connect the dots between people who had lost touch with each other. In January 1850, for example, Sarah Hare (née Quinn) published a request for information on her brother. Anthony (son of Patrick and Catherine Quinn) was a native of Stillorgan, County Dublin, who had left Ireland in December 1847 aboard a vessel called the *Russell Glover* in the company of two young men named Fitzharris. When last heard from, in 1849, Quinn was working in Cincinnati, Ohio. In an effort to spark the memory of anyone who might know her brother, Sarah included some details on his physical appearance. He was, she said, twenty-two years old, of a "dark complexion," approximately five and a half feet tall, "and wants one tooth in front."[32]

To strengthen their chances of receiving a reply, those purchasing space in the Information Wanted columns sometimes enticed their targets with promises of material benefit. In March 1851, Patrick McNally of New Haven, Connecticut, published a notice in the *American Celt*, seeking information on a John Smith, originally of Drogheda, who was supposedly living somewhere between New York and Philadelphia. Any information respecting Smith would be thankfully received by McNally "of whom can be heard something that will be to [Smith's] advantage." Immigrants were not the only ones who purchased Information Wanted ads. When Peter Kennedy died on board the *Avernon* en route to Boston from Cork in the spring of 1849, the local Commissioners of Alien Passengers and Foreign Paupers used the columns of the *Boston Pilot* to try to find the dead passenger's sons, Cornelius and John. They could, the ad promised, "learn particulars in relation to *property* belonging to the *heirs* of said Peter Kennedy" by visiting the commissioners' offices. At other times, ads could be used to track down fugitives and recover stolen goods. In September 1850, Michael O'Hearne and Michael Moran, two farmers in Massachusetts, used the Information Wanted columns of the *Boston Pilot* to offer one hundred dollars for information leading to the arrest of John King, a native of County Clare. Originally detained on suspicion of perjury, King had gone "amongst his countrymen" to collect money to cover his bail but, on the eve of his trial, "got afraid of being punished and made his escape, money and all." King was about forty-five years of age and "rather robust," with a dark complexion and "one tooth out of the front of his mouth."[33]

Although the Irish Australian popular press was much smaller than its North American counterpart (with only one major weekly, the Sydney *Freeman's Journal*, during the Famine years), it too employed its columns as a place where immigrants could search for information on others. As the church was an adhesive in the lives of many Irish Catholics, individual clergymen were often called upon to help people find friends and family. The *Freeman's Journal*, which was founded by an Irish Catholic priest named John McEncroe in June 1850, urged its readers to use the press—not their priests—to find lost people. In the United States, it noted, "the principal Catholic newspapers" all dedicated "a column or two of their journals to the insertion of advertisements in search of friends or relatives," and the *Freeman's Journal* promised to adopt a similar plan to serve those Irish living in Australia. Doing so would increase the chances of success while saving priests from having to spend time and effort on fruitless searches. "As the *Freeman's Journal* is read by the vast majority of Irishmen in this colony," McEncroe explained, "there is more probability of finding out friends through the columns of this journal than by putting clergymen to useless and unnecessary trouble and expense." When immigrants chose to purchase an Information Wanted ad in the Irish Australian press, they sometimes continued to connect their requests for help with the social network of the Catholic Church. In March 1855, for example, a "Notice to Emigrants" published in the *Freeman's Journal* included an ad by a Mary Carey who was searching for her sister, Bridget Carey of O'Brien's Bridge, County Clare. In the original text of her ad, Mary had obviously asked that priests publicize her request on Sundays because in a postscript the newspaper's editor specifically stipulated "that such notices as the above are never read from the altar in Catholic churches."[34]

For desperate immigrants on the edge of destitution, Information Wanted ads could also serve as their last chance for reunion with kin. As fathers were often the breadwinners in their families, advertisements were usually directed at them. One notice, published in the *American Celt* in July 1852, sought information on a Patrick Glynn "who was to meet his father and mother and family, from Kilbride, County Roscommon, in Buffalo" but never showed up. Five months later, the same ad was still being published verbatim in the press. At times, the vagaries of casual employment upset plans for reunion. When Margaret O'Brien arrived in Sydney in early 1855, she sought information on her husband, Cornelius, whom, she had learned, had "left Goulburn for the Victoria [gold] diggings about a month since." It was not unusual for wives and children to find themselves abandoned. Four years after Margaret Cuncanon's husband emigrated from Galway, she followed him to the United States and took out an ad in the *Boston Pilot* as "herself and child are now depending on the benevolence of a few of her old country neighbors." When children got lost, it was up to strangers to reconnect them with their parents. In July 1850, the *Corsair* arrived in Quebec, from Limerick, with two unaccompanied children, Mary and Catherine Cullinane, aboard. Two months later, they were still waiting to be claimed at the local Emigration Office. "No tidings having been heard of [the children's] parents or friends," read a notice in the Quebec *Morning Chronicle*. "This advertisement is inserted in hope that it may meet the eye of some party connected with them." Nor was it unusual that the ad asked other journals "throughout Canada, Vermont, and adjoining states" to reprint the notice. When Fanny McNamara published a request for information on her father in a Boston Irish newspaper, she specifically asked the Dublin *Nation* to copy it in their columns. Meanwhile, Mathew Hughes, who was living in Philadelphia in 1846, took out an ad in the Dublin *Nation* for information on his sister even though she had supposedly emigrated to America.[35]

The columns of the newspapers themselves therefore contained critical content for newly arrived immigrants, but the physical act of mailing issues back and forth across the oceans served as a medium through which the world-scattered Irish reconnected broken bonds of affection and community. To those for whom foreign newspapers were important, the knowledge that family abroad would send them regularly was significant. "William received a letter from his Aunt Margaret a few days ago and two newspapers," John Campbell told his mother back in Donegal in 1846. In exchange, William sent two New York papers and intended to do so regularly. "The papers were a few months old," John admitted, "but by sending two each week, they will soon come up to this present date." For those Irish living abroad, mailed newspapers provided a way to stay in touch with news and opinion from home. In a letter to his brother-in-law in County Derry, John Lindsay encouraged him to write every couple of months. "I would also be glad if you could send me a newspaper as often as you may have an opportunity—I will also send papers to you as often as I can," John promised. "The alarming state of things in Ireland at the present time adds an additional interest to Irish papers, and the one I got yesterday is the only one I have seen for many months." Irish emigrants could also use exchanged newspapers as a way to educate their relations about their new home. After settling in Australia, David Moody resolved to sometimes send some newspapers to his mother back in Ireland so she could "see in them what this land is doing." At other times, mailed newspapers could simply serve as notice that one had made it to the other side of the ocean. Three weeks after arriving in New York in 1850, George Ritchie admitted that his parents might have expected to hear from him earlier but at least "I posted you a paper containing the arrival of the *Hudson* with the names of the cabin passengers."[36]

In sum, the popular press played an important role in helping immigrants get settled in their new homes. Individual issues of any weekly journal served as transferable, affordable media for the transnational communication of ideas and opinions. This was important to the editors and owners of Irish newspapers who, constrained by tight budgets and semiprofessional staffs, relied on exchange agreements with far-flung titles to gather much of the information important to their subscribers. Editors also encouraged readers to send open letters for publication, many of which not only imparted important details but also reified bourgeois values and ideals. Moreover, among the readers themselves, weekly newspapers were a critical way to collect information on a wide range of issues relating to emigration including status updates on particular ships' voyages, advice on how to safely send remittances home, and suggestions on where to settle in their vast new worlds. The weekly press also provided a way for immigrants to project their own voices, concerns, and needs through the Information Wanted columns. Finally, the Irish press offered a venue through which ill-used newcomers could challenge those in positions of power. When an Irish cabin passenger named John McKiernan sailed from Liverpool to New York in 1851, he was overcharged and abused throughout the voyage. After arriving in New York, McKiernan and one of his fellow passengers went to Mr. Tapscott's office to protest their treatment but were unceremoniously expelled onto the street. McKiernan figured their hopes for redress were dashed, but his companion disagreed. "You are wrong," said his friend, "the *Celt* paper is published in Boston." After running McKiernan's experience in its columns, the *American Celt*'s editor hoped his story would be broadly publicized and reprinted in "all papers friendly to the poor emigrants, both here and in Ireland."[37]

"Some True Friend or Old Acquaintance": Friendships and Family in the New World

While fellow passengers, government authorities, and weekly newspapers all proved useful assets to newly arrived Irish immigrants, the most important resource—and the one they strove to rebuild as quickly as possible—were personal relationships with friends and family. These connections were crucial to successful resettlement in the New World. Without friendly faces to greet them, it was harder and more expensive for newcomers to find lodging and employment. Indeed, emigrants were often encouraged to send notice of their impending arrival even before departure. "An old countryman coming over should always, when practicable, apprise some true friend or old acquaintance in our city of his intention and of the name of the vessel wherein he has taken passage," advised one New Yorker in an open letter reprinted in the Irish press in 1849, "so that the arrival of his vessel being announced in the newspapers, he may be sure to meet his friend on the dock when his ship comes up, and be conducted at once to cheap and suitable lodgings." Four years later, a similar letter in the *Limerick Reporter* agreed. Those planning to travel abroad should make arrangements with loved ones before leaving "for if they come out without this precaution, on landing here, weakened by a long voyage, and perhaps with little or no funds, their position is really distressing." This need for personal support upon arrival in a new country often went beyond the bare necessities. Those who successfully reconstituted old networks in their new homes also enjoyed a higher quality of life. Although many experienced great hardships during their first days and weeks after arrival, Daniel Guiney struggled to express how well he and his traveling companions had been treated by their old neighbors who had greeted them. On their first night in their friends' home, "we had potatoes, meat, butter, bread, and tea for dinner and you may be sure we had drink after in Mathew Leary's house." Such was the pleasure of reconnecting with his old friends that Guiney admitted to having "scarcely words to state to you how happy we felt at present."[38]

In their correspondence back and forth across the Atlantic Ocean, the imperial authorities noted that large numbers of Quebec-bound Irish passengers were traveling to rejoin relatives who had already emigrated. Their arrival in Canada, therefore, signified the completion of a new link in chain migration. In December 1846, the colonial secretary, Earl Grey, recognized the pecuniary value of such networks of assistance. Even as their numbers swelled, "newly-arrived emigrants will disperse themselves throughout the various localities where their friends are already established," Grey pointed out, "and where, from the manner in which they are sent for, it may be presumed that they will find the means of subsistence." When asked why more Irish did not head for Australia, Sir Robert Gore-Booth insisted that emigrants "like to go where their friends are. There are very few of them who have not friends in America." In his position as chief emigration officer in

Quebec, A. C. Buchanan tried to help families to reconnect in North America. In 1850, he described the annual arrival of a "very destitute class of the Irish emigrants" whose passages across the Atlantic had been paid for by family scattered as far away as Missouri. Quebec was usually chosen as the port of disembarkation for the simple reason that it was the cheapest route. Before paying for their inland travel with the public funds at his disposal, Buchanan sought, with mixed results, to contact these emigrants' relations. "In all cases where these families were without means, I obtained the husband's address and wrote for immediate assistance to their families," Buchanan reported in his annual account for 1850. "In many cases, money was sent . . . but in several cases, no answer was ever received."[39]

The brief, personal notes scribbled on the backs of some prepaid tickets suggest that most benefactors believed that successful reunification relied on the advance transmission of accurate information. By the mid-1840s, mail crossed the Atlantic on steamships, which took only about two weeks to complete the voyage versus the five or six weeks that emigrants spent on sailing ships. Any passenger who sent a letter on the eve of their departure, therefore, could rest assured that it would arrive several weeks before they did. As the arrival of ships was publicized daily in port cities, those planning on greeting new immigrants could prepare accordingly with only a few details in hand. When eighteen-year-old Catherine Callaghan was preparing to leave home for Philadelphia in 1851, her benefactor reminded her to communicate with them. "We expect you to leave Liverpool on the 12th of April," they wrote on the reverse of her prepaid ticket. "Write a letter and tell us the name of the ship you are coming in." To empower the emigrants to find their own way to safety, other benefactors included detailed descriptions of how to find them upon arrival. "When you land, you must inquire for Walnut Street and then go out until you come to the Schuylkill River," explained Patrick Johnston, "and then inquire for Beach Street No. 2, between [Walnut] and George's Street." Many preferred to personally greet the newcomers. On the eve of Agnes Sharkey's 1851 departure, her benefactor promised to have arrangements in place for her upon arrival. At the very least, they would send a friend "but if I can at all, I will be there myself."[40]

When relatives were not on hand to immediately assist disembarking immigrants, they often found ways to help anyway. This was true even when such family members were hundreds of miles apart. Soon after arriving in Hallowell, Maine, in March 1848, Owen and Honora Henigan sent a letter to their son back in Ireland, recounting their experiences since landing in Canada. Life in New Brunswick had been "almost as bad as Ireland," but thankfully, a family member named Peter had sent money over two hundred fifty miles to support them while in Saint John and then "paid our passage on the coach" to Maine where he lived. They got there to find that Peter "had a good house for us, and the rent of it paid until summer" plus plenty of staples including "two barrels of flour, one barrel of beef, and firewood." Reconnecting with family, and accepting their financial assistance, was not always so easy. For some, inaccurate information and long distances delayed reunion. It took Thomas McGinity some time after landing in New York in 1847 to simply find his sister. "I went to the person with whom she lived and they told me she was married and living out in the country, both she and her husband," McGinity explained in a letter back to Ireland. "I went out of the city and found them about eighty miles up the north river from New York." With his goods held in customs and no money of his own, McGinity was in a tight spot, and yet his pride and family dynamics rendered it difficult for him to accept help. His sister gave him "her bank book to draw the money," McGinity explained, "but I declined on the grounds that her husband could not tell her after that her brother was a beggar coming here."[41]

Having spent the majority of their savings merely getting across the ocean, many immigrants needed to start working immediately. The same people who had facilitated their departure often helped them find work. As Richard Stott has demonstrated in his work on mid-nineteenth-century working-class culture in New York, personal relationships shaped employment in the antebellum urban economy. The first thing immigrant job seekers did was "ask relatives and friends if they knew of openings," explained Stott. "Few of the city's workshops had formal hiring procedures, and most workers found jobs by word of mouth." Those who had already settled abroad often warned prospective emigrants to prepare for hard work and long hours in their new homes. The capitalist work discipline that dictated the pace of employment in North America was strict and impersonal. As seventeen-year-old Mary McKay prepared to sail for Philadelphia, her benefactor scribbled some advice on the back of her prepaid ticket for others to read to Mary. "She will have to be among strangers and work hard and perhaps not see me very often either," they warned. "It don't answer at all times to be together, your employer will not allow you to squander away your time." Destinations, skills, and family often overlapped in any job hunt. As he surveyed a recent batch of Irish emigrants arriving in Quebec in May 1846, Buchanan noted that a few hundred were "going to their friends in different parts of the United States, among whom are a considerable party of miners from Waterford, who are proceeding to the copper and lead mines in the Wisconsin territory." Those already in positions of employment could vouch for newcomers. One day after arriving in New York in 1847, John Burke tracked down an old acquaintance who was employed by a boot maker on Broadway. His friend, "being a good workman," got Burke a job immediately.[42]

Clothes, which had played such a critical role in the safety and comfort of passengers at sea, suddenly became a social liability upon arrival. Many emigrants had started out on their voyage in ill-fitting, old-fashioned, cheap vestments. This, combined with the fact that washing and maintaining clothes over the course of several weeks or months at sea was incredibly difficult, meant that many arrived in outfits that immediately distinguished them from mainstream, respectable society. Some were simply destitute. In 1851, the medical officer at Quebec, George Douglas, noted that a number of the children on one ship in particular were wearing converted bread bags, canvas, and blankets for clothes. "One full-grown man passed my inspection," Douglas added, "with no other garment than a woman's petticoat." Those planning to greet new arrivals often encouraged them to dress well. When James Purcell sent his sister Bridget a remittance to allow her and Purcell's children to join him in Australia, he advised them to each pack "two suits of clothes": a nice outfit for landing and another for day-to-day life at sea. Others were more demanding. Catherine Callaghan was instructed to dress as "neat as she can because you don't know how much mortification some Irish people cause to their friends here." Many offered to dress the new arrivals quickly. As sixteen-year-old John Delaney prepared to sail for Philadelphia in 1851, his benefactor told his parents not to spend extra money on new outfits. He should bring only what he absolutely needed, they promised, "for as soon as I get one sight of him here, I will put a good suit of clothes on him." Then, as now, changing fashion trends could embarrass newcomers. In 1851, a benefactor warned his brother not to wear any frieze or corduroy as "they are not worn in this country by no person . . . [and] bring no knee britches for you would be laughed at here with knee britches."[43]

While immigrants quickly established personal connections with those living in their new homes, they also sent letters and messages back to Ireland as well. In this way, the rebuilding of transnational personal relationships served as an important part of the arrival process. Many sent home hastily written notes or even mere copies of the local newspaper to indicate they had made it alive and would follow up later with more detailed reports. In a June 1849 letter to her friend back in County Down, Jane White apologized for the confused nature of her prose. "I hope you will excuse me," White admitted, "as I merely snatched the opportunity to let you know I am safely landed at last." In his guide for Irish emigrants, John O'Hanlon reminded newcomers not to waste space in their letters on frivolous subjects. Too many emigrants filled their letters with the "uninteresting gossipings of a neighborhood, or public facts, which are always found in the columns of a newspaper [anyway]" instead of the "private details and family affairs of the greatest importance to the correspondent and his absent friend." The letter home was an opportunity to share information, but it was also a place where loved ones could virtually connect by naming each other. This explains, in part, why emigrants often asked their addressees to show their letter to others in the neighborhood. "Best respect to you, dearly beloved father, and mother, brother Patt, and my brother Mick," wrote John Mullawny from New Brunswick in July 1847, "Uncle Martin and wife, Patt Martin, John, Mary, and Nancy, to Mick Hart and aunt and family, Patt Carrane and family . . . and to Thomas Geraghty and family and how he is getting on with his melons and cucumbers, and Patt McGowen, and all the Lissadell Garden Boys." Naturally, requests for information were equally important. "Be pleased to let me know how my two sons are, Patrick and Francis," Thomas Garry told his wife, who was still in Ireland in 1848, "and not forgetting my dear father and mother, friends and neighbors, [and] not forgetting your sister, Bridget."[44]

Those who failed to receive communications from kindred often felt the loss keenly. The Sydney *Freeman's Journal* considered silence from home "one of the most distressing ills attending the separation of friends." Many recognized the fragility of their old relationships. Thomas Reilly rued the thought of never speaking to his friend in Dublin again. Letter writing was, perhaps, the only way they would ever converse in the future, Reilly lamented; "alas, this moment how my heart sinks and tears start into my eyes." Many immigrants found it stressful waiting for a reply to letters they had mailed. "Dear father and mother, I feel uneasy for not getting an answer to the letter I sent you," complained John Mullowney in August 1847. "I went oftentimes to town, expecting a letter from you, and could get no answer." Others sometimes employed guilt as a way to reinvigorate reciprocal exchanges of communication. In June 1847, John Lindsay of Port Clinton, Pennsylvania, told his brother-in-law, William McCullough of County Derry, that his wife Matilda "has never had a letter from her [sister, Jane] yet and it gives her uneasiness thinking that she perhaps had given cause for this silence." Lindsay acknowledged that Jane was probably very busy but trusted "that she will sometimes make an effort to write to her only sister." At other times, a breakdown in communication could encourage an individual emigrant's insecurities to flourish. In a letter to her mother, C. A. McFarland decried the silence from home. "I think you must have forgotten that there is such a one living as me," McFarland wrote from Philadelphia in 1855. She had already sent a letter and two newspapers home but never received a reply. "I do feel so bad when the mails comes in and no letter," she admitted. "I sit down and cry my fill." McFarland hoped that her mother was not like some of her snobby friends who "never answered my letter" after learning that she had taken up employment as a domestic servant.[45]

For those getting settled in their new homes, loneliness was an inescapable part of the experience. In a letter to her cousin, Teresa Lawlor, in Memphis, Tennessee, Sarah Carroll admitted to missing her family since moving to Buffalo, New York. "I hope you will receive this and that we will write often to each other," Carroll pleaded, "for it is the only happiness I can enjoy in hearing from my dear cousins since the Atlantic Ocean separated me from my dearest . . . brothers and sisters. Dear cousin, I hope you will write me." Five years later, Teresa Lawlor received a letter from another cousin who expressed similar feelings. The memory of "that day at noon when I tore myself from your arms . . . has pierced my heart pretty sore," confided Margaret Meehan from Sonora, California, "for I never until lately had the least idea of ever seeing you [again]." At times, other immigrants found their loneliness intermingling with sleep and reverie. In a particularly eloquent letter reprinted in an Irish newspaper in 1854, an anonymous immigrant in Van Diemen's Land wondered if his relatives ever thought of him. "If you don't, I make up for it, for, over 20,000 miles away, my memory is ever with you," he wrote, "and often at nights, in my lonely hut, fancy travels back to home, and in my dreams I visit you all, and I once more seem to be amongst you, telling you my travels." Yet, awakening to find himself still in "the tall, dark, solitary forest by which I am surrounded in deep shadow, I am recalled to the reality of my position, and tears will sometimes start at the disappointment." In the face of such despondency, however, many immigrants still felt that they had made the right choice in moving abroad. Johanna Kelly did admit to her father back in County Tipperary that she sometimes felt "lonesome for the leaving of my friends . . . but, for my own part, if I was in the old country, I would come back again."[46]

In this context of social dislocation, many immigrants went to great lengths to not only stick with any old neighbors who had also moved abroad, but also deepen connections with those who remained in Ireland by sending home updates on their new community. The steady circulation of news drew people closer together. As members of the working poor in a new environment, updates on people's employment were popular in letters. "Ann and Eleanor and Margaret got situations in short after coming here [and] Denny is working with Thomas Redmond, making boots," Michael Hogan told his aunt in 1851. For his own part, he would soon start working in a local foundry for the equivalent of one pound sterling a week. "Thomas Young is [a] clerk over [at] the furnace," explained Hogan. "It was he [who] got me in." After landing in New York in 1848, Eliza Fitzgerald was happy to tell Michael Cahill that "a great many persons from our neighborhood [in Ireland] came out." Several had gone west, but others were living and working nearby. "Peggy Noonan is the same, old style," Fitzgerald related. "John Doyle and brothers and sister are very comfortable." Beyond employment status, emigrants were often simply happy to relate that their friendships had survived the journey. "My dear father and mother, I take this pen with joy to write these few lines to ye hoping to find ye and all inquiring friends in as good health as I am at present thank God," wrote Mary Feeny from New Brunswick in 1847. She had found work soon after arriving in Mispec, about ten miles outside of Saint John, and was happy to report that she now lived very close to John Mullowney and his two sisters, "which makes me feel content [as] John comes to see me very often at night and oftentimes in the day."[47]

It is also true, of course, that leaders in Irish communities abroad sought to build a sense of community based on ethnic nationalism. When Thomas D'Arcy McGee founded his weekly newspaper, the New York *Nation*, in October 1848, he dedicated it to "Ireland and to the Irish Race scattered over this country." McGee subsequently used the paper's columns to publicize the notion that every Irish person in America— howsoever long they had been living there—should band together. In March 1849, he published a letter to the editor that decried the ways in which settled immigrants often treated their recently arrived compatriots. "Many Irishmen in this New World look down with contempt on some of our poor countrymen when they first land here," complained Flood, out of a sense of "false pride and self-conceit, which they pick up here, in their vain attempts to look *Yankeefied*." In so doing, they forgot their shared roots. "All should bear in mind that it was the one dear land that gave them birth," he reminded his readers, "that perhaps the man he looks down on with such contempt has sprung from the very chiefs who have given his country a name in the annals of the world." In Australia, the Sydney *Freeman's Journal*, though much more conservative than McGee's *Nation*, similarly encouraged Irish unity abroad. "Irishmen everywhere, whether high or low, rich or poor," it editorialized in April 1855, "are inheritors of a common instinct that is of an attachment passionate and inflexible as regards their religion and their country." Indeed, when harnessed to notions of religious duty, this ethnic identity often spurred acts of charity. When an Irish mother of five died aboard the *Anglo-Saxon* en route to Boston in early 1847, a local priest took the surviving children to his church on Sunday and appealed to his congregation for help. According to the *Boston Pilot*, $253 was raised "on the spot for their relief!"[48]

These excerpts show that newly arrived immigrants began rebuilding broken bonds of community as soon as they arrived in their new worlds. While the fomentation of an ethnic identity provided one way for leaders to coalesce their prospective constituents, the bonds of friendship and family were far more important, as evidenced by the number of times emigrants mentioned them in their letters. These people used the international postal system to rebuild and repair relationships with their neighbors at home and abroad. Their exchanges were not one-way transmissions but rather reciprocal, transnational networks of news. By sharing, receiving, and responding to updates—both good and bad—Irish emigrants and their relations went some way toward transcending the dislocation caused by the Famine's mass migration. In their letters home, newly arrived immigrants demonstrated to their friends and families that the community feeling they had once enjoyed in Ireland was not completely destroyed but rather changed by the process of migration. An October 1847 letter by Catherine Bradley illustrates the phenomenon. It was, after all, intended for a broad audience. "My dear Uncle, you will please read this to my sisters and other friends," Bradley wrote, "and mind to tell Ann not to grieve or fret after me, for I hope we shall soon meet again." Although sad that her sister had not accompanied her to Canada, Bradley reported being quite satisfied with how things had worked out. "I do feel most happy and content here," she said, "so much so that I sometimes forget Old Ireland for a time." After naming several old neighbors to whom she sent good wishes, Bradley sent updates on those who had emigrated with her including "Charles Henry and Edward Johnston [who] are both as kind to me as brothers." In ending her letter, Bradley encouraged her relations to complete the circuit. "Now, dear Uncle, answer this immediately," she begged, "for I feel anxious to hear how all are that I left behind me."[49]

* * *

In these many and varied ways, the processes of disembarkation and arrival helped to reweave the transnational web of Irish society during the Famine era. A poem titled "The Emigrant," published in the *Galway Vindicator* in 1852, around the height of the migration boom, painted a pessimistic picture of the dislocation facing the average migrant:

> He is leaving the land of his childhood
> The land where his kindred do dwell,
> To live in the waste or the wildwood,
> The desolate valley, and dell.

As the above examples illustrate, however, Irish emigrants often succeeded in mending these damaged relationships. Passengers employed a range of options, for example, in developing and securing local connections. They formed syndicates with fellow passengers for protection and economy during those first hectic days on shore and shrewdly engaged large institutions such as government bureaucracies and the popular press to reunite with family members awaiting them. When their husbands abandoned them, wives used the Information Wanted columns to try to track them down. Emigrants' bonds of solidarity also stretched all the way back to Ireland. By exchanging letters, newspapers, and remittances, newly arrived passengers began the process of reconnecting what "The Emigrant" poem elsewhere referred to as "old ties of affection [in] the land of his fathers." Sharing updates on how old neighbors were faring in the their new communities, while garnering news from home, was critical to maintaining links of reciprocity and affection. Yet, ultimately, it was the transmission of a new remittance—that first step in every emigrant's journey—that also constituted their last. "Come as soon as you can for I shall be expecting you every day from this time," James McGee's benefactor wrote on the back his prepaid ticket in 1852. "I am glad to think that we will meet again, no more to part."[50]

Conclusion

Emigrating means leaving. Tearing asunder bonds of belonging. Yet it can also mean reconnecting. Repairing broken links of solidarity. The letters and diaries of the emigrants themselves demonstrate that the preparation for, experience of, and recovery from a sea voyage were as much about community building as individuals' mobility. During the Great Famine, Irish people at home and abroad rebuilt damaged relationships by using the very tools (remittances, tickets, and ships) that had drawn friends and families apart in the first place. Although there were important and enduring class differences within the Irish diaspora, the project of healing interpersonal relations transcended these disparities. In the summer of 1847, a "beggar boy" named Thomas Garry hid himself aboard a ship carrying Sir Robert Gore-Booth's tenants to New Brunswick. When the crew discovered the stowaway, they prepared to send him back ashore, but the captain was impressed by his pluck and encouraged the passengers, many of whom were indigent themselves, to pool enough money to cover Garry's passage. The following year, having made his way to Peekskill, New York, he sent a letter to his wife in Sligo. In it, Garry enclosed six pounds and vowed he would send the fares for her and their children soon. "Keep your heart as God spared you," he wrote, "you will be shortly in the lands of promise, and live happy with me and our children." Further up the economic scale, in May 1851, Daniel Rountree sent a remittance of seventy dollars to his sister, Ellen, who was living comfortably with another brother, a coal merchant, in Dublin. "I conclude by sending ye all my love and sincere affections," Daniel told her from Washington, D.C., "wishing, if it be the will of Providence, that the few of our family that are yet living can soon enjoy the society of each other in this country." The migration process was a critical circuit in the interpersonal networks of the Irish diaspora during the Famine era.[1]

The restorative power of chain migration manifested itself in different ways throughout the entire journey process. Once individuals and groups had made the decision to leave, they faced the formidable challenge of gathering the necessary means. Over two million people did so, in the teeth of a failing economy, by relying on entangled connections at the local, national, and transnational levels. By eliciting the exchange of money, prepaid tickets, advice, and news, the early stages of the voyage served to bring people living in different parts of the world together in support of a common cause. Once at sea—and temporarily out of touch with their friends and families on land—the process changed. Finding themselves consigned for weeks on end to a weird new environment governed by a handful of strangers enjoying a monopoly over violence, migrants expanded their traditional attitudes of belonging and solidarity along new lines of shared experience. Mealtimes and sleeping arrangements were important, but everyday, silly entertainments could also bring people together. "I gave the [captain's] goat today, amid the laughs of many of the passengers, the following things in succession, all of which it ate with equal relish," diarized Samuel Harvey as he sailed from Belfast to New York in 1849. "Cabbage stalks without leaves, hay, paper, tobacco, shavings of wood, a piece of rope yarn covered in tar, and lastly an old tobacco pipe full of tobacco, which it crumped up in great glee." By encouraging emigrants to broaden how they thought of themselves and others, the sea voyage was the first step in a long, fraught process by which immigrants found their places in new, multivalent societies. Finally, as they arrived in their host countries and built new relationships there, migrants also restitched their connections with home, often by enabling others to follow them. So while migration was undoubtedly, as Cormac Ó Gráda and others have argued, a form of famine relief, it was also a dimension of famine recovery.[2]

The human drama of Irish migration during the Great Famine was, therefore, part of a wider story about the ways in which global networks of communication and exchange reshaped the world in the nineteenth century. This was a time when trade and finance, explains Jürgen Osterhammel, "condensed into integrated and interconnected worldwide webs" capable of drawing distant corners of the globe together in new ways. The international telegraph system, which transmitted messages through a complicated network of cables and relay stations, was coming to fruition, enabling people around the globe to communicate "at the speed of thought." The letters, remittances, and prepaid tickets, which served as fuel for the engine of migration, all traveled on a burgeoning, transnational postal system that became more expansive and reliable during this time period as well. Famine-era migrants traveled in the waning years of the Age of Sail, just a decade or so before steamships began carrying passengers across the oceans, but they followed clear routes that had been established over centuries of capitalist exchange. The packet shipping system attracted merchants by guaranteeing what day their cargo would depart, but it also served migrants well by enabling them to avoid spending precious resources on lodging in port towns. Exiled Irish '48er John Mitchel's caustic snipe that "the sun never sets . . . on British felony" highlights the long reach of the convict transportation system, which also carried thousands of poor Irish (many voluntarily) to new lives in the Australian colonies. The individual vignettes of those who left Ireland during the Great Famine were, in other words, inextricably linked to broader, global stories of capitalist and imperial expansion in the nineteenth century. As the currents of modern life pulled people apart, they also brought them together.[3]

This examination of the Irish emigrant experience suggests new directions for future research on migration both within and beyond Irish Studies. The Great Famine was an epochal turning point in modern Irish history, but its migration lasted only ten years. By expanding their chronological remits, future scholars could use the experiences of Irish migrants before and after the Famine to test the conclusions I have offered here. Does the surviving archival material suggest that eighteenth-century passengers had similar experiences to their Famine-era compatriots? In later years, how did the shorter but more expensive journey upon a transoceanic steamer impact how those headed to Australia and North America thought of themselves and their fellow travelers? As Britain became the preferred destination for Irish migrants in the twentieth century, did the shorter (and cheaper) journey encourage or inhibit shipboard solidarity? Are modern airplanes in any way reminiscent of "that city afloat," which the Reverend James Buck described from the docks of Liverpool in 1853? Historians of migration more broadly could also learn much by focusing their attention on the processes by which people on the move prepared for and handled the sea voyage. Did the complicated agreements between and among indentured servants, their masters, and the authorities change during their time at sea? Countless religious missionaries completed long and complicated sojourns while propagating their faiths. Did those arduous journeys, which had literary precedents in sacred texts such as the Bible, impact how these people thought about their relationships with each other? Did they weaken or strengthen their links to their superiors on land? Finally, Marcus Rediker and others have demonstrated the ways in which racial categorizations were imposed on those treated as human cargoes aboard slave ships. Was it during the course of their sea voyages that Asian laborers became "coolies"?

The emigration of 1847, which for many constituted a headlong flight from hunger and disease, bore the hallmarks of what we would today call a refugee crisis. The panic caused many to leave without adequate resources. The ill, the old, and the young, who would have stayed behind in past years, were often swept along in the rush. Unscrupulous shipowners and agents met the rising demand by pressing unseaworthy vessels and crews into action. Laissez-faire governments on both sides of the ocean held the problem at arm's length. In the midst of all of this, thousands died in squalid conditions. "The unhappy crowds who, in this year of horrors, have fled from Ireland, have not escaped the doom of their brethren," exhorted the Dublin *Nation* in August 1847. "The infection of the land has followed them to the ships, and has not deserted them until they are buried in the depths of the sea, or on the strange shores, which their filmy eyes saw like a dream as they passed out forever from this life." As the late 1840s and early 1850s progressed, however, conditions improved. A. C. Buchanan, the chief emigration officer in Canada, was confident that the 1855 UK Passenger Act would "add materially to the comfort and health of the passengers" by reducing the number of emigrants per ship, increasing the daily food allowance, and providing sufficient medical care. In New York, to which the majority of Irish emigrants sailed after 1847, the establishment of a formal immigrant-processing center on Castle Garden in 1855 was greeted with similar praise. In its first few months alone the depot had, the local commissioners asserted, accomplished "much for the benefit of the emigrant, the shipper, the commission, and the community at large." In his classic study of the passenger laws, Oliver MacDonagh argues that the increased regulation of the emigrant trade during these years was part of a broader revolution in Western governance, characterized by "creative and self-generating" bureaucracies.[4]

Emigration slowed down after the Famine but remained an important dynamic of Irish life for decades afterward. In its annual report for 1855, the New York Commissioners of Emigration pointed out that the total number of "alien passengers" from Europe (the majority of whom were either Irish or German) was less than half the average of the preceding five years and little more than two-fifths of the number in 1854. This sharp decrease was, moreover, "not confined to arrivals at the port of New York but was general throughout the ports of the United States, and it extended to those of British America." The commissioners attributed this steep decline to the enactment of new Passenger Acts by the US and UK governments and the concomitant increase in passenger fares. Raymond Cohn points to other causal factors including generally improved economic conditions in Europe along with the stagnation of real wages and electoral success of nativists in America. Whatever the explanation, the United States remained the first-choice destination of most Irish emigrants until the second quarter of the twentieth century, when the Great Depression and Second World War diverted the flowing tide toward Great Britain. For most western European countries, this was a time of population increase, urban expansion, and industrial growth. In Ireland, the opposite was true. Competition over farmland and limited urban opportunities encouraged many to emigrate. Although most of the seven million men and women who left Ireland in the century and a half after 1855 did so on steamships—and, later, airplanes—the Famine-era sailing ship remained a potent symbol of the emigration experience. Its power is reflected in the popularity of ballads and songs such as Pete St. John's "The Fields of Athenry" (1979) and "Thousands Are Sailing" (1988) by the London Irish punk band, The Pogues.[5]

Enduring popular memories of the Famine and its "coffin ships" certainly eclipsed objective analysis of the experience for many decades, but these emotive recollections also had the positive effect of engraining sympathy for contemporary famine victims and refugees into Irish public discourse. When drought and hunger struck northern Ethiopia in the mid-1980s, Irish nongovernmental organizations such as AFRI (Action From Ireland) and Trócaire received a groundswell of financial support. Twenty years later, in an interview to publicize his 2004 novel *The Star of the Sea*, which was set on a Famine-era emigrant vessel, Irish writer Joseph O'Connor opined that the main lesson to be drawn from Ireland's experience in the 1840s and 1850s was "that we should do more to help those many millions of the world's poor people who are suffering and dying from famine today." As the harrowing images of asylum seekers trying to cross the Mediterranean Sea have flashed on television screens and digital platforms around the world in recent years, similar reflections have emerged. John Roche of the Irish Red Cross has rued that without attention being paid to the humanitarian crises in their home countries, "desperate people will continue to risk their lives on these coffin ships." It must be admitted that not all sectors of the Irish public are sympathetic to the connection. When thirty-nine dead Vietnamese refugees were found crammed into a refrigerated lorry driven by an Irish man in October 2019, a member of Ireland's Parliament, Martin Kenny, publicly expressed his support for asylum seekers, saying that shipping containers like the ones the Vietnamese died in "are the coffin ships of the twenty-first century." Days later, his car was destroyed in an arson attack directly linked to his support for refugees in Ireland. For the most part, however, Irish public opinion is largely dominated by support for vulnerable poor on the move. In the wake of the Essex lorry deaths, *Irish Times* columnist Fintan O'Toole buttressed his argument for stronger laws to protect migrant workers by reminding his readers that "we too had our coffin ships."[6]

Fostering emotional connections with those less fortunate is no small feat. Now, as in the mid-nineteenth century, the centrifugal forces of modernity continue to erode bonds of human solidarity. Economic insecurity, mass migration, and old-fashioned ignorance have encouraged many to turn inward and seek security in race and nation. The digitized, twenty-four-hour news cycle has reduced millions of traumatized human beings into low-resolution refugees. My hope is that by understanding the experiences of Irish emigrants during the Great Famine, we can cut through these sound bites and statistics. In so doing, we might learn to sympathize and support those who are, this very night, heading down to the port with their bundled belongings, to sail into the dark.

ACKNOWLEDGMENTS

I clearly remember the moment this project sparked to life. It was over fifteen years ago and I had just attended an exciting talk at the University of Pittsburgh where Marcus Rediker had sketched out his plan for a new book he was calling *The Slave Ship*. By analyzing the wooden machines that brought enslaved Africans across the Atlantic, Rediker aimed to show one way in which the sea has shaped human history. "That's exactly the kind of fresh perspective we need in Irish Studies," I thought to myself as I walked home that evening. "What would *The Slave Ship*'s equivalent in Irish history be?" A split second later, it dawned on me: "*The Coffin Ship*."

I was a graduate student at the time and still had to finish my dissertation on Irish racial identity and revise it into a book before I could start working on this new project, but I must begin by thanking Marcus for not only inspiring me to write this kind of history but also for always supporting me in many ways as I did so. From the outset, I received critical help from others as well. Kerby Miller generously agreed to share his vast collection of Irish emigrant letters with me and read parts of the manuscript as they developed. Peter Gray introduced me to the DIPPAM database of emigrant primary sources, encouraged me as I made sense of what I found there, and invited me to share those findings with the Irish Studies Seminar at Queen's University Belfast. Kevin Kenny, whose scholarship has shaped my own in many important ways, was always willing to share his thoughts on the project as it progressed and kindly invited me to submit the manuscript to the new Glucksman Irish Diaspora book series, which he founded at New York University Press.

I received lots of help from other friends and scholars as well. Jill Bender, John Bukowcyzk, and Cormac Ó Gráda took the time to read some or all of the manuscript and share their honest opinions. Malcolm Campbell patiently wrote letters in support of my applications for funding and helped me identify sources in the southern hemisphere. Connor Lewis and his wife Lauren kindly hosted me when I visited Columbia, Missouri, to work with Kerby Miller's letter collection.

I got a lot of help and suggestions from a number of other scholars as well including Tyler Anbinder, Colin Barr, Michael Brillman, Ray Cashman, Marguérite Corporaal, Mary Daly, Michael de Nie, Sean Farrell, Matthew Gallman, Darragh Gannon (and the other members of the Irish Studies Seminar at Queen's University Belfast), Ely Janis, Doug Kanter, Sean M. Kelley, Christine Kinealy, Jason King, Jason Knirck, Breandán Mac Suibhne, Mark McGowan, Timothy McMahon, Gerard Moran, Matthew O'Brien, Timothy O'Neil, Jay Roszman, Paul Townend, John Waters, and Nicholas Wolf.

At the University of Nevada, Las Vegas, I have enjoyed the unstinting support of many friends and colleagues, especially Annette Amdal, Greg Brown, John Curry, Austin Dean, Michael Green, Andy Kirk, Noria Litaker, Elizabeth Nelson, Heather Nepa, Jeff Schauer, David Tanenhaus, Michelle Tusan, Paul Werth, Elspeth Whitney, A. B. Wilkinson, and Shontai Zuniga as well as Deans Andrew Hanson, Chris Heavey, Chris Hudgins, Jennifer Keene, and Marta Meana. I was delighted to publish this book with New York University Press and am indebted to my editor, Clara Platter, her assistant Veronica Knutson, Martin Coleman, several other staff, and the two anonymous readers who put so much thought and effort into helping my book reach its potential.

On the Australian side of the ledger, I received help and encouragement from Perry McIntyre, Mary Ramsay, Dianne Snowden, and Val Noone. Having written my dissertation on the Young Irelanders, I must admit that I was a little starstruck when Richard Davis and his lovely wife Marianne took the time to meet with me in Hobart when I was there doing research. I am also grateful to my cousin Conor MacMahon, who flew all the way from Brisbane to Sydney just to share a huge plate of German sausages and a few pints of lager with me one warm December evening.

During the course of this research project, I visited libraries and archives on three continents and was often humbled by the generosity and patience with which I was treated. In Ireland and Britain, I was assisted by the staffs at the Galway County Library (especially Patria McWalter), the Galway Diocesan Archives (especially Tom Kilgarriff), the James Hardiman Library at the National University of Ireland, Galway (especially Kieran Hoare and Margaret Hughes), the Merseyside Museum and Archives in Liverpool, the UK National Archives in London, the National Archives of Ireland, the National Library of Ireland (especially Nora Thornton and Tom Desmond), the National Famine Museum and Archive in Strokestown Park, County Roscommon (especially Caroilin Callery, Ciarán Reilly, and Martin Fagan), and the Public Record Office of Northern Ireland. In the United States, I received much assistance from the staffs of the Historical Society of Pennsylvania, New York Archdiocesan Archives (especially Fr. Michael Morris and Kate Feighery), New-York Historical Society (especially Ted O'Reilly), New York Municipal Archives, New York Public Library, and the University of Nevada, Las Vegas's Lied Library (especially Priscilla Finley, Yuko Shinozaki, and Richard Zwiercan). Two graduate students, Anna Pilz and Leslie Lewis, also assisted me with some of the scanning and photocopying. In Australia, I received great help from the staffs of the State Library of New South Wales (especially David Berry) and the State Library of Tasmania (especially Jessica Walters).

Funding is always one of the biggest challenges facing any scholar working in the humanities, and I was very grateful to receive financial support from a number of programs and agencies. A summer stipend from the National Endowment for the Humanities allowed me to visit Columbia, Missouri, and the Historical Society of Pennsylvania. A Bernadotte E. Schmitt grant from the American Historical Association covered my travel costs to London, where I worked in the UK National Archives. I received a number of grants from the Department of History, College of Liberal Arts, and University Faculty Travel Committee at the University of Nevada, Las Vegas. But this whole project was really kick-started when the Centre for Irish Studies at the National University of Ireland, Galway and Irish American Cultural Institute kindly granted me a Visiting Research Fellowship in Irish Studies to go to Ireland and start conducting research. My family and I thoroughly enjoyed our time in Galway, and I am grateful to Verena Commins, Louis de Paor, Méabh Ní Fhuartháin, and Samantha Williams for supporting us while we were there.

Finally, and most importantly, I have also been blessed with a supportive family. My mother (Sheena), father (Dermot), evil stepmother

(Áine), brothers (Tadhg, Daithí, Milo), sister (Finn), and many kind in-laws (especially Frank and Claudia Clemente) helped me out while I was working on this project in more ways than they know. On the home front, I am glad to finally be able to show my four children (Fionnuala, Dymphna, Clodagh, and Francis) what it is that I have been mysteriously working on all this time, and to thank my wife, Deirdre, for continuing to be so great at raising kids and writing books.

ESSAY ON SOURCES AND METHODOLOGY

As the notes and bibliography of this book suggest, my efforts to understand how Irish emigrants thought and talked about the voyage process during the Great Famine required working with a wide range of primary and secondary sources on multiple continents. Doing so was a great privilege, but it did raise some epistemological and methodological issues, which are worth reflecting on in some detail. Rather than bog down the introduction with scholarly stipulations and academic asides, I wanted to articulate those reflections in a short essay here.

As an international study of human migration, this book builds on the excellent scholarship of many historians working in various fields. Its first debt is, of course, to recent advances in Irish migration studies. Historians of the Irish abroad have, over the past decade or so, begun to meaningfully employ transnational perspectives to write fantastic books. Their ideas, combined with foundational works on the Irish Famine, have contributed much to the intellectual underpinnings of *The Coffin Ship*. My book also owes a lot to those historians (mostly working outside of Irish Studies) who have embraced maritime history as a worthy focus of historical inquiry. Doing so requires snubbing the long-held terracentrism, which Marcus Rediker has attributed to the normative status of modern nationalism and the corresponding, "unspoken proposition that the seas of the world are unreal spaces, voids between the real places, which are landed and national." Beyond the wealth of scholarship dedicated to labor histories of sailors and pirates, a number of these maritime historians have analyzed the sea journey itself. The most vibrant of these voyage studies focus on the slave trade and the ways in which slaves responded to the psychological impact of the Middle Passage. Although *The Coffin Ship* is influenced by these works, it also offers something new in at least one very important way: while most slaves left behind no written record of their travels, many letters, diaries, and newspaper accounts of the Famine-era Irish survive.[1]

These manuscript and printed primary sources are stored in archives and libraries around the world. Multiple trips to Ireland, for example, revealed workhouse ledgers, landlords' papers, emigrant letters, and convict records, which shed light on every stage of the migrant's journey. The UK National Archives in London contained rich collections of official correspondence, and surgeons' reports from emigrant and convict ships headed to Canada and Australia. While such documents represented the official interpretation of conditions at sea, they could also, when read with sensitivity, reveal the voices and motivations of the migrants themselves. The bulk of emigrant letters came from two sources: Kerby Miller's personal collection, which he began amassing when researching and writing his 1985 instant classic, *Emigrants and Exiles*; and the open-access DIPPAM electronic database, which is hosted by the School of History and Anthropology at Queen's University Belfast. Also useful were the shipping records of the Cope family's line of packet ships, held in the Historical Society of Pennsylvania, and various letters and diaries in the New-York Historical Society and New York Public Library. In Australia, the state libraries of New South Wales and Tasmania yielded invaluable passengers' and surgeons' journals. Taken together, these manuscript collections provided the eyewitness accounts that lie at the heart of this "history from the bottom-up" of the migration experience. The main printed primary sources include the British Parliamentary Papers along with countless pages of microfilmed and digitized newspapers, which were especially helpful as the popular press routinely published letters and accounts submitted by their readers. In sum, this wide range of primary sources simultaneously provided firsthand accounts of the migration process along with a sense of the social and cultural milieus in which the voyages occurred.[2]

Histories of migration have traditionally tended to follow their emigrants to one country or another. This book's commitment to synthesize the experiences of those who headed north, south, east, and west does come with certain intellectual jeopardies. It runs the risk, for example, of overgeneralizing the emigrant experience by flattening the real differences between those headed to North America and those traveling to Australia (not to mention between free emigrants and convicted prisoners). One must also be cognizant of the distinctions within the Irish population itself: between north and south, Catholics and Protestants, men and women, young and old, literate and illiterate, English- and Irish-speaking, rich and poor. These differences were tangible and are acknowledged throughout the book. Unlettered, penniless women were undoubtedly more vulnerable to exploitation and disease than well-heeled, male cabin passengers. The Australian emigrant route was definitely much longer, relatively expensive, and more highly regulated than the transatlantic voyage. Convicts often enjoyed better food, clothing, and medicine than passengers crossing to Canada in steerage. Yet the strength of this book lies not in merely listing these multiple differences but rather in its commitment to simultaneously recognize and go beyond them. It does so by employing an analytical framework, which embraces Kevin Kenny's challenge to write "a migration history that combines the diasporic or transnational with the comparative or cross-national." *The Coffin Ship* conceives of the entire voyage process, in other words, as an embodiment of both the local conditions and transoceanic networks that shaped Irish life at home and abroad in the nineteenth century. It is also informed by Roland Wenzlhuemer's point that international links, such as the sailing ship or wireless telegraph, "do not merely bring their endpoints in contact; they interject themselves as mediators and thereby gain a strong bearing on that which is connected." Employing a theoretical net anchored by this transnational framework allows *The Coffin Ship* to expand the notion of "emigrant community" beyond the familiar, landlocked confines of pubs and dance halls.[3]

At the same time, *The Coffin Ship* is, like all books, limited in scope. It does not pretend, for example, to offer a detailed list of the ships themselves, their tonnage, and their crews. This is an interpretation of Irish migration during the Famine, not a catalogue of its wooden machines. Nor is the book a meticulous examination of the legislation, bureaucracy, and politics of migration during this period. While the governments' roles in emigration frequently appear in individual chapters, the focus is on the opinions and attitudes of the emigrants themselves. I did not purposefully limit my collection of emigrant letters and diaries but soon learned that the surviving records do not constitute a perfectly representative core sample of those who left Ireland during the Great Famine. Illiterate travelers, who composed a sizeable fraction of pre-Famine Ireland's rural population, could not write their own letters, and so their thoughts and opinions regrettably appear only occasionally, usually when another person agreed to write on their behalf. Having gone to a *scoil lán-Ghaeilge* as a child, I was eager to find Irish-language letters from the period but to no avail. One can also safely assume that the poorest of the poor (who were underrepresented among emigrants as a whole) are also underrepresented in the evidence base. Men overwhelmingly predominate as the authors of the diaries and journals, although the surgeons' reports on convict ships offer invaluable, if distorted, windows into the thoughts and words of many Irish prisoners (both male and female). Of the emigrant letters cited in this book, one-third were written by women. In sum, the ways in which socioeconomics, region, gender, age, and linguistic differences correlated with illiteracy in mid-nineteenth-century Ireland present a significant epistemological quandary, which—if impossible to resolve—ought at least be acknowledged.[4]

Figuring out how to communicate what I found in these letters presented unique challenges too. In 1847, a poor farmer named Patt Brenan asked his landlord, Charles Wandesforde, to help finance his emigration to the United States. Brenan had read news reports of the fever sheds on Grosse Île and hoped to go to New York "where I will shun this Dreadful Plaigue that is region in Quebeck." The spelling errors, which mar Brenan's petition, give some sense of the difficulties facing any study based on the letters and diaries of nineteenth-century Irish emigrants. Many of the writers cited in this book were semiliterate people for whom the niceties of fine prose were less important than the message being conveyed. Printer's devils setting type by hand also made mistakes in newspaper columns and parliamentary papers all the time. To maintain editorial consistency and avoid interrupting the voices of otherwise thoughtful writers by inserting "[*sic*]" over and over again, I have quietly corrected all spelling and grammatical errors in the sentences cited and employed American English spelling throughout. For those readers interested in the exact spelling of any quotes cited, the endnotes provide all of the information required to track the documents down. Moreover, the conventions of nineteenth-century writing can sometimes sow confusion. Bureaucrats regularly employed abbreviations (such as "inst." and "ult.") and sometimes capitalized common nouns (such as "Passenger") in ways that can baffle today's reader. Words like "burden" could be spelled "burden" by some and "burthen" by others. In the interests of uniformity, therefore, I have elected to keep all common nouns lowercase while spelling the same words the same way every time. In citing Irish place names, I have used the versions employed by the individual writers themselves. All emphases were present in the original quotes.[5]

Interpreting these emigrant letters and diaries opened up bigger, broader methodological issues, which I wrestled with as well. In his 1987 review of Kerby Miller's Pulitzer-nominated *Emigrants and Exiles*, the late David Fitzpatrick was unimpressed by what he saw as the book's "often bland and unchallenging" synthesis. Miller's book drew on a vast array of primary sources including thousands of Irish emigrant letters, but Fitzpatrick charged that his lack of contextual detail for each and every letter quoted "debases his citations of correspondence from historical evidence to mere illustration; while the brevity of his quotations strips these illustrations of *nuance*." How could readers trust Miller's "generalizations" given that he "omits quantitative support and assessment of the respects in which his sample was unrepresentative of the emigrant population"? Miller would have been better off, Fitzpatrick felt, to submit his vast collection of emigrant letters to content analysis. Having classified his correspondents according to time period, occupation, religion, and so on, Miller could have used "the resultant stratified sample" to properly test the strengths and limits of his thesis. Other historians, however, have concluded that a complete contextual understanding of any set of emigrant letters is more or less "completely unknowable." In *Authors of Their Lives*, which analyzes the personal correspondence of nineteenth-century British migrants to North America, David Gerber notes that because we can never measure how many letters were lost or destroyed over the years, the representativeness of a given letter or collection of letters or archive "must remain virtually unresolvable." But the real problem with content analysis of migrant correspondence, Gerber argues, is that even if it succeeds in establishing certain patterns, "it cannot address a much more difficult task— establishing what those patterns mean." Ironically, when Fitzpatrick published his own book on Irish Australian emigrant correspondence in 1994, he built a rich contextual background for his selections of letters but declined to employ "arithmetical 'content analysis' . . . because of its spurious precision in a study not based on a representative sample."[6]

In light of this debate, and based on my familiarity with the strengths and weaknesses of my sources, I concluded that sustained, quantitative content analysis would not suit *The Coffin Ship*. Although I do have some background information on a small number of the correspondents cited in this book, the majority of the letters lack any contextual data. These emigrant diaries and letters are also so remarkably variegated in their length, tone, and focus that they do not lend themselves to numerical scrutiny and comparison. If every document was of a similar length and intended for a similar audience, it might be possible to quantify the emotional impact of, say, seasickness, by calculating what percentage of emigrants mentioned it in their letters. But Samuel Harvey's description of his 1849 sea voyage is over thirty typescript pages long, while Michael Hogan spent only five sentences describing his journey from Liverpool to New York in 1851. I glean useful qualitative information from these sources, but it would be futile to try to compare and contrast them in a systematic, quantitative way. So, in the end, my methodology was rather straightforward. I set out to write a book that used emigrant letters and diaries to offer a sensible account of how Irish people thought and talked about the process of migration during the Great Famine. I spent two years traveling to three continents, collecting as many Irish eyewitness accounts of the emigrant journey as I could find. I then took another two years to read and take notes on each document, trying to make sense of the entangled themes running through them. Once I figured out that "community" was as an important motif for these writers and their readers, I went back over my notes, looking for ways to harmonize the evidence of emigrants' voices into a sensible chorus of interpretation built around that concept. When writing the paragraphs themselves, I deliberately included long, direct quotes from these documents with a view to amplifying the long-lost voices of the emigrants themselves.

In so doing, I hope to have gone some distance toward treating these letters and diaries for what they are: not dry accounts of facts and figures but emotionally charged material objects employed by far-flung friends and family to repair vulnerable relationships.

ABBREVIATIONS

AANY: Archives of the Archdiocese of New York

ADM: Records of the Admiralty

AJCP: Australian Joint Copying Project

BLN: British Library Newspapers database

CLEC: Colonial Land and Emigration Commission

CO: Colonial Office Papers

CON/LB: Convict Letterbooks, Chief Secretary's Office

CRF: Convict Reference File

CSO/OP: Official Papers Series 2 (1832–1880), Chief Secretary's Office

DIPPAM: *Documenting Ireland: Parliament, People, and Migration* database

FS: Free Settlers' Papers

GCL: Galway County Library

GTCM: Galway Town Commissioners Minutes

HC DEB: House of Commons Debate (Hansard)

HO: Home Office Papers

HSP: Cope Family Papers, Historical Society of Pennsylvania, Philadelphia

IFA: Irish Famine Archive, Grey Nun Records database

JHL: James Hardiman Library, National University of Ireland, Galway

KMC: Kerby A. Miller Collection

MMA: Merseyside Museum and Archives, Liverpool

NAI: National Archives of Ireland, Dublin

NLI: National Library of Ireland, Dublin

NYHS: New-York Historical Society

NYPL: New York Public Library

PLMB: Poor Law Minute Book

PRONI: Public Record Office of Northern Ireland, Belfast

QRO: Quit Rent Office Papers

SL-NSW: State Library of New South Wales, Sydney

SL-TAS: State Library of Tasmania, Hobart

SSJ: Surgeon-Superintendent Journal

TDA: *Times* [London] Digital Archive database

TNA: National Archives of the UK, Kew

TROVE: TROVE Digitised Newspapers database

NOTES

1 Davis, *Kennedys*, 9–11.

2 Thomas McGinity to John McGinity and Mary Crosby, October 24, 1847 (T3539/3, PRONI).

3 Scally, *End*, 218. For a full analysis, using digitized databases, of the origins of the phrase "coffin ships" in the nineteenth-century Irish popular press, see McMahon, "Tracking." In 1848, at the height of the Famine, Irish rebel Thomas D'Arcy McGee decried the emigrant packet ships, which "have become sailing coffins, and carried them to a new world, indeed; not to America, but to eternity!" His speech was printed in the Dublin *Nation* on March 18, 1848. In his biography of McGee, David Wilson claims—without primary source evidence—that McGee's reference to "sailing coffins" had an immediate impact and that "before long the boats that carried famine migrants across the Atlantic became known as 'coffin ships'" (Wilson, *Thomas*, 1:192). In fact, my analysis of digitized databases finds no such correlation between McGee's speech and the popularity of the phrases "sailing coffins" or "coffin ships." Beyond the "coffin ships," a rich vein of interdisciplinary scholarship has explored the ways in which the Famine-era migration has been remembered and memorialized in Irish and Irish diasporic history and literature. Key works include Corporaal and King, *Irish Global*, Corporaal, *Relocated Memories*, Corporaal and Cusack, "Rites of Passage," King, "Remembering Famine," Mark-Fitzgerald, *Commemorating*, McGowan, *Creating Canadian*, and McMahon, "Ports of Recall."

For an example of Irish emigrants being portrayed as bereft of agency, see Robert Scally's otherwise thought-provoking and oft-cited 1983 article on nineteenth-century emigration in which he argues that "in the relationship between the emigrant business and the emigrant . . . the latter usually played an almost entirely passive part" (Scally, "Liverpool Ships," 5).

4 *First Report [Emigrant Ships]* (1854), 76. When referencing British parliamentary papers, I follow the University of Oxford Bodleian Library's directions and cite their handwritten, not printed, page numbers because I am actually citing the volume as as a whole, not the individual paper. The argument that emigrant ships should be at least as safe as convict transports was also elucidated around this time in Maury, *Englishwoman* [pt. II], 136 and Anonymous, "Emigration, Emigrants," 446. This delineation of the sea voyage as a connective thread in the Irish diaspora builds on my previous scholarship, which argued that "by connecting the world-scattered Irish, newspapers provided the intellectual basis for an international imagined community" (McMahon, *Global Dimensions*, 5).

5 For more on the chronology and contexts of the Famine, see Ó Gráda, *Black '47*, 13–46. The rundale system and clachans are discussed in Miller, *Emigrants and Exiles*, 54–60 and Scally, *End*, 9–18. The size of pre-Famine farms is examined in Turner, *After the Famine*, 67–68 and Miller, *Emigrants and Exiles*, 380–381. Issues of land and solidarity are discussed more broadly in O'Neill, *Family and Farm*, Huggins, *Social Conflict*, Casey, *Class and Community*, and Mac Suibhne, *End of Outrage*. I am grateful to Áine Hensey and Nicholas Wolf for double-checking my spelling and formatting of Irish words in this book.

6 For statistics on German and Italian immigration to the United States, see Daniels, *Coming*, 145–148 and 188–190, respectively. The 8.5 million statistic is from Kenny, *American Irish*, 89. The *Galway Mercury* is cited in the *Anglo-Celt* (Cavan), April 24, 1851. Kinealy, *This Great*, 294; Kenny, *American Irish*, 90; Crowley, Smyth, and Murphy, *Atlas*, 494. Calculating exactly how many Irish emigrants went to Australia and New Zealand during this time is very difficult because the vast majority embarked at English ports and were not always identified as Irish (or otherwise) in government returns. On page 63 of *The Irish in Australia*, Patrick O'Farrell claims that 23,000 emigrated to Australia between 1841 and 1850, while Kerby Miller's *Emigrants and Exiles* (569) adds that 53,801 moved to Australia and New Zealand between 1851 and 1855. Phillips and Hearn state that the number of assisted emigrants to New Zealand "fell to a trickle" in the mid-1840s (Phillips and Hearn, *Settlers*, 32). These general statistics on Irish Famine-era migration accord with Roger Daniels's estimates in *Coming to America*, 135. The figures on convicts (3,726 men and 2,560 women) are from Bateson, *Convict Ships*, 393–395. For the latest historical survey of the Irish in Australia, see Malcolm and Hall, *New History*.

7 The best data on annual numbers of Irish migrants are scattered across various British Parliamentary Papers: *Sixth General Report* (1846), 46–47 and *Seventh General Report* (1847), 174 (for the year 1845); *Seventh General Report* (1847), 170–171, 174 (for the year 1846); *Thirteenth General Report* (1852–1853), 74 (for the years 1847 to 1850 inclusive); *Seventeenth General Report* (1857, Session 2), 42 (for the years 1851 to 1855 inclusive). I calculated the 1845–1846 data on total Irish migrants by using the CLEC's own formula: "nine-tenths of those who have sailed from Liverpool, and one-third of those who sailed from the Clyde [Glasgow] to North America, in addition to all who have sailed from Irish ports" plus those who headed to Australia (*Thirteenth General Report* [1852–1853], 74). As hard data on Australia-bound Irish emigrants for 1845 and 1846 are difficult to find, I used a round estimate of 500 per year for those years only, based on *Seventh General Report* (1847), 174 and the fact that assisted emigration to Australia was suspended during those years (see Madgwick, *Immigration*, 189–191).

Employing these numbers and formulas, the present study's estimates (and Figure 1.1's data points) for annual emigration (to the United States, British North America, Australia, and New Zealand only) are 77,965 (1845), 108,115 (1846), 219,885 (1847), 181,316 (1848), 218,842 (1849), 213,649 (1850), 254,537 (1851), 224,997 (1852), 192,609 (1853), 150,209 (1854), 78,854 (1855). To this total of 1,920,978 must be added the approximately 300,000 who moved to mainland Britain along with at least 4,000 who went farther afield including the 1,400 to South Africa between 1846 and 1851 (see McCracken, "Odd Man," 254) and the 2,298 who sailed to "other overseas" destinations between 1851 and 1855 (see Miller, *Emigrants and Exiles*, 569). Some undoubtedly went to Asia and South America (especially Argentina) too, but their numbers were very small in these particular years and cannot be accurately calculated. In total, these statistics suggest that at least 2.2 million Irish emigrated abroad between 1845 and 1855, which is slightly higher than the 2.1 million that historians typically cite.

8 This overview of the emigration process between 1845 and 1855 is largely based on MacDonagh, *Pattern* and Spray, "Irish Famine." Although steamships had been ferrying passengers across the Irish Sea since the 1820s, they did not start carrying emigrants to North America and Australia until the 1860s and 1880s, respectively.

9 For useful overviews of these journeys, see Scally, *End*, 184–216 (for the Irish Sea), Cohn, *Mass Migration*, 125–154 (for the Atlantic Ocean), and Haines, *Life and Death*, 123–229 (for the trip to Australia). The "seventy-five percent" estimate is based on the data cited in note 7 (above). The "sickest man in creation" quote is from James J. Mitchell journal, 1853 (Misc. Mss. Mitchell, James J., NYHS).

10 There were 12 pennies in a shilling and twenty shillings in a pound. They were abbreviated as "d.," "s.," and "£," respectively, although a denomination such as £3 5s. 2d. could also be expressed as £3/5/2. Under the conacre system, an agricultural laborer was paid not in cash wages but in plots of fertilized land on which to grow his family's potatoes for the year (Ó Gráda, *Black '47*, 21). By the eve of the Famine, competition for conacre plots was so high that workers were also paying rents of, on average, £10 a year. Kerby Miller has called such arrangements "virtually a speculation in subsistence" (Miller, *Emigrants and Exiles*, 53). In *Black '47*, 108, Cormac Ó Gráda cites a newspaper account from 1847 of a widow who raised the fares for herself and her six children to emigrate by selling her interest in their ten-acre farm (for £15) along with a mare (£5), a cow (£4), a cart and harrow (10 s.), and various "other things." The "dead weights" quote is from Norton, "On Landlord-Assisted," 28. For more on poor law unions' assistance for emigration during the Famine, see Moran, *Sending Out*, 123–158.

11 Ritchie and Orr, *Wayfaring Strangers*, 92–93; Hansen, *Atlantic Migration*, 178–183. For contemporary mentions of the relationship between Irish emigration and the corn, timber, and cotton trades, see *Report [Colonization from Ireland]* (1847), 136, 190, 499; Bateson, *Convict Ships*, 83.

12 For more on the layouts and parts of sailing ships, see Dear and Kemp, *Oxford Companion*. The rule that every ship must have enough lifeboats and lifejackets for every crewmember and passenger did not become international law until after the *Titanic* sank in 1912 (see *Merchant Shipping*).

13 Jefferson, *Clipper Ships*, 5; Coleman, *Going to America*, 89–90; Haines, *Life and Death*, 25; Bateson, *Convict Ships*, 89.

14 *First Report [Emigrant Ships]* (1854), 17. The statistic on 1849 passengers entering New York is from Coleman, *Going to America*, 88. *First Report [Emigrant
Ships]* (1854), 10. For more on the packet ship systems, see Cohn, *Mass Migration*,
62–63 and Albion, *Square-Riggers*, 17–48, 77–105. The pioneering transatlantic
packet company was the Black Ball line, founded in New York in 1818. By the
mid-nineteenth century, its main competitors were the Collins, Cunard, and
Inman lines.

15 The description of steerage as a "high-density urban environment" is in Hassam, *No Privacy*, xviii. By contrast, Hassam argues, life for first-class passengers
"was closely modeled on a polite social gathering at an English country house,
protected and predictable" (xvii). I am not the first historian to suggest that the
sea voyage impacted social relations in the host communities. In the introduction
to his edited volume, *Letters from Irish Australia, 1825–1929*, Patrick O'Farrell believed that the admixture of various peoples at sea "to some extent dissolved their
old social relationships and disposed them to accept more readily the egalitarian
and tolerant Australian environment: the ship was, in some important ways, the
colony in microcosm" (O'Farrell, *Letters*, 2). In his study of seventeenth-century
colonists in New England, David Cressy suggested that the journey across the Atlantic "was a testing experience that set the travelers apart from their landbound
contemporaries and successors" (Cressy, *Coming Over*, ix), while, more recently,
Stephen Berry has argued that the sea voyage constituted "a formative stage" in
the development of collective identification among eighteenth-century Protestants
emigrants en route to North America (Berry, *A Path*, 6). It should be noted that
chapter 5 of this book does not trace the migrants much beyond their first few
days after arrival. For an excellent analysis of the ways in which Famine-era Irish
immigrants employed networks of family, friends, and neighbors to establish financial security in the long term, see Anbinder, Ó Gráda, and Wegge, "Networks
and Opportunities."

16 Ó Gráda, "Next World," esp. 331–336 and *Black '47*, 106–107 and (with Kevin H.
O'Rourke) "Migration"; *Nation* (Dublin), August 14, 1847; "Saranak's 5th Voyage,"
1846, ticket #1432 (Series 1a, Box 62A, HSP). When COVID-19 broke out in March
2020, the Historical Society of Pennsylvania temporarily closed its doors. This prohibited me from returning there to try to track down the names of those anonymous
benefactors who wrote messages on the backs of prepaid tickets on the Cope family
packet line.

1. PREPARATION

1 Hannah Lynch to John Curtis, April 21, 1847 (Balch Institute, Philadelphia [KMC]).
2 The sources for data on total Irish migration between 1845 and 1855 can be found in
note 7 of the introduction (above).
3 James Purcell to Bridget Brennan, August 10, 1846 (35,533/1, NLI); C. H. B. C. S.
Wandesforde, [Reply to questionnaire on effects of emigration], June 14, 1847
(35,533/7, NLI).

4 *Limerick Reporter*, March 30, 1847; *Freeman's Journal and Catholic Register* (New York), January 2, 1847; April 3, 1847; June 2, 1849; Chisholm's letter was originally published in the Sydney *Morning Chronicle* on April 8, 1846 (TROVE) and reprinted in the *Limerick Reporter* on November 3, 1846; *Freeman's Journal* (Sydney), February 12, 1852; *Times* (London), March 23, 1853 (TDA).

5 *Papers [North America]* (1847), 74–75; Affy Griffin to Daniel Griffin, March 10, 1851 (Lewis Neale Whittle papers, Georgia State Archives [KMC]); Mrs. Nolan to Patrick Nolan, October 8, 1850 (T2054, PRONI [KMC]).

6 Affy Griffin to Daniel Griffin, March 10, 1851 (Lewis Neale Whittle papers, Georgia State Archives [KMC]); Hannah Lynch to John Curtis, April 21, 1847 (Balch Institute, Philadelphia [KMC]).

7 Hannah Lynch to John Curtis, April 21, 1847 (Balch Institute, Philadelphia [KMC]); Margaret Masterson to Michael Masterson, October 4, 1850 (Masterson family letters, Kentucky Historical Society [KMC]); "Refunded Passenger Tickets, 1852," ticket #7043 (Series 1b, Box 290, HSP); "Saranak's 11th Voyage," 1847–1848, ticket #2841 (Series 1a, Box 65, HSP).

8 "Saranak's 17th Voyage," 1850, ticket #4530 (Series 1a, Box 68, HSP); "Saranak's 25th Voyage," 1852, ticket #7712 (Series 1a, Box 280, HSP); Mary Duggan to her sister, April 8, 1848 (T2946, PRONI [KMC]).

9 John O'Connor to Judy O'Connor, February 16, 1848 (published in Tuke, *Visit*, 48); "Refunded Passenger Tickets, 1848–1851," ticket #4145 (Series 1b, Box 290, HSP); Bessie Masterson McManus to Michael Masterson, December 24, 1850 (Masterson family letters, Kentucky Historical Society [KMC]).

10 "Saranak's 12th Voyage," 1848, ticket #3091 (Series 1a, Box 65, HSP); Daniel Rountree to Mrs. M. Butler, May 5, 1851 (from Prof. Emeritus Arnold Schrier, University of Cincinnati [KMC]); "Saranak's 11th Voyage," 1847–1848, ticket #2833 (Series 1a, Box 65, HSP).

11 "Saranak's 21st Voyage," 1851, ticket #6201 (Series 1a, Box 69, HSP); John, Dominick, and Mary Fleming to Sarah Humphreys [née Fleming], December 26, 1845 (Department of Manuscripts and University Archives, Cornell University [KMC]); "Saranak's 8th Voyage," 1847, ticket #1999 (Series 1a, Box 63, HSP).

12 Patrick Grant to his mother and siblings, November 3, 1851 (from Prof. Emeritus Arnold Schrier, University of Cincinnati [KMC]); "Saranak's 12th Voyage," 1848, ticket #2951 (Series 1a, Box 65, HSP); Judith Phelan to Teresa Lawlor, May 23, 1849 (Teresa Lawlor letters, California Historical Society, San Francisco [KMC]); James and Elisa Taylor to John Carr, June 6, 1847 (from Professor E. R. R. Green, Belfast [KMC]).

13 James Walsh to Lord Monteagle, September 24, 1851 (13,400/3, NLI). For more on the Monteagle family and assisted emigration, see O'Mahony and Thompson, *Poverty to Promise*. "Refunded Passenger Tickets, 1853," ticket #7555 (Series 1b, Box 290, HSP); James Purcell to Bridget Brennan, August 10, 1846 (35,533/1, NLI); examples of such promissory notes can be found in the Monteagle Papers (13,400/3, NLI); Margaret Kelly to Lady Monteagle, May 1, 1853 (13,400/3, NLI).

14 This biographical sketch of Caroline Chisholm derives from Iltis, "Chisholm, Caroline." Chisholm's best-known pamphlets during this period were *Emigration and Transportation* and *Comfort for the Poor!* See also Walker, *Saviour*. Caroline Chisholm to Earl Grey, January 25, 1847 (Ac 19/1, SL-NSW). Earl Grey served as colonial secretary from July 1846 until February 1852. His immediate successors were John Somerset Pakington (1852), Henry Pelham-Clinton (1852–1854), and George Grey (1854–1855). Caroline Chisholm to T. N. Redington, July 2, 1847 (FS/1847/3, NAI).

15 Patrick Danaher to Lord Monteagle, February 2, 1853 (13,400/3, NLI).

16 Archibald Cunninghame to Lord Monteagle, November 5, 1847 (13,397/2, NLI). These statistics on landlord and workhouse-assisted emigration derive from Hirota, *Expelling*, 30, 37, Miller, *Emigrants and Exiles*, 296, Moran, *Sending Out*, 36, Reilly, "Aspects," 174, and Norton, "On Landlord-Assisted," 39–40. The 22,478 statistic derives from Haines, *Emigration*, 143. Fitzpatrick, "Emigration," 591–596, remains a useful overview of landlord-assisted emigration during this period. Other important secondary sources on the subject include Norton, *Landlords, Tenants*; Moran, *Sending Out*; Kinealy, *This Great*, 309–315. Excellent studies of particular schemes include Anbinder, "Lord Palmerston" and "From Famine"; Lyne, "William Steuart"; Reilly, *Strokestown*.

17 Trench, *Realities*, 123–125; Lyne, "William Steuart," 87–88; Kinealy, *This Great*, 314–315.

18 For details on assisted emigration from these Crown Estates, 1847–1852, see Ellis, *Emigrants*. The leading studies of the Ballykilcline emigration program are Scally, *End* and Dunn, *Ballykilcline Rising*. John Burke to Thomas Coury Knox, February 8, 1848 (QRO/4/3/6/29, NAI); Richard Griffith to Charles Gore, April 11, 1849 (QRO/4/3/1/158, NAI).

19 For more on "Ulster Custom," see Boyce, *Nineteenth-Century*, 111–112. Reilly, "Aspects," 175; Norton, "On Landlord-Assisted," 28.

20 This estimate of almost 600,000 persons evicted can be found in O'Neill, "Famine Evictions," 48. O'Neill's chapter offers a detailed analysis of both the statistics on (and historiography of) Famine-era evictions in Ireland. Lynch, *Mass Evictions*, 66. For more on the Strokestown emigrants, see Reilly, *Strokestown*, 65–77. Papers [North America, and to the Australian Colonies] (1847–1848), 27. Dr. Collins's refutation of the claims of Hugh Reilly (and others) is reprinted on pages 30–31.

21 Trench, *Realities*, 172–173. Although useful as an eyewitness account of assisted emigration during the Famine, Trench's memoirs need to be treated with some skepticism, as suggested in Lyne, "William Steuart." Miller, *Emigrants and Exiles*, 303; Trench, *Realities*, 125; *Limerick Reporter*, August 17, 1852.

22 The Wandesforde emigration statistics can be found in a document entitled "Emigration from Castlecomer Estate" (35,512/8, NLI).

23 C. H. B. C. S. Wandesforde, [Reply to questionnaire on effects of emigration], June 14, 1847 (35,533/7, NLI); James Miley to Kildare Dobbs, August 4, 1845 (35,533/2, NLI); Roderick Miley to Kildare Dobbs, November 14, 1850 (35,533/2, NLI); James Miley to Kildare Dobbs, October 18, 1854 (35,533/2, NLI).

24 James Kelly to Lord Wandesforde, June 15, 1847 (35,526/6, NLI); Thomas Cloase to Lord Wandesforde, January 11, 1847 (35,526/1, NLI); Denis Bowe to Lord Wandesforde, March 29, 1847 (35,526/3, NLI); Biddy Dunleary to Lord Wandesforde, n.d. [1847] (35,526/8, NLI).

25 John Curry to Lady Wandesforde, March 29, 1847 (35,526/3, NLI); James Foley to Lady Wandesforde, March 22, 1847 (35,526/3, NLI); Bryan McDonald to Lady Wandesforde, April 3, 1847 (35,526/5, NLI); Widow Brenan to Lord Wandesforde, March 7, 1847 (35,526/3, NLI).

26 Daniel Bryan to Lord Wandesforde, March 26, 1847 (35,526/4, NLI); Widow Seymour to Lord Wandesforde, March 16, 1847 (35,526/3, NLI); Daniel Flinne to Lord Wandesforde, March 22, 1847 (35,526/3, NLI).

27 James Riley to Lord Wandesforde, March 25, 1847 (35,526/3, NLI); Mary Wallace to Lord Wandesforde, January 28, 1847 (35,526/1, NLI); Margaret Coogan to Lord Wandesforde, March 11, 1847 (35,526/4, NLI). For more on the Wandesforde estate's history, see "Collection List No. 52" in the Prior-Wandesforde Papers, NLI; Nolan, *Fassadinin*; Dunne, "'Humour the People.'" Michael Brenan to Lord Wandesforde, April 13, 1847 (35,526/5, NLI).

28 Donnelly, *Great Irish*, 144; Billy Cantwell to Lord Wandesforde, April 14, 1847 (35,526/5, NLI).

29 *Papers [North America]* (1847), 28–29; Archibald Cunninghame to Lord Monteagle, November 5, 1847 (13,397/2, NLI).

30 T. F. Elliot to James Stephen, January 28, 1847 (CO 384/79, TNA); Kinealy, *This Great*, 305.

31 The "systematic colonization" quote derives from the initial notice of the Godley scheme, which was published in the *Galway Vindicator* on April 10, 1847. The full memorial was reprinted in other newspapers including the *Anglo-Celt* (Cavan), April 16 and 23, 1847. For more on the Godley and Robinson schemes, see Moran, *Sending Out*, 70–80 and 21–28 respectively. Moran, *Sending Out*, 222; *Anglo-Celt* (Cavan), April 23, 1847.

32 *Nation* (Dublin), April 17, 1847 [reprinted in *Boston Pilot*, May 29, 1847]. Maginn's letter enjoyed international attention, being published in *Nation* (Dublin), April 17, 1847, and reprinted in whole in the *Boston Pilot*, May 15, 1847, and in part in the *South Australian Register* (Adelaide), October 16, 1847 (TROVE). *Times* (London), April 6, 1847 (TDA); *Anglo-Celt* (Cavan), April 9, 1847; *South Australian Register* (Adelaide), August 11, 1847 (TROVE).

33 The "thief-colony" quote is cited in Hughes, *Fatal Shore*, 2. The rules and regulations for CLEC assistance were often publicized in handbills and posters, but the popular press published important information too. For an example, see the *Galway Vindicator*, September 8, 1847. For broader overviews of nineteenth-century assisted emigration to Australia, see Haines, "Indigent Misfits," Haines, *Emigration*, and Reid, *Farewell*. Patt Culhane to Lady Monteagle, January 5, 1855 (13,400/3, NLI).

34 This exchange of letters between Stephen Walcott and James Clements can be found in CO 386/42, TNA. For more on the CLEC and assisted emigration, see Richards,

"How Did." Stephen Walcott served as secretary of the CLEC from its foundation in 1840 until 1860.

35 McDonald and Richards, "Workers," 6–11; Haines, "Indigent Misfits," 228, 239. For a useful explanation of the "bounty system" (and the temporary cessation of government-assisted emigration to Australia between 1843 and 1847), see Haines, *Emigration*, 273. Chisholm publicized the government's decision in an open letter to the *Morning Chronicle* (Sydney), April 8, 1846 (TROVE), which was republished in the *Limerick Reporter*, November 3, 1846. For more on the reunion of Irish emigrant and convict families in Australia, see Haines, *Emigration*, 145–148, Madgwick, *Immigration*, 191–192, and McIntyre, *Free Passage*. Stephen Walcott to E. D. Thomson, August 14, 1847 (CO 386/122, TNA).

36 This overview of the poor laws and emigration is based on Moran, *Sending Out*, 123–158, and Kinealy, *This Great*, 309–315. A local poor law officer explained the difference in cost between helping an inmate emigrate versus keeping them in the workhouse in the *Anglo-Celt* (Cavan), March 10, 1848. Kinealy, *This Great*, 310; meeting for week ending August 9, 1851 (Gort PLMB, G01/12/11, GCL); meeting for week ending October 11, 1851 (Mountbellew PLMB [September 12, 1851, to March 19, 1852], GCL); meeting for week ending August 27, 1853 (Galway PLMB [July 30, 1853, to January 7, 1854], GCL).

37 Meetings for weeks ending July 15, August 19, and October 28, 1854 (Galway PLMB [January 14, 1854, to August 5, 1854] and [August 19, 1854, to February 3, 1855], GCL).

38 The "female orphan" statistics are cited in Haines, *Emigration*, 149. For more on the "female orphan" scheme, see McClaughlin, *Barefoot and Pregnant?*, Moran, *Sending Out*, 129–132, Kinealy, *This Great*, 316–327, Madgwick, *Immigration*, 207–213, and Haines, *Emigration*, 148–158. The Australian Monument to the Great Irish Famine (1845–1852), on Macquarie Street in Sydney, Australia, was inspired by the story of the "female orphan" scheme. Its accompanying website contains thousands of details on the women themselves and can be found at www.irishfaminememorial. org. *Limerick Reporter*, September 1, 1848; meetings for weeks ending September 23 and October 21, 1848, and November 3, 1849 (Galway PLMB [January 19, 1848, to November 3, 1848] and [August 31, 1849, to March 29, 1850], GCL).

39 SSJ, *Waverley* (AJCP PRO 3212, SL-TAS); T. N. Redington to Lieutenant Governor of Van Diemen's Land, July 16, 1847 (CON/LB/1, NAI). For more on Irish convict transportation to Australia, see Carroll-Burke, *Colonial Discipline*; Costello, *Botany Bay*; Cowley, *Drift*; Davis, "Not So Bad"; Kavanagh and Snowden, *Van Diemen's Women*; McMahon, *Convicts*; McMahon, *Floating Prisons*; Reece, *Irish Convict*; Shaw, *Convicts*; Williams, *Ordered*.

40 Although it occurred very rarely, children did occasionally travel with their transported fathers. For an Irish example from August 1845, see SSJ, *Samuel Boddington* (AJCP PRO 3209, SL-TAS). The nine voyages for which statistics survive are the *Tasmania [2]*, *Arabian*, *Waverley*, *John Calvin [2]*, *Maria*, *Earl Grey [4]*, *Duke of Cornwall*, *Blackfriar*, and *Midlothian*. The surgeon-superintendent journals for these

journeys can all be found in the AJCP PRO collection at the SL-TAS under the call numbers 3211, 3188, 3212, 3199, 3203, 3193, 3192, 3189, M711, respectively. Only further research will determine whether or not the proportion of non-prisoners traveling on convict transports was abnormally high during the Famine years. For statistics from the Chief Secretary's Office on the high ratio of children to female convicts during the first six months of 1845, see Richard Pennefather to Hon. H. Sutton, December 11, 1845 (CON/LB/1, NAI). SSJ, *Arabian* (AJCP PRO 3188, SL-TAS); SSJ, *John Calvin [2]* (AJCP PRO 3199, SL-TAS); SSJ, *Blackfriar* (AJCP PRO 3189, SL-TAS); SSJ, *Midlothian* (AJCP PRO M 711, SL-TAS). The number in square brackets after a given ship's name refers to the number of journeys it had made as a convict vessel. The name *Tasmania [2]*, in other words, means that this was the *Tasmania*'s second voyage as a convict transport.

41 For more on matrons, see Haines, *Doctors*, 119–121 and *Emigration*, 190–195. T. N. Redington to Archbishop Daniel Murray, January 5, 1848 (CON/LB/1, NAI); T. N. Redington to Governor of the Convict Depot, Grangegorman, January 19, 1848 (CON/LB/1, NAI); T. N. Redington to Governor of the Convict Depot, Grangegorman, January 19, 1848 (CON/LB/1, NAI); Register of Convicts on Convict Ships, 1851–1853 (NAI); T. N. Redington to Lieutenant Governor of Van Diemen's Land, June 24, 1849 (CON/LB/1, NAI); T. N. Redington to Master Commanding the Transport *John Calvin*, January 21, 1848 (CON/LB/1, NAI); T. N. Redington to Lieutenant Governor of Van Diemen's Land, January 21, 1848 (CON/LB/1, NAI); T. N. Redington to Admiralty Agent, March 27, 1849 (CON/LB/1, NAI); Register of Convicts on Convict Ships, 1851–1853 (NAI).

42 SSJ, *Samuel Boddington* (AJCP PRO 3209, SL-TAS); SSJ, *Lord Auckland [2]* (AJCP PRO 3201, SL-TAS); SSJ, *Tory [2]* (AJCP PRO 3211, SL-TAS); SSJ, *Pestonjee Bomanjee [3]* (AJCP PRO 3207, SL-TAS); SSJ, *Blenheim II [1]* (AJCP PRO 3190, SL-TAS); SSJ, *Rodney* (AJCP PRO 3208, SL-TAS); Davis, "Not So Bad," 19; T. N. Redington to Rev. Robert Downing, September 16, 1848 (CON/LB/1, NAI); T. N. Redington to Governor of the Smithfield Convict Depot, n.d. [1848] (CON/LB/1, NAI).

43 This overview of the convict family reunion scheme is based on McIntyre, *Free Passage*. See also Reid, "That Famine." McIntyre, *Free Passage*, 115; William Meredyth Somerville to T. N. Redington, March 4, 1847 (CSO/OP/1847/100, NAI).

44 Archibald McIntyre to Edmond Carr, March 9, 1847 and J. P. Carr to T. N. Redington, July 23, 1847 (FS/1847/3, NAI).

45 Bryan Conlon to Lord Lieutenant of Ireland, April 2, 1850 (FS/1850/2, NAI); "Enquiry into certain irregularities" (Tasmanian Papers 112–113 MAV FM 4/8518, SL-NSW); Con McMahon to Lord Lieutenant of Ireland, n.d. [1850] (FS/1850/1, NAI); T. N. Redington to Con McMahon, June 28, 1850 (FS/1850/1, NAI).

46 Mary and Johanna Kelleher petition, September 3, 1848 (CRF/1848/K39, NAI); Mary Jane Campbell petition, July 1850 (CRF/1850/C68, NAI).

47 Davis, "Not So Bad," 43, 36, 44, 45; meeting for week ending June 7, 1851 (Galway PLMB [December 7, 1850, to July 4, 1851], GCL); *Nation* (Dublin), November 6, 1847.

48 New directions in the historiography of convict transportation consider the Aboriginal Australian experience (Harman, *Aboriginal Convicts*), labor practices (Roberts, "Knotted Hands"), and the system's development beyond Australia (Anderson, *Global History*; Morgan and Rushton, *Banishment*; Ziegler, *Harlots*). Genealogy remains very popular too (Hawkings, *Bound*). The "hard sentence" quote is cited in Hughes, *Fatal Shore*, 129.

49 Mary Hayes to Lord Lieutenant of Ireland, April 29, 1852 (FS/1852/3, NAI).

50 *Third Report* (1849), 619.

2. EMBARKATION

1 James J. Mitchell journal, 1853 (Misc. Mss. Mitchell, James J., NYHS).

2 "Saranak's 15th Voyage," 1849, ticket #4090 (Series 1a, Box 67, HSP).

3 "Saranak's 5th Voyage," 1846, tickets #1441, #1412, #1515 (Series 1a, Box 62A, HSP).

4 *Nation* (Dublin), March 7, 1846.

5 Daniel Rowntree to Mrs. M. Butler, May 5, 1851 (from Prof. Emeritus Arnold Schrier, University of Cincinnati [KMC]); "Saranak's 24th Voyage," 1851, 1852, ticket #7189 (Series 1a, Box 279, HSP); Margaret McCarthy to Alexander McCarthy, September 22, 1850 (published in Ellis, *Emigrants*, 66); John, Dominick, and Mary Fleming to Sarah Humphreys [née Fleming], December 26, 1845 (Department of Manuscripts and University Archives, Cornell University [KMC]); *Boston Pilot*, August 15, 1846.

6 "Saranak's 21st Voyage," 1851, ticket #6348 (Series 1a, Box 69, HSP); "Saranak's 26th Voyage," 1853, ticket #8050 (Series 1a, Box 280, HSP); "Saranak's 11th Voyage," 1847–1848, tickets #2809, #2769 (Series 1a, Box 65, HSP); Nettle, *Practical Guide*, 9.

7 "Saranak's 26th Voyage," 1853, ticket #8109 (Series 1a, Box 280, HSP); "Refunded Passenger Tickets, 1848–1851," tickets #1455, #5891 (Series 1b, Box 290, HSP); "Saranak's 14th Voyage," 1849, ticket #3493 (Series 1a, Box 66, HSP).

8 MacDonagh, *Pattern* offers a book-length of analysis of the UK Passenger Acts and their enforcement during the first six decades of the nineteenth century. For a handy, brief overview of the major changes to the UK and US Passenger Acts in the nineteenth century, see Coleman, *Going to America*, 314–321. "Refunded Passenger Tickets, 1851," ticket #6502 (Series 1b, Box 290, HSP); "Saranak's 20th Voyage," 1851, ticket #5755 (Series 1a, Box 69, HSP); "Saranak's 21st Voyage," 1851, ticket #5734 (Series 1a, Box 69, HSP); "Saranak's 8th Voyage," 1847, ticket #1978 (Series 1a, Box 63, HSP); "Saranak's 11th Voyage," 1847–1848, ticket #2841 (Series 1a, Box 65, HSP); "Saranak's 20th Voyage," 1851, ticket #5884 (Series 1a, Box 69, HSP).

9 "Regulations for the Selection of Emigrants and Conditions on Which Passages Are Granted," 1854 (45,247/5, NLI); O'Hanlon, *Irish Emigrant's*, 25–27. O'Hanlon's guide was published in Boston by Patrick Donahoe, who also owned and edited the *Boston Pilot*. Donahoe reprinted the guide in weekly installments in the *Boston Pilot* between April 12 and June 14, 1851.

10 T. N. Redington to Sir Denis Marchant, January 15, 1848 (CON/LB/1, NAI); meeting for week ending November 20, 1852 (Mountbellew PLMB [November 5, 1852, to

May 6, 1853], GCL); T. N. Redington to High Sheriff (County Waterford), September 17, 1850 (CON/LB/1, NAI).

11 O'Hanlon, *Irish Emigrant's*, 27; "Saranak's 10th Voyage," 1847, 1848, ticket #2557 (Series 1a, Box 64, HSP); "Saranak's 33rd Voyage," 1855, ticket #8050 (Series 1a, Box 281, HSP); "Refunded Passenger Tickets, 1848–1851," ticket #5181 (Series 1b, Box 290, HSP); James Purcell to Bridget Brennan, August 10, 1846 (35,533/1, NLI); *Limerick Reporter*, September 21, 1852. For other favorable comments on pauper emigrants' outfits, see *Galway Vindicator*, May 31, 1848; *Anglo-Celt* (Cavan), December 8, 1848; *Times* (London), March 22, 1849 (TDA); *Nation* (Dublin), February 9, 1850. For an excerpt of clothing advice from *Sidney's Emigrant's Journal* (London) reprinted in an Irish newspaper, see the *Galway Vindicator*, March 31, 1849.

12 James J. Mitchell journal, 1853 (Misc. Mss. Mitchell, James J., NYHS).

13 This overview of nineteenth-century Irish transportation is based on Williams, *Creating*, 7–20. Other useful works on the subject include Nowlan, *Travel*, O'Connor, *Ironing*, and Hoppen, *Ireland*. *Galway Vindicator*, May 4, 1853; the *Clonmel Chronicle* is cited in *Limerick Reporter*, April 3, 1849.

14 Williams, *Creating*, 10; Bianconi's 1848 speech is cited in *Limerick Reporter*, May 25, 1852; *Anglo-Celt* (Cavan), January 26, 1849; *Limerick Reporter*, April 5, 1853; *Anglo-Celt* (Cavan), April 6, 1849; *Limerick Reporter*, April 3, 1849; *Anglo-Celt* (Cavan), January 15, 1852. There were four farthings in one penny, so a "penny farthing" fare meant 1.25 pence (and should not be confused with the first-generation bicycle of the same name, which was invented decades later).

15 Ó Gráda, "Industry," 149–150; Comerford, "Ireland," 374–375. For more on the development of the Irish railway system, see O'Connor, *Ironing*. For information on getting from Limerick to Dublin, see *Nation* (Dublin), August 22, 1846; the Tipperary editor is cited in *Limerick Reporter*, April 20, 1849; *Limerick Reporter*, May 6, 1853; *Galway Vindicator*, August 31, 1853.

16 Williams, *Creating*, 15–17; *Anglo-Celt* (Cavan), July 24, 1851; the Dublin newspapers are cited in *Limerick Reporter*, March 30, 1847.

17 *Second Report [Colonization from Ireland]* (1847–1848), 314; the *Mayo Telegraph* is cited in *Limerick Reporter*, April 4, 1851 and *Anglo-Celt* (Cavan), April 10, 1851; *Galway Vindicator*, August 25, 1847; Galway Town Commissioners meeting on Thursday, November 4, 1847 (GTCM, LA 2/2, JHL).

18 Harris, *Nearest Place*, 189; Scally, *End*, 172.

19 T. N. Redington to Lieutenant General Commanding, January 4, 1848 (CON/LB/1, NAI); *Limerick Reporter*, September 26, 1848; the *Evening Freeman* (Dublin) is cited in *Limerick Reporter*, April 6, 1849; Theobald McKenna to Inspector General, April 10, 1848 (CON/LB/1, NAI).

20 *Limerick Reporter*, June 6, 1854. On August 18, 1854, the same newspaper printed a letter from A. C. Buchanan, the chief emigration officer at Quebec, to the guardians of the Limerick poor law union, stating that the *Theron's* passengers "all were in good health" upon arrival. Meeting for week ending June 24, 1854 (Gort PLMB, G01/12/17, GCL).

21 *Galway Vindicator*, June 18, 1853; February 2, 1853; *Hull Advertiser* cited in *Nation* (Dublin), October 2, 1852 and *Limerick Reporter*, October 12, 1852; Trench, *Realities*, 126.

22 The *Waterford Chronicle* is cited in *Galway Vindicator*, April 11, 1846; *Freeman's Journal* (Sydney), July 23, 1853; the *Waterford Chronicle* is cited in *Anglo-Celt* (Cavan), October 31, 1850. For more on Daniel O'Connell's "monster meetings" of 1843, see Owens, "Nationalism" and McMahon, "International Celebrities," 150–153.

23 Meetings for weeks ending January 1, 1853, and July 17, 1852 (Mountbellew PLMB [November 5, 1852, to May 6, 1853] and [March 26, 1852, to October 23, 1852], GCL). The Mountbellew poor law union was formally established in February 1850, but its workhouse did not open its doors until May 1852.

24 The *Waterford Chronicle* is cited in *Limerick Reporter*, April 20, 1847; *Galway Vindicator*, November 15, 1848 [reprinted in *Limerick Reporter*, November 21, 1848]; T. F. Elliot to James Stephen, June 9, 1847 (CO 384/79, TNA); *Nation* (Dublin), April 11, 1846.

25 The *Freeman's Journal* (Dublin) is cited in *Nation* (Dublin), October 13, 1849, and see also *Limerick Reporter* October 16, 1849; *Nation* (Dublin), April 5, 1851; the *Freeman's Journal* (Dublin) is cited in *Limerick Reporter*, April 18, 1851; *Nation* (Dublin), August 16, 1851.

26 *Anglo-Celt* (Cavan), April 9, 1847; *Limerick Reporter*, June 6, 1854; the *Cork Examiner* is cited in *Limerick Reporter* May 9, 1851.

27 *Galway Vindicator*, March 20, 1847 [reprinted in *Limerick Reporter*, March 23, 1847]; meeting for week ending May 6, 1854 (Galway PLMB [January 14, 1854, to August 5, 1854], GCL).

28 T. N. Redington to Lieutenant Governor of Van Diemen's Land, September 18, 1848 (CON/LB/1, NAI); Major Mylers to Colonel Beresford, May 1, 1849 (CSO/OP/1849/38, NAI). For more on the chronology of Irish convict transportation in the 1840s, and on overcrowding on Spike Island, see Davis, "Not So Bad," 9–10, 17–18.

29 Meetings for weeks ending June 10, June 24, September 30, and October 14, 1854 (Gort PLMB, G01/12/17 and G01/12/18, GCL). The initial report of Kennedy's injury was subsequently reported in the *Galway Vindicator*, July 1, 1854.

30 Bridget Reilly to Lord Wandesforde, May 11, 1847 (35,526/6, NLI).

31 *Anglo-Celt* (Cavan), April 9, 1847; T. F. Elliot to James Stephen, April 28 and June 3, 1847 (CO 384/79, TNA). For more on the *Swatara*, see *Report [Sickness and Mortality]* (1854), 36–37 and Kinealy and MacAtasney, *Hidden Famine*, 87–88. After leaving Belfast, the *Swatara* was forced to put in at Derry City for repairs and eventually sailed for Philadelphia. Dozens died along the way.

32 The *Evening Freeman* (Dublin) is cited in *Limerick Reporter*, March 30, 1847; *Liverpool Mercury*, May 5, 1854 (BLN); Thomas Reilly to John M. Kelly, April 26, 1848 (10,511/2, NLI). In his book *Black '47*, on page 61, Frank Neal estimates that over 1.9 million Irish deck passengers sailed to Liverpool between 1847 and 1854.

33 R. H. Sheil to J. Runge, April 29, 1853 (32,483A, NLI); *First Report [Colonization from Ireland]* (1847–1848), 183–184; *Liverpool Mercury*, January 14, 1853 (BLN). For

more on steamships and the emigrant trade, see Neal, "Liverpool" and Cohn, *Mass Migration*, 223–224. Reports on the *Londonderry* disaster appeared in the *Liverpool Mercury*, December 5, 8, 12, 1848 (BLN) and *Limerick Reporter*, December 8, 1848. For a story of a captain going out of his way to save passengers during a storm on the Irish Sea, see *Galway Vindicator*, February 18, 1852.

34 *Liverpool Mercury*, May 7, 1850, February 10, 1852, and September 10, 1852 (BLN). For more on the runners and frauds of Liverpool, see Coleman, *Going to America*, 66–71. It is true that the high levels of sodium chloride in seawater mean that regular soap does not lather in it. "That soap I bought was no use to me," complained English emigrant David Atkinson in an 1851 letter to his parents. "I was obliged to buy some marine soap. No other kind is any use at sea." David Atkinson to his parents, March 4, 1851 (MLDOC 99, SL-NSW).

35 *Nation* (Dublin), February 26, 1848 [reprinted in *Liverpool Mercury*, March 24, 1848 (BLN)]; *Nation* (Dublin), May 23, 1846; November 3, 1849; *Liverpool Mercury*, March 21, 1848 (BLN).

36 The *Liverpool Albion* is cited in *Nation* (Dublin), July 17, 1847, and *Galway Vindicator*, July 21, 1847; *Nation* (Dublin), July 17, 1847. For more on the deportation of Irish immigrants from Liverpool, see Gallman, *Receiving Erin's*, 30, 65–66 and Hirota, *Expelling*, 171.

37 O'Hanlon, *Irish Emigrant's*, 33, 19; C. Graham to John McGinity, September 5, 1848 (T3539/3, PRONI); MacKenzie, *Emigrant's Guide*, 44.

38 O'Hanlon, *Irish Emigrant's*, 19; *Liverpool Mercury*, May 25, 1847 (BLN).

39 Daniel Rowntree to Mrs. M. Butler, May 5, 1851 (from Prof. Emeritus Arnold Schrier, University of Cincinnati [KMC]); C. Graham to John McGinity, September 5, 1848 (T3539/3, PRONI); *Anglo-Celt* (Cavan), March 23, 1849.

40 *Nation* (Dublin), May 10, 1851; *Limerick Reporter*, September 2, 1851; *Limerick Reporter*, June 20, 1851; *Liverpool Mercury*, January 20, 1852 (BLN). Besides the Dublin *Nation*, the new home was advertised in Irish newspapers including the *Limerick Reporter*, September 26, 1851 (see for "red collars" reference) and *Galway Vindicator*, December 3, 1851. Its opening was also noted in the *Boston Pilot*, June 7, 1851.

41 *Liverpool Mercury*, February 4, 1851 (BLN); *Limerick Reporter*, September 2, 1851; *Nation* (Dublin), February 26, 1848; *Galway Vindicator*, May 24, 1851.

42 Wiley and Putnam, *Wiley & Putnam's*, 38, 30; Byrne, *Emigrant's Guide*, 9.

43 *Liverpool Mercury*, May 14, 1852; July 15, 1851; January 9, 1852 (BLN).

44 "Saranak's 12th Voyage," 1848, ticket #2824 (Series 1a, Box 65, HSP); "Saranak's 33rd Voyage," 1855, ticket #381 (Series 1a, Box 281, HSP); James Purcell to Bridget Brennan, August 10, 1846 (35,533/1, NLI); Wiley and Putnam, *Wiley & Putnam's*, 31–32; "Saranak's 21st Voyage," 1851, ticket #5847 (Series 1a, Box 69, HSP); Byrne, *Emigrant's Guide*, 6.

45 Wiley and Putnam, *Wiley & Putnam's*, 30–31; Nettle, *Practical Guide*, 9–10; MacKenzie, *Emigrant's Guide*, 45; "Refunded Passenger Tickets, 1852," ticket #6553 (Series 1b, Box 290, HSP); "Saranak's 20th Voyage," 1851, ticket #5911 (Series 1a, Box 69, HSP).

46 The "Affectionate Nephew" letter was published in the *Liverpool Mercury*, August 12, 1853 (BLN); O'Hanlon, *Irish Emigrant's*, 40; Wiley and Putnam, *Wiley & Putnam's*, 55. For more on the mess system en route to Australia, see Haines, *Life and Death*, 100, 109.

47 John Burke to Commissioners of Woods, Forest, and Land Revenues, March 21, 1848 (QRO/4/3/6/34, NAI); MacDonagh, *Pattern*, 202–204.

48 MacKenzie, *Emigrant's Guide*, 45; Wiley and Putnam, *Wiley & Putnam's*, 32; SSJ, *George Seymour* (AJCP PRO 3214, SL-TAS).

49 SSJ, *Bangalore* (AJCP PRO 3189, SL-TAS); SSJ, *Lord Dalhousie [1]* (ADM 101/251, TNA); SSJ, *Blackfriar* (AJCP PRO 3189, SL-TAS). For accounts of children being vaccinated on female convict ships leaving Ireland, see SSJ journals from *Tasmania [2]* (AJCP PRO 3211, SL-TAS); *Earl Grey [4]* (AJCP PRO 3193, SL-TAS); *Blackfriar* (AJCP PRO 3189, SL-TAS); *John William Dare* (AJCP PRO M711, SL-TAS). For more on the UK government's policies on vaccinating emigrants and convicts heading to Australia, see Foxhall, *Health, Medicine*, 165–174.

50 *Galway Vindicator*, December 19, 1849; *Liverpool Mercury*, April 29, 1853 (BLN).

51 James J. Mitchell journal, 1853 (Misc. Mss. Mitchell, James J., NYHS); Byrne, *Emigrant's Guide*, 10.

52 Samuel Harvey journal, 1849 (T3258/66/1, PRONI).

3. LIFE

1 Margaret McCarthy to Alexander McCarthy, September 22, 1850 (published in Ellis, *Emigrants*, 66). In his study of eighteenth-century Protestant migrants to North America, Stephen Berry points out that his subjects did not experience the Atlantic Ocean as "a timeless, unitary space." In fact, the sea "represented a complex set of changes masked by a seemingly unvarying appearance" (Berry, *A Path*, 4). In their examination of the ways in which the Famine-era emigrant voyage was portrayed in post-Famine Irish and Irish American literature, Marguérite Corporaal and Christopher Cusack argue that "the coffin ships represent microcosmic Irish 'imagined communities' that function as utopian heterotopia where the cultural clashes experienced in the homeland and the pending assimilation in the New World have to be negotiated" (Corporaal and Cusack, "Rites of Passage," 343).

2 Samuel Harvey journal, 1849 (T3258/66/2 and /6, PRONI); Clark is cited in Moore, *Voyage Out*, 86–87; Mitchel, *Jail Journal*, 23.

3 Connolly, *Priests and People*, 113; James J. Mitchell diary, 1853 (Misc. Mss. Mitchell, James J., NYHS); Samuel Harvey journal, 1849 (T3258/66/18, PRONI); Reid and Mongan, *Decent Set*, 35, 44. William Carleton also describes some rural superstitions in *Traits and Stories*.

4 William McElderry to Thomas McElderry, October 20, 1853 (T2414/11, PRONI [DIPPAM]); Johanna Kelly's letter is printed in *Report [Colonization from Ireland]* (1847), 357; Jonathon Smyth to James Smith, September 24, 1845 (D1828/31, PRONI [DIPPAM]). The *Hercules* originally sailed from Campbelltown, Scotland, en route to Adelaide in late 1852 with Laurence Carey as its surgeon-superintendent but had

to put into Cork in January 1853 when large numbers of its passengers and crew were afflicted by fever. While moored at Cork over the next three months, almost half of its passengers either died (along with Carey) or disappeared. It set sail again on April 12, 1853, with Edward Nolloth as its surgeon-superintendent. For Carey and Nolloth's journals, see SSJ, *Hercules* (AJCP PRO 3213, SL-TAS). The originals are held in TNA as ADM101/77/4 and ADM101/77/5, respectively.

5 SSJ, *John William Dare* (AJCP PRO M711, SL-TAS); SSJ, *Duke of Cornwall* (AJCP PRO 3192, SL-TAS); SSJ, *Blackfriar* (AJCP PRO 3189, SL-TAS); Jonathon Quin to James Quin, December 10, 1849 (MLDOC 3507, SL-NSW). For examples of surgeons reporting good health among the general population of Irish male convicts on their transports, see SSJ, *Samuel Boddington* (AJCP PRO 3209, SL-TAS); SSJ, *Pestonjee Bomanjee [4]* (AJCP PRO 3207, SL-TAS); SSJ, *Blenheim II* (AJCP PRO 3190, SL-TAS). Menorrhagia refers to abnormally heavy menstrual bleeding.

6 "Saranak's 32nd Voyage," 1855, ticket #11 (Series 1a, Box 281, HSP); SSJ, *Kinnear [2]* (AJCP PRO 3200, SL-TAS); Samuel Harvey journal, 1849 (T3258/66/18, PRONI).

7 Thomas Patterson to John Thompson, May 22, 1848 (D2795/5/1, PRONI [DIP-PAM]); *Anglo-Celt* (Cavan), July 22, 1852.

8 James Purcell to Bridget Brennan, August 10, 1846 (35,533/1, NLI); Samuel Harvey journal, 1849 (T3258/66/8–9, PRONI); SSJ, *Tory [2]* (AJCP PRO 3211, SL-TAS); SSJ, *Australasia* (AJCP PRO 3189, SL-TAS); *Sailor's Magazine* [New York] 20, no. 8 (April 1848): 235.

9 Thomas Reilly to John M. Kelly, April 25, 1848 (10,511/2, NLI). Despite being an eloquent nationalist who left Ireland in 1848, this is not the same person as famed Young Irelander Thomas Devin Reilly, who was present at the rising in Tipperary in July 1848. Henry Johnson to Jane Johnson, September 18, 1848 (T2319/1, PRONI). Henry and Jane's correspondence was also published in Wyatt, "Johnson Letters." Jane and her two children sailed to Canada to reunite with Henry, but he died in July 1849, just before they arrived.

10 Moore, *Voyage Out*, 133; Charles Moore diary, 1855 (B 1319, SL-NSW). Meagher's description of the Indian Ocean was published in the *Nation* (Dublin) on July 27, 1850, and reprinted in the *Boston Pilot* and *Irish-American* (New York) on August 17, 1850. The original letter, dated February 16, 1850, is held in the Alan Queale papers (11,705, NLI). It is not clear to which "white bears" Meagher refers as there are no polar bears in Antarctica.

11 William Culshaw Greenhalgh diary, 1853 (DX/1676, MMA); John Burke, "Reminiscences [1839–1891]" (AHMC Burke, John, NYHS); *Armagh Guardian*, February 24, 1846 (DIPPAM). The most famous examples of Irish emigrant ships sunk by icebergs both occurred in 1849: the *Hannah* (Newry to Quebec) and *Maria* (Limerick to Quebec).

12 Meagher's description of boredom at sea was printed in the *Nation* (Dublin) on July 27, 1850, and reprinted in the *Boston Pilot* and *Irish-American* (New York) on August 17, 1850.

13 Samuel Harvey journal, 1849 (T3258/66/17, PRONI); Nettle, *Practical Guide*, 10–11.

14 *Armagh Guardian*, February 24, 1846 (DIPPAM); Witt, "During the Voyage," 193; see Goffman, *Asylums*, especially the "On the Characteristics of Total Institutions" chapter; Rediker, *Between the Devil*, 211–212. For a surgeon's account of the daily schedule aboard an Irish female convict ship, see SSJ, *Maria* (AJCP PRO 3203, SL-TAS).

15 Blunt, *Shipmaster's Assistant*, 13; *Papers [Australian Colonies]* (1850), 260, 263, 267. For more on the historical roots of maritime law, see Witt, "During the Voyage." American and British laws on maritime discipline are discussed in Creighton, *Rites and Passages*, 93–95 and Rasor, *Reform*, 55, respectively.

16 Brand and Staniforth, "Care and Control," 30, 24–25; *Instructions for Surgeons-Superintendent* [Surgeons], clauses 14, 13, and 33; *Instructions for Surgeons-Superintendent* [Masters], clause 6; SSJ, *Lord Auckland [2]* (AJCP PRO 3201, SL-TAS).

17 *Sailors' Magazine* [London] 7, no. 81 (September 1845): 143; *Liverpool Mercury*, April 29, 1853 (BLN); Wiley and Putnam, *Wiley & Putnam's*, 66. For more on the role of religion at sea, see Strong, *Victorian Christianity*.

18 Browning, *Convict Ship*, v–vi; *Limerick Reporter*, April 10, 1849; T. N. Redington to G. Cornwall Lewis, September 12, 1848 (CON/LB/1, NAI).

19 John Burke, "Reminiscences [1839–1891]" (AHMC Burke, John, NYHS); MacKenzie, *Emigrant's Guide*, 63–64; W. Usherwood journal, 1852–1853 (B 784 [CY 1117], SL-NSW).

20 *Papers [North America]* (1847–1848), 320; Bateson, *Convict Ships*, 68; Brand and Staniforth, "Care and Control," 31; SSJ, *Irene* (MLMSS 599, SL-NSW); Hassam, *No Privacy*, 43–44.

21 O'Hanlon, *Irish Emigrant's*, 42; Samuel Pillow journal, 1852–1853 (Ap 115, SL-NSW).

22 *First Report [Emigrant Ships]* (1854), 160, 125; *Report [Sickness and Mortality]* (1854), 16; "Saranak's 32nd Voyage," 1855, ticket #11 (Series 1a, Box 281, HSP); MacKenzie, *Emigrant's Guide*, 65; *Instructions for Surgeons-Superintendent* [Surgeons], clause 13; Stephen Walcott to Samuel Ellis, November 20, 1846 (CO 386/42, TNA).

23 *First Report [Emigrant Ships]* (1854), 180; Reid and Mongan, *Decent Set*, 40; George E. Binsted diary, 1848–1849 (DLMS 137, SL-NSW); James Menzies diary, 1848 (D 6594[L], SL-SA) is also available online at https://bound-for-south-australia.collections.slsa.sa.gov.au.

24 Daniel Molony to H. and A. Cope, September 3, 1851 (Series 1a, Box 69, HSP); T. W. C. Murdoch to Herman Merivale, January 17, 1851 (CO 384/88, TNA); Robert Bunch to T. W. C. Murdoch, November 15, 1851 (CO 384/88, TNA); *Papers [North America]* (1847–1848), 320. For more on the underenforcement of regulations on emigrant ships, see Cohn, *Mass Migration*, 151–152 and Scally, "Liverpool Ships," 22–25.

25 Richard Lynch to John Walpole, February 6, 1849 (CO 384/83, TNA).

26 *Emigrant Ship "Washington"* (1851), 435–436, 439; *South Australian* (Adelaide), April 27, 1849 (TROVE); C. Alexander Wood to T. F. Elliot, October 26, 1849 (CO 386/67, TNA).

27 Captain Theodore Julius to H. and A. Cope, June 27, 1848 (Series 1a, Box 65, HSP) and June 27, 1849 (Series 1a, Box 67, HSP); *Sailors' Magazine* [London] 9, no. 107 (November 1847): 253; Charles Moore journal, 1855 (B 1319, SL-NSW); William Ellery Maxson journal, 1846 (G. W. Blunt White Library, Mystic Seaport Museum [KMC]). References to Lascars appear in Hassam, *No Privacy*, 47 and Elizabeth Hentig journal, 1853 (MLMSS 7657, SL-NSW). For more on East Indian sailors, see Jaffer, *Lascars*. Sailors' resistance and identities is analyzed in Rediker, *Outlaws*.

28 William Ellery Maxson journal, 1846 (G. W. Blunt White Library, Mystic Seaport Museum [KMC]); SSJ, *Irene* (MLMSS 599, SL-NSW); *Emigrant Ship "Washington"* (1851), 435–436.

29 Foucault, *History of Sexuality*; SSJ, *Steadfast* (MLMSS 991, SL-NSW); "Enquiry into certain irregularities said to have occurred on board the Female Convict ship 'Duke of Cornwall' during her voyage from Ireland to this colony in the year 1850" [1851] (Tasmanian Papers 112–113 MAV FM 4/8518, SL-NSW). Emetics were used to induce vomiting.

30 Thompson, "Time, Work-Discipline."

31 James Duncan diary, 1846–1848 (MssColl 859, NYPL).

32 Hassam, *No Privacy*, 46; SSJ, *Bangalore* (AJCP PRO 3189, SL-TAS); Moore, *Voyage Out*, 133. "Dropsy" refers to edema, the accumulation of excess water in a body's soft tissues.

33 *Third Report* (1849), 617; Jonathon Smyth to James Smith, September 24, 1845 (D1828/31, PRONI [DIPPAM]); Samuel Harvey journal, 1849 (T3258/66/6, PRONI). Verses 23–31 of the Bible's Psalm 107 depict God having mercy on sailors caught in a storm.

34 James Duncan diary, 1846–1848 (MssColl 859, NYPL); Thomas Reilly to John M. Kelly, April 25, 1848 (10,511/2, NLI); *First Report [Emigrant Ships]* (1854), 108. Philipps's point about the discord caused by having too many seamen working at the same time was part of a broader campaign being prosecuted by many shipowners at the time to keep their labor costs down by discouraging new government regulations regarding the minimum sizes of crews.

35 H. and A. Cope to Joseph Cope [cousin], August 17, 1852 (Series 1c, Vol. 43, HSP); Christopher Kelly to John Kelly, June 21, 1846 (from Patricia Shaw, San Francisco, CA [KMC]); Andrew Collin to his parents, November 30, 1853 (T2834/1/2, PRONI [DIP-PAM]); "Enquiry into certain irregularities said to have occurred on board the Female Convict ship 'Duke of Cornwall' during her voyage from Ireland to this colony in the year 1850" [1851] (Tasmanian Papers 112–113 MAV FM 4/8518, SL-NSW).

36 Wiley and Putnam, *Wiley & Putnam's*, 61; H. and A. Cope to John Peters, August 16, 1850 (Series 1c, Vol. 43, HSP); Henry Cope to Alfred Cope, May 27, 1851 (Series 1c, Vol. 43, HSP); *Emigrant Ship "Washington"* (1851), 435; Joseph Kidd Walpole journal, 1849 (A 2085, SL-NSW).

37 William H. McCleery to John Orr, July 1, 1847 (Ulster-American Folk Park [DIP-PAM]); Stephen Walcott to J. B. Wilcocks, October 26, 1846 (CO 386/42, TNA); Stephen Walcott to Samuel Ellis, November 7, 1846 (CO 386/42, TNA).

38 *Emigrant Ship "Washington"* (1851), 437–438. The *Galway Vindicator* published excerpts of Foster's letter on May 7, 1851.

39 *Papers [North America]* (1847–1848), 320; Ellen Rountree to Laurence Rountree, August 26, 1851 (from Prof. Emeritus Arnold Schrier, University of Cincinnati [KMC]). The passengers' public letter is cited in Hamrock, *Famine in Mayo*, 138. According to Hamrock, it was published in the *Tyrawley Herald* (Ballina) on September 24, 1846.

40 Wiley and Putnam, *Wiley & Putnam's*, 43–44; Mitchel, *Jail Journal*, 3–4.

41 William Culshaw Greenhalgh diary, 1853 (DX/1676, MMA).

42 O'Hanlon, *Irish Emigrant's*, 40; "Saranak's 20th Voyage," 1851, ticket #5911 (Series 1a, Box 69, HSP); "Refunded Passenger Tickets, 1852," ticket #6553 (Series 1b, Box 290, HSP); James Purcell to Bridget Brennan, August 10, 1846 (35,533/1, NLI).

43 MacKenzie, *Emigrant's Guide*, 59–60; O'Hanlon, *Irish Emigrant's*, 41–42; *Anglo-Celt* (Cavan), March 23, 1849.

44 George Ritchie to his parents, January 10, 1851 (T3292/2, PRONI); Samuel Harvey journal, 1849 (T3258/66/1 and /26, PRONI).

45 Reid and Mongan, *Decent Set*, 39–40; Duffy, *My Life*, 2:131. For more on nineteenth-century Irish funerary practices and wakes, see Brophy, "Keening Community;" Connolly, *Priests and People*, 141–172; Griffith and Wallace, *Grave Matters*; Lysaght, "Hospitality"; Mac Suibhne, *Subjects Lacking*; Ó Crualaoich, "Merry Wake"; Ó Súilleabháin, *Irish Wake*; Tait, *Death, Burial*. William Carleton also describes rural wakes in "Larry M'Farland's Wake" and "The Party Fight and Funeral" in *Traits and Stories*.

46 *Anglo-Celt* (Cavan), March 23, 1849; MacKenzie, *Emigrant's Guide*, 60; Mitchel, *Jail Journal*, 66.

47 The surgeons' instructions are cited in Reid and Mongan, *Decent Set*, 80, f. 17; MacKenzie, *Emigrant's Guide*, 65; SSJ, *Hyderabad [2]* (AJCP PRO 3198, SL-TAS); SSJ, *Irene* (MLMSS 599, SL-NSW); Moore, *Voyage Out*, 70–71.

48 Joseph Carrothers to William Carrothers, July 14, 1847 (T3734, PRONI [DIPPAM]); James Duncan diary, 1846–1848 (MssColl 859, NYPL); Samuel Harvey journal, 1849 (T3258/66/4 and /21, PRONI); James J. Mitchell journal, 1853 (Misc. Mss. Mitchell, James J., NYHS).

49 Rediker, *Between the Devil*, 186; James Menzies diary, 1848 (D 6594[L], SL-SA); Reid and Mongan, *Decent Set*, 36. James Menzies's diary is also available online at https://bound-for-south-australia.collections.slsa.sa.gov.au.

50 Samuel Harvey journal, 1849 (T3258/66/5, PRONI); Moore, *Voyage Out*, 105; David Atkinson to his parents, March 4, 1851 (MLDOC 99, SL-NSW).

51 *Galway Vindicator*, February 18, 1852. Turner first articulated his concept of "communitas" in *Ritual Process*.

52 Byrne, *Emigrant's Guide*, 9; William Culshaw Greenhalgh diary, 1853 (DX/1676, MMA); SSJ, *Tasmania [2]* (AJCP PRO 3211, SL-TAS); O'Hanlon, *Irish Emigrant's*, 41–42; Samuel Harvey journal, 1849 (T3258/66/10–11, PRONI).

53 Samuel Harvey journal, 1849 (T3258/66/8, PRONI); James Duncan diary, 1846–1848 (MssColl 859, NYPL); Henry Johnson to Jane Johnson, September 18, 1848 (T2319/1, PRONI).

54 Hassam, *No Privacy*, 51; *Sailor's Magazine* [New York] 19, no. 4 (December 1846): 125; no. 9 (May 1847): 272.

55 Samuel Harvey journal, 1849 (T3258/66/5 and /30–32, PRONI).

56 *Sailors' Magazine* [London] 9, no. 97 (January 1847): 22; George E. Binsted diary, 1848–1849 (DLMS 137, SL-NSW).

57 William B. Neville journal, 1848–1849 (DLMSQ 148, SL-NSW); George E. Binsted diary, 1848–1849 (DLMS 137, SL-NSW); Daniel Molony to H. and A. Cope, March 31, 1851 (Series 1a, Box 69, HSP); *Sailor's Magazine* [New York] 18, no. 6 (February 1846): 176.

58 Henry Johnson to Jane Johnson, September 18, 1848 (T2319/1, PRONI).

4. DEATH

1 Patt Brenan to Lord Wandesforde, n.d. [1847] (35,526/7, NLI). Wandesforde curtly declined Brenan's request. Michael Collins is cited in the *Irish Times* (Dublin), July 19, 2016. Smallwood, *Saltwater Slavery*, 137.

This "20 percent" estimate has been an enduring part of the conversation on Irish emigrant mortality since the Famine itself. In a debate in Westminster on April 11, 1848, nationalist politician John O'Connell claimed that since 1845, one-quarter of a million Irish people had "been driven to emigrate in such misery that more than 20 per cent of them have died on the passage or immediately after arrival" (HC Deb [April 11, 1848] third series, vol. 98, col. 187). In recent decades, most historians—whether writing for popular or scholarly audiences—have tended to accept the "20 percent" estimate for Canada-bound Irish emigrants in 1847. While admitting that "certainty is impossible because of incomplete records," Oliver MacDonagh believed that "17 percent of the total Irish emigration of 1847 . . . at least 25,000 and possibly as many as 30,000 died" (MacDonagh, *Pattern*, 188n6). In her 1962 best seller, *The Great Hunger*, Cecil Woodham-Smith stated that of the 100,000 emigrants who sailed to British North America in 1847, 17,000 "perished during the voyage" while another 20,000 "died in Canada" soon after arrival (Woodham-Smith, *Great Hunger*, 234). Twenty-three years later, Kerby Miller estimated that "at least 30 percent of those bound for British North America and 9 percent of those sailing to the United States [in 1847] perished on the 'coffin ships' or shortly after debarkation" (Miller, *Emigrants and Exiles*, 292). In his 1996 popular account, *The Famine Ships*, Edward Laxton estimated that of the "more than 100,000" Irish emigrants who sailed to Canada in 1847, "at least 20,000" died (Laxton, *Famine Ships*, 38). "It remains true," Cormac Ó Gráda wrote in 1999, "that the [Irish emigrant] mortality on the Canadian route—about 20 percent—in 1847 was very high" (Ó Gráda, *Black '47*, 106). Mark McGowan's *Death or Canada: The Irish Famine Migration to Toronto, 1847* (2009) does not offer an overall mortality rate but in *1847, Grosse-Île: A Record of Daily Events* (1997), André Charbonneau and André Sévigny state that "around 18 percent (17,477) of the 98,649 emigrants who boarded vessels for Québec City in 1847 died before reaching their final destination." Their statistics encompass, in other words, emigrants of all nationalities, not just the Irish. Moreover, their 17,477 deaths include over 7,500 who died in Montreal, Toronto, and "various cities in Upper Canada" (Charbonneau and Sévigny, *1847, Grosse-Île*, 15, 23). Presumably some of those deaths, however, included people who had emigrated before 1847. It also raises the question of how long after a newcomer's arrival should their deaths continue to be counted as "emigrant mortality."

The bigger problem is that some popular histories, such as William Henry's *Coffin Ship: The Wreck of the Brig St. John*, imply that 1847 (and, thus, the alleged 20 percent mortality rate) was representative of the Famine period as a whole. "About one-fifth of those who sailed from Irish shores during the famine perished en route," Henry claimed in 2009. "Sources indicate that in 1847 alone, some 100,000 people set sail for British North America, with an estimated 20,000 of them either perishing aboard the 'coffin ships' or dying afterwards as a result of conditions on board" (Henry, *Coffin Ship*, 16). Indeed, the term "coffin ship," wrote Henry, "is mainly given to vessels that carried Irish emigrants overseas during the famine of 1845–1850" (Henry, *Coffin Ship*, 52). This intellectual sleight of hand muddies the collective memory of the emigrant experience. As a result, US House of Representatives Speaker Paul Ryan raised few eyebrows in January 2018 when he told an interviewer that his ancestors came from Ireland "on what they called 'coffin ships'" (*Irish Times* [Dublin], January 12, 2018). Professional historians have cautioned against the assumption that emigrant excess mortality was consistently high during the Famine period. Joel Mokyr insisted that the "horror stories" of "'coffin ships'" in 1847 were "not necessarily representative of the emigration movement during the entire period" (Mokyr, *Why Ireland*, 267). Similarly, Cormac Ó Gráda has stated that "the notion that [1847 levels of] mortality was the norm—as implied, for example, in the claim in the *Irish Press* in December 1994 that 'at least [one million] fled the country on the aptly named coffin ships'—is a myth" (Ó Gráda, *Black '47*, 106).

Of the 1,920,978 emigrants who left Ireland for overseas destinations (not including mainland Britain) between 1845 and 1855, perhaps as many as 47,264 (2.46 percent) died. If anything, this estimate of a survival rate of over 97 percent probably understates how many Famine-era Irish emigrants made it to their destination alive. It was calculated by subtracting an average mortality rate of 2 percent from the estimated total number of migrants for every year between 1845 and 1855 inclusive (see note 7 of the introduction, above) except 1847. For 1847, the total number of deaths was calculated by adding the number of Irish deaths en route to Canada (10,820 out of 98,749)—as stated by the emigration officers (see note 11 of chapter 4, below)—to 2 percent of the Irish migrants who did not go to Canada that year (2,423 out of 121,136).

2 *Report [Sickness and Mortality]* (1854), 8; *Second Report [Emigrant Ships]* (1854), 189.

3 *Thirteenth General Report* (1852–1853), 74; *Copies [North American Colonies]* (1854–1855), 140; McInnis, "Population," 386.

4 Cohn, *Mass Migration*, 144–145; Anbinder, *City of Dreams*, 140–141; Rosenberg, *Cholera Years*, 2. For a detailed analysis of the various causes of excess mortality in Ireland during the Famine, see Ó Gráda, *Black '47*, 88–95. Cohn, *Mass Migration*, 144 offers an overview of the spikes in emigrant mortality during the Famine years. Smallpox and yellow fever were by no means eradicated by the mid-nineteenth century, but they had less impact on European migrants, including the Irish (see Brunton, *Politics of Vaccination*). For recent examples of scholarly work on cholera, see Gilbert, *Cholera*; Hamlin, *Cholera*; Whooley, *Knowledge*.

5 Glazier, Mageean, and Okeke, "Socio-demographic," 255; Mokyr, *Why Ireland*, 267; Shlomowitz, "Mortality," 42–45; *Report [Colonization from Ireland]* (1847), 12; *Papers [North American Colonies]* (1852–1853), 479. Although they do not address his comments on emigrant excess mortality, scholars have recently revisited some of Mokyr's main conclusions in *Why Ireland Starved* (see Kelly and Ó Gráda, "*Why Ireland Starved*" and Solar, "*Why Ireland Starved*").

6 T. F. Elliot to James Stephen, August 4, 1847 (CO 384/79, TNA); *First Report [Emigrant Ships]* (1854), 16; Brown, *Passage*, 77–78.

7 Klein et al., "Transoceanic Mortality," 114, 112, 107–108 (for more on slave trade mortality rates, see Eltis, "Mortality," Steckel and Jensen, "New Evidence," and Cohn, "Deaths"); Cohn, "Maritime Mortality," 190; Cohn, *Mass Migration*, 149; Cohn, "Mortality," 297; *Second Report [Emigrant Ships]* (1854), 215; McDonald and Shlomowitz, "Mortality," 89; *First Report [Emigrant Ships]* (1854), 35; Haines, *Life and Death*, 29, 314; Haines, *Doctors*, 7; Bateson, *Convict Ships*, 393–396.

Unless otherwise noted, this chapter's statistics on death include those who died at sea as well as those who died soon afterward (in quarantines and hospitals). When calculating the crude mortality rate of a given population, scholars divide the number of people who died by the number who embarked, and multiply that quotient by 100. Many quantitative historians consider this method to be of limited use when analyzing maritime mortality because it fails to take into account critical dynamics such as the length of the voyage and the relative youth of migrants. As the present chapter seeks to offer a broad, comparative assessment of the issue, however, it limits itself to using such crude mortality rates. For more on the problem of calculating statistics on death, see Cohn, "Maritime Mortality," 160–165.

The annual mortality rates for emigrants en route to Quebec between 1845 and 1855 were calculated using data from Stephen Walcott, "Mortality in Canada Immigration," July 12, 1847 (CO 384/79, NAK) [for 1845]; *Papers [North America]* (1847), 35 [for 1846]; *Papers [North America]* (1847–1848), 393 [for 1847]; *Papers [North America]* (1849), 37–38, 45 [for 1848]; *Copy [Canada]* (1850), 15 [for 1849]; *Copies [North American Colonies]* (1851), 313 [for 1850]; *Papers [North American Colonies]* (1852), 587 [for 1851]; *Papers [North American Colonies]* (1852–1853), 463 [for 1852]; *Papers [North American Colonies]* (1854), 56 [for 1853]; *Copies [North American Colonies]* (1854–1855), 114 [for 1854]; *Copies [North American Colonies]* (1857 Session 1), 899 [for 1855].

8   Cohn, "Mortality," 296–297; Cohn, "Determinants," 390; Ó Gráda, *Black '47*, 106–107. Unfortunately, the annual reports of the New York Commissioners of Emigration include only scattered statistics on emigrant mortality and usually related only to deaths in their local hospitals. The report for 1848 did state that of the 196,511 passengers who sailed for New York in 1848, only 1,002 (0.51 percent) died at sea (*Annual Reports [1861]*, 12).

By twenty-first-century standards, the mortality rates on nineteenth-century sailing ships were very high. One of the world's leading aviation consultants, to70, states there was on average less than one fatal accident per two million commercial passenger flights worldwide during the 2010s. See Adrian Young, "TO70's Civil Aviation Safety Review 2019: A Year of Difficult Questions," https://to70.com. African migrants crossing the Mediterranean Sea in recent years have, however, experienced mortality rates similar to those, which nineteenth-century European migrants faced. According to the International Organization for Migration, an intergovernmental institution operating under the auspices of the United Nations, the mortality rates on the central Mediterranean route were 1.96 percent (in 2017), 3.11 percent (2018), and 3.63 percent (2019). See International Organization for Migration, "Mediterranean Migrant Arrivals Reach 76,558 in 2019; Deaths Reach 1,071," October 11, 2019, www.iom.int.

9   McDonald and Shlomowitz, "Mortality," 89; *First Report [Emigrant Ships]* (1854), 35. Neither McDonald and Shlomowitz nor the *First Report [Emigrant Ships]* (1854) include statistics for 1847 to 1855 inclusive. Calculating the mortality rate for that entire time span, therefore, required combining McDonald and Shlomowitz's statistics for 1847, 1854, and 1855 with the *First Report*'s statistics for 1848 to 1853. In the years for which both sources had overlapping statistical information, the mortality rates were very similar. *First Report [Emigrant Ships]* (1854), 35–36; *Papers [Australian Colonies]* (1850), 41–42; *Papers [Australian Colonies]* (1852), 437–438; *Papers [Australian Colonies]* (1854), 136. Incidentally, while 1849 witnessed a cholera-related spike in mortality among emigrants on the Atlantic Ocean, it seems to have had minimal impact on those assisted emigrants who headed to New South Wales that year. Of the 15,988 who embarked, 360 (2.25 percent) died. The Irish mortality rate that year was below average for that year, at 1.13 percent. See *Copies [Australian Colonies]* (1851), 40–43.

10 Bateson, *Convict Ships*, 393–396; SSJ, *Tory [2]* (AJCP PRO 3211, SL-TAS); SSJ, *Waverley* (AJCP PRO 3212, SL-TAS); Haines, *Life and Death*, 46.

11 McInnis, "Population," 382; *Papers [North America]* (1847–1848), 361, 393, 386, 356. These totals do not include the relatively tiny numbers who sailed to other Canadian ports that year. Buchanan's Table 4 in *Papers [North America]* (1847–1848), 395, includes striking statistics on the mortality rates of those hospitalized soon after arrival. Of the 8,691 emigrants admitted to the quarantine at Grosse Île in 1847, 3,389 (38.99 percent) died, while in the Marine and Emigrant Hospital in Quebec, 712 of the 3,313 (21.49 percent) admitted died. For more on emigrant mortality in Toronto, Montreal, and other Canadian towns, see McGowan, *Death or Canada*, 70 and Charbonneau and Sévigny, *1847, Grosse-Île*, 23.

12 *Papers [North America]* (1847–1848), 386–387, 397–403. The mortality rates based on port of embarkation (other than Liverpool and Cork) were calculated using the data on individual ships listed in Table 8 of *Papers [North America]* (1847–1848). Buchanan provided the statistics for Liverpool and Cork in his letter, although his calculations of the mortality rates for each were slightly off. In his annual report, M. H. Perley states that of the 17,074 emigrants who sailed from Ireland and Liverpool to New Brunswick in 1847, 2,400 (14.06 percent) died either at sea or in quarantine; see *Papers [North America]* (1847–1848), 361. As Mokyr and Ó Gráda point out, "The many vagrants and famine refugees on the roads produced a new term for [typhoid, relapsing fever, and typhus]: 'road fever.'" For this quote, and more on the connection between internal migration and the transmission of infectious diseases, see Mokyr and Ó Gráda, "What Do," 342. For a general overview of typhus in nineteenth-century Ireland, see Crawford, "Typhus."

13 *Papers [North America]* (1847–1848), 397–403, 359, 385.

14 The mortality rates of these individual ships can be found in *Papers [North America]* (1847–1848), 398–399, 401–402. For more on the *Sarah*, see *Copy [Canada]* (1850), 4; *Blanche*, see William Mure to Viscount Palmerston, April 5, 1851 (CO 384/88, TNA); *Fingal*, see *Papers [North American Colonies]* (1854), 64 and *Morning Chronicle* (Quebec), October 25, 1853. For more on the Strokestown emigrants, see Reilly, *Strokestown*, 65–77. The National Famine Museum and Archive, located in the Strokestown Park, organizes commemorative walks along the National Famine Way, a 165-kilometer heritage walking trail, which traces the route taken by the Strokestown emigrants from Roscommon to Dublin in 1847. See Strokestown Park, "National Famine Way," www.strokestownpark.ie.

15 *Papers [North America]* (1847–1848), 385, 393; Cohn, "Determinants," 371, 389; Shlomowitz and McDonald, "Babies at Risk," 86; "Register of deaths and births at sea en route to Australia, 1847–1854" (CO 386/170, TNA). For more on the *Ticonderoga's* fate, see Veitch, *Hell Ship*. The government's restriction of children as assisted emigrants to Australia is discussed in Shlomowitz and McDonald, "Babies at Risk," 87 and *First Report [Emigrant Ships]* (1854), 35–36.

16 Cohn, "Passenger Mortality," 16; *Fifteenth General Report*, 14–15 (for the years 1847–1854) and *Sixteenth General Report*, 419 (for the year 1855); Haines, *Life and Death*, 39. The wrecks of the *Cataraqui*, *Tayleur*, and *Guiding Star* were noticed in the *Boston Pilot*, March 21, 1846, *Anglo-Celt* (Cavan), January 26, 1854, and *South Australian Register* (Adelaide), October 4, 1855 (TROVE), respectively. Bateson, *Convict Ships*, 3, 6. One of the few transports lost at sea, the *Neva*, was carrying Irish convicts from Cork when it sank in 1835. For more on the *Neva*, see McCarthy and Todd, *Wreck* and Bateson, *Convict Ships*, 248–252.

The historical scholarship on shipwrecks (both in Irish historiography and beyond) is relatively scant and overshadowed by sensational narratives of particular disasters (such as Willis, *Shipwreck*) or analysis of archaeologically significant sites (Parker, *Ancient Shipwrecks*). An exception is McMahon, "Shipwrecks," which argues that maritime disasters—and the narratives surrounding them—connected with the Irish reading public during the Famine because they mirrored the great losses, through migration and death, that Irish society was experiencing at the time. Scattered references to Irish Famine-era emigrant shipwrecks can be found in Cohn, *Mass Migration*, 147; Coleman, *Going to America*, 121–131; Guillet, *Great Migration*, 128; Hansen, *Atlantic Migration*, 177; MacDonagh, *Pattern*, 248–250, 266. Famous cases of Irish emigrant shipwrecks during the Famine era included the *Exmouth* (1847), *Ocean Monarch* (1848), *St. John* (1849), *Hannah* (1849), *Maria* (1849), *Caleb Grimshaw* (1849), *Annie Jane* (1853), *Staffordshire* (1853), *Tayleur* (1853), and *City of Glasgow* (1854).

17 *Freeman's Journal* (Sydney), November 21, 1850.

18 *Sailor's Magazine* [New York] 24, no. 4 (December 1851): 484; Dana, *Two Years*, 45.

19 Dr. Fraser is cited in Maury, *Englishwoman* [pt. II], 13. A manuscript copy of Fraser's report is also held in Box 3, Folder 24, Archbishop John Hughes Collection (AANY). SSJ, *Irene* (MLMSS 599, SL-NSW); SSJ, *Kinnear [2]* (AJCP PRO 3200, SL-TAS); *Morning Chronicle* (Quebec), October 18, 1854; Samuel Pillow journal, 1852–1853 (Ap 115, SL-NSW).

20 Samuel Harvey journal, 1849 (T3258/66/24–27, PRONI).

21 SSJ, *Rodney* (AJCP PRO 3208, SL-TAS); SSJ, *Tasmania [2]* (AJCP PRO 3211, SL-TAS); SSJ, *Bangalore* (AJCP PRO 3189, SL-TAS); SSJ, *Hyderabad [2]* (AJCP PRO 3198, SL-TAS).

22 Lysaght, "Women," 23; *Report [Colonization from Ireland]* (1847), 259; *Galway Vindicator*, April 5, 1851. The Mayo eyewitness is cited in Tóibín and Ferriter, *Irish Famine*, 106. For secondary sources on nineteenth-century Irish funerary practices, see note 45 of chapter 3, above.

23 The *Boston Herald* letter is cited in *Nation* (Dublin), June 10, 1854; Moore, *Voyage Out*, 69; Hassam, *No Privacy*, 8.

24 William H. McCleery to John Orr, July 1, 1847 (Ulster-American Folk Park [DIPPAM]); *First Report [Emigrant Ships]* (1854), 122–128.

25 Samuel Harvey journal, 1849 (T3258/66/25–26, PRONI); *Emigrant Ship "Washington"* (1851), 437–438.

26 Frederick W. Hart to William Mure, March 29, 1851 (CO 384/88, TNA); A. D. Crossman to William Mure, April 5, 1851 (CO 384/88, TNA).

27 *Papers [North America]* (1847–1848), 319–323; *Report [Sickness and Mortality]* (1854), 54, 49; *Third Report* (1849), 620. The Black Hole of Calcutta was a dungeon in India where dozens of British soldiers reputedly suffocated to death over the course of one night in June 1756.

28 *Ancien Journal*, vol. 2, 16 and vol. 1, 7, 16 [IFA]. The records ("annals") of the activities of the Grey Nuns of Montreal during the Famine are analyzed and reprinted by Jason King in Kinealy, Moran, and King, *History*, 2:21–27, 197–216.

29 *Armagh Guardian*, August 20, 1849 (DIPPAM).

30 James Duncan diary, 1846–1848 (MssColl 859, NYPL).

31 *Sailors' Magazine* [London] 8, no. 88 (April 1846): 74; Sarah Carroll to Teresa Lawlor, September 16, 1849 (Teresa Lawlor letters, California Historical Society, San Francisco [KMC]); *Boston Pilot*, May 15, 1852.

32 T. W. C. Murdoch to Herman Merivale, February 11, 1853 (CO 386/70, TNA); SSJ, *George Seymour* (AJCP PRO 3214, SL-TAS); SSJ, *Hyderabad [2]* (AJCP PRO 3198, SL-TAS); SSJ, *Earl Grey [4]* (AJCP PRO 3193, SL-TAS); SSJ, *Midlothian* (AJCP PRO M711, SL-TAS).

33 *Report [Sickness and Mortality]* (1854), 38–39; *Sailors' Magazine* [London] 10, no. 109 (January 1848): 7–8; SSJ, *Blackfriar* (AJCP PRO 3189, SL-TAS). For more on miasma theory, the mid-nineteenth-century popular notion that infectious diseases were caused by fatal odors and airs (effluvia), see Vandenbroucke, "1855 Cholera."

34 Henry Johnson to Jane Johnson, September 18, 1848 (T2319/1, PRONI); the account of the *Elizabeth and Sara* is cited in Hamrock, *Famine in Mayo*, 140; Samuel Harvey journal, 1849 (T3258/66/28–29, PRONI).

35 SSJ, *Maria* (AJCP PRO 3203, SL-TAS); *Sailor's Magazine* [New York] 20, no. 2 (October 1847): 43. Nolloth treated other patients with generosity too.

36 George E. Binsted diary, 1848–1849 (DLMS 137, SL-NSW); W. Usherwood journal, 1852–1853 (B 784 [CY 1117], SL-NSW); Charles Moore diary, 1855 (B 1319, SL-NSW); SSJ, *Hyderabad [2]* (AJCP PRO 3198, SL-TAS).

37 *Galway Vindicator*, January 25, 1854. In another account of the *Tayleur*'s accident (published in the *Belfast News-Letter*, January 25, 1854 [BLN]), it was reported that the man who climbed the rigging had "mounted to the topmast for security, and lashed himself there in a sail, where he was some hours afterwards picked off, being at the moment, strange to say, asleep." The *Ocean Monarch* disaster was reported in the *Limerick Reporter*, August 29, 1848. The noble "foreigner" referred to in the article is probably Frederick Jerome, who received many plaudits for his bravery that day.

38 *Copy [Canada]* (1850), 5; *Copies [North American Colonies]* (1854–1855), 116; H. and A. Cope to Enoch Train and Co., December 23, 1846 (Series 1c, Vol. 43, HSP); H. and A. Cope to Mary Bateman, January 19, 1853 (Series 1c, Vol. 43, HSP).

39 *Morning Chronicle* (Quebec), October 4, 1848; *Sailors' Magazine* [London] 8, no. 87 (March 1846): 46–48; *Galway Vindicator*, October 15, 1853. On October 7, 1848, the *Morning Chronicle* published a rejoinder by the captain of the *Hampton* who admitted that M'Fie had abandoned the *Ann*—and defended his decision to do so—but denied that the passengers had been locked below deck.

40 *Nation* (Dublin), June 4, 1853; *Boston Pilot*, July 28, 1849; *Galway Vindicator*, October 15, 1853; *Boston Pilot*, February 18, 1854.

41 *Ancien Journal*, Vol. 2, 17 [IFA]; O'Gallagher and Dompierre, *Eyewitness*, 98; *Ancien Journal*, vol. 2, 106 [IFA].

42 Miller, "Landscape" analyzes pre-Famine Mass attendance figures; Dana, *Two Years*, 45; William B. Neville journal, 1848–1849 (DLMSQ 148, SL-NSW); *Galway Express*, December 31, 1853.

43 Thomas Corby to Lord Wandesforde, March 23, 1847 (35,526/3, NLI); *Galway Vindicator*, June 18, 1853.

44 Liverpool Health of Towns Association to Sir George Grey, March 17, 1847 (HO 45/1816, TNA); James Mathews to William Meredyth Somerville, July 1, 1847 (HO 45/1816, TNA); "A Citizen" is cited in O'Gallagher and Dompierre, *Eyewitness*, 21, 25. Under the poor law system, each union funded itself through rates collected within its boundaries. Paupers were, therefore, entitled to relief only in the union they were originally from. This is why James Mathews demanded that the deportees be sent "to the places on which they are legally chargeable."

45 *Papers [North America]* (1847), 44–45; T. F. Elliot to James Stephen, August 4, 1847 (CO 384/79, TNA); *First Report [Emigrant Ships]* (1854), 5.

46 T. W. C. Murdoch to Herman Merivale, February 11, 1853 (CO 386/70, TNA); *Papers [North America]* (1847), 27, 48–49; *Papers [North America]* (1847–1848), 388–389; *Report [Sickness and Mortality]* (1854), 61.

47 McGee's "sailing coffins" speech was published in the Dublin *Nation* on March 18, 1848. *Freeman's Journal and Catholic Register* (New York), April 1, 1854; *Freeman's Journal* (Sydney), August 6, 1853. For more on the origin of the phrase "coffin ships," see McMahon, "Tracking."

48 Thomas Reilly to John M. Kelly, April 24, 1848 (10,511/2, NLI); "Saranak's 26th Voyage," 1853, ticket #8048 (Series 1a, Box 280, HSP); "Saranak's 21st Voyage," 1851, ticket #6348 (Series 1a, Box 69, HSP); "Saranak's 11th Voyage," 1847–1848, ticket #2795 (Series 1a, Box 65, HSP); "Saranak's 14th Voyage," 1849, ticket #3644 (Series 1a, Box 66, HSP).

49 *Galway Vindicator*, July 3, 1847; July 24, 1847; *Nation* (Dublin), May 3, 1851; John Montgomery to Joseph Searight, January 25, 1849 (D2794/1/2, PRONI [DIPPAM]).

50 *Third Report* (1849), 619; Judith Phelan to Teresa Lawlor, January 24, 1851 (Teresa Lawlor letters, California Historical Society, San Francisco [KMC]); Anne Kelly to John Kelly, July 12, 1850 (from Patricia Shaw, San Francisco, CA [KMC]); Margaret Masterson to Michael Masterson, October 4, 1850 (Masterson family letters, Kentucky Historical Society [KMC]); *Nation* (New York), March 17, 1849.

51 *Galway Vindicator*, June 17, 1846; October 20, 1847; *Limerick Reporter*, January 27, 1854; *Galway Vindicator*, January 25, 1854.

52 H. and A. Cope to George Nichols, November 29, 1853 (Series 1c, Vol. 43, HSP); George Nichols to H. and A. Cope, December 26, 1853 (Series 1d, Box 307, HSP); W. Tapscott and Co. to H. and A. Cope, May 16, 1854 (Series 1d, Box 307, HSP); Stephen Walcott to A. C. Buchanan, September 18, 1847 (CO 386/122, TNA). Throughout August, September, and October 1847, the Quebec *Morning Chronicle* published lists of the names, ages, and vessels of those who died at Grosse Île in the summer of 1847. In November, it also published the names and ages of some of those who died at sea. On October 26 and November 29, 1847, it printed details on "money and effects left by emigrants who died without relatives at Grosse Isle" including "204 boxes and trunks, a large number of feather beds, and great quantity of wearing apparel."

53 *Third Report* (1849), 620; John O'Connor is cited in Tuke, *Visit*, 48; Edward Mc-
   Nally to William McNally, June 8, 1851 (T1448, PRONI [DIPPAM]); Jane Ellen Orr
   to John M. Orr, June 28, 1848 (Ulster-American Folk Park [DIPPAM]).

54 *Third Report* (1849), 620; Daniel Murphy to John Baldwin Murphy, May 1, 1849
   (T3258/23/1, PRONI); Eliza Fitzgerald to Michael Cahill, December 18, 1848 (Ulster-
   American Folk Park [DIPPAM]).

55 Mrs. Nolan to Patrick Nolan, October 8, 1850 (T2054, PRONI [KMC]); Daniel
   Rowntree to Laurence Rowntree, March 23, 1852 (from Prof. Emeritus Arnold
   Schrier, University of Cincinnati [KMC]); "Saranak's 11th Voyage," 1847–1848, ticket
   #2713 (Series 1a, Box 65, HSP).

56 *Morning Chronicle* (Quebec), October 18, 1854; William Hutton to John McCrea,
   October 20, 1854 (D2298/4/2, PRONI [DIPPAM]).

57 James J. Mitchell journal, 1853 (Misc. Mss. Mitchell, James J., NYHS).

5. ARRIVAL

1 John Burke, "Reminiscences [1839–1891]" (AHMC Burke, John, NYHS); Wiley and
  Putnam, *Wiley & Putnam's*, 93. For an excellent, longitudinal study of how networks
  shaped the financial security of Famine-era Irish immigrants in New York, see Anbinder, Ó Gráda, and Wegge, "Networks and Opportunities."

2 Reid and Mongan, *Decent Set*, 47; *Belfast News-Letter*, December 14, 1849 (BLN).

3 Byrne, *Emigrant's Guide*, 12–13; MacKenzie, *Emigrant's Guide*, 99; O'Hanlon, *Irish
  Emigrant's*, 185–187, 43; Wiley and Putnam, *Wiley & Putnam's*, 60.

4 Reid and Mongan, *Decent Set*, 45; Charles Woods journal, 1851 (CON 76/1/1, SL-
  TAS); *Third Report* (1849), 613.

5 Moore, *Voyage Out*, 69; Richard Nuttal Preston to his uncle [Mr. Greaves], n.d.
  [1852] (SAS/3/1/12/e, MMA); John Burke, "Reminiscences [1839–1891]" (AHMC
  Burke, John, NYHS).

6 Begley, "Journal," 46 (KMC); Hassam, *No Privacy*, 61, 8–9.

7 Joseph Claughton diary, 1852 (MLDOC 366, SL-NSW).

8 Andrew Collin to his parents, November 30, 1853 (T2834/1/2, PRONI [DIPPAM]).

9 Henry Johnson to Jane Johnson, September 18, 1848 (T2319/1, PRONI); Edward
  McNally to William McNally, June 8, 1851 (T1448, PRONI [DIPPAM]); James
  Duncan diary, 1846–1848 (MssColl 859, NYPL).

10 *Nation* (New York), May 12, 1849; *Morning Chronicle* (Quebec), June 6, 1851; August
   18, 1853.

11 James J. Mitchell journal, 1853 (Misc. Mss. Mitchell, James J., NYHS); *Anglo-Celt*
   (Cavan), March 11, 1852. Almost identical reports of the *Georgiana* affair were
   published in the *Freeman's Journal* (Sydney), October 28, 1852, and *Limerick Reporter*,
   February 11, 1853.

12 James Duncan diary, 1846–1848 (MssColl 859, NYPL).

13 Foster, "Copy" (D3618, PRONI [DIPPAM]).

14 *Papers [North America]* (1847), 33; *Copies [North American Colonies]* (1851), 333; *Papers
   [North America]* (1847), 47.

15 Stephen Walcott to A. C. Buchanan, July 3, 1847 (CO 386/122, TNA); *Papers [North American Colonies]* (1854), 62–63; *Copies [North American Colonies]* (1854–1855), 140.

16 Stephen Walcott to A. C. Buchanan, August 3, 1847 (CO 386/122, TNA); Caroline Chisholm to T. N. Redington, July 2, 1847 (FS/1847/3, NAI); Archibald Cunninghame to Lord Monteagle, November 5, 1847 (13,397/2, NLI).

17 *Second Report [Colonization from Ireland]* (1847–1848), 271, 273; *Third Report* (1849), 613. The cow Mary Brine was in charge of had been sent aboard the *Yeoman* by Gore-Booth to provide its passengers with fresh milk during the voyage.

18 *Copy [Canada]* (1850), 7, 11; Vere Foster to his mother, September 12, 1851 (D3618, PRONI [DIPPAM]); *Papers [North America, and to the Australian Colonies]* (1847–1848), 96. For Gore-Booth's denial that he had neglected his emigrants or sent them against their will, see Robert Gore-Booth to Stephen Walcott, March 16, 1848 (D4131/H/8, PRONI).

19 *Report [Frauds upon Emigrants]* (1847), 3; *Limerick Reporter*, May 2, 1848; O'Hanlon, *Irish Emigrant's*, 50, 52. Before the founding of Castle Garden in 1855, writes Kevin Kenny, immigrants "simply arrived off the boat onto the streets of Manhattan, with no sense of where they were, where they might go, or how they might get there" (Kenny, *American Irish*, 104). For more on the founding of the Castle Garden depot and on New York's runners and frauds in the nineteenth century, see Coleman, *Going to America*, 266–270, 192–203.

20 Purcell, "New York," 31; *Annual Reports [1861]*, 6, 25, 155.

21 *American Celt* (Boston), September 7, 1850; the Philadelphia Emigrant's Friend Society is cited in Gallman, *Receiving Erin's*, 38; *Nation* (Dublin), August 30, 1851; *American Celt* (Boston), September 14, 1850. For more on emigrant societies in Liverpool and Philadelphia, see Gallman, *Receiving Erin's*, 37–47. The Philadelphia-based American Emigrants' Friend Society, which organized itself on a national basis with branches in major port cities, was founded in 1851. The Irish Emigrant Society (New York) and Irish Emigrant Aid Society (Boston) were both founded in 1841.

22 H. and A. Cope to Captain R. R. Decan, June 30, 1852 (Series 1c, vol. 43, HSP); H. and A. Cope to Patrick McAleer, June 10, 1845 (Series 1c, vol. 43, HSP); H. and A. Cope to Mary B. Thomas, July 24, 1850 (Series 1c, vol. 43, HSP); H. and A. Cope to Thomas Donaldson, August 10, 1847 (Series 1c, vol. 43, HSP).

23 Reid and Mongan, *Decent Set*, 47–48; *People's Advocate and New South Wales Vindicator* (Sydney), March 16, 1850 (TROVE); T. N. Redington to Lieutenant Governor of Van Diemen's Land, September 18, 1848 (CON/LB/1, NAI); Jonathon Quin to James Quin, December 10, 1849 (MLDOC 3507, SL-NSW).

24 Stephen Walcott to A. C. Buchanan, July 17, 1847 (CO 386/122, TNA); Gallman, *Receiving Erin's*, 47.

25 Jane Ellen Orr to John M. Orr, October 13, 1847 (Ulster-American Folk Park [DIPPAM]); John Martin to "Eva" [Mary Anne Kelly], June 6, 1850 (Pos. 1396, NLI); Rev. John G. Mulholland to Rev. George Kirkpatrick, March 21, 1849 (D1424/11/1, PRONI [DIPPAM]). For more on the Irish nationalist press (at home and abroad)

in the mid-nineteenth century, see Andrews, *Newspapers and Newsmakers* and McMahon, *Global Dimensions*.

26 *Boston Pilot*, April 19, 1851; December 3, 1842; September 29, 1849.

27 *Nation* (New York), February 24, 1849; *American Celt* (Boston), October 12, 1850; O'Hanlon, *Irish Emigrant's*, 176–177.

28 *Nation* (Dublin), May 15, 1852; *Belfast Commercial Chronicle*, April 28, 1852 (DIPPAM); *Galway Vindicator*, June 30, 1852.

29 *Nation* (Dublin), June 6, 1846; *Times* (London), May 14, 1850 (TDA).

30 *Limerick Reporter*, March 3, 1846; *Freeman's Journal and Catholic Register* (New York), August 2, 1851; July 6, 1850.

31 *Morning Chronicle* (Quebec), May 18, 1848; *American Celt* (Boston), October 26, 1850; *Boston Pilot*, March 31, 1849; *Galway Express*, August 12, 1854; *Limerick Reporter*, July 22, 1853.

32 *Boston Pilot*, November 6, 1847; January 5, 1850.

33 *American Celt and Adopted Citizen* (Boston), March 1, 1851; *Boston Pilot*, April 7, 1849; September 7, 1850.

34 *Freeman's Journal* (Sydney), December 16, 1854; March 10, 1855.

35 *American Celt and Catholic Citizen* (Buffalo), July 31, 1852; December 24, 1852; *Freeman's Journal* (Sydney), March 10, 1855; *Boston Pilot*, January 5, 1850; *Morning Chronicle* (Quebec), September 16, 1850; *American Celt* (Boston), November 23, 1850; *Nation* (Dublin), October 31, 1846.

36 John Campbell to E. Campbell, February 26, 1846 (D1781/3/6, PRONI [DIPPAM]); John Lindsay to William McCullough, June 21, 1847 (D3305/2/4, PRONI [DIPPAM]); David Moody to his mother, October 16, 1851 (T2901/3/1, PRONI [DIPPAM]); George Ritchie to his parents, January 10, 1851 (T3292/2, PRONI).

37 *American Celt and Adopted Citizen* (Boston), May 24, 1851.

38 *Anglo-Celt* (Cavan), March 23, 1849; *Limerick Reporter*, January 21, 1853; Daniel Guiney to his mother and brothers, August 9, 1850 (QRO/4/3/1/161, NAI).

39 *Papers [North America]* (1847), 21; *Second Report [Colonization from Ireland]* (1847–1848), 279; *Copies [North American Colonies]* (1851), 324.

40 "Saranak's 20th Voyage," 1851, ticket #5755 (Series 1a, Box 69, HSP); "Refunded Passenger Tickets, 1853," ticket #8760 (Series 1b, Box 290, HSP); "Saranak's 20th Voyage," 1851, ticket #5913 (Series 1a, Box 69, HSP).

41 *Third Report* (1849), 621; Thomas McGinity to John McGinity and Mary Crosby, October 24, 1847 (T3539/2, PRONI).

42 Stott, *Workers*, 91; "Saranak's 32nd Voyage," 1855, ticket #10712 (Series 1a, Box 281, HSP); *Papers [North America]* (1847), 41; John Burke, "Reminiscences [1839–1891]" (AHMC Burke, John, NYHS). The emigrating miners Buchanan was referring to may have come from the Prior-Wandesforde estate (see chapter 1).

43 *Papers [North American Colonies]* (1852), 575; James Purcell to Bridget Brennan, August 10, 1846 (35,533/1, NLI); "Saranak's 20th Voyage," 1851, tickets #5755, #5884 (Series 1a, Box 69, HSP); "Refunded Passenger Tickets, 1851," ticket #6122 (Series 1b, Box 290, HSP).

44 Jane White to Eleanor Wallace, June 27, 1849 (D1195/3/5, PRONI [DIPPAM]); O'Hanlon, *Irish Emigrant's*, 189; *Third Report* (1849), 617, 619.

45 *Freeman's Journal* (Sydney), February 24, 1853; Thomas Reilly to John M. Kelly, April 24, 1848 (10,511/2, NLI); *Third Report* (1849), 622; John Lindsay to William McCullough, June 21, 1847 (D3305/2/4, PRONI [DIPPAM]); C. A. McFarland to her mother, March 5, 1855 (D1665/3/6, PRONI [DIPPAM]).

46 Sarah Carroll to Teresa Lawlor, September 16, 1849 (Teresa Lawlor letters, California Historical Society, San Francisco [KMC]); Margaret Meehan to Teresa Lawlor, July 13, 1854 (Teresa Lawlor letters, California Historical Society, San Francisco [KMC]); *Anglo-Celt* (Cavan), January 5, 1854; *Report [Colonization from Ireland]* (1847), 357.

47 Michael Hogan to Catherine Nolan, March 12, 1851 (from Seamus Murphy, Pollerton Little, Carlow, County Carlow [KMC]); Eliza Fitzgerald to Michael Cahill, December 18, 1848 (Ulster-American Folk Park [DIPPAM]); *Third Report* (1849), 621.

48 *Nation* (New York), October 28, 1848; March 24, 1849; *Freeman's Journal* (Sydney), April 21, 1855; *Boston Pilot*, December 5, 1846.

49 *Third Report* (1849), 615.

50 *Galway Vindicator*, July 24, 1852; "Saranak's 24th Voyage," 1852, ticket #7257 (Series 1a, Box 279, HSP).

CONCLUSION

1 *Third Report* (1849), 619. The story of Garry sneaking aboard the ship and having his passage paid by a subscription raised by the captain is in *Second Report [Colonization from Ireland]* (1847–1848), 273. Daniel Rountree to Mrs. M. Butler, May 5, 1851 (from Prof. Emeritus Arnold Schrier, University of Cincinnati [KMC]). The Rountree family background can be found in the accompanying notes within the Kerby Miller emigrant letter collection.

2 Samuel Harvey journal, 1849 (T3258/66/23, PRONI); Ó Gráda, "Next World," esp. 331–336. Ó Gráda also discusses migration as famine relief in *Black '47*, 106–107 and (with Kevin H. O'Rourke) "Migration." In the *Atlas of the Great Irish Famine*, William J. Smyth points out that while the proportions of documented mortalities and rates of emigration almost exactly corresponded between 1846 and 1849, they diverged dramatically over the next three years (1850–1852). Thus did the Great Famine serve, Smyth argues, as the catalyst for a "social revolution" of sustained emigration, which endured into the twenty-first century (Smyth, "Exodus," 494).

3 Osterhammel, *Transformation*, xv; Wenzlhuemer, *Connecting*, i; Mitchel, *Jail Journal*, 8. For more on personal letters and the postal system, see Gerber, *Authors* and Henkin, *Postal Age*.

4 *Nation* (Dublin), August 14, 1847; *Copies [North American Colonies]* (1857 Session 1), 910; *Annual Reports [1861]*, 187; MacDonagh, *Pattern*, 16.

5 *Annual Reports [1861]*, 175; Cohn, *Mass Migration*, 7–8.

6 Éstevez-Saá and O'Connor, "Interview," 166; for the John Roach article, see Irish Red Cross, "Coordinated Approach Needed to Address Tragedy of Mediterranean

Coffin Ships," www.redcross.ie; *Irish Examiner* (Dublin), October 24, 2019; *Irish Independent* (Dublin), October 30, 2019; *Irish Times* (Dublin), October 29, 2019. When the COVID-19 pandemic first broke out in early 2020, many Irish at home and abroad reciprocated an 1847 donation sent by the Choctaw Nation for famine relief by contributing to a GoFundMe account in aid of the Navajo and Hopi communities suffering in the southwestern United States (see *Irish Times* [Dublin], May 5, 2020).

ESSAY ON SOURCES AND METHODOLOGY

1 Scholars working in Irish migration today owe debts to earlier works such as Miller, *Emigrants and Exiles*; Akenson, *Irish in Ontario*; Fitzpatrick, *Oceans*; O'Farrell, *Irish in Australia*; Meagher, *Inventing*. In recent years, groundbreaking new studies have included Barr, *Ireland's Empire* and Barr and Carey, *Religion*; Campbell, *Ireland's New Worlds*; Janis, *Greater Ireland*; Mannion, *Land of Dreams*; O'Neill, *Catholics*; Roddy, *Population, Providence*; Townend, *Road*; Whelehan, *Dynamiters*. Foundational works on the Great Famine include Gray, *Famine, Land*; Kinealy, *This Great*; Ó Gráda, *Black '47*. For Rediker's "unspoken proposition," see *Outlaws of the Atlantic*, 2–3. Important works on the labor histories of sailors and pirates include Rediker, *Between the Devil*; Linebaugh and Rediker, *Many-Headed*; Rediker, *Outlaws*; Vickers, *Young Men*; Appleby, *Women*; Magra, *Poseidon's Curse*; Schoeppner, *Moral Contagion*. Books, which include at least one chapter on migrants' experiences at sea, include Anderson, *New England's Generation*; Berry, *A Path*; Brown, *Passage*; Cressy, *Coming Over*; Kushner, *Battle*; Taylor, *Distant Magnet*. For brief analyses of the Irish emigrant experience at sea, see Scally, *End*, 184–229 and Potter, *To the Golden*, 113–160. In his 1976 Ph.D. dissertation, on which *Emigrants and Exiles* was based, Kerby Miller included an interesting chapter on "The Journey to North America" (see Miller, "Emigrants"). The *Journal of Global History* 11, no. 2 (July 2016): 155–294 is a special issue dedicated to examining nineteenth-century sailing ships as *lieux d'histoire*. Of particular interest to historians of emigrant identity at sea is de Schmidt, "This Strange." Studies of slave ships include Borucki, *From Shipmates*; Kelley, *Voyage*; O'Malley, *Final Passages*; Rediker, *Slave Ship*; Smallwood, *Saltwater Slavery*. Other notable works of non-terracentric history include Christopher, Pybus, and Rediker, *Many Middle Passages*; Lipman, *Saltwater Frontier*; Perl-Rosenthal, *Citizen Sailors*; Rafferty, *Republic Afloat*.

2 In order to eschew the controversies surrounding their authenticity, neither Gerald Keegan's nor Robert Whyte's alleged "famine diaries" were employed during the course of research for this book. For a discussion of the debates surrounding those books, see McGowan, "Famine, Facts" and King, "Genealogy." Christine Kinealy, Gerard Moran, and Jason King have recently co-edited a four-volume set of primary sources relating to the Great Famine. Volume 2, edited by Jason King, contains a number of Famine-era voyage narratives (see Kinealy, Moran, and King, *History*, vol. 2). For background information on the Cope family's line of packet ships, see Killick, "Early."

3 Kenny, "Diaspora," 135; Wenzlhuemer, "Ship," 165. Other important works of trans-national migration history include Bender, *Rethinking*; Choate, *Emigrant Nation*; Gabaccia, *Italy's*; Tyrrell, "Reflections." The *Journal of American History*'s special issue on "The Nation and Beyond" (86, no. 3 [December 1999]) is very useful too, as is, of course, the "*AHR* Forum: Oceans of History" in *American Historical Review* 111, no. 3 (June 2006): 717–780. Future studies of Irish emigrant voyages could put more focus on the differences and varied experiences within the Irish emigrant population. How did varying points of departure and arrival impact the migration process?

4 For adroit analyses of the US and UK governments' migration policies, see Mac-Donagh, *Pattern*; Gallman, *Receiving Erin's*; Hirota, *Expelling*.

5 Patt Brenan to Lord Wandesforde, n.d. [1847] (35,526/7, NLI).

6 Fitzpatrick, "Irish," 273–275; Gerber, *Authors*, 9, 39–40; Fitzpatrick, *Oceans*, 28. Andrew Hassam also offers interesting insights into the form and function of voyage diaries in *No Privacy*, xiii–xiv.

BIBLIOGRAPHY

MANUSCRIPT COLLECTIONS

Australia
   State Library of New South Wales
      Caroline Chisholm papers (1833–1854)
      Charles Moore diary (1855)
      David Atkinson letters (1851)
      Elizabeth Hentig journal (1853)
      George E. Binsted diary (1848–1849)
      John Henry Read journal (1848–1849)
      Jonathon Quin letter (1849)
      Joseph Claughton diary (1852)
      Joseph Kidd Walpole journal (1849)
      Samuel Pillow journal (1852–1853)
      Tasmanian Papers (1803–1890)
      Thomas Willmott journal (1852)
      William B. Neville journal (1848–1849)
      W. Usherwood journal (1852–1853)
   State Library of Tasmania
      Australian Joint Copying Project (Surgeon-Superintendents' Journals)
      Charles Woods journal (1851)
Ireland
   Galway County Library
      Galway Poor Law Minute Books
      Gort Poor Law Minute Books
      Mountbellew Poor Law Minute Books
   James Hardiman Library, National University of Ireland, Galway
      Galway Town Commissioners Minutes
   National Archives of Ireland
      Convict Letterbooks, Chief Secretary's Office
      Convict Reference Files
      Free Settlers' papers
      Official Papers Series 2 (1832–1880), Chief Secretary's Office
      Quit Rent Office papers
   National Library of Ireland
      Alan Queale papers
      Inchiquin family papers

      Kelly family papers
      Monteagle family papers
      Prior-Wandesforde family papers
      Richard Henry Sheil papers
United Kingdom
    Merseyside Museum and Archives, Liverpool
      Richard Nuttal Preston letters (1852–1854)
      William Culshaw Greenhalgh diary (1853)
    National Archives, Kew
      Colonial Office papers
      Home Office papers
      Records of the Admiralty
    Public Record Office of Northern Ireland
      George Ritchie letter (1851)
      Henry Johnson letter (1848–1850)
      Lissadell family papers
      McGinity family papers (1847–1850)
      Miscellaneous Emigrant letters
      Murphy family letters (1849)
      Samuel Harvey journal (1849)
United States
    Archives of the Archdiocese of New York
      Archbishop John Hughes Collection
    Columbia, Missouri
      Kerby A. Miller Collection
    Historical Society of Pennsylvania
      Cope Family papers (Collection 1486)
    New-York Historical Society
      James J. Mitchell journal (1853)
      John Burke "Reminiscences" (1839–1891)
    New York Public Library
      James Duncan diary (1846–1848)

MICROFILMED NEWSPAPERS

Australia
  Freeman's Journal (Sydney)
Canada
  Morning Chronicle (Quebec)
Ireland
  Anglo-Celt (Cavan)
  Galway Express
  Galway Vindicator
  Limerick Reporter

Nation (Dublin)
United States
  American Celt (Boston)
  American Celt and Adopted Citizen (Boston)
  American Celt and Catholic Citizen (Buffalo)
  Boston Pilot
  Freeman's Journal and Catholic Register (New York)
  Irish-American (New York)
  Nation (New York)

ELECTRONIC DATABASES

British Library Newspapers (Gale Cengage Learning)
Documenting Ireland: Parliament, People, and Migration (Queen's University Belfast)
Irish Famine Archive, Grey Nun Records (Jason King, 2015; National University of
  Ireland, Galway)
Times [London] Digital Archive, 1785–1985 (Gale Cengage Learning)
TROVE Digitised Newspapers (National Library of Australia)

PRINTED PRIMARY SOURCES

Annual Reports of the Commissioners of Emigration of the State of New York, from the Organization of the Commission, May 5, 1847, to 1860, Inclusive. New York: John F. Trow, 1861.

Anonymous. "Emigration, Emigrants, and Emigrant Ships." *Irish Quarterly Review* (Dublin) 4, no. 14 (June 1854): 430–471.

Begley, Donal, ed. "The Journal of an Irish Emigrant to Canada." *Irish Ancestor* 6, no. 1 (1947): 43–47.

Blunt, Joseph. *The Shipmaster's Assistant, and Commercial Digest.* 5th ed. New York: Harper & Brothers, 1851.

Browning, Colin Arrott. *The Convict Ship, and England's Exiles: In Two Parts.* London: Hamilton, Adams, 1847.

Byrne, J. C. *Emigrant's Guide to New South Wales Proper, Australia Felix, and South Australia.* London: Effingham Wilson, 1848.

Carleton, William. *Traits and Stories of the Irish Peasantry.* 1st series. London: George Routledge & Sons, 1877.

Chisholm, Caroline. *Comfort for the Poor! Meat Three Times a Day!! Voluntary Information from the People of New South Wales.* London: John Ollivier, 1847.

———. *Emigration and Transportation Relatively Considered.* London: John Ollivier, 1847.

Copies or Extracts of Any Despatches Relative to Emigration to the Australian Colonies, in Continuation of Papers Presented to the House of Commons, in February 1850. 1851 (347): xl.

Copies or Extracts of Any Despatches Relative to Emigration to the North American Colonies; in Continuation of Papers Presented to the House of Commons in July 1849. 1851 (348): xl.

Copies or Extracts of Despatches Relative to Emigration to the North American Colonies (in Continuation of Papers Presented April 1851). 1854–1855 (464): xxxix.

Copies or Extracts of Despatches Relative to Emigration to the North American Colonies (in Continuation of Parliamentary Paper, no. 464, of Session 1855). 1857 Session 1 (14): x.

Copy of a Despatch Transmitting Report from the Chief Agent of Emigration in Canada for the Year 1849, and Other Documents. 1850 (173): xl.

Dana, Richard Henry. *Two Years before the Mast: A Personal Narrative of Life at Sea.* New York: Harper and Brothers, 1846.

Duffy, Charles Gavan. *My Life in Two Hemispheres.* 2 vols. London: T. Fisher Unwin, 1898.

Emigrant Ship "Washington." Copy of a Letter from Lord Hobart to the Colonial Land and Emigration Commissioners. 1851 (198): xl.

First Report from the Select Committee of the House of Lords, on Colonization from Ireland; Together with the Minutes of Evidence. 1847–1848 (415): xvii.

First Report from the Select Committee on Emigrant Ships; with the Minutes of Evidence Taken Before Them. 1854 (163): xiii.

Foster, Vere. *Copy of a Letter Addressed by Mr. Vere Foster to the Directors of the American Emigrants' Friend Society of Philadelphia.* 1851.

Hassam, Andrew, ed. *No Privacy for Writing: Shipboard Diaries, 1852–1879.* Melbourne: Melbourne University Press, 1995.

Instructions for Surgeons-Superintendent on Board Convict Ships Proceeding to New South Wales, or Van Diemen's Land: And for Masters of Those Ships. London: W. Clowes for Her Majesty's Stationary Office, 1840.

MacKenzie, Eneas. *The Emigrant's Guide to Australia, with a Memoir of Mrs. Chisholm.* London: Clarke, Beeton, & Co., 1853.

Maury, Sarah Mytton. *An Englishwoman in America.* London: Thomas Richardson and Son, 1848.

Merchant Shipping (Convention). A Bill to Make Such Amendments of the Law Relating to Merchant Shipping as Are Necessary or Expedient to Give Effect to an International Convention for the Safety of Life at Sea, Signed in London on January the twentieth, Nineteen Hundred and Fourteen, and for Purposes Incidental Thereto. 1914 (273): iv.

Mitchel, John. *Jail Journal.* Edited by Thomas Flanagan. Dublin: University Press of Ireland, 1982.

Moore, Bruce, ed. *The Voyage Out: 100 Years of Sea Travel to Australia.* Freemantle: Freemantle Arts Centre Press, 1991.

Nettle, George. *A Practical Guide for Emigrants to North America, Including the United States, Lower and Upper Canada, and Newfoundland.* London: Simpkin, Marshall, and Co., 1850.

O'Hanlon, Rev. John. *The Irish Emigrant's Guide for the United States.* Boston: Patrick Donahoe, 1851.

Papers Relative to Emigration to the Australian Colonies. 1850 (1163): xl.

Papers Relative to Emigration to the Australian Colonies. 1852 (1489): xxxiv.

Papers Relative to Emigration to the Australian Colonies. 1854 (436, 436-I): xlvi.

Papers Relative to Emigration to the British Provinces in North America. 1847 (777, 824): xxxix.

Papers Relative to Emigration to the British Provinces in North America. 1847–1848 (932, 964, 971, 985): xlvii.

Papers Relative to Emigration to the British Provinces in North America. 1849 (1025): xxxviii.

Papers Relative to Emigration to the British Provinces in North America, and to the Australian Colonies. 1847–1848 (50, 50-II): xlvii.

Papers Relative to Emigration to the North American Colonies. 1852 (1474): xxxiii.

Papers Relative to Emigration to the North American Colonies. 1852–1853 (1650): lxviii.

Papers Relative to Emigration to the North American Colonies. 1854 (1763): xlvi.

Report of the Select Committee Appointed by the Legislature of New-York to Examine into Frauds upon Emigrants. Albany: C. Van Benthuysen, 1847.

Report of the Select Committee of the House of Lords on Colonization from Ireland; Together with the Minute of Evidence. 1847 (737, 737-II): vi.

Report of the Select Committee of the Senate of the United States on the Sickness and Mortality on Board Emigrant Ships. Washington, D.C.: Beverley Tucker, 1854.

Sailors' Magazine and Nautical Intelligencer (London).

Sailor's Magazine and Naval Journal (New York).

Second Report from the Select Committee of the House of Lords, on Colonization from Ireland; Together with the Further Minutes of Evidence. 1847–1848 (593): xvii.

Second Report from the Select Committee on Emigrant Ships; Together with the Proceedings of the Committee, Minutes of Evidence, Appendix, and Index. 1854 (349): xiii.

Seventeenth General Report of the Emigration Commissioners. 1857, Session 2 (2249): xvi.

Seventh General Report of the Colonial Land and Emigration Commissioners. 1847 (809): xxxiii.

Sixth General Report of the Colonial Land and Emigration Commissioners. 1846 (706): xxiv.

Third Report from the Select Committee of the House of Lords on Colonization from Ireland; Together with an Appendix; and an Index to Minutes of Evidence Taken in Sessions 1847 and 1847–8. 1849 (86): xi.

Thirteenth General Report of the Colonial Land and Emigration Commissioners. 1852–1853 (1647): xl.

Trench, W. Steuart. *Realities of Irish Life.* London: Longmans, Green, 1869.

Tuke, James H. *A Visit to Connaught in the Autumn of 1847.* London: Charles Gilpin, 1848.

Twenty-Fourth General Report of the Emigration Commissioners. 1864 (3341): xvi.

Wiley, John, and George Putnam. *Wiley & Putnam's Emigrant's Guide.* London: Wiley & Putnam, 1845.

SECONDARY SOURCES

Akenson, Donald H. *The Irish in Ontario: A Study of Rural History.* Montreal: McGill-Queen's University Press, 1984.

Albion, Robert Greenhalgh. *Square-Riggers on Schedule: The New York Sailing Packets to England, France, and the Cotton Ports.* Princeton: Princeton University Press, 1938.

Anbinder, Tyler. *City of Dreams: The 400-Year Epic History of Immigrant New York*. New York: Houghton Mifflin Harcourt, 2016.

———. "From Famine to Five Points: Lord Lansdowne's Irish Tenants Encounter North America's Most Notorious Slum." *American Historical Review* 107, no. 2 (April 2002): 351–387.

———. "Lord Palmerston and the Irish Famine Emigration." *Historical Journal* 44, no. 2 (2001): 441–469.

Anbinder, Tyler, Cormac Ó Gráda, and Simone A. Wegge. "Networks and Opportunities: A Digital History of Ireland's Great Famine Refugees in New York." *American Historical Review* 124, no. 5 (December 2019): 1591–1629.

Anderson, Clare, ed. *A Global History of Convicts and Penal Colonies*. London: Bloomsbury, 2018.

Anderson, Virginia DeJohn. *New England's Generation: The Great Migration and the Formation of Society and Culture in the Seventeenth Century*. Cambridge: Cambridge University Press, 1991.

Andrews, Ann. *Newspapers and Newsmakers: The Dublin Nationalist Press in the Mid-Nineteenth Century*. Liverpool: Liverpool University Press, 2014.

Appleby, John C. *Women and English Piracy, 1540–1720: Partners and Victims of Crime*. Woodbridge, UK: Boydell Press, 2013.

Barr, Colin. *Ireland's Empire: The Roman Catholic Church in the English-Speaking World, 1829–1914*. Cambridge: Cambridge University Press, 2020.

Barr, Colin, and Hilary M. Carey, eds. *Religion and Greater Ireland: Christianity and Irish Global Networks, 1750–1969*. Montreal: McGill-Queen's University Press, 2015.

Bateson, Charles. *The Convict Ships, 1787–1868*. Sydney: A. H. & A. W. Reed, 1974.

Bender, Thomas. *Rethinking American History in a Global Age*. Berkeley: University of California Press, 2002.

Berry, Stephen R. *A Path in the Mighty Waters: Shipboard Life and Atlantic Crossings to the New World*. New Haven, Conn.: Yale University Press, 2015.

Borucki, Alex. *From Shipmates to Soldiers: Emerging Black Identities in the Río de la Plata*. Albuquerque: University of New Mexico Press, 2015.

Boyce, D. George. *Nineteenth-Century Ireland*. Dublin: Gill & Macmillan, 2005.

Brand, Ian, and Mark Staniforth. "Care and Control: Female Convict Transportation Voyage to Van Diemen's Land, 1818–1853." *Great Circle* 16, no. 1 (1994): 23–42.

Brophy, Christina Sinclair. "Keening Community: Mná Caointe, Women, Death, and Power in Ireland." Ph.D. diss., Boston College, 2010.

Brown, Kevin. *Passage to the World: The Emigrant Experience, 1807–1940*. Barnsley, UK: Seaforth Publishing, 2013.

Brunton, Deborah. *The Politics of Vaccination: Practice and Policy in England, Wales, Ireland, and Scotland, 1800–1874*. Rochester: University of Rochester Press, 2008.

Campbell, Malcolm. *Ireland's New Worlds: Immigrants, Politics, and Society in the United States and Australia, 1815–1922*. Madison: University of Wisconsin Press, 2008.

Carroll-Burke, Patrick. *Colonial Discipline: The Making of the Irish Convict System*. Dublin: Four Courts Press, 2000.

Casey, Brian. *Class and Community in Provincial Ireland, 1851–1914*. Basingstoke: Palgrave Macmillan, 2018.

Charbonneau, André, and André Sévigny. *1847, Grosse-Île: A Record of Daily Events*. Ottawa: Minister of Canadian Heritage, 1997.

Choate, Mark. *Emigrant Nation: The Making of Italy Abroad*. Cambridge, Mass.: Harvard University Press, 2008.

Christopher, Emma, Cassandra Pybus, and Marcus Rediker, eds. *Many Middle Passages: Forced Migration and the Making of the Modern World*. Berkeley: University of California Press, 2007.

Cohn, Raymond L. "Deaths of Slaves in the Middle Passage." *Journal of Economic History* 45, no. 3 (September 1985): 685–692.

———. "The Determinants of Individual Immigrant Mortality on Sailing Ships, 1836–1853." *Explorations in Economic History* 24 (1987): 371–391.

———. "Maritime Mortality in the Eighteenth and Nineteenth Centuries: A Survey." *International Journal of Maritime History* 1 (June 1989): 159–191.

———. *Mass Migration Under Sail: European Immigration to the Antebellum United States*. Cambridge: Cambridge University Press, 2008.

———. "Mortality on Immigrant Voyages to New York, 1836–1853." *Journal of Economic History* 44, no. 2 (June 1984): 289–300.

———. "Passenger Mortality on Antebellum Immigrant Ships: Further Evidence." *International Journal of Maritime History* 15 (December 2003): 1–19.

Coleman, Terry. *Going to America*. Garden City, N.Y.: Anchor, 1973.

Comerford, R. V. "Ireland 1850–70: Post-famine and mid-Victorian." In *A New History of Ireland*, vol. 5: *Ireland Under the Union, 1801–1870*, edited by W. E. Vaughan, 372–395. New York: Oxford University Press, 2010.

Connolly, S. J. *Priests and People in Pre-famine Ireland, 1780–1845*. Dublin: Four Courts Press, 2001.

Corporaal, Marguérite. *Relocated Memories: The Great Famine in Irish and Diaspora Fiction, 1846–1870*. Syracuse, N.Y.: Syracuse University Press, 2017.

Corporaal, Marguérite, and Christopher Cusack. "Rites of Passage: The Coffin Ship as a Site of Immigrants' Identity Formation in Irish and Irish American Fiction, 1855–85." *Atlantic Studies* 8, no. 3 (September 2011): 343–359.

Corporaal, Marguérite, and Jason King, eds. *Irish Global Migration and Memory: Transatlantic Perspectives of Ireland's Famine Exodus*. New York: Routledge, 2017.

Costello, Con. *Botany Bay: The Story of the Convicts Transported from Ireland to Australia, 1791–1853*. Cork: Mercier Press, 1987.

Cowley, Trudy Mae. *A Drift of "Derwent Ducks": Lives of the 200 Female Irish Convicts Transported on the Australasia from Dublin to Hobart in 1849*. Hobart: Research Tasmania, 2005.

Crawford, E. Margaret. "Typhus in Nineteenth-Century Ireland." In *Medicine, Disease, and the State in Ireland*, edited by Greta Jones and Elizabeth Malcolm, 121–137. Cork: Cork University Press, 1999.

Creighton, Margaret S. *Rites and Passages: The Experience of American Whaling, 1830–1870*. Cambridge: Cambridge University Press, 1995.

Cressy, David. *Coming Over: Migration and Communication between England and New England in the Seventeenth Century.* Cambridge: Cambridge University Press, 1987.

Crowley, John, William J. Smyth, and Mike Murphy, eds. *Atlas of the Great Irish Famine.* New York: New York University Press, 2012.

Daniels, Roger. *Coming to America: A History of Immigration and Ethnicity in American Life.* 2nd ed. New York: HarperCollins, 2002.

Davis, John H. *The Kennedys: Dynasty and Disaster.* New York: S. P. I. Books, 1992.

Davis, Richard. "'Not So Bad as a Bad Marriage': Irish Transportation Policies in the 1840s." *Tasmanian Historical Research Association Papers & Proceedings* 47, no. 1 (March 2000): 9–65.

Dear, I. C. B., and Peter Kemp, eds. *The Oxford Companion to Ships and the Sea.* 2nd ed. Oxford: Oxford University Press, 2016.

de Schmidt, Johanna. "'This Strange Little Floating World of Ours': Shipboard Periodicals and Community-Building in the 'Global' Nineteenth Century." *Journal of Global History* 11, no. 2 (July 2016): 229–250.

Donnelly, James S., Jr. *The Great Irish Potato Famine.* Phoenix Mill, UK: Sutton, 2001.

Dunn, Mary Lee. *Ballykilcline Rising: From Famine Ireland to Immigrant America.* Amherst: University of Massachusetts Press, 2008.

Dunne, Terence M. "'Humour the People': Subaltern Collective Agency and Uneven Proletarianization in Castlecomer Colliery, 1826–34." *Éire-Ireland* 53, nos. 3–4 (2018): 64–92.

Ellis, Eilish. *Emigrants from Ireland, 1847–1852: State-Aided Emigration Schemes from Crown Estates in Ireland.* Baltimore: Genealogical Publishing, 1983.

Eltis, David. "Mortality and Voyage Length in the Middle Passage: New Evidence for the Nineteenth Century." *Journal of Economic History* 44, no. 2 (June 1984): 301–308.

Éstevez-Saá, José Manuel, and Joseph O'Connor. "An Interview with Joseph O'Connor." *Contemporary Literature* 46, no. 2 (Summer 2005): 161–175.

Fitzpatrick, David. "Emigration, 1801–1870." In *A New History of Ireland,* vol. 5: *Ireland Under the Union, 1801–1870,* edited by W. E. Vaughan, 562–622. New York: Oxford University Press, 2010.

———. "The Irish in America: Exiles or Escapers?" *Reviews in American History* 15, no. 2 (June 1987): 272–278.

———. *Oceans of Consolation: Personal Accounts of Irish Migration to Australia.* Ithaca, N.Y.: Cornell University Press, 1994.

Foucault, Michel. *The History of Sexuality,* vol. 1: *An Introduction.* New York: Vintage, 1990.

Foxhall, Katherine. *Health, Medicine, and the Sea: Australian Voyages, c. 1815–1860.* Manchester: Manchester University Press, 2012.

Gabaccia, Donna. *Italy's Many Diasporas.* Seattle: University of Washington Press, 2000.

Gallman, J. Matthew. *Receiving Erin's Children: Philadelphia, Liverpool, and the Irish Famine Migration, 1845–1855.* Chapel Hill: University of North Carolina Press, 2000.

Gerber, David A. *Authors of Their Lives: The Personal Correspondence of British Immigrants to North America in the Nineteenth Century.* New York: New York University Press, 2006.

Gilbert, Pamela K. *Cholera and Nation: Doctoring the Social Body in Victorian England.* Albany: State University of New York Press, 2008.

Glazier, Ira A., Deirdre Mageean, and Barnabus Okeke. "Socio-demographic Characteristics of Irish Immigrants, 1846–1851." In *Maritime Aspects of Migration,* edited by Klaus Friedland, 243–278. Cologne: Böhlau Verlag, 1989.

Goffman, Erving. *Asylums: Essays on the Social Situation of Mental Patients and Other Inmates.* New York: Anchor, 1961.

Gray, Peter. *Famine, Land, and Politics: British Government and Irish Society, 1843–50.* Dublin: Irish Academic Press, 1999.

Griffith, Lisa Marie, and Ciarán Wallace, eds. *Grave Matters: Death and Dying in Dublin, 1500 to the Present.* Dublin: Four Courts Press, 2016.

Guillet, Edwin C. *The Great Migration: The Atlantic Crossing by Sailing Ship since 1770.* Toronto: University of Toronto Press, 1963.

Haines, Robin. *Doctors at Sea: Emigrant Voyages to Colonial Australia.* Basingstoke: Palgrave Macmillan, 2005.

———. *Emigration and the Labouring Poor: Australian Recruitment in Britain and Ireland, 1831–1860.* London: Macmillan, 1997.

———. "Indigent Misfits or Shrewd Operators? Government-Assisted Emigrants from the United Kingdom to Australia, 1831–1860." *Population Studies* 48, no. 2 (July 1994): 223–247.

———. *Life and Death in the Age of Sail: The Passage to Australia.* Sydney: University of New South Wales Press, 2006.

Hamlin, Christopher. *Cholera: The Biography.* Oxford: Oxford University Press, 2009.

Hamrock, Ivor, ed. *The Famine in Mayo, 1845–1850: A Portrait from Contemporary Sources.* Castlebar: Mayo County Council, 2004.

Hansen, Marcus Lee. *The Atlantic Migration, 1607–1860.* New York: Harper, 1961.

Harman, Kristyn. *Aboriginal Convicts: Australian, Khoisan, and Māori Exiles.* Sydney: University of New South Wales Press, 2012.

Harris, Ruth-Ann M. *The Nearest Place That Wasn't Ireland: Early Nineteenth-Century Irish Labor Migration.* Ames: Iowa State University, 1994.

Hawkings, David T. *Bound for Australia: A Guide to the Records of Transported Convicts and Early Settlers.* Stroud, UK: History Press, 2012.

Henkin, David M. *The Postal Age: The Emergence of Modern Communications in Nineteenth-Century America.* Chicago: University of Chicago Press, 2006.

Henry, William. *Coffin Ship: The Wreck of the Brig St. John.* Cork: Mercier Press, 2009.

Hirota, Hidetaka. *Expelling the Poor: Atlantic Seaboard States and the Nineteenth-Century Origins of American Immigration Policy.* New York: Oxford University Press, 2017.

Hollett, David. *Passage to the New World: Packet Ships and Irish Famine Emigrants, 1845–51.* Gwent, UK: P. M. Heaton, 1995.

Hoppen, K. Theodore. *Ireland since 1800: Conflict and Conformity.* London: Pearson, 1989.

Huggins, Michael. *Social Conflict in Pre-famine Ireland: The Case of County Roscommon.* Dublin: Four Courts Press, 2007.

Hughes, Robert. *The Fatal Shore: The Epic of Australia's Founding.* New York: Vintage, 1986.

Iltis, Judith. "Chisholm, Caroline (1808–1877)." In *Australian Dictionary of Biography.* http://adb.anu.edu.au.

Jaffer, Aaron. *Lascars and Indian Ocean Seafaring, 1780–1860: Shipboard Life, Unrest, and Mutiny.* Woodbridge, UK: Boydell Press, 2015.

Janis, Ely M. *A Greater Ireland: The Land League and Transatlantic Nationalism in Gilded Age America.* Madison: University of Wisconsin Press, 2015.

Jefferson, Sam. *Clipper Ships and the Golden Age of Sail.* London: Bloomsbury, 2014.

Kavanagh, Joan, and Dianne Snowden. *Van Diemen's Women: An Irish History of Transportation to Tasmania.* Dublin: History Press, 2015.

Kelley, Sean M. *The Voyage of the Slave Ship Hare: A Journey into Captivity from Sierra Leone to South Carolina.* Chapel Hill: University of North Carolina Press, 2016.

Kelly, Morgan, and Cormac Ó Gráda. "*Why Ireland Starved* after Three Decades: The Great Famine in Cross-Section Reconsidered." *Irish Economic and Social History* 42, no. 1 (December 2015): 53–61.

Kenny, Kevin. *The American Irish: A History.* Harlow, UK: Longman, 2000.

———. "Diaspora and Comparison: The Irish as a Case Study." *Journal of American History* 90, no. 1 (June 2003): 134–162.

Killick, John. "An Early Nineteenth-Century Shipping Line: The Cope Line of Philadelphia and Liverpool Packets, 1822–1872." *International Journal of Maritime History* 12, no. 1 (June 2000): 61–87.

Kinealy, Christine. *This Great Calamity: The Irish Famine, 1845–1852.* Lanham, Md.: Roberts Rinehart, 1994.

Kinealy, Christine, and Gerard MacAtasney. *The Hidden Famine: Hunger, Poverty, and Sectarianism in Belfast, 1840–50.* London: Pluto Press, 2000.

Kinealy, Christine, Gerard Moran, and Jason King, eds. *The History of the Irish Famine.* 4 vols. New York: Routledge, 2019.

King, Jason. "The Genealogy of *Famine Diary* in Ireland and Quebec: Ireland's Famine Migration in Historical Fiction, Historiography, and Memory." *Éire-Ireland* 47, nos. 1–2 (Spring/Summer 2012): 45–69.

———. "Remembering Famine Orphans: The Transmission of Famine Memory between Ireland and Québec." In *Holodomor and Gorta Mór: Histories, Memories, and Representations of Famine in Ukraine and Ireland,* edited by Christian Noack, Lindsay Janssen, and Vincent Comerford, 115–114. New York: Anthem Press, 2012.

Klein, Herbert S., Stanley L. Engerman, Robin Haines, and Ralph Shlomowitz. "Transoceanic Mortality: The Slave Trade in Comparative Perspective." *William and Mary Quarterly* 58, no. 1 (January 2001): 93–118.

Kushner, Tony. *The Battle of Britishness: Migrant Journeys, 1685 to the Present.* Manchester: Manchester University Press, 2012.

Laxton, Edward. *The Famine Ships: The Irish Exodus to America.* New York: Henry Holt, 1996.

Linebaugh, Peter, and Marcus Rediker. *The Many-Headed Hydra: Sailors, Slaves, Common-ers, and the Hidden History of the Revolutionary Atlantic.* Boston: Beacon, 2000.

Lipman, Alan. *The Saltwater Frontier: Indians and the Contest for the American Coast.* New Haven, Conn.: Yale University Press, 2015.

Lynch, Matthew. *The Mass Evictions in Kilrush Poor Law Union during the Great Famine.* Miltown Malbay: Old Kilfarboy Society, 2013.

Lyne, Gerard J. "William Steuart Trench and the Post-famine Emigration from Kenmare to America, 1850–1855." *Journal of the Kerry Archaeological and Historical Society* 25 (1992): 51–137.

Lysaght, Patricia. "Hospitality at Wakes and Funerals in Ireland from the Seventeenth to the Nineteenth Century: Some Evidence from the Written Record." *Folklore* 114, no. 3 (2003): 403–426.

———. "Women and the Great Famine: Vignettes from the Irish Oral Tradition." In *The Great Famine and the Irish Diaspora in America,* edited by Arthur Gribben, 21–47. Amherst: University of Massachusetts Press, 1999.

MacDonagh, Oliver. *A Pattern of Government Growth, 1800–1860: The Passenger Acts and Their Enforcement.* London: MacGibbon and Kee, 1961.

Mac Suibhne, Breandán. *End of Outrage: Post-famine Adjustment in Rural Ireland.* Oxford: Oxford University Press, 2017.

———. *Subjects Lacking Words? The Gray Zone of the Great Famine.* Cork: Cork University Press, 2017.

Madgwick, R. B. *Immigration into Eastern Australia, 1788–1851.* Sydney: Sydney University Press, 1969.

Magra, Christopher P. *Poseidon's Curse: British Naval Impressment and Atlantic Origins of the American Revolution.* New York: Cambridge University Press, 2016.

Malcolm, Elizabeth, and Dianne Hall. *A New History of the Irish in Australia.* Sydney: University of New South Wales Press, 2018.

Mannion, Patrick. *A Land of Dreams: Ethnicity, Nationalism, and the Irish in Newfound-land, Nova Scotia, and Maine, 1880–1923.* Montreal: McGill-Queen's University Press, 2018.

Mark-Fitzgerald, Emily. *Commemorating the Irish Famine: Memory and the Monument.* Liverpool: Liverpool University Press, 2013.

McCarthy, Cal, and Kevin Todd. *The Wreck of the Neva: The Horrifying Fate of a Convict Ship and the Irish Women Aboard.* Cork: Mercier Press, 2013.

McClaughlin, Trevor. *Barefoot and Pregnant? Irish Famine Orphans in Australia.* 2 vols. Melbourne: Genealogical Society of Victoria, 1991, 2001.

McCracken, Donal. "Odd Man Out: The South African Experience." In *The Irish Dias-pora,* edited by Andy Bielenberg, 251–271. Harlow, UK: Pearson Education, 2000.

McDonald, John, and Eric Richards. "Workers for Australia: A Profile of British and Irish Migrants Assisted to New South Wales in 1841." *Journal of the Australian Population Association* 15, no. 1 (May 1998): 1–33.

McDonald, John, and Ralph Shlomowitz. "Mortality on Immigrant Voyages to Australia in the 19th Century." *Explorations in Economic History* 27 (1990): 84–113.

McGowan, Mark. *Creating Canadian Historical Memory: The Case of the Famine Migration of 1847.* Ottawa: Canadian Historical Association, 2006.

——. *Death or Canada: The Irish Famine Migration to Toronto, 1847.* Toronto: Novalis, 2009.

——. "Famine, Facts, and Fabrication: An Examination of Diaries from the Irish Famine Migration to Canada." *Canadian Journal of Irish Studies* 33, no 2 (Fall 2007): 48–55.

McInnis, Marvin. "The Population of Canada in the Nineteenth Century." In *A Population History of North America,* edited by Michael R. Haines and Richard H. Steckel, 371–432. Cambridge: Cambridge University Press, 2000.

McIntyre, Perry. *Free Passage: The Reunion of Irish Convicts and Their Families in Australia, 1788–1852.* Dublin: Irish Academic Press, 2011.

McMahon, Anne. *Convicts at Sea: The Voyages of the Irish Convict Transports to Van Diemen's Land, 1840–1853.* Hobart, Australia: Anne McMahon, 2011.

——. *Floating Prisons: The Irish Hulks and Convict Voyages to New South Wales, 1823–1837.* Ultimo, Australia: Halstead Press, 2017.

McMahon, Cian T. *The Global Dimensions of Irish Identity: Race, Nation, and the Popular Press, 1840–1880.* Chapel Hill: University of North Carolina Press, 2015.

——. "International Celebrities and Irish Identity in the United States and Beyond." *American Nineteenth Century History* 15, no. 2 (2014): 147–168.

——. "Shipwrecks and Society: Press Reports of the Irish Emigrant Passage to Canada, 1845–1855." In *Canada and the Great Irish Famine,* edited by William Jenkins. Montreal: McGill-Queen's University Press, forthcoming.

——. "Tracking the Great Famine's 'Coffin Ships' across the Digital Deep." *Éire-Ireland* 56, nos. 1–2 (Spring/Summer 2021).

McMahon, Colin. "Ports of Recall: Memory of the Great Irish Famine in Liverpool and Montreal." Ph.D. diss., York University, 2010.

Meagher, Timothy J. *Inventing Irish America: Generation, Class, and Ethnic Identity in a New England City, 1880–1928.* Notre Dame, Ind.: University of Notre Dame Press, 2001.

Miller, David W. "Landscape and Religious Practice: A Study of Mass Attendance in Pre-Famine Ireland." *Éire-Ireland* 40, nos. 1–2 (Spring/Summer 2005): 90–106.

Miller, Kerby A. *Emigrants and Exiles: Ireland and the Irish Exodus to North America.* New York: Oxford University Press, 1985.

——. "Emigrants and Exiles: The Irish Exodus to North America, from Colonial Times to the First World War." Ph.D. diss., University of California, Berkeley, 1976.

Mokyr, Joel. *Why Ireland Starved: A Quantitative and Analytical History of the Irish Economy, 1800–1850.* London: George Allen and Unwin, 1983.

Mokyr, Joel, and Cormac Ó Gráda. "What Do People Die of During Famines: The Great Irish Famine in Comparative Perspective." *European Review of Economic History* 6, no. 3 (December 2002): 339–363.

Moran, Gerard. *Sending Out Ireland's Poor: Assisted Emigration to North America in the Nineteenth Century.* Dublin: Four Courts Press, 2004.

Morgan, Gwenda, and Peter Rushton. *Banishment in the Early Atlantic World: Convicts, Rebels, and Slaves.* New York: Bloomsbury, 2013.

Neal, Frank. *Black '47: Britain and the Famine Irish.* London: Macmillan, 1998.

———. "Liverpool, the Irish Steamship Companies, and the Famine Irish." *Immigrants and Minorities* 5, no. 1 (1986): 28–61.

Nolan, William. *Fassadinin: Land, Settlement and Society in Southeast Ireland, 1600–1850.* Dublin: Geography Publications, 1979.

Norton, Desmond. *Landlords, Tenants, Famine: The Business of an Irish Land Agency in the 1840s.* Dublin: University College Dublin Press, 2006.

———. "On Landlord-Assisted Emigration from some Irish Estates in the 1840s." *Agricultural History Review* 53, no. 1 (2005): 24–40.

Nowlan, Kevin B., ed. *Travel and Transport in Ireland.* Dublin: Gill & Macmillan, 1973.

O'Connor, Kevin. *Ironing the Land: The Coming of Railways to Ireland.* Dublin: Gill & Macmillan, 1999.

Ó Crualaoich, Gearóid. "The 'Merry Wake.'" In *Irish Popular Culture, 1650–1850,* edited by J. S. Donnelly Jr. and Kerby A. Miller, 173–200. Dublin: Irish Academic Press, 1999.

O'Farrell, Patrick. *The Irish in Australia.* Sydney: University of New South Wales Press, 1986.

———. *Letters from Irish Australia, 1825–1929.* Sydney: New South Wales University Press, 1984.

O'Gallagher, Marianna, and Rose Masson Dompierre, eds. *Eyewitness. Grosse Ile. 1847.* Quebec: Carraig Books, 1995.

Ó Gráda, Cormac. *Black '47 and Beyond: The Great Irish Famine in History, Economy, and Memory.* Princeton: Princeton University Press, 1999.

———. "Industry and Communications, 1801–45." In *A New History of Ireland,* vol. 5: *Ireland Under the Union, 1801–1870,* edited by W. E. Vaughan, 137–157. New York: Oxford University Press, 2010.

———. "The Next World and the New World: Relief, Migration, and the Great Irish Famine." *Journal of Economic History* 79, no. 2 (June 2019): 319–355.

Ó Gráda, Cormac, and Kevin H. O'Rourke. "Migration as Disaster Relief: Lessons from the Great Irish Famine." *European Review of Economic History* 1, no. 1 (April 1997): 3–25.

O'Grady, Desmond. *The Road Taken: Poems, 1956–1996.* Salzburg: University of Salzburg Press, 1996.

O'Mahony, Christopher, and Valerie Thompson. *Poverty to Promise: The Monteagle Emigrants, 1835–58.* Darlington: Crossing Press, 1994.

O'Malley, Gregory. *Final Passages: The Intercolonial Slave Trade of British America, 1619–1807.* Chapel Hill: University of North Carolina Press, 2014.

O'Neill, Ciaran. *Catholics of Consequence: Transnational Education, Social Mobility, and the Irish Catholic Elite, 1850–1900.* Oxford: Oxford University Press, 2014.

O'Neill, Kevin. *Family and Farm in Pre-famine Ireland: The Parish of Killashandra.* Madison: University of Wisconsin Press, 1984.

O'Neill, Tim P. "Famine Evictions." In *Famine, Land, and Culture in Ireland*, edited by Carla King, 29–70. Dublin: University College Dublin Press, 2000.

Osterhammel, Jürgen. *The Transformation of the World: A Global History of the Nineteenth Century*. Princeton: Princeton University Press, 2015.

Ó Súilleabháin, Seán. *Irish Wake Amusements*. Cork: Mercier Press, 1997.

Owens, Gary. "Nationalism without Words: Symbolism and Ritual Behavior in the Repeal 'Monster Meetings' of 1843–5." In *Irish Popular Culture, 1650–1850*, edited by James S. Donnelly and Kerby A. Miller, 242–269. Dublin: Irish Academic Press, 1999.

Parker, A. J. *Ancient Shipwrecks of the Mediterranean and the Roman Provinces*. Oxford: British Archaeological Reports, 1978.

Perl-Rosenthal, Nathan. *Citizen Sailors: Becoming American in the Age of Revolution*. Cambridge, Mass.: Belknap, 2015.

Phillips, Jock, and Terry Hearn. *Settlers: New Zealand Immigrants from England, Ireland, and Scotland, 1800–1945*. Auckland: Auckland University Press, 2008.

Potter, George. *To the Golden Door: The Story of the Irish in Ireland and America*. Boston: Little, Brown, 1960.

Purcell, Richard J. "The New York Commissioners of Emigration and Irish Immigrants." *Studies: An Irish Quarterly Review* 37, no. 145 (March 1948): 29–42.

Rafferty, Matthew Taylor. *The Republic Afloat: Law, Honor, and Citizenship in Maritime America*. Chicago: University of Chicago Press, 2013.

Rasor, Eugene L. *Reform in the Royal Navy: A Social History of the Lower Deck, 1850–1880*. Hamden, Conn.: Archon Books, 1976.

Rediker, Marcus. *Between the Devil and the Deep Blue Sea: Merchant Seamen, Pirates, and the Anglo-American Maritime World, 1700–1750*. Cambridge: Cambridge University Press, 1987.

———. *Outlaws of the Atlantic: Sailors, Pirates, and Motley Crews in the Age of Sail*. Boston: Beacon, 2014.

———. *The Slave Ship: A Human History*. New York: Penguin, 2007.

Reece, Bob, ed. *Irish Convict Lives*. Sydney: Crossing Press, 1993.

Reid, Richard. *Farewell My Children: Irish Assisted Emigration to Australia, 1848–1870*. Sydney: Anchor, 2011.

———. "'That Famine Is Pressing Each Day More Heavily upon Them': The Emigration of Irish Convict Families to NSW, 1848–1852." In *Poor Australian Immigrants in the Nineteenth Century: Visible Immigrants*, vol. 2, edited by Eric Richards, 69–96. Canberra: Australian National University Press, 1991.

Reid, Richard, and Cheryl Mongan, eds. *A Decent Set of Girls: The Irish Famine Orphans of the* Thomas Arbuthnot, *1848–1850*. Yass: Yass Heritage Project, 1996.

Reilly, Ciarán. "Aspects of Agency: John Ross Mahon, Accommodation, and Resistance on the Strokestown Estate, 1845–1851." In *Ireland's Great Famine and Popular Politics*, edited by Enda Delaney and Breandán MacSuibhne, 172–185. New York: Routledge, 2016.

———. *Strokestown and the Great Irish Famine*. Dublin: Four Courts Press, 2014.

Richards, Eric. "How Did Poor People Emigrate from the British Isles to Australia in the Nineteenth Century?" *Journal of British Studies* 32, no. 3 (July 1993): 250–279.

Ritchie, Fiona, and Doug Orr. *Wayfaring Strangers: The Musical Voyage from Scotland and Ulster to Appalachia*. Chapel Hill: University of North Carolina Press, 2014.

Roberts, David Andrew. "The 'Knotted Hands That Set Us High': Labour History and the Study of Convict Australia." *Labour History* 100 (May 2011): 33–50.

Roddy, Sarah. *Population, Providence, and Empire: The Churches and Emigration from Nineteenth-Century Ireland*. Manchester: Manchester University Press, 2014.

Rosenberg, Charles E. *The Cholera Years: The United States in 1832, 1849, and 1866*. Chicago: University of Chicago Press, 1987.

Scally, Robert. *The End of Hidden Ireland: Rebellion, Famine, and Emigration*. New York: Oxford University Press, 1995.

———. "Liverpool Ships and Irish Emigrants in the Age of Sail." *Journal of Social History* 17, no. 1 (Autumn 1983): 5–30.

Schoeppner, Michael A. *Moral Contagion: Black Atlantic Sailors, Citizenship, and Diplomacy in Antebellum America*. Cambridge: Cambridge University Press, 2019.

Shaw, A. G. L. *Convicts and Colonies: A Study of Penal Transportation from Great Britain and Ireland to Australia and Other Parts of the British Empire*. London: Faber and Faber, 1966.

Shlomowitz, Ralph. "Mortality and the Pacific Labour Trade." *Journal of Pacific History* 22, no. 1 (January 1987): 34–55.

Shlomowitz, Ralph, and John McDonald. "Babies at Risk on Immigrant Voyages to Australia in the Nineteenth Century." *Economic History Review* 44, no. 1 (1991): 86–101.

Smallwood, Stephanie. *Saltwater Slavery: A Middle Passage from Africa to American Diaspora*. Cambridge, Mass.: Harvard University Press, 2007.

Smyth, William J. "Exodus from Ireland: Patterns of Emigration." In *Atlas of the Great Irish Famine*, edited by John Crowley, William J. Smyth, and Mike Murphy, 494–503. New York: New York University Press, 2012.

Solar, Peter M. "*Why Ireland Starved* and the Big Issues in Pre-famine Irish Economic History." *Irish Economic and Social History* 42, no. 1 (December 2015): 62–75.

Spray, William A. "Irish Famine Emigrants and the Passage Trade to North America." In *Fleeing the Famine: North America and Irish Refugees, 1845–1851*, edited by Margaret M. Mulrooney, 3–20. Westport, Conn.: Praeger, 2003.

Steckel, Richard H., and Richard A. Jensen. "New Evidence on the Causes of Slave and Crew Mortality in the Atlantic Slave Trade." *Journal of Economic History* 46, no. 1 (March 1986): 57–77.

Stott, Richard B. *Workers in the Metropolis: Class, Ethnicity, and Youth in Antebellum New York City*. Ithaca, N.Y.: Cornell University Press, 1990.

Strong, Rowan. *Victorian Christianity and Emigrant Voyages to British Colonies, c. 1840–c. 1914*. London: Oxford University Press, 2017.

Tait, Clodagh. *Death, Burial, and Commemoration in Ireland, 1550–1650*. Basingstoke: Palgrave Macmillan, 2002.

Taylor, Philip. *The Distant Magnet: European Emigration to the U.S.A.* London: Eyre and Spottiswoode, 1971.

Thompson, E. P. "Time, Work-Discipline, and Industrial Capitalism." *Past & Present* 38 (December 1967): 56–97.

Tóibín, Colm, and Diarmaid Ferriter, eds. *The Irish Famine: A Documentary*. New York: Thomas Dunne Books, 2001.

Townend, Paul A. *The Road to Home Rule: Anti-imperialism and the Irish National Movement*. Madison: University of Wisconsin Press, 2016.

Turner, Michael. *After the Famine: Irish Agriculture, 1850–1914*. Cambridge: Cambridge University Press, 1996.

Turner, Victor. *The Ritual Process: Structure and Anti-Structure*. Chicago: Aldine, 1969.

Tyrrell, Ian. "Reflections on the Transnational Turn in United States History: Theory and Practice." *Journal of Global History* 4, no. 3 (November 2009): 453–474.

Vandenbroucke, Jan P. "The 1855 Cholera Epidemic in Ferrara: Lessons from Old Data Reanalysed with Modern Means." *European Journal of Epidemiology* 18, no. 7 (2003): 599–602.

Veitch, Michael. *Hell Ship: The True Story of the Plague Ship Ticonderoga, One of the Most Calamitous Voyages in Australian History*. Crows Nest: Allen and Unwin, 2018.

Vickers, Daniel. *Young Men and the Sea: Yankee Seafarers in the Age of Sail*. New Haven, Conn.: Yale University Press, 2007.

Walker, Carole Ann. *A Saviour of Living Cargoes: The Life and Work of Caroline Chisholm*. Brisbane: Connor Court, 2011.

Wenzlhuemer, Roland. *Connecting the Nineteenth-Century World: The Telegraph and Globalization*. Cambridge: Cambridge University Press, 2015.

———. "The Ship, the Media, and the World: Conceptualizing Connections in Global History." *Journal of Global History* 11, no. 2 (July 2016): 163–186.

Whelehan, Niall. *The Dynamiters: Irish Nationalism and Political Violence in the Wider World, 1867–1900*. Cambridge: Cambridge University Press, 2012.

Whooley, Owen. *Knowledge in the Time of Cholera: The Struggle over American Medicine in the Nineteenth Century*. Chicago: University of Chicago Press, 2013.

Williams, John. *Ordered to the Island: Irish Convicts and Van Diemen's Land*. Sydney: Crossing Press, 1994.

Williams, William H. A. *Creating Irish Tourism: The First Century, 1750–1850*. London: Anthem Press, 2011.

Willis, Sam. *Shipwreck: A History of Disasters at Sea*. London: Quercus, 2009.

Wilson, David A. *Thomas D'Arcy McGee*. 2 vols. Montreal: McGill-Queen's University Press, 2008, 2011.

Witt, Jann M. "'During the Voyage Every Captain Is Monarch of the Ship': The Merchant Captain from the Seventeenth to the Nineteenth Century." *International Journal of Maritime History* 13, no. 2 (December 2001): 165–194.

Woodham-Smith, Cecil. *The Great Hunger*. New York: Harper & Row, 1962.

Wyatt, Louise, ed. "The Johnson Letters." *Ontario History* 40 (1948): 27–52.

Ziegler, Edith M. *Harlots, Hussies, and Poor Unfortunate Women: Crime, Transportation, and the Servitude of Female Convicts, 1718–1783*. Tuscaloosa: University of Alabama Press, 2014.

INDEX

Action From Ireland (AFRI), 237

Adelaide, Australia, 102, 115, 117, 120, 124, 138, 142, 198

Admiralty (UK), 62, 110, 111

advice, 3, 21, 56, 234; from authority figures, 212; from emigration agents, 58–59; in newspapers, 58–59, 222; on emigration process, 22, 57–58, 60, 85, 86, 97; on expenditures, 21; on life abroad, 226; on life at sea, 57, 94, 96; on sailors, 99, 116; on the packet system, 57–58; to other emigrants, 129

Ahascragh, County Galway, 56

alcohol: alcoholism, 19; and German emigrants, 184; and law enforcement, 76, 78; and sailors, 90, 99, 112, 120, 171; as entertainment, 137, 223; as irritant at sea, 94; as luxury at sea, 62, 103, 128, 131; as medicine, 162, 163, 174, 200

American Celt (Boston), 214, 217

American Celt and Adopted Citizen (Boston), 218, 222

American Celt and Catholic Citizen (Buffalo), 220

American Emigrants' Friend Society (Philadelphia), 203

ancestry, 3, 35–36, 66, 270n1

Anglo-Celt (Cavan), 40, 66, 104

Antarctica, 107

anti-Irish bigotry, 87, 141–142, 166–167, 172–173, 183–184

Antrim, 102, 106, 141, 145, 162, 173, 200, 201

Ardnaglass, County Sligo, 18

Armagh, 169, 212

Armagh Guardian, 169–170

assisted emigration: as convict family reunification, 46–48, 49–52, 53–54, 64; by landlords, 27–38, 59, 72, 78–79, 146, 181, 190, 197, 203–207, 212; by Family Colonization Loan Society, 25–26, 46, 114, 133, 135; by poor law unions, 38, 42–45, 59, 62, 64, 71; Earl Grey scheme, 44–45; Godley scheme, 38–40; Robinson scheme, 39; to Australia through CLEC, 10, 38, 40–42, 59, 62, 64, 129, 151, 152–153, 158, 159

Athy, County Kildare, 79

Atlantic Ocean, 3, 106, 199; and commerce, 8, 82; and underregulation, 7, 53, 116, 118, 130, 148, 173; beauty of, 100, 108; fear of, 56; emigrant mortality on, 150–151, 158, 182, 185, 186; emigrant solidarity on, 135, 141, 145, 223, 224, 228; in historiography, 2

Auburn, New York, 23

Aughamucky, Co. Kilkenny, 36, 78–79

Australia, 2, 3, 15, 18, 58, 66, 100, 107, 120, 134, 135, 139, 140, 144, 175, 180, 182; advice regarding, 56, 86, 91, 92, 94, 104, 132, 133, 226; and convict transportation, 8, 40, 46–54, 70, 77, 93, 111, 127; arrival in, 196–198, 210–212; as less popular destination, 5, 223; assisted emigration to, 24–26, 27, 33, 37, 38, 40–42, 44–45, 49–50, 59, 62, 63, 64, 101, 135; distance from Britain, 6, 101, 106, 154, 235, 245; gold rush, 198–199, 202; Irish connections with, 8, 9, 12, 205–206; Irish identity in, 230; mortality en route to, 148, 150–159, 172, 183, 188; newspapers in, 18, 72–73, 120, 160, 213, 219–220, 221;

ABOUT THE AUTHOR

Cian T. McMahon is Associate Professor of History at the University of Nevada, Las Vegas, where he specializes in migration and identity in the nineteenth century. He is the author of *The Global Dimensions of Irish Identity: Race, Nation, and the Popular Press, 1840–1880* (2015).